Acclaim for Laura Fairchild Brodie's

BREAKING OUT

Laura Fairchild Brodie

BREAKING OUT

Laura Fairchild Brodie, who served on one of VMI's assimilation committees, received her B.A. from Harvard and her Ph.D. from the University of Virginia. She has taught at the University of Virginia, Hollins College, VMI, and Washington and Lee University. With her husband and three young daughters, she lives in Lexington, Virginia.

BREAKING OUT

VMI AND
THE COMING OF WOMEN

Laura Fairchild Brodie

VINTAGE BOOKS
A Division of Random House, Inc.
New York

In memory of

Erika S. and Glen A. Fairchild

First Vintage Books Edition, May 2001

The Library of Congress has cataloged the Pantheon edition as follows:
Brodie, Laura Fairchild.
Breaking out / Laura Fairchild Brodie.
p. cm.
1. Virginia Military Institute—History—20th century.   2. Sexism in higher education—United States—Case studies.   3. Feminism and education—United States—Case studies.   4. Educational equalization—United States—Case studies.
LC 212.862.B75 2000
379.2'6—dc21

Vintage ISBN: 0-375-70581-3

Author photograph © Fran Fevrier/Images Out of the Ordinary
Book design by Deborah Kerner

www.vintagebooks.com

Printed in the United States of America
10 9 8 7 6 5 4 3 2 1

CONTENTS

Contents

ACKNOWLEDGMENTS

MUCH OF THE INFORMATION IN THIS BOOK COMES FROM sixty-six interviews that I conducted with cadets, administrators, faculty, and staff of the Virginia Military Institute, as well as with visiting cadets from Norwich and Texas A&M Universities, between January 1997 and March 1999. I have also relied heavily on nonconfidential information and documents distributed at meetings of VMI's Executive Committee for the Assimilation of Women—the group charged with overseeing VMI's transition to coeducation—which I was invited to join in August 1996 by the Institute's Superintendent, Major General Josiah Bunting III. I attended the weekly meetings of this committee through May 1997, and I continued my regular participation as the committee met on a biweekly basis throughout the 1997/98 school year. I also attended over a dozen meetings of subcommittees at VMI charged with studying specific aspects of the assimilation process.

Nevertheless, this book is not intended to be a scholarly work based on exhaustive research. A book of that nature would be premature at this early stage in VMI's transition to coeducation. Rather, the chapters that follow bring together the stories, opinions, and concerns of the members of a unique college community (and I count myself among those members) facing a new and challenging time in VMI's institutional history. The opinions and conclusions presented here, when not directly attributed to other people, are my own and are not necessarily shared by the Virginia Military Institute and its administration.

I am deeply grateful to the many members of the VMI community who have shared their time and impressions with me. Special thanks go to General Bunting, for his generosity and open-mindedness in authorizing my research, and to Colonel N. Michael Bissell, the man charged with handling VMI's assimilation of women, who approached my project with enthusiastic support.

I would also like to thank Brian and Frances Richardson and Molly Petty for their comments on early versions of this manuscript; my editor at the Knopf Publishing Group, Jane Garrett, for recognizing the potential in this project; Jeanette Coleman and Catherine Tomlin, for providing free and loving child care; and especially my husband, Colonel John A. Brodie, Ph.D., for his unfailing warmth, insight, and sense of humor.

INTRODUCTION

I AM THE BAND DIRECTOR'S WIFE.

At first glance, that might seem irrelevant. This is not a book about snare drums and spit valves and John Philip Sousa. What lies ahead is an insider's view of a deliberately anachronistic Southern institution confronting the facts of sexual equality in the twenty-first century. More specifically, this is the story of the Virginia Military Institute, and the internal challenges it faced as it relinquished its status as the last all-male military college in the United States. The key players are a group of young women tackling a male-oriented system of education, and a community of administrators, alumni, faculty, and male cadets, all struggling to integrate women into their world, on their terms.

Why does my own background matter? Because no one can talk about VMI without getting personal. In the seven years that the Institute spent waging a legal war to defend its males-only admissions policy, neutrality was a luxury few could afford. The issues were too emotional, too inflammatory. Should women be at VMI? How far should our nation's military colleges, as well as the armed services, go to accommodate women? What does equality between the sexes really mean when translated into practical terms?

Answers to these questions depend on each individual's perspective. Are you a man or a woman? Were you born and bred in Virginia? Are you a Yankee? Have you ever fought in a war? What do you know about military training? Have you ever seen VMI? The questions quickly become accusations.

I come to this story with as much personal baggage as any human being. My biases are all the more relevant because I was not only a witness to, but an occasional participant in, several of the events at hand—joining in committee debates, mingling at cocktail parties, teaching English to the last all-male "rat mass" in VMI's history. In the pages that follow I will occasionally metamorphose from narrator to character, Jekyll to Hyde, stepping out of the shadows to provide a more intimate, first-person view. To make that view clear, an introduction is necessary.

And so, as I was saying, I am the band director's wife.

I am also a doctor of English literature, a part-time professor, a full-time mother. But for my present purposes, these facts are secondary. What matters is that for the past ten years I have attended every Parents' Weekend concert at VMI. I have traveled with the band to Paris, to New York, to Mardi Gras in New Orleans (imagine thirty-eight hours round-trip on a bus with fifty cadets). I have watched VMI's Corps march in full regalia at dozens of Friday afternoon parades, framed on the left by the flat peak of House Mountain, and on the right by the early twilight reflected in the windows of the barracks. I have sat within ear-splitting distance of the VMI pep band at basketball and football games, cheering for the "Keydets," and I once spent $120 on a long white dress and a pair of elbow-length gloves, so that I could stand next to my husband underneath a giant replica of the VMI Class Ring, as he was dubbed an honorary member of the Class of 1992.

In other words, I am a member of the VMI Family.

Many colleges use a family metaphor to describe the relations among students, faculty, alumni, parents, and staff, but few take the metaphor as seriously as VMI. One former VMI official used to invoke the Family so often—"We must communicate with the Family," "The Family will not like this"—that a conversation with him felt like a scene from *The Stepford Wives*.

At VMI, "Family" is a literal term. Many of the cadets are sons, grandsons, nephews, or cousins of former graduates. Most of the administrators are alumni, as are many of the professors. In 1995 the Dean of the Faculty distributed a memo stating that VMI's faculty needed to hire more women, more minorities, *and* more alumni (none of whom were women, and few of whom were minorities). The memo confirmed a larger institutional belief that only those who have lived through VMI's system can understand it. VMI is a cloistered society, full of private rituals, complex rules, and a language of confusing acronyms. It can take months to distinguish between the EC, the GC, SRC, and the VFT. It can take years to fathom why any college freshman would voluntarily submit to VMI's seven-month system of daily abuse known as the "ratline."

Hand-in-hand with this elusive spirit comes a wariness toward outsiders. During its long road to the Supreme Court, VMI was often vilified by commentators whose knowledge of the school was superficial. As a result, the Institute began to circle its wagons even tighter.

Without some status as a VMI insider, I would never have been allowed to research this book. The last female intellectual whom VMI welcomed into its fold was an anthropologist who impressed a few administrators with her tribal interpretations of the school's muddiest rituals. But as the court case neared completion, this short-term visitor to the Post was touted in the papers as an expert on VMI, espousing a viewpoint so full of doubts that the Commandant who had befriended her thought "Never again." Indeed, anyone who has ever read Susan Faludi's scathing critique of The Citadel* might wonder why any military college would allow a feminist writer into its midst.

And I am a feminist. Not a man-hater, not a witch, not an inflexible opponent of all things patriarchal, but a supporter of a society equally fair to its mothers and fathers, brothers and sisters. I intentionally described myself as "feminist" in a letter submitted to VMI's Superintendent, Major General Josiah Bunting III, shortly after the Supreme Court ruled against VMI, when I sought his permission to undertake an oral history of the Institute's transition to coeducation. I knew that the word triggers alarm bells in the minds of most VMI officials. Bunting, however, did not flinch. Instead, he invited me to join his committee on coeducation, adding "You have read Carol Gilligan, haven't you?" Apparently Bunting thought it would be useful to have someone with a knowledge of women's studies joining the debate, someone who knew Gilligan's theories about the self-esteem problems among female adolescents. Not to mention the fact that my presence on the committee would double the number of women in the room. Bunting did not seem fazed by the knowledge that the person now chronicling VMI's actions would be coming from a feminist background. After all, I was Mrs. Brodie. I was the band director's wife.

---

* "The Naked Citadel," *The New Yorker,* September 5, 1994.

I mention my ideological background for two reasons: to lay my cards on the table and to emphasize that what follows is not a piece of propaganda for VMI. Despite my ties to the Institute, my husband's occasional refrain of "please don't get me fired," my fondness for most of the people involved (believe it or not, VMI is filled with well-intentioned, intelligent, likable people), my role has always been that of a concerned skeptic, committed to honesty, not adulation.

Like most people who are well acquainted with VMI, I have spent my moments loathing the place. But I have also witnessed events that were fascinating, funny, and admirable. None more admirable than the manner in which hundreds of people on VMI's Post—from cadets, to faculty, to laundry workers—all came together to prepare for the arrival of women. Many did not agree with the Supreme Court's ruling that nullified the Institute's single-sex admissions policy. Many feared that the mixture of women and men in VMI's barracks would be explosive. But the vast majority determined to try their best to make coeducation work. This book is about them. In keeping with my original plans for an oral history, the narrative that follows is filled with the voices of administrators, cadets, and faculty. Their stories and opinions color the first half, which covers VMI's year of planning for coeducation, and they are especially prominent in the second half, which looks at the women's first year at VMI.

The pages ahead provide only the opening chapters in an ongoing story. Whether VMI's transition to coeducation will ultimately result in success or scandal, whether its first female graduates will look back on their alma mater with devotion or disillusionment, will remain for the future to determine. However, the first act in this drama has been played out. The role of this book is to offer a window into an unusual institutional culture, to describe what was involved in bringing women into that culture, and to survey some of VMI's earliest responses to a new era in its history.

WHEN LIEUTENANT GENERAL WINFIELD S. SCOTT, former Superintendent of the Air Force Academy, visited VMI in the spring of 1997, he declared that no other military college had done so much to prepare for the arrival of women. At the same time, no other military college planned to do so little to alter its system. In its determination to offer women the same harsh model of physical and mental stress applied to men, VMI became a case study in higher education and a microcosm for national debate about men and women, single- and dual-sex military training, and the benefits and drawbacks of tradition and change.

These are the issues that drive the narrative that follows, but to approach them we must first survey VMI's history. For it is the culture of VMI that will dominate the pages ahead, and to appreciate the Institute's present, you must know something about its past.

Let us go then, you and I, to the place where I take all visitors who come to Lexington, Virginia—the doors of Jackson Memorial Hall, at the center of VMI's Post.

SETTING
THE STAGE

1

WHAT IS/WAS VMI?

JACKSON MEMORIAL HALL STANDS AT THE UPPER-RIGHT-HAND corner of the parade ground. For cadets at the Virginia Military Institute, this oak-carved auditorium serves as a threshold to Heaven and Hell. It is the setting for Sunday church services and the first stop in the indoctrination rites of Hell Night. On the outside, JM Hall features the same tan stucco walls, small-paned windows, and fluted parapets that make the entire VMI Post resemble a storybook castle. But if you step inside, beyond the wooden lobby, you will find yourself in a wide middle aisle, where rows of pews are paralleled, overhead, by two lines of state flags, all leading the eye forward to a large stage. There, on the back wall, a twenty-three-foot arch-shaped painting hangs in bold color.

This painting, the masterwork of Benjamin West Clinedinst, Class of 1880, portrays a scene sacred to VMI history. In it, a crowd of young VMI cadets is charging into an artillery barrage at the Battle of New Market. The action took place on May 15, 1864, after 241 cadets marched eighty miles up the Shenandoah Valley to join the Confederate forces of General John C. Breckenridge. Originally intended as a reserve battalion, the cadets played a decisive role in the battle, filling a large gap in the center of Breckenridge's line and turning back the Union troops in a muddy wheat field, which they later dubbed the "Field of Lost Shoes."

In Clinedinst's painting the cadets are running forward in midstride, some with their rifles brandished in the air, others with weapons still balanced at their shoulders. On the far right, you can see the bare foot of one cadet whose boot was swallowed in the mud. On the left, a shell

INTERIOR OF JACKSON MEMORIAL HALL. *(Peter Howard Photographer Inc.)*

explodes into orange fire, sending billows of smoke through the cadets' crowded ranks. Two fallen Union soldiers lie in the path of the oncoming charge.

The focal point of the painting, however, rests in the middle, where a blonde cadet in the front line lurches backward under the impact of a blow, his body arching into a semicircle while his red mouth and shocked blue eyes gape at heaven in an expression of mortal terror. Behind him, a dark-haired cadet turns his face away from the charge, away from his dying classmate, toward the viewer of the painting. In his face we see a pink-cheeked adolescent, running forward into a volley of gunfire, with his head averted and eyes closed.

It seems incongruous, and somewhat portentous, to watch young couples pledge their marriage vows before Clinedinst's scene of battle during VMI's summer wedding season. But it was also incongruous, in the spring of 1993, to hear the radical Beat poet Allen Ginsberg recite his famous "Howl" with this painting as a backdrop. And incongruity (or, as he put it, "circumstantial surrealism") inspired a local photographer, Patrick Hinely, to capture an image of the Boys Choir of Harlem singing

4

CANDLELIGHTING BEFORE CLINEDINST'S NEW MARKET PAINTING. *(Jim Richardson/Harmony House)*

before the painting, with their hands raised to heaven in a moment of musical joy and their young black faces uplifted to meet the rebel yell of those Confederate boys.

Incongruity, however, is one of VMI's most redeeming features. Anyone whose acquaintance with the Institute is limited to newspaper clippings and television sound bites is liable to place this four-year, formerly all-male military college into one of two categories: either a stronghold of integrity and honor in a culture marred by compromise and political correctness, or an archaic bastion of macho conservatism, where misogyny is masked by a veneer of Southern gentility. While each stereotype contains its iota of truth, the reality behind VMI is much more complex.

Images of the Institute as an exclusive realm of conservative thinking cannot incorporate a professor such as Gordon Ball, youthful friend to Jack Kerouac and Allen Ginsberg, who, in 1996, nominated Bob Dylan for the Nobel Peace Prize. Similarly, visions of the VMI cadet as a burly Southern white male do not account for the significant contingent of students from Taiwan and Thailand, who can occasionally be found in the barracks cooking their native dishes on illegal hot plates.

True, VMI is no mecca of diversity. Like all military institutions, its method of discipline relies on a culture of homogeneity, expressed in its uniforms, its haircuts, even its architecture. The ostensive purpose of the school's infamous ratline is to "break down" individual freshmen into one "rat mass" and rebuild them as "VMI Men." But the "VMI Man" has never been as monolithic as his title implies. Within the Institute's homogenizing system, cadets strive to establish their individuality. And in a society where most eighteen-year-olds prefer to dress down, sleep late, and absorb hours of MTV, any young person who seeks out a life of daily hardship—without television, without telephones, without privacy—has a lot of individuality, or at least idiosyncracy, to express.

These idiosyncracies are important to the story at hand, for if you want to learn about VMI, you must be willing to engage in a temporary suspension of disbelief, setting aside knee-jerk impulses toward condemnation or celebration long enough to appreciate the oddities of the place and its people. And one of the Institute's oddest features, especially for those who live outside the South, is its lingering homage to heroes of the Confederacy.

Stepping back from Clinedinst's painting, you will notice that it is flanked on the right and left by two floor-level portraits—a side view of Robert E. Lee and a full-front rendering of Thomas "Stonewall" Jackson. On Sunday mornings, with a cross standing in front of the New Market painting, these three artworks form their own Holy Trinity. They provide a staunch reminder that, despite the fact that a typical VMI class attracts cadets from over forty states and several countries, the Institute remains a distinctly Southern institution, committed to a pious preservation of its history.

VMI's Confederate heritage frames every school year. Each fall, the rats' first formal duty as freshmen involves traveling to New Market, to parade through the streets of the sleepy town. Afterward, they gather at VMI's Hall of Valor, a museum on the battlefield, where they learn about the events at New Market from upperclass reenactors dressed in Confederate costumes. To cap the excursion, the rats stage their own charge across the battlefield.

A more somber remembrance occurs at the end of each year, on the anniversary of the battle. Each May 15, the Institute holds a review parade in memory of the ten New Market cadets who died of wounds incurred on the "Field of Honor." Leaders of the Corps place wreaths on the graves of six of these young men, who are buried next to JM Hall beneath a statue of "Virginia Mourning Her Dead." A cadet rifle squad fires a three-volley salute, followed by a rendering of echo taps, with one bugler standing on the library rooftop and another answering from across the parade ground, inside the barracks.

On the same day, VMI also remembers one of its most valued heroes, Stonewall Jackson, who died exactly one year before the Battle of New Market. Jackson is the patron saint of VMI. His sacred relics are displayed in the VMI Museum (housed in the basement of JM Hall). There one can see the bullet hole in the leather coat that Jackson was wearing when he was accidentally shot by one of his own men at the Battle of Chancellorsville. Nearby, Jackson's horse, Little Sorrell, stands in a taxidermic time warp; the bare patches on his coat testify to a century of souvenir mongers. At the museum's exit, Little Sorrel toys and refrigerator magnets are on sale for the kids.

Jackson served as a professor of natural philosophy at VMI before the Civil War. The cadets viewed him as a sort of kook—a religious fanatic and third-rate professor who read from his notes and could scarcely look up to answer a question. They gained a new respect for him, however, with the onset of war. The awkward professor proved to be a brilliant military strategist, whose campaign in the Shenandoah Valley is required reading in military classrooms worldwide.

Today, a statue of Jackson presides over VMI's twelve-acre parade ground, standing just opposite the barracks' main entry, "Jackson Arch." Tradition requires that every rat salute the statue each time he or she leaves the barracks—in other words, several times a day. Returning to the arch, cadets face an engraved quote from the General that serves as the Institute's motto: "You May Be Whatever You Resolve to Be."

VMI's administrators are quick to explain that the Institute's homages to Jackson and the New Market cadets are not designed to cele-

STONEWALL JACKSON, SCULPTED BY SIR MOSES EZEKIAL, CLASS OF 1866.
(Andres R. Alonso/fotoVISION)

brate the Confederacy, but to recognize the values of honor, duty, and discipline embodied in praiseworthy individuals. In addition, they insist that VMI's rituals, like the rituals on any college campus, enable today's cadets to maintain a sense of continuity with all of the graduates who have gone before.

Still, one wonders what must run through the minds of VMI's black cadets, as they participate in the Institute's Southern rituals. Saluting a Confederate General, parading in honor of Confederate dead, and charging up the "Field of Honor" all have a surreal quality today, made all the more strange when one adds the element of race. Whenever I have asked, the answers have been as varied as the individuals to whom I was speaking. For Finnie Coleman, a black alumnus now teaching African-

RAT SALUTES JACKSON ON A FOGGY MORNING. *(Jim Richardson/Harmony House)*

American literature at Texas A&M University, his response to VMI's rituals was a matter of evolving awareness:

> As a rat I wanted to be everything that VMI was about. I didn't necessarily agree with the Confederacy, but for me it was a nonissue. This was the school that I had chosen to go to; therefore the traditions were sacrosanct. . . . In hindsight, the entire New Market process, with the parade and the actual march up there, is problematic on a number of different levels. As a new cadet I wasn't sophisticated enough to understand what those things meant. It was sort of like when I was a kid, I would draw Confederate flags. I didn't know what they meant.

Coleman was looking back with the benefit (some might say "detriment") of years of graduate education. By contrast, one of the young black women in VMI's first coed class assessed her school's Southern traditions with a less contemplative and more humorous approach. She loved VMI's sense of history and enjoyed reenacting the New Market charge. The constant salutes to Jackson, however, did try her patience, in part because his statue faces away from the barracks, surveying the parade ground. As she put it: "Here I am saluting this Confederate General's rear end."

Today, VMI has relinquished the most controversial symbols of the Confederacy. As of 1992 the Confederate flag no longer appears on VMI's class ring, and Dixie has been off the band's repertoire for the past few decades. Cadets who object strongly to the New Market Parade can usually find ways to avoid it, but most accept VMI's argument for tradition. Indeed, few would have attended the Institute if they had no stomach for the Old South, because in Lexington, Virginia (the quaint college town in which VMI resides), memories of the Confederacy extend well beyond the Institute's gates.

Lexington natives are born in Stonewall Jackson Hospital and buried, along with the General himself, in Stonewall Jackson Cemetery. Some live on Jackson Avenue in houses sold through "Stonewall Country Properties." The oldest locals boast an even closer tie to the General; several were born in Jackson's house when it served as the town's hospital.

Although for many Americans "Stonewall" now serves as the name of the largest gay-rights movement in the United States, named after the Stonewall Inn in Greenwich Village, where police squared off against gays during a massive riot in 1969, in Virginia the word still evokes visions of one of the South's greatest heroes, and most of Lexington's oldest residents do *not*—thank you—appreciate the irony behind its more recent connotations.

Stonewall Jackson's influence over Lexington is rivaled only by that of Robert E. Lee, who retired to the town after the War, where he served as President of Washington College, now Washington and Lee University. Lee and his family are buried on that university's campus, which is adjacent to VMI. Outside the family crypt, visitors leave pennies on the grave of Traveler, Lee's beloved horse.

All in all, VMI is a very Southern school in a very Southern town.

Why does this matter in a book about coeducation? It matters because VMI's Southern heritage and reverence for tradition have influenced its legal struggles, its planning for coeducation, and its approach toward men and women.

When the U.S. military academies admitted women in 1976, they did so, however unwillingly, at the order of Congress—a federal body dictating policy to federal institutions. By contrast, the challenge to VMI's single-sex admissions policy came in 1989 from a group of "outsiders"—officials at the U.S. Department of Justice, once again telling the Commonwealth of Virginia what to do. Never mind the fact that the Justice Department was responding to a legitimate complaint from an anonymous female high-school student. Never mind that at least 347 other women had been turned away when requesting admissions information from VMI between 1988 and 1990. And never mind that most of the people at VMI had been expecting a legal challenge for years. When that challenge came, the reaction was emotional and fractious. In the eyes of many VMI adherents, the case was a matter of states' rights vs. federal intrusion, Southern tradition vs. Northern self-righteousness.

As the case moved back and forth between District and Appellate courts, eventually concluding in a landslide Supreme Court decision against VMI, the Civil War was especially poignant in the VMI collective mind, not only because of New Market, not only because VMI trained officers for the Confederacy, but because in 1864 General David Hunter marched his Union troops down the Shenandoah Valley, placed his cannons near the Maury River directly across from VMI, shelled the Institute and then entered its grounds and burned almost every building, including its library and scientific collections. The attack nearly closed VMI's doors forever; it took decades to rebuild the school. But from its ashes VMI rose like a small, defiant Phoenix, all the more stubborn when the federal government once again came knocking at its gates, demanding that it surrender its males-only enclave, and all the more determined to handle coeducation in its own way once the Supreme Court had spoken.

In the rhetoric of many VMI officials, the court case hearkened back to the Civil War, while the subsequent planning for coeducation was analogous to the Reconstruction. When General Josiah Bunting III, VMI's Superintendent, addressed the Richmond Kiwanis Club in April 1997, he compared VMI's preparations for women to the efforts of the defeated Confederate forces: "We must do our fame and name credit, even as the ragged remnants of General Lee's noble army did our Commonwealth inestimable credit when they obeyed their commander in the dark days of April 1865."

Meanwhile Thomas Moncure, a member of the Institute's Board of Visitors, had a biting message for the Northern intruders:

> It is no accident that the ire of the politically correct has been directed at the VMI and The Citadel. These are Southern institutions, in the twin pillars of Southern civilization, Virginia and South Carolina. We are entirely too used to the smug and sanctimonious Yankee, whose preferences are always superior to ours, sitting in pharisaical judgment of the South. . . .
>
> It is our sense of continuum, rooted literally and figuratively in the soil that separates Southerners from other Americans. We are a people with a past. Our past is both a physical presence and an innate feeling that engenders in us deep appreciation for an occasional backward glance. Our knowledge of history allows us to view squarely the inconsistencies of the human condition. . . .
>
> The politically correct will gloat at the demise of an institution that has served Virginia and this nation well for more than 150 years. They will not hesitate to speak of the death of tradition. But do not expect the voices of glee to come with Southern accents.*

Most VMI grads do not share Moncure's antipathy for "sanctimonious" Yankees. Many are Yankees themselves. Nor are Moncure's opinions representative of VMI's entire Board of Visitors. Moncure was one of the Board's most short-lived members. Appointed in June 1996, he remained on the Board long enough to cast a vote for VMI's privatization, then resigned in January 1997 in protest over the Institute's plans to admit women. In his letter of resignation he stated that he could not "continue to be a party to what must ultimately be a sham on the good people of Virginia."

But while Moncure's rhetoric is atypical, many VMI alumni share his belief that the United States' appetite for "political correctness" is devouring all respect for tradition. And chief among the Southern traditions that VMI had hoped to preserve was an element of decorum in the relations between men and women. What did it mean to be a gentleman

---

* "VMI Ruling a Loss for Reason," *Fredericksburg Free Lance-Star,* June 27, 1996.

in 1997? What did it mean to be a lady? Could any sense of gentility survive a coed ratline? These were important questions to alumni, parents, and administrators, anxious to reestablish behaviors, or discover panaceas, that might smooth the rough edges of today's adolescents.

In fact, VMI was founded through a few citizens' search for gentility. In 1839 a group of Lexington residents wanted to rid their town of the raucous soldiers who were guarding the local arsenal. The citizens reasoned that if they were to build a military college on the site, the students could protect the arms while pursuing their education. Young officers-in-training were bound to be more polite, quieter, and more genteel than your average enlisted man. Thus the nation's first state military college was born—a monument to one town's desire for propriety.

Today, VMI clings to the superficial remnants of a more decorous age. VMI's Code of a Gentleman, memorized by all cadets, still includes the following admonitions:

> A Gentleman:
> Does not speak more than casually about his girlfriend . . .
> Does not go to a lady's house if he is affected by alcohol . . .
> Does not hail a lady from a club (Barracks) window . . .
> Never discusses the merits or demerits of a lady . . .
> Does not slap strangers on the back nor so much as lay a finger on
> a lady.

For VMI's first coed class, these words were destined to sound peculiarly archaic, and peculiarly relevant. Translated into modern parlance, they could form the starting point for a sexual harassment policy. But was a rat a lady? And how many of the cadets were gentlemen?

MY OWN ACQUAINTANCE with VMI's version of gentlemanliness began when my husband first introduced me to some of the Institute's officials, most of whom were VMI grads. Each man had his own way of greeting a new spouse. The Commander of the Marine Corps detachment kissed my hand; the Commandant of Cadets (a sort of Dean of Students) hugged me and kissed my cheek; the Deputy Commandant remarked that my husband had never mentioned what a pretty wife he had, and went on to praise his own "bride."

Some women would have been thoroughly annoyed at such behavior. Having spent most of my youth in North Carolina, I was not offended. I was amused. This theatrical friendliness was distinctively Southern, a complement to the cadets' ongoing tradition of tipping their hats to civilian women and saying "Good Evening, Ma'am," "Afternoon, Ma'am."

Of course, those hugs and kisses happened ten years ago. The administrators who were in place by the time VMI's first female cadets arrived were not so physically demonstrative. Had they been inclined to kiss a hand or two, the temptation would have been squelched by the hours of sexual harassment training they received prior to the onset of coeducation. Nevertheless, they valued the principles behind VMI's gestures of gentlemanliness. They valued tradition; they respected old-fashioned courtesies; and they sympathized with one of the prevailing characteristics among VMI alumni—a pervasive opposition to change.

The concept of "change" is an anathema to many VMI grads. Whenever the subject came up in conversation, General Bunting liked to quote W. C. Fields: "The only person who wants a change is a wet baby."

VMI's grounds radiate an aura of immutability. According to Paul Maini, Executive Vice President of the VMI Alumni Association:

> I can bring Harry Byrd from the Class of '35 back here. I can sit him up on the balcony. He can look out across the parade ground and see the same barracks that he lived in. He can see the same architecture, the same trees, and the same grass, generally, that he remembers from his cadetship. He can look out over a parade and see the same uniforms. And until this year he could see an all-male group that was exactly like his except for the number that are out there.

Although the experiences of today's cadets are, in Maini's words, "universes apart" from those recalled by the school's oldest alumni, when it comes to outward appearances, stepping onto VMI's Post is like entering the land that time forgot.

Hand-in-hand with this ambience of structural stability comes the belief that VMI's intrinsic nature should remain constant—something many people felt would not be possible if the school admitted women.

When explaining their opposition to coeducation, many cadets insisted that women could never get the VMI experience, because the moment women entered the school, the VMI they sought would be lost for all time.

This brand of fatalism (or realism, depending on one's perspective) was not limited to cadets. VMI's lawyers used the same argument, as did George F. Will in his nationally syndicated newspaper column. In the days immediately following the Supreme Court's June 26 ruling, Will distributed an article in which he stated that the Supreme Court had given women "the right to enroll in an educational institution which, the moment they enter it, will essentially cease to exist."

Behind these statements lay the belief that VMI's single-sex culture was, prior to 1997, one of the defining characteristics of the school. According to VMI's administrators, no other college in the United States had a system of education that relied so heavily on the assumption of a single-sex student body. Whether it came to the cadets' open living conditions, or the "adversary system" of verbal abuse and physical stress that upperclassmen heap on new indoctrinees—a system that no other military college had maintained after going coed—VMI's world, so its adherents argued, was not meant to accommodate both sexes.

Throughout VMI's legal bid to remain all-male, the Institute's single-sex status was all the more precious to its supporters because of its rarity. Alumni often pointed out that if VMI and The Citadel (South Carolina's similar, all-male military school) were required to admit women, single-sex military colleges for men would be extinct, and only three civilian colleges for men would remain in the United States: Hampden-Sydney in Virginia, Morehouse College in Georgia, and Wabash College in Indiana. "Save the Males" swiftly became the most popular slogan on bumper stickers in VMI and Citadel territory, as merchandisers coopted the language of environmentalists to promote these schools as an endangered species. Doug Chase, a popular newspaper columnist in Lexington, put the matter succinctly: "I wonder why we're worried about the one-of-a-kind snail darter and not the one-of-a-kind VMI."*

"Diversity" was another liberal cause that VMI supporters adapted

---

* Quoted by Sandy Banisky, "Admit Women to VMI? Town Says No, Politely," *Baltimore Sun,* May 13, 1996.

to defend their position. When required to prove that the school's exclusion of women served an important governmental objective, the Institute's lawyers argued that VMI helped to diversify Virginia's system of higher education, and within that system there were other opportunities for collegiate women in search of publicly funded military training.

Virginia Polytechnic Institute, a large and prestigious public university about eighty miles south of Lexington, includes a Corps of Cadets that has been coed since 1973. Although VPI's military regimen is not as intense as VMI's, its cadets wear uniforms throughout the school day, they learn to march and drill, they maintain good standards of appearance, fitness, and military decorum, and new arrivals undergo months of high-pressure indoctrination. Prior to 1997, any Virginia daughter who wanted a state-supported, military-style education could join VPI's Corps or take ROTC classes at another of Virginia's many public colleges. It would be a shame, VMI alumni argued, to put their school's system at risk to meet the interests of a small number of female students who wanted something more.

But would women really threaten the Institute's intrinsic nature? Was maleness itself an essential factor in the VMI ethos?

One group of cadets circulated their own crude response to this question in the early 1990s, designing a T-shirt that featured the silhouette of a VMI cadet in full-dress uniform, with his saber thrust forward from his waist in a not-so-subtle phallic symbol. The caption read: VMI. You Need a Member to Be a Member.

But when Charles Bryant, '69, gave the keynote address at a kickoff ceremony for VMI's orientation sessions on coeducation (March 11, 1997), he stressed that the rules for membership in VMI's Corps had never been absolute. Prior to 1859 all cadets were Virginians. Today, roughly forty-four percent hail from other states or countries. Prior to 1912, the Institute catered solely to chemistry and engineering majors. Today, cadets receive B.S. and B.A. degrees in thirteen disciplines, with half of the Corps majoring in the liberal arts or economics. From the early 1940s until the end of the Cold War, all entrants had to qualify for a military commission, and the majority of graduates went into the armed services. Today, thirty-five to forty percent receive a commission, with almost half of these opting for reserve status. Finally, prior to 1968

African-American men could not attend the Institute. As the new millennium nears, approximately seven percent of VMI's Corps is black.

All of these changes were initially greeted with resistance, inspiring lamentations about the school's decay. But VMI survived. And while the admission of women would undoubtedly require major adjustments, some observers wondered which sort of cadet was more removed from VMI's traditional mission: a Virginia daughter pursuing an Army commission, or a New Jersey son with no interest in a military career, sitting with sullen resentment through his mandatory ROTC classes?

This question was only one among many batted back and forth from 1989 to 1996, in courtrooms and in living rooms, in Washington and in Lexington. Not that the arguments in Lexington were ever very heated. Lexington residents rarely stage protests. Even those who viewed VMI's admissions policy as overtly unconstitutional tended to sympathize with the school's desire to be left alone. As General Bunting put it: "If you have things that plainly are working well, and have worked well, and have spoken to the needs of succeeding generations, things that transcend computers or electric typewriters, you should not put them at risk provided they are doing their work honorably."

But was VMI, in its all-male days, such an honorable place?

In the eyes of many women's groups, the Institute's single-sex admissions policy represented something more pernicious than a simple desire for diversity in higher education. The Institute's exclusion of women was an attempt to preserve a chauvinistic men's club, one that promoted constrictive notions of women's abilities and their role in society. After all, what sort of attitudes toward women were being cultivated in this public institution?

This is a valid question and one especially difficult to answer, since, on the subject of women, the attitudes of VMI cadets tend to range from absolute egalitarianism to blatant pigheadedness. I sampled something of the latter quality in the fall of 1988, when walking with my husband through the underground concourse that connects VMI's barracks with the student activities building. The concourse, like all of the barracks, was off-limits to women without a special escort, a fact which explained, but did not excuse, the dimly lit bulletin board that hung on the wall. There, under the headings of Alpha, Bravo, Charlie, Delta, each of VMI's companies had posted its favorite pinup photos of women. They included women in string bikinis; women in thongs; women in leather underwear and studded collars, straddling Harley-Davidsons. Large-breasted women arched their backs while hoses splashed water over their T-shirts.

In a private wall locker such photos would have been tame, even predictable. But in the hallway of a public institution they were inflammatory. It did not matter that VMI removed the pictures a few weeks later; I had seen the underside of VMI's gentlemanliness, and it would be several weeks before I could watch a cadet tip his hat and say "Afternoon, Ma'am" without a dark sense of irony.

Among VMI's older adults, ideas about gender tend to resemble those among America's moderate-to-conservative citizens. Most of the school's administrators have highly educated wives and ambitious young daughters, and these men would never suggest that women's educational or career opportunities be curtailed in any significant way. The only exception, of course, was Dad's beloved alma mater, and when it came down to it, most alumni daughters were happy, in years past, to remain exempt from pressures to uphold the family tradition by attending VMI. After all, to most women (and men), the "VMI Experience" was not even remotely appealing. In the last few years of the court case several alumni wives touted bumper stickers that read: Any Woman Who Wants the VMI Experience Should Marry a VMI Man—a slogan as cautionary as it was conservative.

VMI's official position on the different natures of women and men was expressed, in part, in the statements of expert witnesses whom the Institute recruited during the court case. Dr. David Riesman, from Harvard University, and Dr. Richard C. Richardson, from Arizona State, testified in 1991 before the U.S. District Court for Roanoke, Virginia. They offered their opinions on gender-based developmental differences, and questioned whether VMI's adversative method of education would be appropriate for women. The presiding judge summed up their arguments in his "Findings of Fact," stating, among other things, that: "Males tend to need an atmosphere of adversativeness or ritual combat in which the teacher is a disciplinarian and a worthy competitor. Females tend to thrive in a cooperative atmosphere in which the teacher is emotionally connected with the students."* VMI's critics responded by attacking the school's propagation of outdated sexual stereotypes, but the Institute's lawyers stuck to their guns, claiming that the fundamental differences between the sexes legitimated Virginia's support for single-sex military education for men.

It is important to note that not everyone associated with VMI was opposed to coeducation. When Captain Blair Turner, Head of VMI's Department of History, polled the school's faculty in March 1990, sixty-two percent of the respondents favored the admission of women. Some hoped that coeducation would enhance VMI's academic environment, increasing the school's applicant pool and producing a more competitive atmosphere in the classroom. Others saw it as a simple case of civil rights; although they were happy teaching an all-male corps, they didn't see how VMI could continue to keep women out.

Among the eighty-four replies that Turner received, only a handful of faculty members offered vociferous objections. One respondent stated that any faculty member who did not agree with the school's admissions policy should leave the Institute. Another claimed that simply taking the poll was a disservice to VMI. And a few complained that they were never given a chance to vote. But Turner, who was then serving as President of VMI's chapter of the American Association of University Professors (AAUP), felt that it was important for those professors who responded to the poll to have their say. VMI's chapter of the AAUP released the results of the poll to the press, resulting in a brief flurry of newspaper articles and radio shows, followed by an extended winter of alumni disgruntlement about the school's "disloyal" professors.

Meanwhile, the court case dragged on.

I LEAVE THE LEGAL NUANCES of the case to writers more qualified to analyze them. For the purposes of the narrative that follows, only a few points require emphasis. First, one must note the role played by Judge *Jackson* Kiser, of the U.S. District Court in Roanoke. Kiser ruled in VMI's favor during the first round of the legal battle in April 1991, and

---

* Judge Jackson L. Kiser, *United States v. the Commonwealth of Virginia,* June 14, 1991, Appendix.

he backed the Institute again when the case was remanded to him in October 1992. He later served as the presiding judge in the ongoing skirmishes between VMI and the U.S. Department of Justice, as VMI carried out what it called its "assimilation" of women.

Following Kiser's original decision for VMI, the Justice Department appealed its case to the U.S. Court of Appeals for the Fourth Circuit, in Richmond, Virginia. That court determined that Virginia must either admit women to VMI, renounce public funding for the school, establish a parallel program for women, or find another creative solution. It was here that the case became especially interesting, for in a new test of the doctrine of "separate but equal," VMI chose the last option.

By September 1993 the VMI Foundation (which manages the Institute's endowment) had agreed to help establish the Virginia Women's Institute for Leadership at Mary Baldwin College—a four-year women's school thirty miles north of Lexington. If VMI ultimately won the court case, the Foundation's ongoing financial contributions to VWIL would top $5 million.

Like VMI, VWIL would receive public support, with the State of Virginia providing equal financial assistance for in-state cadets at both institutions. VWIL students would take leadership courses, complete an off-campus leadership externship, and participate in community service projects. They would learn to march and drill as part of a ceremonial Virginia Corps of Cadets, and they would attend ROTC classes at VMI. In most other areas, however, their college experience would differ significantly from the VMI model.

VWIL students would live in dormitories, not barracks. They would not be required to eat meals together, and they would wear their uniforms three days a week, as opposed to VMI's round-the-clock schedule. Most notably, when a task force of faculty and staff from Mary Baldwin sat down to design the VWIL program, they agreed that for most women VMI's confrontational style of military training was entirely inappropriate. Rather than breaking down VWIL cadets through an adversarial system, these educators favored a method of character development that emphasized cooperation and promoted self-esteem. In other words, there would be no ratline at Mary Baldwin.

From the outset, the VWIL proposal drew harsh criticism from observers who viewed it as a weak ploy to avoid true gender equity. The

Justice Department stressed that Mary Baldwin and VMI were in no way comparable: the average combined SAT score for entrants at Mary Baldwin was about 100 points lower than the score for VMI freshmen; Mary Baldwin's faculty held significantly fewer Ph.D.s; its course offerings in science and math were less extensive; and Mary Baldwin's alumni network and endowment could not begin to approach VMI's.

Nevertheless, Judge Kiser was satisfied that VWIL and VMI could achieve similar outcomes. "If VMI marches to the beat of a drum," he wrote in his ruling on April 29, 1994, "then Mary Baldwin marches to the melody of a fife, and when the march is over, both will have arrived at the same destination." Feminists deplored this statement as idiotic, but the Appellate Court in Richmond upheld Kiser's ruling, and in August 1995, even as the Supreme Court was deciding whether to review the matter, forty-four women enrolled in VWIL.

Meanwhile, down in Charleston, South Carolina, administrators at The Citadel were watching these events with keen interest. Earlier that month Shannon Faulkner had entered their barracks, the first woman to infiltrate The Citadel's all-male environment. Although she had resigned within a few days, Faulkner had opened the floodgates to subsequent legal challenges, and The Citadel was now investigating the possibility of starting its own VWIL equivalent at the all-female Converse College.

By October of that same year, however, after the Supreme Court had decided to review VMI's case, it seemed unlikely that the nation's chief justices would accept VWIL as a remedy to VMI's constitutional troubles. No one doubted that VWIL had some impressive young women in its ranks, women who thrived under the VWIL system. At the end of the program's inaugural year one of VWIL's strongest students, Trimble Bailey, was named by VMI's Air Force ROTC department as their top first-year cadet, outperforming 127 male classmates. Small victories of this kind, however, would ultimately do little to bolster VMI's legal position.

The Supreme Court heard oral arguments on VMI's case on January 19, 1996, and handed down its ruling on June 26. In a seven-to-one vote, the Court decreed that VMI could no longer continue as a publicly supported, single-sex institution. Clarence Thomas abstained from the vote because his son was attending VMI at the time.

Ruth Bader Ginsburg wrote the majority opinion, forever inscribing herself as a nemesis in the hearts of VMI's most reactionary alumni.

Within her opinion she described the legal standards for intermediate and strict scrutiny, and the need for an "exceedingly persuasive justification" for any form of gender discrimination in public institutions. She also surveyed several of the inequities that women had faced in the past, noting Virginia's protracted fight to exclude women from the University of Virginia in Charlottesville prior to 1970, and the comparatively slim resources the state had used in the past to found single-sex colleges for women, all of which had subsequently gone coed. It seemed that in Ginsburg's view, Virginia had a long history of discriminatory practices when it came to providing for the higher education of its daughters.

Ginsburg also pointed to VMI's own mission statement, finding nothing gender-specific in its aims:

It is the mission of the Virginia Military Institute to produce educated and honorable men, prepared for the varied work of civil life, imbued with love of learning, confident in the functions and attitudes of leadership, possessing a high sense of public service, advocates of the American Democracy and free enterprise system, and ready as citizen soldiers to defend their country in time of national peril.

"Surely," she wrote, "that goal is great enough to accommodate women."

Finally, Ginsburg concluded by stating that: "There is no reason to believe that the admission of women capable of all the activities required of VMI cadets would destroy the Institute rather than enhance its capacity to serve the 'more perfect Union.' "

Within these last words, and others like them, VMI found some cause for solace. Ginsburg's opinion was peppered with remarks implying that VMI need not substantially alter its system to accommodate the average woman. Instead, its legal obligations were directed toward "women capable of all the activities required of VMI cadets." In later months VMI would make particular use of those passages where Ginsburg reiterated statements made in the District and Appellate Courts:

In contrast to the generalizations about women on which Virginia rests, we note again these dispositive realities: VMI's "implementing methodology" is not "inherently unsuitable to women," 976 F. 2d, at 899; "some women . . . do well under [the] adversative model," 766 F. Supp., at 1434 (internal quotation marks omitted); "some women, at least, would want to attend [VMI] if they had the opportunity," id., at 1414; "some women are capable of all of the individual activities required of VMI cadets," id., at 1412, and "can meet the physical standards [VMI] now impose[s] on men," 976 F. 2d, at 896. *It is on behalf of these women that the United States has instituted this suit, and it is for them that a remedy must be crafted.* (italics mine)

In other words, VMI would later insist, the Institute was not required to modify its adversative system to accommodate women, nor, more controversially, to adjust its physical standards.

Ginsburg's opinion did not specify whether separate public educational programs for men and women could ever withstand legal scrutiny. Chief Justice William Rehnquist, however, clearly believed this to be true. Rehnquist wrote a concurrent opinion in which he stressed that a state could provide separate educational institutions for men and women, as long as it devoted comparable resources to both sexes. The problem in VMI's case was that after the Supreme Court first ruled against a publicly funded single-sex school in 1982,* the state of Virginia did not move promptly to establish a single-sex program for women. Such a school would not have had to mirror VMI; it could have been altogether different. Rehnquist even suggested that Virginia might have met its constitutional obligations by channeling more financial support into the state's private women's colleges:

Had the State provided the kind of support for the private women's schools that it provides for VMI, this may have been a very different case. For in so doing, the State would have demonstrated that its interest in providing a single-sex education for men, was to some measure matched by an interest in providing the same opportunity for women.

---

* See *Mississippi Univ. for Women v. Hogan.*

Accordingly, the remedy should not necessarily require either the admission of women to VMI, or the creation of a VMI clone for women. An adequate remedy in my opinion might be a demonstration by Virginia that its interest in educating men in a single-sex environment is matched by its interest in educating women in a single-sex institution.

VWIL was simply too little, too late.

Of course, Rehnquist was stating his own opinion. Whether a majority on the Supreme Court would support a "separate but equal" approach to single-sex education would remain for the future to decide.

The lone voice of dissent in all of this debate was Justice Antonin Scalia, who attacked his colleagues' ruling against VMI as a matter of "politics smuggled into law." In Scalia's opinion, the Court was usurping power not specified in the Constitution; VMI's fate should have been determined by the people of Virginia, not by the courts. The first paragraph of Scalia's dissent merits reading, because it captures the sentiments of many VMI alumni:

Much of the Court's opinion is devoted to deprecating the closed mindedness of our forebears with regard to women's education, and even with regard to the treatment of women in areas that have nothing to do with education. Closed minded they were—as every age is, including our own, with regard to matters it cannot guess, because it simply does not consider them debatable. The virtue of a democratic system with a First Amendment is that it readily enables the people, over time, to be persuaded that what they took for granted is not so, and to change their laws accordingly. That system is destroyed if the smug assurances of each age are removed from the democratic process and written into the Constitution. So to counterbalance the Court's criticism of our ancestors, let me say a word in their praise: they left us free to change. The same cannot be said of this most illiberal Court, which has embarked on a course of inscribing one after another of the current preferences of the society (and in some cases only the counter majoritarian preferences of the society's law trained elite) into our Basic Law. Today it enshrines the notion that no substantial educational value is to be served by

an all men's military academy—so that the decision by the people
of Virginia to maintain such an institution denies equal protection
to women who cannot attend that institution but can attend others.
Since it is entirely clear that the Constitution of the United States—
the old one—takes no sides in this educational debate, I dissent.

Scalia was not entirely accurate in referring to a "decision by the people of Virginia" to maintain an all-male military college. A statewide ref-
erendum on VMI's admissions policy had never been proposed, and had
there been such a vote, it is not at all clear which side would have won.
But Scalia touched a popular chord at VMI when he asserted that the
High Court was intruding in affairs that were none of its business.

Once the Supreme Court had spoken, VMI's strongest supporters
experienced the common stages of mourning—shock, anger, denial, bargaining. For several cadets, the immediate response was disbelief. Some
had been lulled into assurance by the early courtroom victories. Others
had maintained an unwavering faith in what they viewed as a just cause.

Lieutenant Ryan McCarthy, '97, who would later serve as an administrative aide during VMI's first semester of coeducation, remembered
the startling impact when he first heard the news. He was in the midst of
biochemical training at Fort Bragg, standing in a tent, learning how to
clear hazardous material out of his gas mask. At the moment when the
instructors took the masks away, leaving their troops to inhale riot gas,
one mischievous noncommissioned officer leaned over to McCarthy and
said: "You lost the court case." McCarthy gasped, sputtered, and ended
up crawling out of the tent on his hands and knees.

"The first impression you get," he later explained, "is that everything
will change. They will tear the barracks down and build new ones. . . .
We'll wear different uniforms, we'll act differently, talk differently. . . .
You devote four years of your life to something, you give up four years
of the easy fraternity-guy life, and then you say, 'For what?' "

Among those faculty and administrators who had long anticipated
this outcome, the only surprise was the margin of defeat. After all of the
legal maneuvering, the final vote hadn't even been close. Nevertheless, it
was good to have the case decided. For seven years, much of VMI's emotional and financial energy had been diverted toward the legal struggle.
The Institute had spent approximately $10 million from its endowment,

money that covered everything from legal fees to public relations expenses. (No public money was spent on VMI's private lawyers and consultants, and the school's efforts to solicit alumni funds specifically for the court case netted less than $500,000.)

Along with this financial price had come the cost to the Institute's spirit. VMI had spent several years in a holding pattern. According to Captain Turner of VMI's history department, a professor could scarcely change the carpeting in his office without feeling that he should consult with the Institute's legal advisors. Now, the school could begin to move on.

The direction VMI would take was not immediately apparent. As the next two chapters will show, VMI's most influential supporters responded to the Supreme Court decision with widely divergent visions of the school's future. But one point was clear to everyone—the Institute had turned a page in its history, and with this new leaf our story begins in earnest.

2

C O E D U C A T I O N :
T H E   I N I T I A L   B L U E P R I N T S

WHEN BILL STOCKWELL, VMI'S ASSOCIATE DEAN OF THE FAC-ulty, first heard of the Supreme Court's ruling, his immediate thought was "Oh crap. I can't imagine the amount of work that is before us." As Colonel Stockwell recalled, "I didn't lament the fact that women were coming because it was going to be good or bad for the Institute. My initial reaction was: the next couple of years are going to be hell."

The hell that Stockwell envisioned included a mountain of administrative chores—establishing policies, modifying facilities, addressing complaints—with each new decision preceded by days, sometimes weeks, of committee debate. Within twenty-four hours of the Supreme Court's June 26, 1996, judgment, VMI's administrators had launched into a daily routine of three-hour meetings, followed by all-day work sessions, designed to draft blueprints for a new coed era. During the early weeks, however, the work had to be done discreetly, for in July 1996 the Institute had not yet accepted coeducation as an inevitability. In fact, a last-ditch effort was under way to try to ensure that women never attended the "Mother I."

Immediately following the Supreme Court's decision, some alumni began to speculate publicly about the possibility of making the school private. A Contingency Planning Committee, composed of representatives from the Institute's alumni agencies and Board of Visitors, had been investigating the ins and outs of privatization for several months. Now, with Justice Ginsburg's opinion before them, those alumni who supported the idea brought the issue squarely into the public arena. Commenting for the press, Edwin Cox III, then-President of the VMI Alumni

Association, assessed the alumni's never-say-die spirit with Confederate aplomb: "You always fight for what you think is right until you've been badly whipped, like General Lee was the day before Appomattox. . . . If you took an overly cautious approach, we'd still be British."*

Nothing in Justice Ginsburg's opinion specifically prohibited privatization. Although the U.S. Department of Justice had gone on record as opposing the idea back in 1992, from a legal standpoint privatization remained a possibility. The principal barrier lay in the price tag. VMI's officials estimated that it could take anywhere from $200 million to $400 million to buy or lease the Institute's campus from the state and to establish an endowment to replace the approximately $10.8 million in state funds that VMI receives annually.

When these totals were first batted about in the spring of 1996, General Bunting joked that "I could raise that in eleven phone calls," a hyperbole that lost its humor when some people began to take him at his word. By July, the Superintendent's rhetoric was more subdued. Speaking to Allison Blake of the *Roanoke Times,* Bunting explained that in his "heart of hearts" he expected VMI to admit women, adding that "I'm very conscious of what we have to do when the dust settles: to admit women or raise ten zillion dollars and keep it all male."†

VMI's Board of Visitors, however, was not willing to rule out privatization. In the summer of 1996 this Board was composed of two women and fifteen men, all appointed by the Governor of Virginia and all opposed to coeducation. Most of them were Institute graduates, and when they met in mid-July they decided to allow their fellow alumni two months to investigate the feasibility of going private. At the same time, they instructed VMI's administrators to present to them, within the next two weeks, their initial plans for accommodating women. The Board's final decision on the future of the Institute would be announced on September 21. In the meantime, VMI's Admissions Office was told to record the names and addresses of women requesting applications, and to inform these prospective cadets that they would hear from the Institute after the September 21 vote.

---

* David Reed, Associated Press Newswire, June 28, 1996.
† "VMI Aware of Hurdles," *Roanoke Times,* June 29, 1996.

Some observers viewed this deferment as a stalling tactic, designed to grant VMI one final year of all-male glory. They pointed to The Citadel, which, only two days after the Supreme Court ruling, had announced that it would "enthusiastically accept qualified female applicants into the Corps of Cadets." The words of The Citadel's Public Relations Officer, Terry Leedom, rang like an admonition in VMI's ears: "The Court spoke as loudly and clearly as it possibly could. That's now the law of the land, and we didn't want to go through with more delays that would not have fit into the spirit of the ruling." Leedom went on to assert that "They may not like her," referring to the male cadets' attitude toward the next female cadet to enter The Citadel, "but she's not going to know it. They will have respect for the individual. That is drilled into cadets from Day 1. It will work here, and it will work well."*

In retrospect, The Citadel clearly acted with destructive haste. The same Corps of male cadets who cheered and hooted as Shannon Faulkner left The Citadel the previous fall were not prepared to make such a swift about face. Whether the judge presiding over The Citadel's legal affairs would have allowed that college a year to plan for women was doubtful. But by January 1997, after two of the school's first four female cadets had left amidst allegations of hazing, it would be easy for observers to condemn The Citadel's abrupt launch into coeducation while praising VMI's measured approach. It seemed that the race would go to the tortoise, not the hare.

In the summer of 1996, however, the view was quite different. The Citadel's swift admission of women was hailed in the press as a sign of goodwill, while VMI was criticized for dragging its feet.

Why didn't VMI's Board of Visitors promptly acknowledge coeducation as the wave of the future? Why was the Board willing to expose VMI to months of negative PR, while its alumni pursued a privatization campaign that seemed to face insuperable obstacles?

There were several reasons. First of all, VMI needed time to prepare for coeducation. Unlike The Citadel, which for years had included women in its night courses and had formulated a remedial plan to prepare for Shan-

---

* See Michael Janofsky, "Citadel, Bowing to Court, Says It Will Admit Women," *New York Times,* June 29, 1996.

non Faulkner, VMI had made no previous efforts to accommodate female students. It remained a college where, for example, there were no women's locker rooms in the main athletic building. Whenever I, as a faculty spouse, joined my husband at VMI's swimming pool, he used the indoor entry via the men's dressing room, while I entered through an outside exit. He placed his clothes in a locker; I left mine in a bag by the wall. Afterward, he showered and dressed in the men's facilities; I joined the other spouses in a small coach's office next to the pool, dripping on the desk and filing cabinets. We knew that the men's locker room was nothing to be envied. Like the rest of the athletic building, it was reputed to be old and filthy. But we were always surprised that the Institute could maintain such blatant inequities, despite the presence of female faculty members for the past few decades. Apparently, none of the female professors were swimmers.

VMI's structural problems were merely the superficial manifestation of deeper, attitudinal barriers that had to be addressed before women could be received as cadets. With this in mind, the Institute's Board of Visitors wanted at least one year to lay the groundwork for coeducation. Timing, however, was not the Board's chief motivation in allowing the alumni to investigate privatization. They were also inspired by the unique relationship between VMI's alumni agencies and the Institute.

VMI's alumni agencies consist of three main organizations: the Alumni Association, which is responsible for organizing reunions, publishing the alumni review, and generally "perpetuating memories of cadetship"; the VMI Foundation, which handles all of the Institute's fundraising and manages the school's endowment; and the Keydet Club, which is a booster organization for VMI's athletic teams. These three units enjoy an independent and powerful status at VMI. They are private corporations, connected to the Institute only through their mission and legacy of cooperation. And because they hold the purse strings for all VMI funds not provided by the Commonwealth of Virginia, they are a force to be reckoned with.

Paul Maini of the VMI Alumni Association readily admits that the setup "is not the optimum situation for a college president":

> When disagreements arise, we have the ability to tell the President of the college, "No we don't agree." Our own Board is who we answer to . . . and this is relatively unique. . . . We benefit a great

deal from it because of our independence, but the college President sees his endowment controlled by someone else.

And what an endowment it is. VMI enjoys the biggest endowment per capita of any public college in the United States. While the total endowment at larger universities might dwarf VMI's treasure chest (estimated at over $250 million in January 1998), if you compare the size of the endowment to the size of the school, VMI's funds per student remain the highest in the country. The Institute's graduates are not more wealthy than their peers nationwide, but their emotional commitment to their alma mater translates into hard cash, and that cash gives them a great deal of influence.

Faculty members often lament the amount of power that VMI's alumni wield over the workings of the Institute. So do the many administrators who find their Brother Rats camping at their doors whenever emotional issues are at hand. And everything at VMI is emotional. Coeducation merely raised the stakes.

In July 1996 VMI's Board of Visitors was anxious to maintain the school's tradition of strong alumni support, and was determined to lay the groundwork for a reconciliation of the entire VMI Family after the September 21 vote. They felt that they should not endorse coeducation without first allowing the private alumni agencies to pursue their vision of VMI's future. Because of these agencies' independent status, the Board could allow them to examine privatization while the Institute's administration moved forward with plans for a coed Corps. Very little time would be lost in the process, and something might be gained.

No one on the Board of Visitors wanted coeducation; as they saw it, the September 21 vote would be a choice between two evils. Still, the decision would be theirs. On a symbolic level, the investigation of privatization stole some of the Supreme Court's thunder; it gave the impression that VMI's fate was in its own hands (even though any final decision on privatization would have been up to the Virginia General Assembly). The Board of Visitors' September 21 vote would ultimately vie with the Supreme Court's June 26 ruling as a decisive date in determining VMI's future. Meanwhile, from July through September 1996, two separate factions were charting a course for VMI, preparing to lay their cases before the Board of Visitors. To understand their positions, let us begin with a behind-the-scenes look at the work of the first faction: VMI's administrators.

VMI'S ADMINISTRATION had been facing the possibility of coeducation for years, and once the Supreme Court had spoken, time was of the essence. As noted above, a group of the Institute's top officials had begun meeting to construct a skeletal plan for coeducation on the first morning after the High Court's ruling. According to Colonel Mike Bissell, who eventually was to head the effort, a covert aura surrounded their initial work:

> We were very secretive during those days, because we didn't want to send the signal that we were emphatically going coed. . . . We all met in Carroll Hall, so that we wouldn't be conspicuous. Well, in fact it was almost more conspicuous in some cases because you had all of the administrators walking down there. But the point was not to let people know that we were meeting to that extent.

Carroll Hall is an academic building on the opposite end of the Post from VMI's chief administrative offices. In order to reach it, the administrators had to traverse the full length of the parade ground, past the library, past the barracks, and past almost all of the school's academic buildings. Anyone looking out of an office window on a summer morning could not mistake this daily migration of the Institute's top brass—which included the Dean of the Faculty, the Chief Business Executive, the Superintendent with all of his attendant colonels. Had their enterprise truly required concealment, they would have been better off remaining in their usual enclave behind the closed doors of VMI's Smith Hall.

But was secrecy necessary? Any reasonable person might assume that in July 1996 VMI's officials would have been engaged in an all-out planning effort for coeducation. Anything less would have been irresponsible. But in the emotional atmosphere that followed upon the Supreme Court's decision, the mere thought of admitting women could raise hackles. After seven years of arguing that VMI's educational system could not survive a transition to coeducation, the Institute's administrators did not want to advertise the fact that they were mapping just such a future.

So secretive was the atmosphere at the earliest meetings, that when

Lieutenant Colonel Kathleen Bulger-Barnett, a professor of Spanish, was asked to join the planning committee, she was not told its purpose. In the spring of 1996 Bulger-Barnett received a phone call from Colonel Bissell, asking if she would help with a big project that might be coming up. She agreed, not knowing what the project was about. That was the last she heard until the summer, when she received a call from Colonel Leroy Hammond, Headquarters Executive Officer. As she recalled,

> I didn't realize what I was getting into. . . . Colonel Hammond called and said "Would you come to this meeting tomorrow?" I didn't know who the meeting was with; I didn't know what the meeting was about. I thought it was just a typical VMI meeting during the summer. So I walked into Hammond's office with shorts and a T-shirt, to find Si Bunting and every head administrator. I thought "Oh! Now I know what this is about."

Bulger-Barnett was the only woman, as well as the only faculty member, on the original Executive Committee for Coeducation, a status that left her somewhat confused: "I wasn't sure what my role was . . . I didn't know if I was the token faculty or the token female. I didn't know why I was there." She was used to a certain tokenism at VMI. Bulger-Barnett is an attractive, young professor, and film clips from her classroom regularly appear in PR videos to prove that yes, VMI does have female faculty members. Now she was serving as the sole voice of womanhood in the Institute's earliest deliberations on coeducation.

At the other end of the spectrum, the Committee had invited a conservative male student, Scott Grogan, to represent the Corps of Cadets. Grogan was appalled at the thought of women coming to VMI. How could cadets, as gentlemen, subject women to the same abuse that they regularly heaped on one another? No matter what the subject—women's housing, women in the ratline—Grogan could be relied upon to voice the most virulent objections. And that was what General Bunting wanted. According to Bulger-Barnett:

> Bunting was very clear at the start of the meetings that we were all to speak our minds. Regardless of what we said, one side or the other was going to hate us, so we should go ahead and speak. . . . He made sure that we were very open. . . . You know how it is

when you sit with a bunch of administrators, it's sort of hard to be open; but I think for the most part everybody was.

The committee's immediate goal was to produce a report by July 30 for the Board of Visitors, outlining actions necessary to make VMI a coeducational school. Haircuts, pull-ups, skirts, showers—everything that the Institute was to debate over the coming year was now laid on the table. But as they pondered which aspects of VMI's routine would need to be changed, the Committee found itself equally questioning which aspects of VMI life could *never* be changed.

This latter issue was of primary interest to Bunting, a man more attuned to philosophical questions than administrative details. Bunting was one of VMI's most successful graduates—a Rhodes scholar; an accomplished author; an educator who had assumed his first college presidency at the age of thirty-three (at the all-female Briarcliff College in New York), and who had gone on to lead the all-male Hampden-Sydney College in Virginia before moving to New Jersey to oversee the first few years of coeducation at the prestigious Lawrenceville School. He was also a veteran, having served as an Army intelligence officer in the Mekong Delta in Vietnam.

Bunting had resigned from the military shortly after writing a novel about the war, *The Lionheads,* in which he presented the Army's top brass in an unflattering light. Now, his rank of Major General was not in the U.S. Army, but in the Virginia Militia, which continues to function in a regular, uniformed capacity only at VMI.

No one familiar with Bunting's youth would have pegged him as the future president of a Southern military college. Born into a well-to-do family on the Philadelphia Main Line, he had been thrown out of one boarding school after another before receiving permission to take his exams at the Salisbury School in Connecticut. A subsequent enlistment in the Marines had led him to VMI, with a tattoo of the Corps' eagle, globe, and anchor on his right forearm. (VMI is perhaps the only college in the United States where both the President and the Dean of the Faculty sport prominent tattoos.)

Once in VMI's unyielding grip, Bunting had thrived, eventually earning the top cadet rank—Regimental Commander. Since then he had credited VMI with turning his life around, a service that he felt the Institute still specialized in for young men of his bent, i.e., "the idle, not to say shiftless, but possibly talented youngster who for a variety of reasons has not done well in high school":

> I'm not sure exactly why that is, but I think VMI does extremely well with that kind of kid because it says to him: "We're going to give you complete structure. We're going to insist that you compete every day, not only with yourself, but with all your Brother Rats. We're going to remove from your calculus of excuse every conceivable excuse that you might have. You are going to make it on your Mother Wit, on your energy, on your heart, and we'll be here to push you very hard, but we'll also probably be here to pick you up when you fall down."

Bunting did not recommend VMI's system for everyone. When asked whether there are young men who are ruined by VMI, his response was candid:

> I am sure that there are. I do not know who they are. . . . But even with all of the system's doctors and nurses, so to speak, who are interested individually in the cadets, I am sure that there are some kids who drop through that net, and are hurt by it, and who are seriously bruised by it, and who find it cold and heartless and full of a kind of false masculinity.

Nevertheless, Bunting's faith in what VMI had done for his own life made him all the more determined that coeducation should not alter the Institute's essential nature. As he looked toward the years ahead, he wanted his Executive Committee to first determine "What are the irreducibles of VMI?" ("My first question," according to Kathleen Bulger-Barnett, "was What is an irreducible?") Bunting went so far as to ask the committee members to go home and write a paragraph about what they considered to be the key elements that made VMI unique. The roomful of colonels returned the next morning with their paragraphs in hand and dutifully read them aloud. It was a school-marmish exercise—Bunting tended to chair his committee as if he were leading one of his classes in Victorian literature—but the homework assignment had its purpose.

The question of VMI's "irreducibles" was not Bunting's pet project, but a central matter that had been troubling the Institute's Board of Visitors for several years. As the possibility of coeducation neared, VMI's leaders recognized that the admission of women would involve issues far greater than "potty parity" and jewelry policies. In the years ahead, VMI was fated to embark upon a lengthy effort of institutional soul-searching. What would be the nature of the Institute as it approached the twenty-first century? How would it attract young women, while also maintaining the traditional base of young men on which it relied?

Ever since the integration of women into the federal academies in 1976, VMI and The Citadel had rested much of their reputations on their status as all-male institutions. They had served as refuges for young men who wanted a single-sex military education with all of the physical and psychological "rigors" (some would say "hazing") that had been abandoned at most of the nation's coed military schools. With the onset of coeducation, what remained to make VMI distinctive?

As the committee members attempted to outline the essential qualities of VMI, a few responses emerged again and again. These were the core items that would be at stake in the coming years, and as such they merit attention. At the top of the list was the Institute's cadet-run honor system.

VMI's HONOR CODE states simply that A CADET WILL NEITHER LIE, CHEAT, STEAL NOR TOLERATE THOSE WHO DO. On the surface, it seems a rather basic rule to live by, not very different from honor codes at other colleges. The distinction, however, rests in the gravity with which VMI cadets approach the subject of honor.

If you ask a new group of VMI rats why they made their rather odd college choice, you're liable to be surprised by the number that will immediately cite the Institute's Honor Code. Unlike most college applicants, who tend to be drawn by a school's academic specialties, its social life, or the beauty of its campus, many of VMI's cadets seem driven to invest their youthful faith in old-fashioned concepts such as Duty, Discipline, and above all, Honor. Even after four years of college, occasionally tarnished by the memory of cheating scandals, many of them manage to graduate with this faith intact—faith in honor, faith in their ideals, faith in themselves.

It can be tempting to dismiss a young person's earnest references to honor as a sign of naivete or an unreflective repetition of the "company line," but for General Alan Farrell, VMI's Dean of the Faculty, it was their commitment to abstract ideals that tended to make the Institute's best graduates into good fighting men. Farrell had served under many officers since his years as an enlisted Green Beret in Vietnam, and he was particularly impressed with VMI's product:

> The difference is that they believe. Inside the machine that is constructed around an ideal, they believe. And they will be the last ones to abandon the ideal. They believe in the system. They believe in the perfectability of human beings. They believe that by willpower you can overcome obstacles, you can overcome human weakness in the first place, but you can overcome odds, even. And in combat the only way you stay alive is by believing you can beat odds. You can't change odds, but you can beat odds. That's how wars are won, by desperate people who don't know they are beaten.

With honor, as with most other objectives at VMI, the Institute's method of instilling "belief" is to transform an abstract concept into a concrete reality—by codifying it, by posting the details of the Code in every cadet room and classroom, and by imposing the severest penalty upon anyone found guilty of a breach.

At VMI, the single sanction for an honor violation is dismissal—known to cadets as a "bongo furlough" because of the ominous drumming-out ceremony that accompanies a cadet's expulsion. Back in 1910, a drumout was a very public and humiliating event. According to historian Henry A. Wise, "the Corps paraded in full dress at 4 p.m. The 'prisoner' was brought before it, stripped of his uniform, took a thorough beating on his posterior, and was escorted to the limit gates after being warned never to return."*

Today, drumouts occur in the middle of the night, with the guilty cadet conspicuously absent. The Corps wakes to the ominous sound of a snare and bass drum duo, starting then stopping, starting then stopping, signaling that a fellow cadet is gone. Within seconds, doors are unceremoniously kicked open by members of the cadet guard team, and the

---

* Henry A. Wise, *Drawing Out the Man: The VMI Story.* Charlottesville: Published for the VMI Alumni Agencies by the University Press of Virginia, 1978.

Corps is told, by a voice on the barracks intercom, to get up. The cadets, clad in bathrobes, step out of their rooms, onto the four levels of "stoops" (or porches) overlooking the Old Barracks Courtyard. Once the Corps has assembled, the drums stop on the call, and the nine members of the Honor Court seemingly float into the middle of the square, with only the swift motion of their white trousers visible in the darkness. Pacing around the sentinel box at the center of the Courtyard, the Honor Court President announces the name of the guilty party, cites his crime, and concludes with the following words: "He has placed personal gain above personal honor and has left the Institute in shame. His name will never be mentioned in the four walls of Barracks again." With that, all of the cadets turn their backs, walk into their rooms, and shut their doors, without comment, without hesitation. Until graduation, most will adhere to the injunction against speaking the name of the dismissed cadet or discussing his or her actions.

Draconian? Perhaps. But the impact of the ritual is inescapable. One female exchange student from Norwich University, who witnessed a drumout in the fall of 1997, was so impressed that she determined to lobby for the same ceremony at her own college.

While VMI's honor system has its admirers, it also inspires detractors. Some observers argue that the Institute's Code, as enforced by VMI's investigative hierarchy of cadet prosecutors, does not inspire honor so much as it instills paranoia, teaches surveillance, and rewards a rigid adherence to rules that do not promote a greater sense of integrity. On one hand, rats are told that if they pocket a penny that they find on the ground, they will be dismissed for theft (a perversion of the old adage: "Find a penny, pick it up, all the day you'll have good luck"). But so long as they act "en masse," avoiding the strict definition of lying, cheating, or stealing, rats can indulge in more serious crimes—burning mattresses, smashing tables, looting the mess hall during "rat riots"— with comparatively minimal punishment.

Another objection leveled against VMI's Honor Code stems from the subtleties of its application. A visiting student once complained that a cadet who successfully "runs the block" (sneaks out of the barracks after taps without getting caught) and goes into town wearing civilian clothes, receives no penalty, but a cadet who signs out of the barracks under a "permit" and wears unauthorized civilian clothes, must either turn himself in for punishment or be dismissed from the Institute for a "false official statement." Because the cadet signed a form specifying a uniform, he or she is honor-bound to dress correctly. The lesson, according to the system's critics, seems to be that cadets can behave in any manner they choose, so long as they put nothing in writing and make no verbal statements.

In response to such criticisms, many alumni argue that adherence to a rigid system of honor helps eighteen-year-olds develop the behaviors that lead to a broader sense of integrity as they mature. "Honor," as General Farrell likes to say, "is a habit," and although the Institute's habitualized system might seem archaic, VMI remains a school where employees leave their wallets in unlocked rooms, and where cadets take pride in the absence of second chances.

What does this have to do with coeducation? Why should the arrival of women make any difference to VMI's Honor Code?

During the court case, many VMI alumni expressed fears that romantic relationships would weaken the Institute's honor system. How could a cadet turn in a cheater or thief with whom she was in love? Others questioned whether VMI's Honor Court would seem unjust to women, if it contained no female members. Honor Court members are traditionally chosen by their peers, and although no one wanted a quota system, some administrators wondered: if women were not eventually elected to key positions, would the court seem discriminatory?

VMI's honor system was destined to encounter its first minor obstacle related to coeducation in the spring of 1997, when the U.S. Department of Justice suggested that the Institute add a clause to its Code making sexual harassment an honor offense. The level of indignation triggered by this short-lived instance of federal interference can only be appreciated if one understands VMI's institutionalized reverence for its Code.

The second feature of VMI life that the school's administrators determined to preserve was the "ratline," or, in its original form, "rat line." The name comes from the sole path that rats are allowed to walk inside VMI's barracks, a route they must follow with their chins buried in their necks and their arms stiff at their sides in the traditional VMI "straining" posture. This path is so well-worn that one can see its texture rubbed into the barracks' concrete floor. Any rat who wants to stray from it must be escorted by an upperclassman or a VMI official.

Today the compound term "ratline" frequently replaces its two-word equivalent, glossing over the separate concept of a "line" to better encompass the six to seven months of physical exertion, minimal sleep, and in-your-face harassment endured by new indoctrinees. (The worst thing about the ratline, new arrivals often say, is having your face showered with spit from the deliberately precise punctuation of an obnoxious upperclassman.)

Most VMI administrators believe that the ratline's "adversative" training leaves its survivors with a sense of accomplishment and confidence. It encourages habits of time management under severe stress and promotes lifelong friendships forged through commiseration. Parents who arrive to watch VMI's Friday afternoon parades often credit the Institute's system with turning their surly teenagers into mature young men. And if you ask Jim Berger, a Lexington local, he'll tell you that the ratline was one of the factors that enabled him to survive six-and-a-half years of captivity in North Vietnam.

Still, not everyone at VMI values the manner in which the ratline has been administered in recent decades. Professors complain about the futility of teaching exhausted students. Administrators complain about upperclassmen's penchant for plaguing rats with silly, degrading tasks. And perhaps no one is more critical of the system than Colonel Lee Lewane, a Lexington resident who graduated from the Institute in 1950.

No one can question Lewane's devotion to his alma mater. While teaching in VMI's Army ROTC department from 1959 to 1962, Lewane volunteered to help train a cadet ranger unit, a tank platoon, a combat arms unit, and a judo team, earning an Army Commendation Medal for his extra efforts. Since then, his enthusiasm for the Institute has been unfailing. At VMI's 1995 alumni reunion parade, Lewane arrived with a chestnut stallion named Jason and rode the length of the parade ground next to his Brother Rat, Jones Felvey III, as they commemorated their years in one of VMI's last cavalry troops.

But although Colonel Lewane loves the "Mother I," he has never loved the ratline. Throughout VMI's planning for coeducation, Lewane was going to avail himself of every opportunity to urge VMI to switch to a more positive style of leadership training. He even antagonized some fellow alumni by writing a letter that was published in Lexington's *News-Gazette* on August 13, 1997:

The demeaning and degrading verbal treatment of new cadets and, worse yet, physical humiliation that is sadistic in nature, is disgusting and antiquated. It must be immediately replaced with a style of cadet leadership that is inspiring, yet no less demanding. A mixture of velvet and steel. Gen. Creighton Abrams, former Army Chief of Staff, once remarked "Build on what a man is, don't tear him down." Those who subscribe to a philosophy that a person should be shorn of his dignity and personality and then built back up again midst shouts and screams is an affront to parents. By and large, mothers and fathers who send their sons and daughters to VMI have discharged their parental responsibilities of inculcating in them such sterling qualities of integrity, loyalty, commitment and recognition between right and wrong.

It is perhaps a sign of institutional health that some of the ratline's sharpest critics are to be found within VMI's own ranks.

To the Institute's credit, VMI's administrators did not attempt to muzzle Colonel Lewane during their planning for coeducation. Instead, they invited him to serve on a committee that reviewed the co-curricular side of VMI life. (Co-curricular is a common phrase at VMI, used to describe the school's daily military regimen, including its ratline, its cadet-run government, and almost all of the features of barracks life.) Although the Co-curricular Committee did not have a mandate to effect major reforms in the ratline, Lewane had the opportunity to share his views with the rising cadet leaders.

Lewane was, in his own words, a "voice crying in the wilderness." Although many VMI alumni support calls for an increased "professionalization" of the ratline, few share Lewane's enthusiasm for "positive leadership." One theme that would be repeated by several VMI officials in the year to come was the belief that the federal academies, and other military colleges that have abandoned their adversarial methods of training since the admission of women, are sliding down a slippery slope into a "feel good" military, sacrificing combat readiness for the sake of political correctness. According to this view, the positive style of leadership instilled at the academies promotes better human relations in times of peace, but does not produce better fighters in times of war. At a public hearing on privatization, one VMI alumnus went so far as to assert that if the Institute could preserve its single-sex, adversative system, "VMI may be the saviour of the military of the world!"

To academy graduates, such criticism from a small college in Virginia is liable to sound like the voice of a mouse squeaking into a lion's ear. Most VMI grads, however, prefer to think of themselves in terms of David and Goliath. According to Paul Maini, who keeps a constant finger on the alumni pulse, maintenance of an adversative system is VMI's chief way of remaining strong and unique:

> You tend to hang on to identities that make you "the most" or "the best," and ours is as "the toughest." We are the toughest military school probably in the world. . . . And our alumni don't want to let loose of that because we're not the best academic institution, we're not the biggest, we don't have the best football team. So that's something that can be a special identity for us.

Every military college lays its own claims to toughness, but when it comes to sheer ferocity, VMI and The Citadel have long enjoyed a unique position, maintaining a grueling style of training that has been a rare phenomenon in American culture since the mid-1970s. Only a small minority of eighteen-year-olds have ever been interested in such training. But for those young people who deliberately sought VMI's mixture of bonding and bondage, the Institute's administrators wanted to keep the ratline intact.

Hand-in-hand with preservation of the ratline came the final, less tangible goal for Bunting's committee: continuance of the present culture within VMI's barracks. This meant maintaining an open atmosphere in a Spartan environment; preserving the "dyke system," in which senior cadets establish a familial, mentoring relationship with rats who perform menial chores; and, above all, allowing the Corps to police itself through its "class system"—a plan of self-governance, in which cadets exert authority and enjoy privileges based on their places in the chain of existence, from first classmen down to rats.

What would romantic relationships, and the daily tensions of male–female contact, do to this cloistered society? For Paul Maini, that was the key question:

> Most alumni believe that the co-curricular environment of VMI is the critically important ingredient that does something to us, that

helps us become successful, that creates the bond of friendship or creates the memories. There are so many intangibles inside the barracks, that to bring women into that environment would—and here the alumni's choice of words vary: "change," "destroy," "eradicate"—but in many cases "destroy" whatever it is that VMI is doing. And based upon how firmly people felt that, you could chart their commitment to privatization.

In order to keep alumni from defecting into the privatization camp, and to fulfill their own visions for their alma mater, VMI's administrators had to map a future in keeping with the past. And so, as General Bunting's Executive Committee compiled its July 30 report for the Board of Visitors, page after page highlighted all the features of VMI life that should remain untouched. Change was inevitable but should be limited, as much as possible, to matters practical, not spiritual.

These practical matters presented more than enough challenges. What sort of haircuts and uniforms should women have? Where should they be housed? Should VMI replace its pull-up requirement on the VMI fitness test (VFT) with a flexed arm hang? What efforts should be made to recruit women and men?

In the days between June 27 and July 30, 1996, the members of Bunting's committee knew that they could not answer all of these questions. Nor did they want to. In order for a transition to coeducation to succeed, the decision-making process could not be dominated by one insular group. The process needed to involve representatives from the entire VMI Family—faculty and administrators, alumni and staff members, and, above all, cadets. If the cadets did not feel a sense of ownership in the plan, it would never work. At VMI, administrators can dictate policy until their faces are as blue as their "Blue Book" of regulations, but the Corps will ultimately act according to its will. And so, one of the chief tasks of VMI's administrators in the summer of 1996 was to outline a structure of committees and subcommittees, including cadet representatives, that would discuss issues and recommend policies throughout the upcoming year.

There was no question of who would manage this bureaucracy. The operation was to be headed by Colonel N. Michael Bissell, '61, who had served for the past year as the Commandant for the Virginia Women's

Institute for Leadership at Mary Baldwin College, helping to coordinate that program from VMI's end. While General Bunting acted as the public spokesman for VMI, selling the press and the alumni on the Institute's future and exerting final control over all policy decisions, Colonel Bissell would play the chief supporting role. His job was to manage all of the details involved in the transition to coeducation. Whatever happened with VMI's first female cadets, most of the praise or blame would fall on Bissell's shoulders.

Anyone curious about Bissell's character and qualifications needed only to glance at the coffee table in his office. There, in full view, were the two predominant symbols of his life: a model of a black Commanche stealth helicopter, and a Bible. The contrast between these images of war and faith epitomized the energies of a man, who, in 1996, was at once VMI's most highly decorated living alumnus and a devout Catholic, loving husband, and father of seven children, including three sons who had attended VMI.

Bissell had received the Distinguished Service Cross, the Army's second highest honor, during his years as a combat helicopter pilot in Vietnam. But like most veterans at the Institute, he rarely spoke about the war. Instead, he preferred to focus on the subsequent decades he had spent commanding numerous Army aviation units in the United States and Korea.

Bissell had returned to VMI in 1991 to serve as the Institute's first full-time Commandant of Cadets—a position that included overseeing daily life within the barracks—but he had given up the position in 1995 after undergoing triple-bypass surgery following a major heart attack. Now, the only concern anyone felt in watching him take up the reins of coeducation was for his health. No one doubted his abilities. Bissell not only had the military experience for the job, he also had two personal qualifications rare at VMI: the patience necessary to manage a bureaucracy with the U.S. Department of Justice looking over his shoulder and, more importantly, a vocal respect for the capabilities of female cadets.

Like most of his fellow alumni, Bissell had consistently opposed the idea of coeducation at VMI. He had nothing against women. He simply knew that VMI's educational method had been crafted to meet the needs of young men, and that men's opportunities for single-sex education were rare in the United States. At the same time, however, he championed the cause of the young women at VWIL and expressed faith in the leadership abilities, academic prowess, and physical strengths of the female cadets he had met at other military colleges. He did have a tendency to conclude his praise of female cadets by noting that most were "cute as a button"—a comment he shared with VMI's male cadets to persuade them that young women could be tough, professional, *and* feminine. In Bissell's case, this paternalistic praise seemed to derive from generational differences, not from any pernicious form of sexism. It was the language of a grandfather commenting on eighteen-year-olds.

With Bissell in place at the head, VMI's administrators went on to outline a pyramid of committees designed to consider the impact of coeducation on every aspect of Institute life. At the top of the structure was a spinoff from Bunting's Executive Committee, with the Superintendent passing the chairman's torch to Colonel Bissell. Throughout the 1996/97 school year, this group of faculty and administrators would hold luncheon meetings every Tuesday at noon in VMI's board room, discussing policy over an unhealthy repast of sandwiches, cookies, potato chips, and soda. Beneath this umbrella group were seven sub-committees: Recruiting, Facilities, Academics, Athletics, Orientation, Public Relations, and Co-Curricular Activities. To fill these committees Bunting's group came up with a list of over 120 members of the VMI Family. Every committee would include faculty and alumni, cadets and administrators, men and women. One member of the Board of Visitors was also assigned to each group, although most could never attend the meetings. A cadet Committee-at-Large was created later to spread information among the Corps and to gauge cadet responses to all of the plans for coeducation.

None of the people who, unbeknownst to them, were being assigned to these committees during the summer of 1996 had any experience guiding a college from a single-sex to a coed environment. VMI would have to educate its employees as the planning process unfolded. To do this, Bunting's group outlined a plan to send teams of faculty, cadets, and administrators from all of the proposed committees to visit military and civilian colleges throughout the country, hoping to learn from other schools' experiences of coeducation. The list of colleges to be visited included the U.S. Coast Guard Academy, the U.S. Merchant Marine Academy, The Citadel, Virginia Tech, Culver Military Academy, Texas

A&M University, New Mexico Military Institute, and Norwich University in Vermont. After every trip, the travelers would be expected to provide written and oral after-action reports.

VMI's leaders had hoped to visit the federal academies, for despite the Institute's determination to follow its own path, its administrators knew that the academies had decades of experience from which they could benefit. But because the academies were tied to the federal government, and because VMI was still a party in a federal lawsuit, the Justice Department had decreed that there should be no contact between VMI and the nation's top military colleges without its approval. Throughout their planning for coeducation, VMI's administrators would be constrained from consulting with academy officials—a limitation that they found annoying. The federal ROTC officers then posted at VMI were also instructed not to advise the Institute on any of its decisions about women. The Institute would have to chart its course without federal assistance.

In addition to learning from military colleges, VMI also planned to send a few of its people to visit civilian schools, such as Davidson, to absorb their lessons of coeducation. The most useful civilian model, however, proved to be right next door at Washington and Lee University.

Washington and Lee's campus is immediately adjacent to VMI's. Tourists who visit Lexington are often surprised by the sudden contrast between the former's colonial, brick buildings and the latter's fortresslike architecture. Although the two colleges maintain a sometimes bitter rivalry, in the 1996/97 school year, faculty and administrators from W&L were happy to offer advice to their next-door neighbors. W&L had only begun to admit women in 1985, and memories of its own graduates' "Better Dead than Coed" bumper stickers remained fresh. Since those years, W&L's transition to coeducation had brought significant academic benefits, sparing that college, in the words of one W&L professor: "the fate of descending into a Southern gentlemen's drinking school." Of course W&L is a very different place from VMI, more readily able to accommodate women. But its officials still had useful suggestions for VMI.

In addition to consulting with other colleges, Bunting's group planned one more strategy for learning from the outside world; they intended to invite national experts to VMI to meet with the Institute's many committees. Lieutenant General Winfield Scott (no relation to the hero of the

Mexican War) was at the top of the list. Scott had served as Superintendent of the Air Force Academy and the New Mexico Military Institute, and he was a firm believer in the positive role that female cadets had played at the federal academies. At the other end of the spectrum, VMI planned to invite Elaine Donnelly, President of a small conservative think tank called the Center for Military Readiness, which served primarily to point out the problems raised by women's presence in the U.S. military.

In the coming months VMI also intended to invite teams of cadets and administrators from Norwich and Texas A&M Universities to hold panel discussions and help critique VMI's efforts. Their involvement was part of a larger plan to start an exchange program, designed to bring male and female cadets from each of these schools to VMI for one semester. The young women, it was hoped, could act as "big sisters" for VMI's first female rats, and, together with their male classmates, could help VMI's upperclassmen understand how coeducation functioned at other military institutions. At the same time, VMI cadets would study in Vermont and Texas, hopefully returning to the Institute with new lessons about life in a coed Corps.

When the exchange program was first proposed, not everyone at VMI was pleased. Objections often resounded with a tone of defensiveness: How could outsiders appreciate the ratline? Would the exchange students be critical of VMI's normal routine? Would upperclass women challenge the authority of VMI's first classmen?

The fact that the U.S. Department of Justice liked the idea did little to recommend the exchange program in the eyes of Institute alumni. (In the spring of 1997 the Justice Department encouraged The Citadel to implement a similar program. Working hastily, Citadel officials established contacts with Norwich and Texas A&M, but had only recruited two outside visitors by the fall of 1997.) Despite reservations, VMI's administrators moved forward with their plans for an exchange, believing that upperclass female cadets could serve as useful role models for female rats.

Bunting's committee also recognized that more female administrators, faculty, and staff would be necessary to serve as role models in a coed college. In the summer of 1996 VMI had only one woman among its uniformed administrators, and only eight percent of its full-time faculty were women, as compared to approximately twenty-seven percent nationwide (a figure that includes civilian colleges, which are more appealing to female professors). Women did play key roles in VMI's Personnel, Public Relations, and Accounting offices, and helped to run the alumni agencies. They were also ubiquitous as secretaries, clerical staff, and laundry and mess hall workers, but with the pending arrival of female cadets VMI wanted to place more women in leadership positions.

The most immediate priority was to hire an Admissions Officer to spearhead the recruitment of young women. Other new positions that Bunting's committee anticipated included: an Assistant Dean, Assistant Commandant, Assistant Director of Cadet Affairs, Counselor, Physical Education Instructor, and Part-Time Physician. All of these positions were eventually filled by women during the 1996/97 school year. To handle the increased flow of paperwork, additional clerical workers were also going to be needed, and in the fall of 1997 the Institute planned to hire a Deputy Title Nine Coordinator, to specialize in federal guidelines for gender equity.

The salaries and benefits for these new employees would not be a one-time expense. Clearly, the admission of women was going to entail a lot of new, ongoing expenditures, and one of the biggest questions for VMI's administrators as they sketched their early plans was, How much was the whole thing going to cost?

When Colonel John Rowe, VMI's Chief Business Executive, sat down with his calculator, he estimated that after the first coed class matriculated, VMI's operating costs would increase by $1.8 million a year. Adding this to the totals for construction projects, changes in publications, the travel schedule described above, recruiting costs, and various other items, Rowe's office came up with a projected start-up budget of over $5 million.

Rowe had little doubt that the state would come up with the money. The federal lawsuit against VMI is titled *The United States vs. Virginia,* not *The United States vs. the Virginia Military Institute.* The Commonwealth of Virginia had a vested interest in making sure that VMI's transition to coeducation was well done. The main financial obstacle came from the fact that the Virginia General Assembly, which had to approve any allocation of state funds, would not be meeting again until January 1997. VMI, meanwhile, was going to need a considerable amount of money in the next few months in order to initiate and complete construction projects before the arrival of women.

The Institute's idea for the necessary funds was creative. Because the Commonwealth of Virginia budgets for two years at a time and the state was then in the first year of its biennial cycle, VMI planned to ask then-Governor George Allen to transfer the funds from the state's budget for the Institute for the next year. The Governor, a long-time VMI supporter, could do this without legislative approval. Then, in January 1997, the Governor could submit a budget amendment to the General Assembly, restoring the funds that had been transferred.

The plan worked well. Ultimately, the state gave VMI $5.2 million, enough to carry out the transition to coeducation with thorough attention to details. (By contrast, The Citadel received less than $1 million from South Carolina for its initial foray into coeducation. That college, however, did not need to undertake major construction projects.)

The itemized breakdown of this budget, along with detailed recruitment schemes, computerized images of possible accommodations for women, membership lists for the various committees, and a mass of other material, were all included in the report that Bunting's Executive Committee ultimately compiled for the Board of Visitors on July 30, 1996. General Bunting's introductory remarks to the Board outlined the philosophy VMI would follow in the coming year:

> . . . if we're going to do it, we're going to do it well—*extraordinarily* well. We will have to effect a cultural change, an attitudinal change, many of us in ourselves: doubt, skepticism, cynicism, sorrow are not a fertile soil in which to plant the seeds of a new coeducational VMI. Once you have spoken, we will act; and I need not remind you of my own position in the long struggle that has brought us to this point. Healing and building will have to occur simultaneously. (emphasis in original)

To appreciate Bunting's words, one must keep in mind the perspective of the speaker and his audience. This statement was not issued for the benefit of the media or anyone outside VMI. These were the remarks of a man who opposed the admission of women to VMI, addressing a Board who unanimously shared that opposition. Given those facts, Bunting's words were noteworthy for their determination. True, he qualified his statement by alluding to his personal objections to coeducation.

This caveat was to become a standard feature of Institute rhetoric in the upcoming year, with cadets and administrators constantly reiterating the message that "*I* didn't want coeducation, but now that it's here I'm going to see that it's done right."

Notably, in July 1996 Bunting did not hesitate to use the words "cultural change," an unpopular concept at VMI. (By September he would be espousing the concept of "minimal change," a vague term that satisfied no one.) At this early stage, however, the Superintendent was prepared to affirm a commitment to a new order, with one substantial qualification. VMI's "adversative" style of education had to remain untouched:

> The Supreme Court opinion, which has in effect brought us to this meeting, bristles—literally—with testimonials to the "incomparable" efficacy of the VMI way of educating young men for lives of leadership and service; and also, with considered assertions of the ability, desire, will, and fitness of some young women to participate fully in that VMI culture. I take the Supreme Court at its word. I am not especially impressed that other military schools, since coeducation, have abandoned their adversative systems. We are VMI and we will go our own way as we always have.

With these words, Bunting drew his line in the sand. Whether or not the Institute could defend that line remained to be seen. How could VMI effect an attitudinal change without making changes in the ratline? In maintaining an educational model specifically designed for men, would VMI be hindering the full acceptance of women? These questions would have to be answered by the young women who accepted VMI's challenge.

One final point distinguished Bunting's remarks to the Board of Visitors. The Superintendent knew that the Board's September 21 announcement would attract a brief national spotlight, and he wanted to make the most of it. He encouraged the Board to use that moment in VMI's history to effect an academic and admissions renaissance at VMI.

The Institute sorely needed such an initiative. In the post-Vietnam era, single-sex military colleges had little appeal for most eighteen-year-olds. While the federal academies enjoyed international prestige and offered free tuition, VMI had fewer incentives to attract top-quality students. As a result, the intellectual caliber of its applicants had gradually dwindled. It had been decades since VMI had produced a Rhodes Scholar; Bunting was one of the last. And for a man of his scholarly bent, who spent his spare hours writing a book about his vision of the ideal university (a modern return to Cardinal Newman's Victorian project), it had to be disappointing to encounter college-aged students who had not mastered subject–verb agreement.

And so, VMI's administrators included a recruiting wishlist in their report to the Board of Visitors. They wanted more full academic scholarships, athletic scholarships, and financial aid. They mentioned plans to cultivate 105 new feeder schools, to "develop intrastate and interstate institutional partnership programs," to "design the nation's best counselor tour program," and to conduct a marketing study to profile VMI's new target audience. Several, though not all, of their wishes would come true in the upcoming year.

On the academic front, Bunting's committee suggested ways to expand the Institute's curriculum, looking at items that would benefit both male and female students. Two ideas that had been discussed for years at VMI—a new major in psychology and a teacher certification program, managed in conjunction with a well-established program at nearby Mary Baldwin College—were scheduled for adoption in the fall of 1997. The administrators also considered adding a criminal justice major to their offerings, noting that law enforcement was a career choice for one percent of VMI's graduates, and that criminal justice was the most popular major at Norwich University among both men and women. But in the minimal-change atmosphere that would soon prevail, this suggestion was placed on a back burner.

On the whole, the working papers that VMI's administrators placed before the Board of Visitors in the summer of 1996 approached coeducation with a serious and comprehensive vision. Most important, they resounded with the pervasive assumption that VMI *would* admit women. Although Bunting's committee knew that a parallel alumni group was exploring the chances of going private, most of VMI's administrators did not view privatization as a credible option. At orientation sessions for new faculty in August 1996, VMI's top administrators stated that the Institute would definitely be admitting women the following year.

As it turned out, these officials underestimated the emotional force of their opponents. As September 21 neared, privatization expanded from an apparent pipe dream into an administrator's worst nightmare. Most VMI officials believed that an attempt to go private would have disastrous, even fatal, consequences for the Institute, far outweighing the dangers of coeducation. Many Board members, however, did not agree. By September 1996, with one Board member after another choosing to "rally round the flag" of privatization, the atmosphere in VMI's Smith Hall shifted from smooth confidence to mild alarm. The Institute's early blueprints for coeducation were on the table. Whether they would be used remained to be seen.

3

THE CASE

OF THE "PRIVATEERS"

WE NOW COME TO THE MATTER OF PRIVATIZATION, A COURSE
that VMI's Board of Visitors came very close to endorsing. It might seem
far-fetched and somewhat mean-spirited—the idea of transforming a
public college into a private institution simply to avoid the admission of
women. But to many VMI graduates, privatization was no more improb-
able, and no more potentially destructive to their alma mater, than the
idea of female cadets living in VMI's barracks. As they saw it, coeducation was fraught with perils: romantic relationships could erode Corps
discipline and the honor system; sexual harassment might sap Corps
morale; increased supervision in the barracks might threaten VMI's system of cadet self-governance; and "institutional denial" could destroy
VMI's credibility. Many alumni also believed, realistically or not, that the
federal government might impose a recruiting mandate on VMI, requiring the school to alter its system to attract women. And the first item on
the chopping block, most graduates assumed, would be the ratline.

Writing for the *VMI Alumni Review* in the winter of 1997, George
H. "Skip" Roberts, '68, Executive Vice President of the VMI Foundation, summed up the threat that coeducation posed to the Institute's
"adversative method":

No one has ever introduced women into such an environment
without it ultimately being abandoned. Whether one follows the
models of VPI, Texas A&M, Auburn, Clemson or the federal military academies, the results have been the same. The cross gender
relations among college aged students, heightened even more in

today's hazy definition of sexual harassment, have led to the aban-
donment of the adversative system at the federal academies and at
the remaining state military colleges. No college nor any educator
has ever recommended the use of such a system for 17–18-year-
old young women. Few recommend its use for young men.*

With these visions of darkness in their minds and a sincere love for
the Institute in their hearts, several of VMI's alumni leaders decided to
investigate the possibility of going private. Their work began in earnest
after the Supreme Court heard oral arguments on VMI's case in January
1996. Facing the possibility of a legal defeat, the VMI alumni agencies
formed an eight-man "Contingency Planning Committee," composed
of two VMI grads from each of the three agencies and the Board of
Visitors.

Steve Fogleman, who would soon succeed Edwin Cox as President of
the VMI Alumni Association, stressed that no one on the committee
actually wanted privatization. For most, the matter boiled down to
"which was of paramount importance": continuance of VMI's current
method of education—a method that these men felt could not be sustained in a coed environment—or the existence of the Institute itself.
According to Fogleman, the committee members recognized that the
financial burden of privatization—estimated at anywhere from $200 mil-
lion to $400 million—might eventually cause the Institute to fail. But as
they saw it, the Supreme Court's actions had backed them into a corner.

Over the next several months, the committee sought advice from outside educators, lawyers, and accountants, and hired the nationally recognized firm of Barnes and Roche to conduct an independent assessment
of the fundraising issues surrounding privatization. At the same time,
they asked Skip Roberts to join with his Chief Financial Officer, David
Prasnicki, to compile documents, crunch numbers, and ultimately produce an extensive assessment of the numerous issues surrounding privatization.

Roberts was a capable man for the job. On his office door his colleagues
had placed a sign reading "Master Fleecer," an apt title for a lawyer,
fundraiser, and executive who had watched VMI's endowment grow from

---

* "The Issues Before the Board," *VMI Alumni Review*, Winter 1997, pp. 46–47.

$100 million to $250 million under his seven-year tenure. Roberts was eminently pragmatic, seldom swayed by emotion. When it came to the privatization of VMI, he viewed himself and Prasnicki as the double-edged voice of reason in an atmosphere of heated sentiment: "Our job was to strip out the emotion, so that the policy makers had the facts in front of them."

The facts were daunting. From the outset Roberts knew that privatization was "a very long shot." Still, the project offered an exciting intellectual challenge: "It was fascinating. No one has ever done it in America. No one has ever launched the privatization of a state educational institution. We were flying in uncharted territory."

Some would question whether they were ever flying at all. The obstacles to privatization were so numerous, many observers doubted that the scheme could get off the ground.

The mere consideration of privatization required VMI's alumni to engage in rhetorical backtracking. During the court case, VMI had argued that a ruling against the Institute would affect not only public colleges, but any form of public subsidy for single-sex private colleges. VMI had attempted to persuade several private women's colleges to file amicus briefs on its behalf, telling these schools that their tax exemptions, federal grants, and federal student loans were at risk should VMI lose its case. Although a few women's colleges signed on in support of VMI, most dismissed the Institute's arguments as scare tactics, noting a clear distinction between public and private colleges. Justice Antonin Scalia, however, lent some credence to VMI's doomsaying when, in his dissent, he claimed that the Supreme Court's majority opinion could also apply to a private male college.

Now, the supporters of privatization had to assume that an independent VMI could receive all of the public subsidies that private colleges presently enjoy. And with or without these public funds, the larger legal question remained of whether VMI could avoid the Supreme Court's judgment by going private. The Justice Department's opposition to the idea guaranteed that a private VMI would face another round of courtroom battles. That is, if the issue ever made it to the courts.

Before facing legal challenges, the plan would have required approval by Virginia's General Assembly, and at least one state senator objected to the whole idea. Talking to Allison Blake of the *Roanoke Times*, Senate Democratic Leader, Richard Saslaw, gave a blunt assessment of privatization: "I would not vote for that. Why should we sell off VMI? Why not UVA and William and Mary? . . . When are we handing off state assets because alumni don't like a Supreme Court decision?"* Although some VMI alumni insisted that their cause had strong backers in the General Assembly, it was difficult for anyone to distinguish between staunch support and the promises of politicians telling their constituents what they wanted to hear.

Nevertheless, a few VMI alumni believed that regardless of the likelihood of success, the matter should be placed before the General Assembly. If the politicians struck down the idea, so be it. VMI should not be the party to give up the fight.

But even if privatization had survived the legislative process and legal challenges, what sort of college would have remained?

The Department of Defense had already written to VMI, asking the school to certify that it would not unlawfully discriminate against women. Many administrators assumed that if the Institute went private, DOD would remove its large ROTC contingent from the school. At the present time, some thirty-five federal ROTC employees work at VMI each year, a number that does not include their administrative and support personnel. All VMI cadets must take twelve hours of ROTC classes, and approximately forty-five percent of the Institute's graduates receive commissions in either active or reserve units.

VMI without ROTC was a bleak prospect. If the federal government pulled out, the Institute would lose its ability to commission officers and to recruit students planning military careers. General Bunting advised the privatization committee that direct costs from the removal of ROTC would approach $2 million annually in lost scholarship aid, and another $2 million in lost support from ROTC faculty, staff, and equipment provided by the Armed Services. Writing for the Winter 1997 issue of the *VMI Alumni Review,* Skip Roberts noted that: "The intangible costs were described by some as taking the 'M' out of VMI."[†]

Some alumni were willing to sacrifice that letter of the alphabet if it would free the Institute from all obligations to the federal government,

---

* "Alumni Panel at Work on Plans," *Roanoke Times,* June 28, 1996.
† "The Issues Before the Board," *VMI Alumni Review,* Winter 1997, 46.

but fewer were willing to remove the "V" from VMI. Many graduates felt that the loss of the school's status as a Virginia institution would be more devastating to the Institute's character than the inclusion of women.

Meanwhile, VMI's business-minded alumni kept their eyes on the bottom line. For them, the issue revolved around one key question: was privatization financially feasible?

Had VMI been willing and able to raise tuition substantially, the answer might have been yes, but the Institute prides itself on being accessible to a middle-class student body. (VMI cadets enjoy their status as "rats," as opposed to the "minks" at neighboring Washington and Lee. The difference in mammals highlights the distinction between scrappy cadets and sleek fraternity brothers.) At a time when many private colleges were charging $25,000 a year, VMI's total tuition, fees, and quartermaster charges (which include uniforms and laundry) amounted to $9,485 for Virginia residents and $15,950 for those from out of state, with approximately seventy percent of the student body receiving some form of financial aid. In order to maintain VMI's traditional applicant pool, leaders of the privatization campaign hoped to limit any tuition increases to no more than $2,000. Money would have to come from other sources.

But who was going to foot the bill? Normally, VMI looks to its wealthiest alumni in times of crisis, and when Barnes and Roche conducted their privatization feasibility study, they interviewed nine of VMI's top givers. The results weren't promising. As Skip Roberts put it: "Those who had the greatest capacity to fund the privatization of VMI were those in fact who said that 'I cannot get from A to B and be at C five years from now, and I am not prepared to put the kind of seven figure numbers on the table that it would take.' "

Plenty of smaller donors approached Roberts with checkbooks in hand, and were unhappy to be rebuffed:

A lot of those who were emotionally involved had a very difficult time with this. They were saying "What do you mean? I'm ready to give everything I've got. I will commit. I will make my $5,000 gift."

But that's the widow's mite. It may have been a great contribution and a great percentage of their resources, but that was the one $5,000 that they were ever going to give.

After studying VMI's fundraising possibilities, Barnes and Roche determined that the Institute had neither the fundraising capacity nor the lead gift potential to make privatization feasible. Their message was clear: from a financial perspective, privatization was a dead end.

The Contingency Planning Committee responded to Barnes and Roche's news like a patient who has just been informed that his condition is terminal; they wanted a second opinion. The source they consulted was not exactly unbiased—the committee spoke with some of VMI's most influential alumni, leaders of the VMI Campaign, which had raised $80 million in cash and $75 million in commitments for the Institute from 1978 to 1990. Not surprisingly, these men approached privatization with a can-do spirit. In their experience, VMI had tended to exceed all expectations whenever it came to fundraising. They did not believe that Barnes and Roche's top-down approach—relying on major donors within the VMI community—was the only way to tackle the project. Many believed that the privatization of VMI was a national cause—one that could generate broad-based financial support from outside donors. In the emotional atmosphere of the time, with VMI enjoying national attention while conservative factions deplored the Supreme Court's deathblow to single-sex, public military schools, privatization supporters were willing to bet that the nation's conservative leaders would put their money where their mouths were.

To understand how they might have reached this conclusion, one need only read the open letter that Phyllis Schlafly addressed to VMI's alumni in the midst of the debate, a letter that was published on the VMI Alumni Unofficial Web Site on July 11, 1996:

THIS IS AN OPEN LETTER to Virginia Military Institute Alumni.

Dear Alumni:

Your VMI training not only taught you to be tough, courageous and honorable, but also to survive humiliation and harassment. You are now facing your greatest challenge.

You've lost a major battle. Are you going to be survivors, or are you going to let the enemy wipe you and your kind from the face of the earth, pour salt in the soil that produced you, and drop you down the Memory Hole?

The most important factor in any confrontation is the ancient maxim "Know your enemy." I'm not sure you ever understood the nature of your enemy.

The massive government lawsuit against VMI wasn't about "ending sex discrimination" or "allowing women to have access to the same educational benefits that men have at VMI." It was a no-holds-barred fight to feminize VMI waged by the radical feminists and their cohorts in the Federal Government. . . .

The VMI decision was wholly predictable when Clinton appointed Ruth Bader Ginsburg to the Court. Her activist determination to write her radical feminist goals into the Constitution was all laid out in her published writings, but no Senator questioned her about them. Every Senator who voted for her confirmation shares in the shame of this decision.

VMI Alumni, your response to this Supreme Court defeat should be to reject the state subsidy and embark on a national fundraising drive to raise the money to keep VMI functioning exactly as it always has. If the still-existing single-sex colleges, such as Wellesley and Smith, can survive on private fundraising plus government student loans, and if Hillsdale College can survive without any government funds at all, there's no reason why VMI and The Citadel can't do this, too.

Don't make the mistake of changing VMI's unique lifestyle to try to accommodate Sister Rats. The women who seek a military career based on dual standards and gender norming can go to West Point, Annapolis, or the Air Force Academy.

VMI Alumni, if you allow Ginsburg et al. to do to VMI what Pat Schroeder et al. have done to the United States Navy, you are not the exemplars of manhood we thought you were. And that goes for Citadel alumni too.

Schlafly's tactics were striking. Here was a woman challenging the masculinity of VMI's alumni. The admission of female cadets would be equivalent to the Institute's defeat at the hands of women—Ginsburg, Schroeder, and the membership of NOW.

Schlafly's letter voiced the most extreme side of the privatization argument, and as such it did not represent the views of the majority of

VMI alumni. As Paul Maini once noted: "Most people here don't like extremists about anything." Her remarks, however, help to explain why, in the summer of 1996, some alumni believed that the privatization of VMI could become a national conservative rallying point.

These "privateers," as they came to be called by a few VMI administrators, received a boost on September 10, when the Justice Department filed a petition demanding that VMI immediately begin mailing applications to women. Although VMI was already processing applications from men, at the beginning of the 1996/97 school year it would not even send information to their sisters, telling them instead that they would have to await the outcome of the September 21 vote—a response that left DOJ indignant.

DOJ's timing could not have been worse. With the Board of Visitors' vote only eleven days away, VMI viewed the federal petition as a form of harassment. The petition would never make it through the legal system prior to September 21, and by that time the matter was likely to be moot. The only purpose it seemed to serve was to bolster the argument for privatization.

Throughout the court case, whenever the Department of Justice did something that Institute officials deemed rude or overreaching, VMI's alumni responded by digging in their heels. According to Paul Maini: "Everything that the Justice Department did that was embarrassing or accusatory in its tone to VMI brought more people on board to say 'OK, the federallies are here again. The carpetbaggers are coming in, so we've got to stand up.' "

In this case, "privateers" waved the federal petition at those VMI Board members who were sitting on the fence and essentially said: "See, I told you so." In their opinion, this action was only a slight taste of the federal micromanagement VMI would experience if it admitted women. Meanwhile, in the corridors of Smith Hall, General Bunting muttered that no one was doing more to ensure that VMI would *not* go coed than the U.S. Department of Justice.

THE EMOTIONS SURROUNDING privatization reached their highest pitch in the week preceding September 21, as two key meetings brought matters to a boil. First, on September 13, 1996, the Boards of the VMI Alumni Association and the VMI Foundation held a joint meeting in

Richmond. They intended to survey the options facing VMI and to vote on a recommendation to present to the Board of Visitors. Given the alumni's enormous influence at the Institute, and their status as the only group capable of acquiring the school, this vote was going to be important. The meeting, which was closed to the public, was packed with VMI's most vocal supporters.

Among them was Skip Roberts, who outlined four options facing the Institute: "full-blown" civilian coeducation, accommodative coeducation, privatization, and closing the school.

"Full-blown" coeducation was a fate that several alumni had predicted would befall VMI down the road. If the Institute could not attract enough women who wanted to suffer through the ratline and live in the existing barracks, many people believed that the federal government would insist that VMI change its system. The Institute's adversative method would lie on the trash heap of history, and what remained would be just another civilian college, competing with similar schools throughout Virginia.

A few pessimistic alumni believed that VMI should save itself considerable trouble and become a civilian college from the outset. The fate was inevitable, so why go through the sham of trying to integrate women into a system that would not survive in a dual-sex environment? For that matter, a few alumni insisted, why not close the school altogether? As some die-hard grads surveyed the obstacles to privatization, they had begun to despair of success and had called for the Institute's end. According to Paul Maini: "I had fifty-year-old, mature, educated, normally conservative-minded people who said 'Burn it down!' And they weren't kidding."

To those individuals, Skip Roberts wanted to convey a simple message:

> Some of you are talking about shutting it down. Let's just get that off the table. The State of Virginia is not going to shut VMI down. It's got too big an economic investment in the Lexington community. The state government subsidizes a lot of inefficient operations, and it is unlikely that it would pull a $30 million economic engine out of Lexington.
>
> Close your eyes and put a chain link fence around VMI. Now

put that facility in the heart of the Valley's tourism business. Do you honestly believe today, in this context, that the state would close VMI?

As always, Roberts was attempting to fight fiery emotions with chilly economics, and his efforts were only partially successful. Talk of closing VMI would continue to surface well into the winter of 1997, with some alumni believing that the Institute might be gradually dismantled. One such alumnus explained his rationale in a letter to the editor of the *Richmond Times-Dispatch*:

> To most VMI alumni, VMI's system is not one to be tampered with even lightly, without totally twisting it out of shape, unlike a university where big changes can occur without destroying the basic university ideals of education and scholarship. Many alumni believe that there are standards or rules and morality regarding the VMI system that must be defended, even to the point of closing the school by slowly scuttling it. This would indeed be trouble and not without pain, but no more than the Board now has, given that it has no real view for the future except "do what we have been doing, only with women in the Corps," which cannot be done.*

Talk of closing the school resonated with dark irony. According to VMI's fight song, the Institute's "battle cry is Never, Never Die." The same sentiment appears in the VMI Doxology—a reworded version of the Christian liturgical rite, performed, in this case, by VMI cadets and alumni at the end of every basketball and football game. Where churchgoers sing: "Praise God from whom all blessings flow / Praise him all creatures here below," VMI sports fans resound with "Red, white and yellow floats on high / The Institute shall never die." Now, faced with the possible admission of women, some alumni were ready to throw in the towel.

These, however, were a small minority. For most, the issue came down to privatization vs. "accommodative" coeducation.

---

* "VMI Follows Path to Destruction," *Richmond Times-Dispatch,* January 30, 1997.

"Accommodative" was an odd name for a plan that involved as few accommodations as possible. In essence, it meant opening the Institute to those women seeking VMI's current style of education, with minimal adjustments—the path that VMI ultimately would follow. On that September evening in Richmond, however, privatization was clearly the people's choice, with one speaker after another rising to champion the idea.

Among the supporters was Elaine Donnelly, President of the Center for Military Readiness, who painted a particularly gloomy picture of VMI's future, should it admit women:

> In order to achieve a "critical mass" of ten to fifteen percent women, political pressures will be applied to achieve proportional representation, i.e., quotas, for admissions and promotions of women to leadership positions. . . .
>
> To attract women in significant numbers, the spartan VMI environment, featuring plain wood furniture, unlocked doors, and mattresses that are rolled up each morning, will have to be modified and eventually eliminated. . . .
>
> Because intentional random stress will be perceived as sexual harassment when applied to women, VMI will eventually have to eliminate it. . . .
>
> Mandatory sensitivity courses—probably designed by feminist advocates—will be necessary to reduce young men's resistance and to accommodate women's need for emotional support. . . .
>
> Highly-publicized embarrassments at a coed VMI are as predictable as hurricanes in August . . . *

Meanwhile, Skip Roberts tried to infuse a tone of pragmatism into the debate. Looking back, he recalled his words as a message of caution:

> Folks, you have to be serious about this. This is not a game. It's not a raw emotional thing. You're not going to trump it with some people in Richmond walking around with VMI buttons on. You have to understand the politics, the finances, the state retirement

---

* "A Coed VMI: What to Expect," reprinted in the Winter 1997 issue of the *VMI Alumni Review*.

system, the state benefits system, the nature of the faculty, the impact of the state employees lobbyists, and where they are going to be in this process.

Roberts' matter-of-fact approach won him no friends that day. At the end of the meeting, when the Board of the VMI Foundation decided to take no vote on VMI's future, realizing that they could not support privatization, some alumni blamed Roberts. The leaders of the VMI Alumni Association, however, voted unanimously to present a proposal to the Institute's Board of Visitors, asking that they endorse a plan to take the school private.

BY THE TIME THE BOARD members arrived in Lexington on September 18, emotions were running wild. Feelings reached their climax on the afternoon of Friday, September 20, when the Board held its only public hearing on VMI's future. The hearing took place in the Turman room of VMI's library, with portraits of the Institute's former Superintendents looking on. General Bunting sat at the front of the room next to William Berry, the Chairman of the Board, who presided over the session. Beside them, the entire Board of Visitors was gathered around a U-shaped group of tables, with a podium at the open end backed by rows of spectators. Television cameras lined the room, recording, on one side, the pleading faces of emotional speakers, and on the other, the varied expressions of Board members, some nodding, some poker-faced.

Of the twenty-three individuals who spoke, only three believed that women should be admitted to VMI. Among them was Colonel Lee Lewane, once again evangelizing for positive leadership as well as coeducation.

For everyone else, the admission of women was an appalling prospect. One speaker urged the Board to "save the last vestiges of civility between men and women," and compared VMI's position to the Spartans at Thermopylae. Another invoked Robert Frost's "The Road Not Taken," a poem often used by VMI officials to persuade young people to enroll at the Institute. In the eyes of this alumnus, privatization and coeducation were two roads diverging in a yellow wood; it would "make all the difference" if VMI would choose the less traveled, private road.

Two alumni had conducted informal polls of their fellow grads, finding overwhelming support for privatization. As Scott Sayer, '86, put it, the issue boiled down to "combat readiness vs. gender equity," and he deplored what he saw as a two-tiered system in the present Army. For several other speakers as well, the present argument was not only about VMI, but about women in combat.

Several Lexington women also spoke in support of privatization. Sis Warner, whose husband, Harry, was one of the leaders of the privatization campaign, deplored the thought of a "VMI headed by Ms. Ginsburg." She compared a vote for coeducation to the death of Stonewall Jackson: "Don't let VMI be killed by her own." By contrast, Ms. Edna Pickral, widow of a 1943 grad, tried to inject some humor into the tense situation: "They are all interested in sex," she said, speaking of today's college students. "They'll get a much better education if they don't have to think about it all the time."

That evening the Board settled into a long night, and longer morning, of intense debate. They excused General Bunting from their deliberations, a decision that he welcomed as a great favor. Before they rendered their vote, however, William Berry asked Bunting to say a few words at lunch. The Superintendent left the Board with one final message:

> Whichever way you go I will do the very best I can for you . . . but you should remember that if you do vote to take the school private, so far as my own work is concerned, I will not be a normal college president. I will not be teaching, or leading, or working with students or faculty on this Post. My entire effort will be to raise this huge sum of money and to evangelize publicly on behalf of what you would like VMI to become.

Some alumni had been encouraging Bunting to resign in protest, should VMI admit women. But that, he explained, "would not have been a good thing." Nor did he plan to quit if the school went private. Either way, as he informed the Board, he would do as he was "ordered."

Shortly after lunch the Board held its vote, followed by a one o'clock press conference in the library of VMI's George Marshall Museum. The room was too small for the large audience; listeners peered in from beyond the door. But the setting was appropriate. In the upcoming year the United States and Europe would be celebrating the fiftieth anniversary of the Marshall Plan, and for many people in the room, Marshall, VMI's most famous graduate, embodied the heritage that they felt was now at stake.

Fewer of the people assembled that afternoon realized that Marshall had left a lesser-known legacy that tied him to the day's events. He was the founder of DACOWITS, the Defense Advisory Committee on Women in the Services, which acts today as the most powerful political advocate for U.S. servicewomen, leading the charge for Congressional repeal of combat exclusion laws. Marshall had formed the civilian committee in 1951 to advise the Defense Department on ways to enlist and retain women during the manpower crisis of the Korean War. Although the far-sighted General might never have imagined that female cadets would someday attend his alma mater, it seemed fitting for his spirit to preside over the current scene.

By the time the press conference began, television cameras, newspaper reporters, and print photographers filled the library. Alumni who had played key roles in the privatization campaign sat in a front row with their "Go Private" buttons clearly displayed. Before them, the seventeen members of the Board of Visitors assembled in a semicircle around a podium stacked with microphones.

When William Berry stepped forward to speak, he cut to the heart of the matter: By a 9 to 8 vote, the Board of Visitors had decided to accept women into VMI's Corps of Cadets, beginning in August 1997.

The closeness of the vote was a surprise to many. For those who opposed privatization (few could be described as supporting coeducation), it seemed that a catastrophe had been narrowly averted, like a near miss between two airplanes. For the supporters of privatization, however, the numbers showed just how close they had come to carrying the day. Now, most were choked by a wave of bitter disappointment.

"As you can see by the closeness of the vote," Berry continued, "this resulted from a thorough and often difficult debate. Our intent is to comply fully with the 26 June decision of the Supreme Court, and we will immediately send applications to young women who have inquired about attending VMI." Within hours, applications for women would be in the mail, and the Justice Department's petition for an injunction against VMI would be laid to rest.

In his next breath, Berry affirmed the Institute's intent to maintain its present system. Women were welcome, so long as they were willing to play by VMI's rules:

> The Board made this decision with the full understanding that VMI will not change the military and academic features of its culture that have distinguished the Institute since its founding. In doing so, the Board finds support in the opinion of the Supreme Court that "VMI's implementing methodology is not inherently unsuitable to women," that "some women do well under the adversative model," that "some women, at least, would want to attend VMI if they had the opportunity," and that "some women are capable of all of the individual activities required of VMI cadets . . . and can meet the physical standards VMI now imposes on men."

With this, the reporters perked up their ears. Did VMI intend to be the first college ever to apply the same physical standards to women and men?

Berry elaborated on nothing. Instead, he made a brief statement designed to bring the supporters of privatization back into the fold:

> Much has been made—in some quarters—of division among us. I would say they don't know us very well. There have been differences, honest differences expressed honestly by honest people. And all of them stem from a deep loyalty and affection for this institution.
>
> I am confident that our family will stand united, and God willing will always be so.
>
> From motives of heart and conscience, we have fought a long campaign together. It is now the challenge for General Bunting and his staff to lead VMI into the new millennium in which VMI will graduate its first class of educated and honorable men and women. I am absolutely confident of VMI's future and in its ability to address this new challenge. We will do our best.

General Bunting then took the podium and reiterated VMI's commitment to nurturing the "vigorous virtues" in young people.

When the prepared statements were over, the reporters launched an onslaught: "How long would the women's hair be? Would the women be required to do pull-ups?" To the backers of privatization, some of whom were now crying, the questions seemed as grotesque and invasive as an interrogation at a funeral. General Bunting responded with tough talk of buzz-cuts and unchanged physical standards, defiant rhetoric that soothed some alumni, while giving the reporters plenty of material to take to NOW and the ACLU for their critique.

In fact, Bunting's stance was more rigid than the motion that the Board of Visitors had approved. The Board's resolution stated that there would be no changes to the VMI methodology except "alterations necessary to afford members of each sex privacy from the other sex in living arrangements, and to adjust aspects of the physical training programs." This last exception seemed to acknowledge that some adjustment of physical standards might be necessary in the future.

With the conference adjourned and the microphones turned off, Anita Blair, a member of the Board of Visitors who staunchly opposed coeducation, read a statement to a circle of reporters on behalf of several Board members:

> We regard this as the worst possible choice. . . . By electing to modify VMI and admit women, the Board of Visitors has guaranteed that the Virginia Military Institute will be fundamentally changed in such a way that neither young men nor young women will obtain the benefits formerly associated with a VMI education.
>
> Today's majority decision is a disservice not only to Virginia's sons and daughters, but to Virginia as well. The majority of the Board of Visitors has chosen a course that wastes Virginia's educational resources. The financial cost of modifying VMI's physical plant is vastly disproportionate to the benefit of educating a tiny number of women who might be interested in attending VMI. . . .

After listening to Blair, the press gathered comments from cadets and alumni. David Zirkle, a first classman from Virginia, offered the usual comparisons to the Civil War: "VMI has been through a lot. It was burned in the Civil War, shelled by Union artillery. It survived that. We will endure this."* Robert Patterson, '43, VMI's lead attorney during the court case, was less optimistic: "It's a sad day for VMI. It's a sad day for the state and it's a sad day for the nation as far as I'm concerned."†

In the weeks to come, several observers delivered postdecision analyses. Wes Allison from the *Richmond Times-Dispatch* argued persuasively that the Board had split along generational lines, with the younger members more staunchly supporting privatization.‡ Paul Maini, on the other hand, assessed the entire privatization campaign as a matter of "the heart vs. the head. People who tended to trust more in their heart, said 'We can do this.' People who trusted more in the numbers, and their heads, said 'It can't be done.'"

Whatever the reason, the vote was in. It did not offer a warm welcome for women, nor did it give VMI's administration a mandate for change. Quite the opposite. The closeness of the vote, and the lingering opposition of several Board members, meant that the Institute's governing body would be monitoring VMI just as meticulously as the Justice Department, but with a different agenda. At the same time, the federal government would use the vote, and the defiant tone of VMI's statements, to argue that the Institute needed to be watched carefully in the months ahead.

Despite its reluctant tenor, the vote gave Colonel Bissell the green light to set in motion all of the committees, the travel plans, and the construction projects that had been outlined by VMI's administrators over the summer. In the months to come, VMI's faculty, cadets, and administrators would embark upon the largest planning effort for coeducation known to any military college. The questions they pondered and the decisions they made occupy the next section of this book.

---

* Quoted by Mike Allen, "Cadets and Others Say It's Time to March On," *Richmond Times-Dispatch,* September 22, 1996.
† Quoted by David Reed, Associated Press, "VMI Ends All-Male Tradition," September 22, 1996.
‡ "VMI Vote Split Along Age Lines," *Richmond Times-Dispatch,* September 24, 1996.

PREPARING
FOR WOMEN

4

THE LANGUAGE
OF ASSIMILATION

THE FIRST ITEM OF BUSINESS WAS NOT HAIRCUTS, NOT SWIMSUITS, not showers—not any of the seemingly innocuous details that would grow into little monsters as discussions unfolded. For the more than 100 cadets, faculty, administrators, and alumni who sat down to discuss the specifics of VMI's future, the initial challenge rested in something more fundamental—their own choice of words.

Words, after all, can foster goodwill or civil suits; they are the starting points for friendship and for sexual harassment. In their July 1996 report for the Board of Visitors, VMI's administrators explained that "attrition data from other colleges reflects that language and vulgarity are the main causes of attrition with female cadets, not the toughness of the system." The same lesson emerged when a VMI team attended a 1997 national conference on "Leadership in a Gender-Diverse Military." There they listened as one speaker after another stressed the importance of inclusive language in creating a productive work environment for women and men. Male-centered terminology, sexist jokes, gendered profanity—all could contribute to a hostile atmosphere, and all existed, to a greater and lesser degree, on the VMI Post. In preparing for the arrival of female cadets, VMI faced a variety of semantic challenges: cleaning up the locker-room language in the barracks; correcting the gender bias in official documents and daily conversations; and determining which of the Institute's awkward, but historically significant terms, such as "dyke," "boned," and "run a period," should survive the axe of political correctness. At the same time, administrators needed to develop a discourse flexible enough to appease VMI's most difficult audiences—insistent reporters, skeptical alumni, and a hawkish Department of Justice.

In the ensuing struggles for the linguistic high ground, "coeducation" was an early casualty. By October 1996 VMI had decided that "coeducation" implied more change than the school desired to undertake. The Supreme Court's decision did not require the Institute to implement a new system of education jointly designed for men and women. Rather, VMI was charged with integrating women into its existing, male-oriented program. "Integration," however, carried its own political baggage. And so, Colonel Bissell, who made no claims to a silver tongue, searched his brain for synonyms.

The word he eventually settled upon was "assimilation"; VMI would "assimilate" women into its culture. Shortly thereafter, a sign reading "Assimilation Office" appeared outside Bissell's door. For the undertaking VMI had in mind, "assimilate" was an accurate term, with a history of use at other military institutions. But the word had a sinister ring.

Ironically, VMI's determination to "assimilate" women coincided with the release of *Star Trek: First Contact*. In that film, as in the television series, the greatest threat to civilization comes from a half-organic, half-mechanical alien race called the Borg, whose sole objective is the assimilation of other cultures. Borg creatures lumber about in zombie fashion, informing their victims that "We are Borg. You will be assimilated. Resistance is futile." In the fall of 1996, the Borg's mission of creating a homogeneous "collective" provided a grotesque counterpoint to VMI's project of "breaking down" new cadets to form one cohesive "rat mass."

The Borg analogy emerged again in the spring of 1997, when every person on VMI's Post, from laundry workers to top administrators, began attending training sessions on sexual harassment, fraternization, and new "assimilation policies." Between sessions, a few administrators could be heard exchanging Borgian greetings: "I have been assimilated. Have you been assimilated? Resistance is futile."

Most of the reporters covering VMI embraced the concept of "assimilation" with a swift and uncritical fervor, reminiscent of the speed with which the term "adversative method" had saturated the public debate during VMI's earlier legal struggles. Several military colleges use the phrase "adversative method" to describe the mental harassment and physical exertion faced by new indoctrinees. The two words lend a scientific air to an unscientific process, enabling the schools to argue that there is, indeed, a "method" to their madness. Although "adversative method" had been heard at VMI in the past, during the court case the term increased in popularity. Today, "adversative method," "assimilation," and "close-cropped" (the deliberately vague term used by VMI administrators to hold critics at bay while the Institute fine-tuned its haircut policy) constitute the most prevalent linguistic legacy of VMI's admission of women.

Meanwhile, the term "women" itself received only partial currency at VMI. During the earliest meetings of the Institute's Executive Committee on Assimilation (previously "Coeducation"), administrators referred to prospective female cadets as "girls," "gals," "women," "females," and "ladies," prompting calls for a standardized terminology. All parties agreed that the gender-neutral term "cadet" was preferable wherever possible, with "women" acknowledged as the most professional alternative. "Girls," however, remained the most commonly used term on Post, preferred by cadets, older employees, and several visiting consultants who, owing to generational differences, tended to view college-age students as "boys," "girls," and "kids."

"Young ladies" also remained popular, largely because of the Institute's Southern heritage. In March 1997, NPR's Linda Wertheimer was clearly amused when VMI's rising First Class President, Kevin Trujillo, referred to the prospective female cadets as "the young ladies." When Wertheimer asked whether VMI would refer to the women as "young ladies" after their arrival on Post, Trujillo did not miss a beat. He stated matter-of-factly that the women would be "cadets" and "rats."

More specifically, the women would be known as "*Brother* Rats," the appellation VMI cadets have applied to their classmates ever since the nineteenth century. No administrator was willing to tamper with that sacred title. If the Corps of Cadets decided someday to dub its women as "sisters," that was fine, but "Brother Rat" would be left to its own, natural evolution.

In the meantime, some faculty members wondered how to address the women in class. Throughout the Institute's history, VMI cadets have been referred to as "Mr. Smith" or "Mr. Jones." Should the women be hailed as "Ms." or "Miss"? Or should all students be addressed as "Cadet Smith" and "Cadet Jones"?

The written word proved just as tricky as spoken language. As VMI prepared for the arrival of women, it had to revise stacks of Institute publications, from recruitment brochures to Rat Bibles (the pocket-sized guides to VMI history and trivia that all rats must memorize). In the end, the revisions for each publication reflected the biases of individual authors. VMI's academic regulations were edited with the meticulous sensitivity to language typical of people with Ph.D.s; "he and she" appeared in all the appropriate places. By contrast, VMI's "Blue Book" of co-curricular regulations, which covers everything from haircuts to furloughs, was prepared by military officers and cadets who had little interest in his's and hers'. As long as the Blue-Book policies were adjusted to account for the presence of women, pronouns were of secondary import. And so, the 1997/98 Blue Book opened with a one-page bold-faced "DISCLAIMER: . . . Words importing the masculine gender shall be deemed to include the feminine unless the context of usage necessarily requires otherwise." Whether this linguistic Band-Aid would stick for more than a year or two remained to be seen.

These efforts got little play in the press. Most reporters were concerned with VMI's plans to address the double meanings in several of its traditional terms, such as "dyke" and "boned."

VMI cadets have long served as "dykes" within the Institute's "dyke system." Awkward as the word might sound, the etymology of "dyke" rests in sartorial matters. Mike Burke, '73, who now serves as a Lieutenant Colonel in the U.S. Army and an Assistant Professor of English at West Point, researched the term for a 1981 graduate linguistics paper on "Cadet Slang at the Virginia Military Institute":

> In an 1856 work, *A Collection of College Words and Customs,* by B. H. Hall, "diked" appears, the spelling used at VMI until around World War II. Hall defines the term:
>
>> At the University of Virginia, one who is dressed with more than ordinary elegance is said to be *diked out.* Probably corrupted from the word decked, or the nearly obsolete *dighted.* Samuel Johnson's *Dictionary* and the *OED* define *dight* as

meaning to "dress, bedeck, adorn," and "to get a person ready, to dress."*

In today's Corps, the term "dyke" can refer to any uniform worn by cadets, such as "class dyke," "gym dyke," etc. More specifically, "dyke" refers to the various straps and sashes on cadet uniforms, which hold up items such as sabers and band boxes. Because it is impossible for a cadet to adjust these straps without assistance, rats were originally assigned to first classmen to help them dress, or get "dyked out."

This assignment eventually evolved into VMI's "dyke" system—one of the unique features of life at VMI. In a typical dyke relationship, a rat performs menial tasks for a designated "first" (folding laundry, rolling up mattresses), and, in exchange, is taken under wing and indoctrinated into the ways of the Institute. Rats and upperclassmen paired in this mentoring system are known reciprocally as one another's "dykes," a word that has raised eyebrows for years, and seemed especially troublesome with the coming of women. Most administrators believed that "dyke" could be preserved, if the Institute was careful to inform incoming cadets of the term's derivation, but one Colonel did object to the phrase "cross-gender dyking," noting that it sounded like "something that would go on in New York City."

"Boned" is another oddity in the VMI lexicon. When a VMI cadet is reported for misconduct, he is said to have been "boned." A faculty member might "bone" a cadet for disruptive behavior, with the penalty assigned to the cadet also referred to as his "bone." No one can say where "bone" originated. The U.S. Army's nearest equivalent is "gig," which means "to spear or jab." Some VMI old-timers speculate that "bone" may have derived from women's whale-bone corsets, and their efficacy in straightening out a wayward body with one sharp stab. Mike Burke associates the word with fish and the act of removing their bony skeletons. Regardless of its derivation, the word was a minor sticking point. Some people questioned whether male faculty and staff would feel comfortable informing female cadets that they intended to "bone" them. Few acknowledged that "boning" a male cadet involved equally awkward connotations.

---

* Virginia Military Institute Archives, Lexington, Virginia.

One final phrase that inspired some debate was "running a period." At VMI "period" refers to each grading period, originally a term of thirty days, shortened, in recent decades, to twenty-eight. A cadet who remains free of demerits (or "bones") in a given cycle is said to have "run a period." This phrase became controversial in the fall of 1996 when a female reporter from the *Roanoke Times* interpreted the words as a clear allusion to the female menstrual cycle. Several cadets and alumni protested that the words had never before been used in that fashion. According to Keith Gibson, Director of the VMI Museum, the term originally had very practical and positive connotations:

> It was a very desirable thing to run a period, and I can't ever imagine it having any sexual implications at all. It had to do with the calendar. In the mid-70s, VMI was a more cloistered community than it is today. We have become that thing that I think many old alumni feared, in essence a suitcase college. Cadets have all sorts of things to take them away from here on the weekends. But even as recently as the '70s, that wasn't the case at all. As a first classman, you received six weekends that you could take, ostensibly looking for a job. One of the only ways that you could get away was to perform this rather significant effort of going twenty-eight days without receiving a demerit. I was always very anxious to do that. I can remember as a cadet, you would go twenty days and then you would get a demerit for something silly and disaster had befallen you. One of the things that kept the Corps in conformity with the Blue Book was the hope and prospect of running a period. Today cadets have so many weekends that it's immaterial.

When it came to the double meanings in "period," Gibson stressed that "It was never suggested. Cadets didn't even kid around about it; it just didn't occur to anyone." Once the reporter's article had appeared, however, the term raised plenty of snickers.

Faced with these and other awkward phrases, VMI's officials originally contemplated the pros and cons of altering the Institute's traditional parlance. General Bunting, however, settled the issue in a brief memo dated December 19, 1996. His stance was unequivocal:

Gentlemen:

Please note that I do not want the VMI stoop lingo changed, not a word of it, in order "to accommodate" women. You might think these small items, but they are important and significant, historical accretions that help us sustain the legacies of our predecessors: The words are hardy old *VMI* words. *They are not to be excised from the Rat Bible, etc., during my time as Superintendent.* (emphasis in original)

Bunting's insistence on the preservation of VMI's traditional lexicon conformed to his own propensities as a wordsmith with a flair for Victoriana. In his syllabus for an undergraduate course, he once referred to a text as the class's historical "enchiridion," a word alien to most English speakers, but typical of a man who liked to keep his students and colleagues reaching for their dictionaries. Whether one viewed Bunting's use of multisyllabic words as a formula for confusion or a refreshing antidote for a language dumbed-down to the level of "lite" and "luv," his linguistic flourishes proved useful in disarming and charming the multitude of reporters and alumni that he faced day after day.

So long as Bunting served as the verbal gatekeeper, words such as "dyke," "boned," and "Brother Rat" would enjoy the status of protected speech. But there were plenty of other, nontraditional terms that needed to be exorcised from the VMI vocabulary.

After 158 years of single-sex freedom, the language in VMI's barracks had sunk to a dismal level. Profanity was commonplace, with "fucking" used as an all-purpose adjective. During his tenure as Commandant, Colonel Bissell was once confronted by an angry father only hours after matriculation. The father had gone into the barracks to help his son move in, and was so appalled at the litany of "fuck this . . . fuck that" coming from cadets' mouths that he packed his son back into the car. After venting his disgust to Bissell, the irate dad and his would-be cadet drove off and were never seen again.

Bissell was troubled by the incident, but some of the embarrassment wore off when he drove his own son to college. There, on the dormitory steps of a well-respected university, Bissell also heard his share of the "f-word"—language all the more surprising to him because it was used by women as well as men. (In fact, VMI's first women would arrive at the Institute with a repertoire of obscenities rivaling their male counterparts'.)

Profanity is nothing new to American culture. VMI's Rat Bible contains an admonition regarding the problem in a section titled "Words to Live By," chosen by members of the Cadet Corps:

> The General is sorry to be informed that the foolish, and wicked practice of profane cursing and swearing (a vice heretofore little known in an American Army) is growing into fashion; he hopes the officers will, by example as well as influence, endeavor to check it, and that both they and the men will reflect that we can have little hopes of the blessing of Heaven on our Arms if we insult it by our impiety and folly; added to this, it is a vice so mean and look [*sic*], without any temptation, that every man of sense, and character, detests and despises it.
>
> General George Washington, 1776

One difference between Washington's day and our own is that obscenities are no longer the prerogative of sailors and soldiers. Among today's teenagers, profanity is so common, so casual, and so brutal that it appears symptomatic of a growing coarseness in American society. Despite the efforts of VMI's administrators, who admonished and sometimes "boned" cadets for their language, the Institute could not hope to rid its barracks of profanity. Nor could VMI hold its cadets to a higher standard than its own employees, most of whom had their own favorite expletive deleteds. (Prior to the arrival of women, one faculty member was noted for regularly referring to his students as "you assholes.") However, VMI clearly needed to draw the line when it came to inappropriate and profane terms regarding women and sex.

Some crude sexual terms had been ingrained for years. Whenever cadets peeled apart the stiffly starched legs of a new pair of white trousers, they referred to the act as "raping your virgin ducks"—a phrase that one alumnus dated back to midcentury. Other problematic terms were more recently acquired. In December 1996 a reporter asked Colonel Bissell whether the Institute would be getting rid of phrases such as "dyke," "boned," and "roll your hay tight as a tampon." (Cadets must roll up their thin mattresses, or "hays," every morning.) For a brief moment, Bissell looked blank. He had never heard that last phrase before, and he was not going to repeat it at a press conference. The Colonel replied in a dead-pan tone that VMI intended to keep those traditional words that had a legitimate derivation. After the reporters had dispersed, he asked a few cadets if they had heard this latest bit of "tampon" vulgarity; they claimed to be equally surprised. Bissell suspected that, with all the talk about women, some wise-guy cadets were coining new phrases.

The October 18, 1996, issue of *The Cadet* (the Corps newspaper) contained its own satiric list of the top fifteen words that wouldn't be heard on Post after the arrival of women (explanations are mine):

Top Fifteen Words That Won't Be Used Next Year

15. **Blow Co.**—euphemism for Band Company
14. **Dyke**
13. **Virgin Night**—when rats who have not yet been summoned before the Rat Disciplinary Committee must go en masse
12. **Stop, Nut**—the crude equivalent of "Stop, Rat"
11. **Nuts to Butts**—also known as "nose to necks," a formation required of rats, where they stand single file with their bodies pressed against one another.
10. **Brother Rat**
9. **Rat Rub**—defined by one cadet as "shaved head against a rat's girlfriend's . . . er . . . well . . . you know . . . it's a sex thing."
8. **Boned**
7. **Roll hay as tight as a tampon**
6. **Grab a sac**
5. **Suck it up**
4. **Raping your virgin ducks**
3. **Run the period**
2. **Put out**
1. **Ratline**

In fact, most of these terms were destined to survive well past the arrival of women, probably because they were tame compared to the language of VMI's crudest cadets.

Some cadets had been known to belittle rats by calling them "bitches," or any of several obscene terms for female genitalia. These were the types of words that gave VMI's administrators the most heartburn. When Susan Faludi, author of *Backlash,** encountered a similar use of profanity at The Citadel (upperclassmen calling a freshman a "pussy" or "fucking little girl"), she described it as "a submerged gender battle":

> A bitter but definitely fixed contest between the sexes, concealed from view by the fact that men play both parts. The beaten knobs were the women, "stripped" and humiliated, and the predatory upperclassmen were the men, who bullied and pillaged. If they couldn't re-create a male-dominant society in the real world, they could restage the drama by casting male knobs in all the subservient feminine roles.[†]

Although VMI prides itself on being more civilized than its arch rival, The Citadel—less harsh, less zealous, and, according to VMI cadets, much less prone to physical violence—when it came to language, the Institute was an equally open target for feminist critique.

All in all, the language in VMI's barracks was not very different from what you might hear in fraternity houses nationwide, i.e., widespread profanity, crude references to women, and detailed descriptions of sexual acts. As one cadet explained:

> Outside of barracks people turn on their gentleman face. If they're in a uniform, nine times out of ten you'll see a cadet act better outside the barracks than you'll see inside. Of course. Inside of barracks it's like a very big boys' locker room. And I stress the word boys, because men don't talk like that. You hear explicit details on dates that you really didn't need to know. You could have probably slept better that night not knowing what happened with Johnny and his girlfriend.

---

* *Backlash: The Undeclared War Against American Women* (New York: Crown, 1991).
† "The Naked Citadel," *The New Yorker,* September 5, 1994.

One benefit that some cadets and administrators foresaw from the arrival of women was the opportunity to professionalize the language of VMI's Cadre (cadet leaders who train rats). In a coed atmosphere, cadets would need to think before they spoke and find ways to exert pressure on rats without resorting to obscenities. Whether the majority of VMI's cadets would be able to maintain a professional demeanor once the women arrived was unclear. When asked about profanity, cadets often responded that, just as they would never use vulgar language in front of their mothers, sisters, and girlfriends, so they expected to be able to restrain themselves once women were introduced into the barracks. But this reply missed the point, since articulated words are less significant than the sentiments behind them. Some faculty members expressed the hope that an increased respect for women's strengths, intelligence, and character would develop among male cadets, and be manifested in their speech, once women were promoted from "dates" to "Brother Rats."

In the meantime, VMI's efforts to lessen profanity assumed the tangible form of belt-sanders, as the Institute's Buildings and Grounds crews began sanding and refinishing classroom desktops, many of which displayed obscene graffiti. On a symbolic level, this attempt to replace decades of masculine prejudice with a new coat of varnish resembled the Institute's efforts to swiftly transform years of anti-coed rhetoric into new words of welcome. It was an awkward game of anagrams. But at least, as VMI's first female rats sat down to their opening classes, they would not be greeted with insulting furniture. For that, they had a fellow student to thank. A young male cadet suggested that the graffiti be removed, and in this small act of consideration, joined with similar good deeds from other well-intentioned cadets, VMI rested its hopes for the future.

RECRUITING

FOR A NEW ERA

HAVING PROGRESSED ALL THE WAY TO THE BELT-SANDING of desktops, we should step back to consider a few preliminary questions. For instance: Who was going to be sitting at those desks? Are we talking about a lot of effort for a very small number of female cadets? After all, what woman would want to attend VMI?

In the text of Justice Ginsburg's majority opinion, she had quoted the U.S. District Court in Roanoke as stating that if VMI went coed, it should eventually be able to "achieve at least ten percent female enrollment." In other words, she expected that VMI should be able to find approximately forty women each year who would be willing to endure the ratline. Compared to the number of women at the other military colleges in the United States—and we'll look at those numbers below—ten percent was a modest figure. Nevertheless, a lot of people associated with VMI viewed it as unlikely.

Many alumni, who knew best about the daily hardship of VMI life, doubted that their alma mater would ever attract more than a handful of female cadets. Eight or nine women might enroll the first year, maybe fifteen in the years to come. But as they looked toward the decades ahead, the question remained: Would VMI ever appeal to more than a token number of females?

A partial answer came on April 5, 1997, when forty-four girls, ages nine to thirteen, arrived at VMI with their young brothers and cousins, excited to attend the Institute's first coed Legacy Day. Legacy Day is an annual event at VMI, when alumni offspring are invited to explore their parents' alma mater. These children constitute a precious future applicant pool for VMI; multigenerational ties draw roughly eighteen percent of each new class into the Institute's life of discipline and deprivation. In some Virginia families "VMI Men" recur like a genetic anomaly, marking every generation back to the Civil War. With the Supreme Court's 1996 decision, the women of these families faced no legal bars to following in their fathers' footsteps. Some still faced parental bars; a few alumni swore that their daughters would never attend the Institute. But as VMI's 1997 Legacy Day showed, that sentiment was not universal.

The forty-four girls who joined in the day's festivities constituted over thirty percent of the total number of participants. They listened to talks from Mr. and Mrs. J.T.L. Preston, VMI's nineteenth-century founder (courtesy of Museum Director Keith Gibson and his wife, Pat). The children also watched a "phun with physics" demonstration, ate in the mess hall, and went home sporting VMI hats. Afterward, Liza Mundy, an alumni daughter whose young siblings had attended, assessed the significance of the day:

> From now on, young women in my family are going to have to take VMI seriously. Rather than viewing VMI as a source of anecdotes, a pigheaded men's club or, in dark moments, the root of all evil, girls are going to have to entertain it as an option. Which is no small thing. Like many children of alums, I come from a multigenerational VMI family, a family in which at some point each boy has had to ask himself: Do I want to be like Dad and go to VMI? Or not? This can be a tough question, maybe more so for VMI sons than for legacies of other schools, because you don't really graduate from VMI, you survive it, and enrolling at VMI means seeing whether you can survive what your dad survived. . . .
>
> And now girls will experience the anxiety of influence too. Now girls will have to decide: Do I want to be like my dad, or my mom, or neither, or both? This is true not just at VMI but everywhere. While parental oppression, and inspiration, are by no means gender-bound, it used to be—I think—that when men were figuring out how to pattern themselves, what to embrace and what to defy, they looked to their fathers, while girls looked to their moms. Now the opportunity for oppression, and inspiration,

is much wider. At VMI, boys will someday have to imagine them-selves into a tradition that includes their mothers, and girls will have to imagine themselves into a tradition that includes Stone-wall Jackson.*

The girls who explored VMI that April day seemed to have no problems imagining themselves in the Institute's world. In the faces of children, where aspirations knew no limits of gender, the prospects for a coeducational VMI looked bright.

Optimism also surfaced in the more than 200 applications for provisional appointments that VMI alumni submitted for their daughters, granddaughters, and nieces during the 1996/97 school year. Provisional appointments are small, ceremonial certificates, hailing a child's designation as a future cadet. They do not guarantee admission into VMI. Instead, they exist for the pleasure of parents, some of whom frame and hang these pieces of paper in their children's rooms, where they can inspire curiosity, anticipation, or dread. A list of provisional appointees appears quarterly in the Institute's *Alumni Review,* and in the spring of 1997 nothing symbolized the new era at VMI more concretely than the names of newborn sons and daughters, listed side-by-side—"Class of 2018: Jonathan Andrews Collins, Jr., David Patrick D'Antonio, Mallory Dest, Jane Audrey Ferrara, James Edward Gooding, Rebecca Carter Saunders Griffin. . . ."

But if VMI's future shared the same bright promise as these new lives, its present was more cloudy. In the fall of 1996, the new generation of provisional appointees remained years away from Jackson Arch. For the present, VMI's Admissions Office faced the formidable task of attracting women into the Class of 2001—a group destined to contain no female legacies.

Overseeing the effort was Colonel Vernon Beitzel '72, VMI's Director of Admissions. Beitzel knew first-hand about political upheaval at the Institute, having matriculated with the first class to include black cadets. But as he remembered it, the arrival of African-Americans in the fall of 1968 had drawn minimal public attention. By contrast, the advent of

---

* "Daughters of VMI," *Washington Post,* May 18, 1997, W07, © 1997, The Washington Post. Reprinted with permission.

women was being heralded by a steady media crescendo, and like most VMI alumni, Beitzel did not welcome the fuss.

The Supreme Court's decision had initially left Beitzel stunned and disappointed: "For the first time, it became a reality . . . You think about the loss of a parent, or something like that. You know it's going to happen, but when it actually does, then it really hits you." Soon afterward, however, a heartening encounter inspired a "really quick turnaround" in his attitude:

A couple of days after the decision I was walking in, in the morning, and I met a mother and daughter. They were visiting Washington and Lee. The decision had just been announced, and the daughter said "I wanted to just come by and pick up some material." She was almost shy and reluctant to say anything. They came here thinking that we were going to give them some material and just get them out the door. Well, we spent basically the whole day with them.

In talking to her and asking her why she was interested in VMI, the types of things that she said made me realize that there were women out there looking for the same outcomes in a VMI education as the young men. I said: "If there are a lot of women out there like her, then this is going to be fine."

That particular daughter chose not to attend VMI—and therein lay the problem. While curiosity might draw young women to VMI's gates, few would take the risk of committing themselves to four years in a harsh military environment.

Meanwhile, VMI recognized that coeducation could not succeed with only a handful of women. As General Bunting often explained to reporters, the Institute needed to attract "a genuine cohort" to form a support system for all of its members. Initial target numbers for this cohort ranged from twenty to fifty, with administrators hoping to place at least two to four women in each of VMI's nine companies, in order to "assimilate" each unit.

Reaching that goal was going to be difficult. Twenty years of coeducation at the federal academies had left those institutions still laboring to maintain a strong contingent of women. In January 1999 the Offices of

ACADEMY	'80 ENROLLEES/GRADS/ATTRITION	'98 ENROLLEES/GRADS/ATTRITION
Army		
MEN	1400/ 855/ 39%	993/ 781/ 21%
WOMEN	119/ 62/ 48%	154/ 102/ 34%
Navy		
MEN	1214/ 892/ 26.5%	1024/ 733/ 23%
WOMEN	81/ 55/ 32%	190/ 138/ 27%
Air Force		
MEN	1441/ 802/ 44%	1111/ 797/ 28%
WOMEN	156/ 97/ 38%	197/ 150/ 24%

Institutional Research at each of the academies offered the above numbers on male and female matriculants and graduates for their first coed class and their most recent alumni:

According to these figures, women constituted approximately 8.5 percent of the first coed class at West Point, 7 percent at the U.S. Naval Academy, and 11 percent at the U.S. Air Force Academy. Sixteen years later these percentages were considerably higher, ranging from fifteen to 18 percent, with the Navy more than doubling its originally low number of female enrollees. But this rise in percentages occurred in part because the Department of Defense—faced with a shrinking military—reduced total enrollment by admitting fewer men. In addition, the totals for women did not always rise at a steady rate. According to the Office of Media Relations at the Air Force Academy, the number of female matriculants arriving in Colorado Springs each fall has varied dramatically from year to year, rising to 224 for the Class of 1984, dropping to 158 for the Class of 1996—almost back to the school's original count sixteen years earlier.

Average enrollment for a new class at VMI traditionally ranges from 400 to 420 students. The Institute was planning for an especially large "rat mass" in 1997, hoping to recruit 30 women and 420 men. (The "rat mass," incidentally, does not achieve the status of a "cadet class" until after completing the ratline.) Some sources at VMI explained this large "mass" size by saying that VMI did not want to reduce its usual number of male cadets. Others said that VMI was increasing its number of matriculants to compensate for high attrition rates and to maximize tuition intake. Whatever the reason, if VMI reached these enrollment figures its women would constitute 6.6% of the incoming class—a percentage not too far from that achieved in the first year of coeducation at the federal academies. The academies, however, enjoy the advantages of international repute and free tuition. Attracting women to a small military college in Virginia, where, as noted earlier, tuition, fees, and quartermaster charges for the Class of 2001 would total $9,485 for in-state students and $15,950 for out-of-state, posed a considerable challenge.

To appreciate the enormity of the task, one might consider the enrollment history of Norwich University, a small college in Northfield, Vermont, that educates both military and civilian students. When Norwich voluntarily admitted women into its Corps of Cadets two years before the federal academies, it found the process of recruitment painstakingly slow. During its first year of coeducation, in 1974/75, the Norwich Corps of Cadets included 8 women and 906 men. The following year the women's ranks, including freshmen and sophomores, had only increased to 11.* The numbers crept upward at a snail's pace before reaching their current figure of approximately fifteen percent, which is roughly the proportion of women that most military colleges can hope to attract today. Annual female enrollment at the New Mexico Military Institute (NMMI), a junior military college in Roswell, currently averages around ten to fifteen percent, and approximately seventeen percent of Virginia Tech's Corps of Cadets is female. The U.S. Coast Guard Academy boasts some of the highest numbers for female matriculants, often topping thirty percent.

Persuading women and men to enroll in a military college is one thing; getting them to stay is another. Historical data show that roughly thirty-four percent of VMI's matriculants do not graduate. Typically, the attrition rate for the fourth class, or freshman, year hovers around twenty-two percent, dropping to twelve percent for the combined span of the third through first class years. Attrition for women was likely to be higher. The first class of women to attend West Point lost almost half of its female matriculants, and the attrition rate for West Point's women is typically ten percent higher than the rate for men. (Interestingly, women at the Air Force Academy often have a lower rate of attrition than men.)

---

* Norwich University News Release, Public Relations Office, September 21, 1995.

Attrition poses problems at other military schools as well. During the 1996/97 school year, as VMI planned for coeducation, Texas A&M had an especially difficult time holding on to its women. The Aggie Corps lost approximately fifty percent of its female "fish," or freshmen—a disturbing statistic for which no single cause could be found. Because cadets can leave the Aggie Corps while remaining at A&M as civilian students, the attrition rate at that University was liable to be higher than at VMI, where the consequences of quitting were more disruptive to a student's life. Still, attrition rates at other military colleges worried VMI's administrators as they planned for women, especially since the Institute intended to present its female cadets with one of the toughest training programs in the country. VMI was searching for female candidates who were willing to tackle (although not necessarily pass) a men's physical fitness test, and who could look in the mirror at a shorn head without losing their self-esteem. Such women were bound to be rare.

Scholarships provided one avenue for attracting such women. Although some of the Institute's smaller scholarships were designated for men, the larger funds were immediately open to both sexes. Women were prime candidates for full four-year Institute Scholarships, and VMI's track-and-field coach hoped to offer at least two partial scholarships to female athletes.

VMI used scholarships as a specific tool to attract female transfer students from the New Mexico Military Institute. Mia Utz, who would eventually join VMI's Class of 2001, explained that she had never considered attending the Institute until one fall day in 1996, when her Commandant called her into his office. There she learned that VMI would provide her with a full two-year scholarship if she chose to finish her bachelor's degree in Virginia, a challenge she decided to accept. Utz was one of two NMMI women who were given free room, board, tuition, and books at VMI. The Institute also offered the women free admittance to the Institute's Summer Transition Program—a four-week precursor to the ratline described later in Chapter 10. When one of the women chose to attend summer school in Louisiana, the Institute paid for that as well. A third transfer student from NMMI came to VMI without the perks.

VMI initially sought transfer students from NMMI to serve as big sisters in the assimilation process—a role later assigned to exchange students from Norwich and Texas A&M. VMI was particularly interested in

NMMI because that junior college was founded by a VMI alumnus who had based its program on the Institute's model. In fact, VMI's administrators were so enthusiastic about strengthening their ties to NMMI, that by the spring of 1998 they had established a plan to offer full scholarships every year to two of NMMI's top graduates, female or male.

The two female scholarship recipients for 1997 were bound to be a special pair. They were going to be arriving at VMI with commissions in the U.S. Army Reserve and with experience from NMMI's own military system. Melissa Graham, the second scholarship recipient from NMMI, would be one of the first two female cadets to graduate from the Institute, completing her course work in two years. (The other woman destined to graduate from VMI in 1999 was Chih-Yuan Ho, from Taipei, Taiwan. Ho had been a long-time admirer of Li-Jen Sun, a Taiwanese General who had studied at VMI for a year-and-a-half in the mid-1920s, and when Ho learned that the General's old stomping ground was accepting women, she quickly signed up, even though she had already completed almost all of the course requirements necessary for a college degree.)

In all, eight members of VMI's initial "cohort" of women would be coming to the Institute as transfer students. Although they would wear the ring of the Class of 2001, several of these women would be graduating early—much to the chagrin of some male cadets, who bitterly resented the fact that women would be "walking the stage" with VMI's last two all-male classes.

VMI'S FACE-TO-FACE RECRUITMENT of the women from NMMI was a rarity. In general, the Institute was relying on the U.S. Postal Service to send its message. During the fall of 1996, VMI's Admissions Office sent recruitment materials to 35,082 high-school women from lists obtained from the College Board, the National Research Center for College and University Admissions, and the American College Testing Service. VMI also gave the Department of Defense information to mail to 3,700 young women who were applying for ROTC scholarships nationwide, and sent a trial mailing to the 1,400 women believed to constitute the entire female membership of the Civil Air Patrol.

By VMI's standards, these mailings constituted a huge, one-time effort, larger than any campaign ever directed toward young men (even though VMI was seeking nine times as many men as women). Some alumni complained that VMI was recruiting women too vigorously; a few especially disgruntled souls felt that the Institute should limit its efforts to begrudging responses for those women who sought the school out. But VMI's Admissions Office had higher aspirations, and the admissions officers knew that they were playing a difficult game of catch-up. By October 1996 most high-school seniors had already decided where to apply for college, and many had mailed their applications. Among those women who had not yet made their choices, most had never heard of VMI.

As a result, VMI was trying to blanket the field, using what Colonel Beitzel called a "shotgun approach." At the same time, the Admissions Office was fine-tuning a search for the Class of 2002—an effort more indicative of how VMI would recruit women in the future. As part of that search, VMI planned to distribute approximately 30,000 direct mail pieces in February and March 1997, 9,000 of which would be directed toward women. A drop from 35,000 mailings to women in 1996 to 9,000 in 1997 might seem precipitous, but VMI's admissions officers knew that when recruiting prospective female cadets, it was the quality of a mailing list, not its size, that mattered.

The message also mattered, and this was a particular problem for VMI, since all of its recruitment materials were geared toward men. In the coming year the Institute would be revising all of its recruitment brochures to welcome "he and she." Photographs of female cadets and coed footage for recruitment videos were planned for the future. In the interim, VMI hastily produced a glossy eight-page brochure aimed at its first female prospects.

Opening the brochure, young women faced a snapshot of General Bunting, accompanied by the following sales pitch:

A New Challenge:

Throughout its 158-year history, VMI has provided a superior military education grounded in the development of personal qualities such as honor, integrity, and character. The results can be measured by the remarkable level of success attained by its graduates. Now, as we undertake our new mission, we extend to women an invitation to share in this storied tradition. The method of this education remains unchanged. For a select group of outstanding young women, however, the experience represents a historic opportunity to stand with the more than 16,000 honorable citizen-soldiers who have gone before.

The key sentence, sandwiched in the middle of the paragraph, regards the unchanged status of VMI's adversative method. It was a sentence intended as much to soothe alumni spirits as to woo prospective applicants. In essence, VMI was looking for a few good women—women who could acclimate themselves to a method of education specifically designed for men.

To emphasize this point, VMI included, in the middle of its brochure, two pages of quotes. Some were from male cadets, downplaying gender differences: "Of course women can succeed at VMI. This doesn't have as much to do with gender as it does with the will to succeed." Other quotes came from VMI's earliest female applicants, including one favorite among the Institute's officials: "When I heard VMI say that they were going to hold girls to the same standards as the guys, I went to my guidance counselor that day and got an application."

VMI's MESSAGE WAS CLEAR; all it needed now was a messenger, someone who would serve as the primary contact for prospective female cadets and their parents. The person who ultimately accepted the job was Terri Reddings, an outspoken woman with a good sense of humor, both essential qualities when selling buzz cuts and pull-ups to high-school girls.

Prior to joining VMI, Reddings had served as the Assistant Director of Admissions at Radford University, a small school in southwest Virginia, where she had originally been hired by Vern Beitzel. She was newly married and looking forward to settling down in August 1996, when she received a call from her old boss. When Beitzel explained that, pending the Board of Visitors' vote, VMI might need someone with her credentials to help in the recruitment of women, Reddings was skeptical:

I said "Vern, to be honest with you, I do not expect that you all will be in a situation where you will be forced to take women. Whatever you all have to do, it probably won't come to that." I just was satisfied in my mind that enough money would be raised. Whatever needed to be done would be done so that VMI could always and forever remain exactly the way it was.

Reddings' response was typical for a native Virginian who had known the single-sex VMI all her life and had even dated a cadet during her undergraduate years at nearby Hollins College. She was very surprised when Beitzel called again within hours of VMI's September 21 press conference, inviting her to visit the Institute's Post. Although Reddings knew that a job at VMI would entail living as a "weekend wife," residing in Lexington Monday through Friday and returning to Radford on weekends, the opportunity was too rare to miss. With the support of her husband she joined VMI's administration on November 11, 1996— Founder's Day.

For Reddings, as for several of the women who would be hired over the next year to meet the needs of a newly coed Corps, working at VMI involved not only a career change but a cultural change. Although she did not, as her friends assumed, have to cut her hair and perform calisthenics at 5:30 A.M., she was required to don the uniform of the Virginia Militia—attire very similar to that of the U.S. Army, except for the brass "V.A." that appears where one normally finds "U.S." (VMI employees are sometimes mistaken for uniformed representatives of the Veterans' Administration.) Reddings' new title of "Major" also required some getting used to, especially since her father had devoted twenty-seven years of his life, in active and reserve service, to earn the same rank in the U.S. Army.

On a deeper level, VMI's devotion to its Confederate heritage constituted a cultural challenge for Reddings as a black female:

When you come on Post you sort of feel awed by the sense of history and the preservation of that history. . . . The great attention to Southern history is interesting to me as a black woman from a black family. My great-great-grandfather was one of the last persons to be sold as a slave in the state, so I guess I think that Southern history was not the most pleasant experience for lots of people.

I don't know how well that's being included in what's being preserved around here. When you talk about Southern history you need to include *all* those who played a part. Not just the glorious figures, but all those who were involved.

When Reddings joined VMI she was one of only three African-Americans in the Institute's administration and faculty, as well as being one of the first female administrators. But her unique position didn't faze her. Questioned by reporters, Reddings suggested that VMI's cadets could benefit from a little diversity: "the world is not full of twenty-two-year-old white gentlemen."

Although Reddings' colleagues were happy to welcome her on board, some alumni were openly skeptical about her task:

> I had a call from an alum, who I think in his own way was attempting to welcome me into the fold. But he said, "I don't know why on earth you think you can do this job. From what I've heard and read it's going to be tough and I can't imagine any young women wanting to come. But nevertheless I'm glad you're there. Somebody's got to take it on . . . I wish you luck, but I don't think this is going to be very successful."
>
> It was a strange encounter; it wasn't at all humorous . . . It was interesting that people think, "Well, you're there to try to do a job, but you're not going to be very successful no matter how hard you try, because there may be some factors that you're not aware of coming into play."

This brand of pessimism was especially worrisome to VMI's Admissions Office, because the Institute relies heavily on the enthusiasm of alumni to help recruit new cadets. VMI alumni sponsor tables at college day and college night programs. They host large banquets and individual dinners for prospective cadets and their parents. They provide admissions officers with the names of interested students and submit application fee vouchers for young people whom they encourage to apply, free of charge. VMI also suggests that all applicants submit a letter of recommendation from an alumnus, and the Institute lists almost

100 alumni nationwide on its application form, to simplify the match-making process.

With the coming of women, doomsayers predicted that this entire network of alumni involvement would collapse. Many alumni, it was feared, would not want to recruit for a coed college. As Vern Beitzel recalled:

> There was some fear that when we made the decision to admit women there would be a mass exodus and a loss of all the support we have had. And I know about three alumni who said "I can no longer in good conscience recruit. Take my name off the list, I'm not going to help you." But there have been very few of those. Most of the alumni have gotten right in and taken the attitude that we have here at VMI—that they didn't necessarily like the decision, but let's do it better than anybody. Let's find some good women.
>
> What's interesting for me to see is that alumni who very adamantly opposed coeducation, once they got to meet a couple of these women, would call and invariably say "Vern, I never thought I'd do this, but I'm recommending a woman to VMI. I met her and she's sharp . . ."
>
> Some of the alumni are angry, and some have basically said: "I don't feel I can recruit for VMI now because I'm not sure what VMI is now. Give me a couple years to see what's happened and I might be back helping you again." But further away from VMI and Virginia, they have a tendency to look at it a little bit differently.

In fact, during the 1996/97 school year more alumni participated in the recruitment process than ever before. As one delighted official explained, the alumni "felt that they were needed," and rallied to the cause of their school.

This positive spirit also marked VMI's fundraising efforts. From July 1, 1996, to June 30, 1997, the Institute's alumni-sponsored endowment agencies received almost $10.6 million in donations—the third highest fundraising year ever. The school's annual giving program (an unrestricted subset of the larger total), set a new record of $2.66 million, surpassing its previous high of $2.61 million. In the next few years, the numbers were going to get even better.

This was all very welcome news, especially since VMI had been bracing for a drop in financial support. Prior to the Board of Visitors' decision to admit women, VMI's alumni agencies had polled several colleges, including Dartmouth, the University of Virginia, the Naval Academy, and Princeton, asking how coeducation had impacted alumni giving. In each case, the school had experienced a substantial drop in donations that lasted from four to five years after the admission of women. Princeton officials informed VMI that their alumni giving had plummeted by thirty percent in their early years of coeducation. Most of these schools, however, had chosen to admit women, alienating alumni who disagreed with the decision. In VMI's case, the vast majority of alumni felt that their alma mater had fought the good fight, doing all that it could to remain single-sex. They were willing to stick by their school as it faced a task that it had not invited.

WITH ITS ALUMNI NETWORK INTACT, a direct-mail campaign under way, and Terri Reddings on the telephone, VMI's Admissions Office began to see its efforts bear fruit in a steady trickle of female applicants. One final weapon remained to win these women over—the Institute's open-house weekends.

Each year VMI attracts roughly 550 applicants to six open-house events. These weekends provide would-be cadets with an opportunity to sleep in the barracks, dine in the mess hall, attend a class, and view a parade. Open-house attendees who come in the fall and winter see the ratline in full swing and can talk to rats and upperclassmen about VMI's unusual method of training its freshmen.

VMI's first coed open house took place on the weekend of October 19, 1996, attracting two women, fifty-four men, and a throng of reporters, who trailed the female high-schoolers from building to building. It was an historic occasion, but not as significant to the VMI mindset as the November open house, when nine female attendees actually spent the night in VMI's barracks. In the past, the only women to manage this feat had been rare girlfriends, smuggled in at a cadet's peril. Now, prospective female cadets were sleeping next door to VMI's upperclassmen, with an extra cadet sentinel posted in the Old Barracks'

Courtyard to answer their questions and escort them to the bathroom. Afterward, VMI's male cadets explained that they were less disturbed by the presence of women in the barracks than by the arrival of reporters on Post—a frequent complaint that cemented VMI's determination to limit media access the following year.

Most of the young women who came to VMI's open houses were surprisingly enthusiastic about the place. Jennifer Boensch, from Virginia Beach, explained after the April open house that she was "sold on the first night . . . I really liked the school, how small it was, how everything was so tight, it seemed so perfect." Kendra Russell, from Chattanooga, Tennessee, had a similar response. She and her mother had been planning to follow up their visit to VMI with a trip to Charlottesville to look at the University of Virginia. But after spending a weekend at the Institute, Russell told her mother that "We don't even need to go to UVA."

If anything, the women's responses to the open houses were overly optimistic. Alexis Abrams, from Alexandria, Virginia, gave a particularly cheerful assessment of the November weekend: "Cadets came up to us and said, 'Congratulations,' and 'We wish you the best of luck.' . . . I think the school really wants us here." *

This sense of being wanted probably came from VMI's admissions officers, who were trying hard to present a welcoming face. "The first thing we had to do," Vern Beitzel explained,

> was combat the view that one woman had when she walked through the door, which was: "You guys don't really want me. I know that." We had to quickly convey to them, "Wait a minute, yes we do. We need you. We want you." Our staff did an excellent job of making applicants and inquiries feel at ease. I think one of the prime examples is that two girls came up to one of our staff members at a program as a joke. They wanted to give him a hard time, but not in a malicious way. He started talking about VMI, and they had no intention of coming. Now she's coming to VMI this fall and her sister is coming with her (to Washington and Lee).

---

* "VMI Impresses Possible Female Cadets, They Say," Associated Press report, *Richmond Times-Dispatch,* November 18, 1996.

VMI's Admissions Office was determined to make female applicants feel comfortable. But would a woman who had recently considered VMI a joke make a good cadet? And how could a recruitment officer explain— without spooking female candidates—that their message of "We need you, we want you," would not be echoed by many of the 1,300 male cadets that these women would face come August?

Very few cadets actually *wanted* women at VMI. Privately, their reactions ranged from anger, to apathy, to determined professionalism, but rarely did a male cadet voice enthusiasm for VMI's fate. Cadet Sergeant Gabriel Hubble, who guided Alexis Abrams and several other young women around VMI's Post in November, offered a typical assessment of the situation: "Most of us are really disappointed with the way things have gone. But all we can do is make the most of it."*

In the coming school year there would continue to be a clear distinction between the attitudes of women and men, with women often sounding a cheerful note while male cadets remained more glum. The disparity highlighted one of the most pervasive questions during VMI's recruiting process: Did these women understand what they were getting into?

The question is equally applicable to VMI's men. Each year, some students arrive at Jackson Arch with very little understanding of what VMI and the ratline are all about. General Bunting often tells the tale of one short-lived rat who responded to upperclassmen's commands with an understandable, but unacceptable, "kiss my ass" and "go fuck yourself." The young man was soon sent packing. Another student arrived at VMI with several trunks of civilian clothes, explaining to his roommates that he had assumed that the Institute's military regimen was a part-time affair. He was gone before the end of the first year, presumably in search of a college where he could enjoy his wardrobe.

Some of VMI's women were equally naive. One female rat confessed to her roommates in the fall of 1997 that she had not realized that this would be the Institute's first year of coeducation until after she had been accepted.

Most of the women, however, realized from the outset that if they joined VMI's first coed class, they would be embarking on a very diffi-

---

* "VMI Impresses Possible Female Cadets, They Say," Associated Press Report, *Richmond Times-Dispatch*, November 18, 1996.

cult journey. When confronted with these women's toughest questions, Terri Reddings tried to be honest:

> Women are asking: "Am I going to be really made to feel that VMI now will belong to me as much as it always has to other cadets? Is it going to be equal and fair treatment?" And I have responded this way:
>
> I go into the whole routine of explaining all of the painstaking effort associated with this assimilation—examination of policies, facilities and attitudes—and I say that "just as there are no guarantees in life, there are no guarantees with this situation. However, if you come here with the same determination and preparedness as young men have been coming with all these years and do not perceive yourself as intrinsically different, you will maximize your opportunities for the same success everybody else is enjoying. I can't guarantee everybody is going to have a welcoming attitude towards you—I think some will, some will be indifferent, and some flat out won't. But these things take time."

It is hard for eighteen-year-olds, most of whom desperately want to fit in, to anticipate the emotional impact of an environment where one's silent presence is enough to evoke resentment. Nor could VMI's administrators accurately gauge how much hostility their female cadets might face in the coming years, because for every male cadet who seemed openly antagonistic to the prospect of coeducation, there were many others who were determined to be as fair and accepting of the women as possible. But if VMI's first female cadets could endure the daily harassment of rat life, they could probably endure any other form of antagonism that might come with their status as pioneers. And so, in the spring of 1997, most of VMI's concerns for the Class of 2001 were focused on the question of whether these students would be prepared—insofar as that is possible—to become rats.

THE RATLINE RECEIVES little mention in VMI's admissions materials. Most of the school's brochures emphasize the romance of VMI, showing photographs of formal parades, one-on-one student–teacher exchanges, and mountains ablaze with fall foliage. There are no shots of upperclassmen yelling into the faces of rats or dropping them for push-ups at predawn sweat parties. One brochure does include a tiny picture of a group of rats "straining," their backs arched, arms straight, chins tucked against their necks. Beneath the photo, the ratline is ambiguously described as "an immersion experience . . . designed to instill and reinforce personal character traits that will serve a cadet throughout his life."

Applicants must witness the ratline in action to have any understanding of its nature, and here again, VMI's open-house weekends play an important role. VMI often stages skits on these weekends, with upperclassmen enacting typical scenes from a rat's day (e.g., insults heaped on a red-faced rat, seen running in place, while a classmate next to him is quizzed on the names of those New Market cadets who "Died on the Field of Honor, Sir!"). High-school students often respond to such skits with nervous laughter: "You guys don't really *do* that, do you?" Any doubts that remain are usually dispelled after VMI's officials leave the visitors alone in a room for an hour with several rats. Freed from the observation of upperclassmen and administrators, rats tend to pour out their stories, and the results, as Vern Beitzel explains, are blunt:

> We close the door, leave, and let them talk about whatever they want—tell the horror stories . . . and they don't pull any punches. They tell the straight stuff, and that gives them (prospective applicants) a pretty good view of what the ratline's all about. Alumni also tell their horror stories, but when you look back on the ratline it comes across as much more playful, and much more of a joke, than what it is when you are in there feeling it. I think our applicants have a pretty good sense of what the ratline is about.

Some administrators, however, weren't so certain. Not all applicants attend the Institute's open-house weekends, and VMI wanted to ensure that the Class of 2001 was especially prepared for the ratline, if only so that these students could distinguish between sexual harassment and the routine degradation of rat life. In light of this concern, the Institute's administrators determined to take one extra step in the spring of 1997. They decided to produce a new video, showing clips from Hell Night, midwinter sweat parties, and other intimidating and inspirational moments in the life of a rat. The intent was not to rob VMI's rituals of their mystery, but to provide incoming men and women with a taste of what to expect when they matriculated in August. Some administrators questioned the wisdom of producing a film that would inevitably fall into the hands of reporters, in which many of the activities could be viewed as brutal. But, they reckoned that in the upcoming year, most of VMI's rituals would be bared to the public anyway, and for now, a video seemed the best means of offering words of warning and welcome to the Class of 2001.

The key to the film was its editing. VMI's administrators attempted to view early footage with the eyes and ears of the innocent, trying to gauge the impact of words and activities to which they had become inured. When they noticed, for instance, that injured rats, exempt from physical activities, were standing against the wall in the background of clips from Hell Night, they quickly cut those scenes. Although the rats' injuries had nothing to do with the night's events, the image of young men being "worked out" by loud-pitched upperclassmen, while their classmates stood in the back with crutches and arm casts, gave an unpleasant impression of cause and effect.

Even after the initial round of editing, Vern Beitzel stated frankly that the film "scared" him. He was especially worried about scenes from Breakout—an annual ceremony in which rats graduate from the ratline by crawling across a muddy field and forming a human chain to scramble up a hill of mud, while upperclassmen alternate between physically tormenting them and helping them up. In the end, VMI kept the footage from Breakout down to a minimum.

By the time the film was ready, the final result was a production that showed glimpses of the ratline's tribulations while showcasing its rewards. Scenes from Breakout were followed by footage of successful cadets conquering VMI's obstacle course. Images from Hell Night were balanced with clips from a tug-of-war. A symphonic score, accompanying visions of rats "squaring their corners" (turning at stiff right angles) as they moved through the barracks and pattering, double-time, up the stairs, gave the mundane indignities of the ratline a Hollywood flair.

Student reactions to the film varied. One woman described the video as "a turn on." "I was scared but I was smiling through the whole thing. . . . The adrenaline rush when you get done with things like that is unbelievable." Another woman explained that the video proved more disturbing for her mother than for herself: "She was just in awe the whole time. She had her mouth hanging open . . . shaking her head, saying 'I can't believe you're going to be doing this.'" One male athlete who had never heard of VMI before being recruited for football and track admitted to finding the tape an eye-opener. He recalled watching the film with his grandfather: "He was laughing at me. I was terrified. I thought 'they're just going to run up in my face like that, and start yelling?'" Overall, VMI found the responses to the film to be overwhelmingly positive. Several parents thanked the school for giving them a visual image of what their children would be up against.

But why did their children choose this life in the first place? Why would anyone, male or female, seek out VMI's daily routine of harassment and hardship?

One woman, at the end of her rat year, acknowledged the extremity of the choice she had made:

> What am I doing here? Am I crazy? All of these girls out there, they are so beautiful. They can wear whatever they want to wear. They can drive a car. They can go to any kind of college they want to. What am I doing here? It's like being in prison.

This same woman, however, enjoyed the uniqueness of the challenge she had accepted, a sentiment that seemed to be shared by several of VMI's first female cadets.

As with most of VMI's male applicants, the women who applied to the Institute were looking for something out of the ordinary. Some admired VMI's uncompromising Honor Code; some were attracted by its physical rigor; others liked its small size and sense of history. Many voiced support for VMI's males-only admissions policy, insisting that they had had no special desire to see it end. But now that the school was open to women, they wanted to reap its benefits.

None of the women accepted into VMI were daughters or granddaughters of Institute alumni. Kim Herbert, from Herndon, Virginia, had an older brother who matriculated in 1993, but he had died in an automobile accident during his rat year. Although his tragedy did not determine her college choice—"You don't go through something like this just to do it for somebody else"—Herbert later acknowledged that "It helped me a lot, knowing that his spirit was always there to protect me."

Almost one-third of VMI's women shared some experience as military brats. Erin Claunch, a 4.0 honor student and cross-country runner from Round Hill, Virginia, told Victoria Benning of the *Washington Post* that: "I've lived in a military environment all of my life, so I know what to expect . . . I'm really looking forward to the challenge. I'm anxious to test my limits and see how far I can go."* Claunch, who hoped to follow her father's lead as an Air Force pilot, and possibly become an astronaut, gave up a chance to attend the Air Force Academy for an appointment to VMI, preferring the Institute's small size and the opportunity to stay close to her family. VMI sweetened the pot by offering her a full four-year Institute scholarship.

The most unlikely candidate among VMI's first women came from Russia, a country hitherto unrepresented among VMI's Corps. Yulia Beltikova, from Krasnodar, near the Black Sea, heard about VMI while studying as an exchange student in Northern Virginia. Her father had served in the Russian military's rocket corps, and she had always wanted to attend a military college, but the academy in Moscow was closed to women. For Beltikova, admittance to VMI was a dream come true: "In Russia, when I was waiting for the response from VMI, whether to be admitted or not, I will tell you the truth, I was crying for the last three days before I got the letter." When the letter finally arrived, Beltikova was thrilled.

BY THE SUMMER OF 1997, statistics seemed to show that VMI's efforts to recruit women had paid off. As of June 19, the Institute's Admissions Office had received 12,181 overall inquiries, 1,688 from women. VMI had offered appointments to a total of 852 applicants, including 66 women, 31 of whom had made deposits (30 would eventually matriculate in August). Of these women 13 came from Virginia; 15 hailed from states ranging from Oregon to Michigan. Cadets Ho from Taiwan and Beltikova from Russia would be traveling the farthest to attend VMI.

---

* "Loudon Girl Enrolls at VMI," *Washington Post,* June 26, 1997.

Seventeen of these women received full or partial academic scholarships—a very large number, considering that only 38 of their 430 male classmates were granted the same honor (fourteen percent of VMI's men traditionally receive athletic scholarships; two women got the same award). General Bunting insisted that the disproportionate number of academic scholarships for women reflected their high-school records, rather than an attempt to induce women to enroll. Meanwhile, VMI's Board of Visitors instructed it not to publish any comparisons between the men's and women's academic credentials, citing the need to promote solidarity among the Class of 2001.

Reflecting upon the thirty-one women who had placed deposits, Vern Beitzel offered these final thoughts:

> If I could sit down and talk with every male cadet I'd tell them that they need to be grateful for these thirty-one women, because these women have said "I'm coming on your terms." If these women didn't say that, you would have other women here wanting to come on their terms, or somebody else's terms. These thirty-one women want VMI as those cadets know it, and they've got to realize that they should not take it easy on the women, but they should not do anything that is going to make the ratline any more difficult.

Gratitude was not the most common sentiment expressed by VMI's male cadets as they looked toward these women's arrival. But if VMI's first female rats were willing to suffer the same trials that VMI's men had traditionally endured, most of the male cadets were ready to acknowledge the possibility of mutual respect.

SWEATING THE DETAILS:

MODIFICATIONS TO FACILITIES

AMONG THE MOST IMMEDIATE QUESTIONS FACING VMI AS it prepared for the arrival of its first thirty women were where they would live and what modifications would be needed to accommodate them throughout the Post.

VMI's administrators had long argued that their barracks was not suitable for two sexes. Life in the barracks, they explained, was centered on the concept of zero privacy. Cadets showered in open bays. They used toilets without stall doors. They lived in four-man rooms (sometimes three, sometimes five), in a deliberate departure from the two-man arrangement found at other military colleges. Nine-paned windows spanned the upper half of the doors to these rooms, so that anyone could look inside at any time. As a result, it was almost impossible to be alone at VMI. According to Colonel Bissell, the most privacy a cadet could find on the Institute's Post was in a library study carrel.

When describing these living conditions to acquaintances unfamiliar with VMI, I have twice received the same response: "It sounds like a Victorian scheme for preventing masturbation." Crude as this response might sound, it is not unreasonable, given that some features of the Institute's class system and ratline resemble life in the nineteenth-century English public (i.e., private) schools for adolescent boys. VMI cadets, however, offer a more philosophical rationale for their mode of living.

Within VMI's barracks, they explain, young people can bond together as brothers in an atmosphere of emotional and physical openness. Cadets see each other cry, just as they see each other laugh, and ideally, they develop the sense of living in a large family. Most male cadets would prefer private showers, and some modest young men assiduously avoid the barracks' bathrooms, waiting to use the comparatively luxurious facilities in VMI's academic buildings. But for the majority of them, the Institute's open style of life is preferable to an outside world where Americans huddle within their separate houses, their separate cubicles, their emotional shells.

Skeptical observers are quick to note that what VMI describes as "openness" many other people would call "surveillance." Indeed, the architectural design of VMI's barracks resembles the plans for one of the late eighteenth century's most innovative models of surveillance—Jeremy Bentham's panopticon.

The panopticon was Bentham's vision for the ideal prison. Within it, prisoners' rooms form a cylindrical structure surrounding a central guard tower. From the tower, an unseen observer can peer into a prisoner's cell at random intervals. Because prisoners never know when they are being watched, they internalize the possibility of perpetual surveillance and begin to police their own behavior. In this way the panopticon succeeds, through psychological pressure, in establishing a level of discipline previously achieved through brute force.

The design of VMI's Old Barracks follows a similar principle. The Old Barracks consists of four stories that form an even square surrounding an open courtyard. All four stories are lined by open porches called "stoops," a word that also refers to each level of the building. Cadets inhabit a stoop according to their class, with first classmen on the ground floor and rats at the top. The windowed doors to cadet rooms face the interior of the courtyard, which is dominated by a sentinel box that looks like a miniature castle tower. From anywhere the sentinel stands within the courtyard, he can monitor activities on each stoop, and if he wants a closer look, he can stroll on the stoops and peer into the bedrooms at close range or walk inside, often without knocking. (In 1949 VMI built a rectangular New Barracks, connected to the old structure by a wide opening known in military circles as a "sally port." The New Barracks has a design similar to the old one, minus the sentinel box.)

To many people, the prospect of living in such a building, ever-visible to the eyes of the Officer of the Day, would resemble an Orwellian nightmare. Still, as VMI tells it, the ultimate goal is not to empower Big Brother, but Big Brothers. One of the advantages of the barracks' design is that it helps facilitate the school's system of Corps self-governance, in which cadets have considerable responsibility for policing their peers, and where all students are responsible for enforcing the tenets of VMI's Honor Code. What they sacrifice in privacy, the cadets regain in both the responsibilities and rewards of community.

The idea of bringing women into this environment was upsetting to many alumni. Some based their objections solely on nostalgia and exclusivity. Women had traditionally been barred from crossing the inner threshold of Jackson Arch (the barracks' main entrance) except on special occasions—pep rallies, graduation, the glee club's holiday "Carols in the Courtyard." Even on matriculation day, fathers and brothers helped new cadets move into their rooms, while mothers were asked to remain outside the barracks' walls. In the minds of some alumni, the daily presence of women within this fraternal sanctum would be a desecration.

Others, however, offered arguments for the status quo that were less emotional and more practical. In a coed environment, allowances would have to be made for privacy between the sexes, and while the adjustments might be small, over time they were liable to eat away at the open spirit that distinguished VMI life. It is hard, General Bunting once said, to measure the long-term psychological effects of slight alterations in behavior, such as standing behind a wall when one might otherwise have been standing out in the open. The ultimate result of such alterations might be beneficial, but in the accumulation of these minor details, something precious would be lost.

So strong was some graduates' attachment to the idea of a single-sex barracks that an unfounded rumor circulated in September 1996, to the effect that the "privateers" would scuttle their opposition to coeducation if the Institute agreed to house women elsewhere. And VMI's administrators did consider their alternatives. One July morning in 1996 General Bunting's Executive Committee toured the Post, exploring every possible option for housing women. They looked at the wards in VMI's hospital and at the guest rooms on the upper floor of the student activity building. But none of them liked the idea of keeping female cadets in quarters entirely separate from the barracks. Such an arrangement would not have increased the women's safety. As Colonel Rowe, VMI's Chief Business Executive, had learned in consultation with Washington and Lee, if you house women in a separate area "you might as well put up a neon sign saying 'Here they are, come and get 'em.' "

More important, barracks life is a crucial part of the VMI education. Institute officials often point out that VMI's barracks is not a college dormitory, but a "leadership laboratory," where cadets absorb lessons just as important as anything covered in the classroom. Within the barracks cadets serve on guard teams, hold committee meetings, endure the tribulations of the ratline, and learn, as upperclassmen, not only how to torment rats but how to teach them. To deny young women full access to this environment would diminish their cadetships.

In view of this perspective, VMI's administrators quickly dismissed any thought of housing women outside of the barracks and considered instead how they might bring female cadets into the structure, while separating the sexes. They looked at the concourse in the barracks' lower level, an area that could be cordoned off to ensure the women's privacy. But that space was out of sight, out of mind, and VMI's officials had decided up front that they did not want to install surveillance cameras or any other security equipment not used for the men. Besides, female cadets would surely resent being relegated to the basement.

Bunting's Executive Committee also pondered various construction programs, examining some architectural sketches and computerized images. They considered four possible locations for a new women's wing that would have jutted out from the existing barracks, and although none of the drawings was ideal, a few were tempting.

However, all of the construction programs were prohibitively expensive; one extension that added twenty-six rooms was estimated at almost $10 million. Plans for a new wing would also have required approval from Virginia's Art and Architectural Review Board, since VMI's Old Barracks is a National Historic Landmark. In addition, most of the other military colleges with which VMI consulted insisted that men and women should not be segregated in any way.

Visitors from Texas A&M University were particularly adamant about the need to house men and women door to door. During A&M's early years of coeducation in the mid-1970s, its female cadets had not only lived in separate housing, they had drilled in separate platoons and, in one case, had worn different uniforms. "What they found over a period of time," explained Colonel Bissell, "was that the women started to complain, saying 'This is not coeducation. We don't know what's going on. We don't feel comfortable with it. This is a sham.' " When Bissell visited A&M in 1994 as part of an accreditation team, he found that some of the female cadets still did not feel fully integrated into the Aggie Corps. Problems continued, in part, because female cadets lived on separate dormitory floors from their male counterparts, an arrangement popular at civilian colleges, but detrimental in military schools. According to Bissell: "In all cadet corps an awful lot goes on at night—meetings, discussions on what they are going to do about parades, and so forth. . . . I found that at the other schools, too, the women were saying that, 'We've got to be right there or we are not part of the Corps.' "

Ultimately, VMI decided to place its first female cadets on the fourth stoop of the Old Barracks, right alongside their Brother Rats. Rats normally live in blocks of rooms according to their companies (Alpha, Bravo, Charlie, Delta, etc.). VMI intended to "bookend" the women's rooms, so that the last room for Bravo Company and the first room for Charlie would contain women. In this way, women could be clustered together for support.

VMI originally intended to place three or four women in each of its nine companies, hoping that after attrition there would still be at least two women per unit. But that plan didn't materialize, since eight of VMI's female cadets chose to join Band Company. In the upcoming year, Alpha and Golf companies would contain upperclass female exchange students, but no female rats.

ONCE THE IDEA of any major structural additions to the barracks had been abandoned, one might imagine that VMI's housing troubles would have been minimized. Renovations, however, are often more difficult than new construction, and over the next year VMI was going to find that even the most minor alterations in its barracks could provoke major headaches.

For instance, take the matter of those large windows on the cadets' doors. To grant the cadets some privacy when changing clothes, VMI's administrators decided to install shades. The shades could be pulled down whenever anyone was dressing, otherwise they were to remain up. Even this minor adjustment provoked complaints from traditionalists, who viewed the shades as the first step toward the demise of VMI's open community. Everyone agreed, however, that in a coed environment some privacy was necessary.

The problem with shades was finding a product sturdy enough for cadet life. As most of VMI's Buildings and Grounds officials will tell you, no object in the barracks can survive unless it is nailed to the floor, and shades are very fragile items. Nevertheless, these officials tried hard to find something that would serve. They looked at cardboard tubes, wooden tubes, and metal tubes. They planned for twelve inches of extra material, so that the shades wouldn't be yanked right off their rollers. But according to Brownlee Tolley, the good-natured "Director of Capital Outlay" who directs most maintenance projects at VMI, the experiment was doomed from the start:

> Sometimes when the guys go into a rat's room they want the element of surprise, so WHAM!, they run in all at once, and the door hits the wall. Naturally it hits the shade first, and this started bending the shades and the brackets. So we had to go in and put in doorstops. Some of the rooms had them, but I think we still put in over 200 doorstops just to protect the shades.

As it turned out, the shades were not worth protecting. By the end of the first month of the 1997/98 school year, many of them had fallen apart, leaving Tolley philosophical: "With these problems that you run into, these challenges you have to address, you try to do the best thing that you know. Sometimes it works, sometimes it's a total fiasco."

A similar nuisance emerged in the form of toilet stall doors, which, as I've already mentioned, were missing from most of the bathrooms in the barracks. The absence of stall doors had never been a philosophical issue for VMI. The stalls had included doors in the past, but they had been torn down so often that VMI's maintenance workers had eventually stopped replacing them. Now, when a few male cadets learned that the women's toilets were going to be built with saloon-style swinging doors, they insisted that their restrooms be similarly fitted. For the sake of "potty parity," VMI's administration complied, dispatching Tolley's crews to hammer doors onto the men's stalls. The end product looked rather silly, since the stalls were only about five feet high. Stepping into a men's restroom, one could immediately see over the tops of the stalls, with or without doors. But this was what the men wanted, or so they thought.

As it turned out, the older stalls were so tight that the new swinging doors banged against the users' knees. Within the first few weeks of the 1997/98 school year, the cadets had begun to tear them down again.

These were relatively minor problems compared to the troubles raised by the women's bathrooms. VMI could not simply redesignate some of the men's bathrooms for women, since each stoop in both the Old and New Barracks contained only one central bathroom and showering area shared by hundreds of men. (The barracks contains a few other toilets for men, but all were needed for VMI's large male population.) The Institute's administrators decided that a block of cadet rooms, accessible to both the Old and New Barracks, and extending from the first stoop to the fourth, would have to be transformed into women's bathrooms and showers. (One alumnus later complained of the indignity of taking a friend to visit his old room in the barracks and finding that it was now "the women's head.")

The change was particularly annoying for those cadets who, one morning after class, returned to their rooms to find unexpected eviction notices taped to their doors. Effective immediately, they were to vacate the premises to make way for the new construction. The young men understood the need for their removal; what they resented was the administration's failure to inform them of the imminent switch. VMI's officials responded with a belated "Oops, sorry."

Building the women's facilities, and especially their showers, proved troublesome on both a practical and a philosophical level. Male cadets at VMI currently take "gang" showers, gathering in 20 × 15-foot tiled rooms where six metal poles offer four shower heads, pointing north, south, east, and west. Following rat "sweat parties" (high-pressure workouts) or afternoon intramurals, these facilities can host a crowd of bodies vying for the hot water, an experience hailed as part of the no privacy philosophy.

The women's showers, however, were not going to follow the same design. Because the cadet rooms that were to be converted into showers were not meant to accommodate extensive plumbing, no one could vouch for the structural integrity of the floors, once they had been punctured with several three- to four-inch drains. It seemed that at least one dividing wall would be needed to strengthen the framework. And where there was one wall, there might as well be more, since most of VMI's administrators did not like the idea of group showers for women.

Women, so they argued, required extra time and privacy when showering. They were acculturated to a level of physical modesty not shared by their brothers, and they had "special hygienic needs." Colonel Bissell was particularly adamant on the subject:

When I was acting Chief of Staff of the 101st Division, I took the division on an exercise in Germany, where we moved into tents for two months. I was directly responsible for the headquarters element. During the first two weeks approximately ninety percent of the women in headquarters (we had about thirty of them) came down with urinary tract infections because they couldn't clean themselves properly. We had these little field showers out there; it was like a duffel bag over your head that water plopped out of. I ended up sending ninety percent of the women back on sick call . . . We finally decided to rent a Gasthaus every two or three days, where we ended up sending the women so they could properly wash themselves. So I became a firm believer in this.

"Blood pathogens" was the favorite term used by VMI administrators whenever the subject of women's showers arose, and while VMI's Post Physician explained that women ran no risk of catching hepatitis or AIDS from a group shower, the consensus seemed to be that VMI's female cadets should not spend four years in a setting where they might feel too embarrassed to clean themselves adequately.

Some people might dismiss these concerns as a matter of old-fashioned men being squeamish about women's menstrual cycles. When I asked a female Army veteran about women's needs for privacy, she scoffed: "There was no privacy in Desert Storm. When I needed privacy, I asked the guy standing next to me to turn his back." But a college is not a combat zone, and many officials at the other colleges with which VMI consulted shared the Institute's reasoning.

Next door, at Washington and Lee University, the Physical Education Department had held similar discussions when constructing a new athletic facility, ultimately opting for private showers for women. Based on their combined experience at various colleges, the professors concluded that when faced with communal showers, women tended to wash less frequently than necessary.

The problem in VMI's case was that private showers for one sex grated against the Institute's egalitarian ideal. Insofar as possible, VMI tries to treat all of its cadets equally, and several male cadets viewed the women's showers as an unfair luxury. Why, they asked, were women being granted the privacy that they were systematically denied?

VMI's officials replied by explaining the physiological rationale for the design of the women's showers, a tactic that left many cadets dissatisfied but silenced, since most eighteen- to twenty-two-year-old males will fall into embarrassed acquiescence when faced with the word "menstruation." The school's administrators also decided to allow male cadets living on the barracks' first and third floors to use the women's facilities during the 1997/98 school year, as no women would be residing on those levels. But although these responses tended to mollify VMI's Corps, they did not placate the Institute's most vocal alumni.

In the upcoming months, heated debates over the women's showers occurred in the alumni "electronic turnouts"—a branch of VMI's official Web site where opponents of the school's new mission routinely chose to vent their frustrations. The most striking feature of the shower debate was the degree of emotion generated by a relatively small matter. One supporter of private showers for women accosted his fellow grads with some especially graphic imagery:

> I guess you really need this spelled out, don't you? OK, go to your local gym, go into the open showers, and give yourself an enema—right there in front of everybody. Then maybe you'll understand what a woman would feel like having to douche in the old VMI showers. Not all women need this sort of privacy (as some will no doubt tell you), but some will. [October 16, 1997]

(One of the dubious marvels of today's Internet is that it enables a female reader such as myself to quietly listen while VMI alumni discuss feminine hygiene.)

As it turned out, building separate shower stalls for women was easier said than done. VMI decided to build the stalls with solid four-inch concrete blocks, in line with the notion that all new construction in the barracks must be "cadet proof." Concrete blocks, however, would place a heavy burden on an old building, and the floors of the showers were already going to be weakened by the drilling necessary for the drainpipes. Without reinforcement, these blocks were liable to send each newly porous floor crashing down upon the one below it. And so the construction crews embarked upon an excavation in the barracks' foundation, opening up a large hole, which, to the untrained eye, resembled an archaeological dig. One administrator remarked that the crews were liable to uncover the remains of the old arsenal that had preceded VMI at the site. The construction workers poured a massive footing into this hole and built the shower stalls as a series of concrete walls extending from the barracks' basement up to the top floor.

The undertaking proved much more complex than VMI's administrators had anticipated at the policy stage. To further complicate matters, a few officials began to second-guess the original decision months later, after returning from a trip to the U.S. Merchant Marine Academy. It seemed that the women at USMMA, wanting no favoritism in their bathroom facilities, had dismantled their private shower stalls, attacking them with sledge hammers in the middle of the night. When VMI's team innocently asked these women whether they required privacy when menstruating, the response was blunt. As Colonel Leroy Hammond explained: "They literally laughed in our faces."

Hammond's after-action report provoked a brief flurry of renewed debate at an April Executive Committee meeting. Seated around the large wooden table in VMI's chief Board Room, the Institute's administrators batted the old issue back and forth, with some officials lamenting the perils of treating men and women differently in any respect. "Just give all the new bathrooms to the men," one voice finally interjected, at which point Colonel John Rowe had had enough. Holding up a manila file on which he had drawn what appeared to be a large slice of Swiss cheese, he indicated that the sketch represented the twenty-some holes that had been drilled into the barracks floor in order to construct the women's shower stalls. Clearly, a decision had been made and acted upon; now was not the time to question earlier logic. If the cadets attempted to knock down the structure, Rowe added, the whole place would "pancake."

In the end, the design of the women's showers was less important than the questions that it raised. How much privacy should be allowed in a coed VMI? What did equal treatment of the sexes mean when it came down to bricks and mortar? And how could VMI's administrators approach the subject of feminine hygiene without blowing it out of proportion?

Every time VMI's officials raised menstruation as a potential issue, they risked reinforcing popular stereotypes about women being incapacitated by their bodies—notions especially prolific in the masculine world of military culture. (I once had a Marine Corps private explain to me, with great solemnity, that women could not be in combat because they needed regular showers, and if they did not get them, they smelled *bad*.)

VMI's cadets were particularly susceptible to mistaken notions about women's health—a point I can best illustrate with a brief digression.

At an April meeting of one of VMI's many assimilation committees, Colonel Gordon Calkins—a Physical Education professor and U.S. Marine officer whose talk is as blunt as his crewcut—decided to give VMI's rising cadet leaders a briefing on the physiological differences between men and women. In the coming year these male cadets would be leading young men and women in numerous exercise sessions, morning runs, and forced marches; they had never trained female recruits, and Calkins felt that they should be aware of women's physical limitations, when compared to men. And so he began to read through a list of those facts which, he felt, might affect the women's ability to keep up:

Men are ten percent taller.

Women are ten percent fatter.

Women have wider pelvises.

Women have shorter limbs.

Women have less muscle mass.

Women have smaller hearts.

Maximum oxygen uptake for women is twenty to thirty percent less than for men.

Women have higher heart rates at submaximal levels.

Men have ten to fifteen percent more hemoglobin.

At the same workload, women work at a higher percentage of their physical capability (e.g., oxygen uptake) and may therefore be less tolerant of exercise in the heat.

Women are more susceptible to stress injuries than men (fractures, strains, sprains, etc.).

At the end of his list, Calkins arrived at the subject of menstruation. He noted that extreme physical exertion can cause a temporary cessation of menstruation, known as "amenorrhea," a condition he felt should be monitored, but not fretted over. Finally, he concluded by questioning whether women's periods would affect their ability to participate in sweat parties and forced marches.

This last question, appended to an already daunting list of negatives, made me wince. Looking around the room, I suspected that many of the cadets who were now sitting in embarrassed silence could easily succumb to the fallacy that women were incapable of physical exertion during their periods. I therefore interjected that if any woman was so debilitated by cramps that she could not participate in ratline functions, she should go to the infirmary, but such a case was no different than a male cadet suffering from a severe stomach ache. For most women, it should be a nonissue.

A few days later I was dismayed to find the exchange jumbled in the cadet newspaper as part of an article about changes to the VMI system necessitated by the arrival of women:

> Other changes will include a new SOP [standard operating procedure] on forced marches and "gim" status for women during periods of menstruation. This will pose a difficulty [*sic*] due to high stress, a female's cycle can become off balance, posing a health problem that could prove difficult for sweat parties and other physical activities.*

The term "gim" refers to those cadets who, owing to health reasons, are temporarily excused from any physical or military duty, including most of the physical exertion of the ratline. The term originated in the 1860s, when VMI's assistant surgeon owned a horse named "Old Gimlet," and cadets who visited the hospital were said to be "riding the Gim."† Cadets

---

* Steve Nichols, "Class of '98's RDC and OGA," *The Cadet*, April 25, 1997.
† Mike Burke, "Cadet Slang at the Virginia Military Institute," Virginia Military Institute Archives, Lexington, Virginia.

who spend too much time on the gim tend to be viewed as slackers, and are often singled out for abuse. The suggestion that VMI's female cadets would be "riding the gim" each month was not only absurd, but detrimental to their acceptance within the Corps.

Because VMI's cadet-run newspaper has traditionally abounded in grammatical and factual errors, I consoled myself with the hope that the article would not be taken seriously. A few days later, however, a male faculty member stated with matter-of-fact credulity that he noticed that VMI's female cadets would be given medical exemptions from the ratline during their periods. The idea had not struck him as ridiculous; it seemed in keeping with his knowledge of his wife's moods. All of this left me to wonder how many cadets had read the same article and nodded their heads, their suspicions confirmed that VMI's women would be retreating to the hospital every month. (In the opening months of the 1997/98 school year VMI's Post Physician reported that no women had checked into the hospital because of their periods.)

ONE THING THAT THE INSTITUTE'S administrators learned as they prepared for women was that controversy could arise not only from changes to the normal routine, but from things left unchanged. Take, for example, the matter of door locks for cadet rooms. During the summer session, when VMI's cadet-run class system is not available to help enforce discipline, the Institute encourages students to purchase padlocks for their doors. Throughout the regular school year, however, locks are deemed offensive to the Institute's open ethos and its honor system.

With the imminent arrival of women, many people questioned this no-locks policy. Most military colleges have installed locks on their doors. Female cadets at the Coast Guard Academy explained to a team of VMI visitors that, as an unwritten code, they tended to use their locks only during furloughs and weekends, when intoxicated fellow cadets might be returning from liberty. At VMI, locks would serve a similar purpose. Because the Institute is situated in a small town with little crime (population around 7,000 without the college students), outsiders pose a minimal threat to cadet safety. Locks would primarily ensure that drunk upperclassmen could not barge into women's rooms.

Drunkenness is not a daily problem at VMI. On the whole, the Institute's restrictive atmosphere results in less substance abuse than one finds on other college campuses. Alcohol is forbidden to all cadets on Post regardless of age; everyone must pass a one-credit substance abuse course in order to graduate, and a study by the State of Virginia in the late 1980s and early 1990s found that there was significantly less use of illicit drugs at VMI than at other Virginia schools. Binge drinking on weekends, however, does present serious problems. Cadets imbibe freely off campus and sometimes sneak liquor into the barracks, as attested to by the trash cans on a Monday morning. "On weekends there are intoxicated cadets around," admits Colonel Bill Stockwell, the Associate Dean who teaches VMI's substance abuse course, "and frankly I don't know a good way to control that."

Still, few people liked the idea of locks. When it came to women's safety, VMI felt that the barracks' open design was the surest buffer against any form of sexual assault or physical abuse. At most times, hundreds of other cadets remain within easy yelling distance, including members of VMI's twenty-four-hour cadet guard team. Anyone approaching a cadet room can be easily observed from most angles in the barracks, and because of the barracks' crowded quarters, a young man entering a woman's room at night would most likely encounter three or four female cadets.

Still, several of the female exchange students who attended VMI in the fall of 1998 were surprised by the absence of locks, and lobbied for them as an important precaution. In response, Colonel Bissell reopened the debate, asking an upperclass cadet committee to review the subject during VMI's first year of coeducation. These young men took their charge seriously. "It concerned me very greatly to make a recommendation to Colonel Bissell for no locks," explained third classman Tom Craig, "and then maybe have someone get hurt because of a decision we had made. That kept me up at night." But the female rats whom Craig consulted didn't want locks, and neither did their male peers.

VMI did, however, embark upon other safety measures without hesitation. Security lighting, for example, appeared throughout the Post during the summer and fall of 1997.

Prior to the arrival of female cadets, VMI was a very dark place at night, with pitch-black staircases, shadowy parking lots, and dimly lit streets, where cars swerved to avoid cadets in their dark gray winter uniforms. Additional lighting had long been a goal of the Post police, even though cadets complained bitterly at the prospect of any outdoor lights that might shine into the curtainless windows of their rooms.

To help determine the darkest and most threatening locations on Post, Lieutenant Colonel Kathleen Bulger-Barnett, then serving on VMI's Facilities Committee, organized teams of women to tour the Post at night. Guided by a Post policeman and a Buildings and Grounds official, these groups of female faculty and staff were asked to use their safety instincts to make recommendations for the placement of security lights.

With eight to ten people trailing one flashlight, the tours had the flavor of a children's ghost hunt and resulted in the conclusion that lights were needed *everywhere*. Ultimately, VMI decided to place lights around its academic buildings, above its central cadet parking lots, and along the road that loops its parade ground. Dark-green Victorian style lampposts would line VMI's main avenue, while the barracks would be fitted with brass-carved lanterns abutting from each arch and corner.

After submitting blueprints to the state's Art and Architectural Review Board, VMI learned that its lighting scheme would produce a campus twice as bright as the University of Virginia in Charlottesville, a situation that was not ideal. (Some cadets later complained that they missed the haunting quality of crossing a dark parade ground on a foggy night.) But VMI's administrators moved forward with their plans, hoping that the lights would showcase the Institute's architecture, while ensuring that anyone walking the Post's main thoroughfares at night could identify the face of any person encountered.

As with most of VMI's renovations, the execution of the lighting scheme proved more difficult than the planning. Each lamppost had to be planted in a forty-two-inch-deep hole—a particular problem since the Institute did not have complete maps of all of the underground gas, water, phone, and power lines. As Brownlee Tolley from Buildings and Grounds explained:

There's stuff in the ground, and some of it's marked, some of it's not . . . It's been a real challenge. When you look at the surface and you see the lamps, you think "that's a nice light." But it's behind the scenes where all of the dollars are, doing all of this searching, and digging, and in several cases, repairing. They've hit gas lines, they've hit telephone lines and this has to be repaired.

Power shutdowns continued on VMI's Post well after the arrival of the women, as construction crews installed a line of lampposts behind the school's library, near a 7,200-volt power line.

Buildings and Grounds crews also worked diligently during the summer of 1997 to clear the shrubs that surrounded one particularly dark stairway extending from the lower cadet parking lot up to the main Post, via a wooded hillside. Workers removed one layer of growth after another and added seven lights, so that a Post policeman passing the site could look up or down into the woods and distinguish anyone walking on the stairs.

Finally, for the first time in its history VMI planned to install eleven emergency call boxes, giving the user a direct link to Lexington's 911 system. This system had been in operation for only a few years prior to the arrival of women at VMI, and during those years the dispatching service had been plagued with problems. Still, the fact that Lexington, Virginia, survived until 1995 without a 911 service testifies, in part, to the town's low crime rate.

The location of the call boxes was determined in a typically unscientific fashion. VMI's Facilities Committee examined a large aerial photograph of the Post, and placed small scraps of yellow Post-its on all the potential call-box sites. The photograph was then displayed for public comment, and all the members of the VMI community were invited to place additional Post-its, marked with their initials and a date, wherever they believed another phone was needed. One additional phone was suggested.

ONLY A FEW OTHER construction projects still remained to be done. The most important one involved the renovation of Cocke Hall, an old athletic building that houses VMI's Department of Physical Education.

Cocke Hall had been designed exclusively for men. No locker rooms had ever been constructed for female faculty members, some of whom responded to the inequity by making lewd jokes about the building's apropos name. Although women's showers had been planned in the past, they had never fully materialized. "There were absolutely no locker facilities in Cocke Hall for women," explained Brownlee Tolley. "There were supposed to be showers in one area, but when I went in there and looked, the water was off, and it was just some storage area, jumbled up." Colonel Rowe acknowledged the problems bluntly:

Title IX is most visible in college athletics, but it really applies across the board ... You've got to have equal facilities for both students and for faculty and staff, and we sure didn't have it. The men's faculty locker room was not so great either. Cocke Hall was just a mess. We're lucky the fire marshal didn't go in there and shut it down.

Bringing this building up to date proved to be the most expensive undertaking in VMI's entire assimilation process, costing over $2 million. The end product evoked some grumbling from male faculty members, who found that their locker room had been sacrificed in order to build facilities for women. Now they would have to shower alongside their students. Still, compared to their female colleagues, who had waited two decades for the change, the men had little cause for complaint.

Other construction projects proved comparatively minor. Cormack Fieldhouse, the site of VMI's indoor track, was equipped with a new women's locker room as well as updated plumbing in the men's showers, where a sewage line tended to back up every time the water was turned on. Two private examination rooms were also added to the Post hospital, a renovation that highlighted another oddity of VMI life. Prior to the arrival of women, VMI doled out medical care with the same open spirit found in the barracks. When Dr. David Copeland took on the duties of Post Physician in 1993, he was surprised by the conditions:

For innumerable years, sick call was held in a large room, and there would be as many as fifteen cadets in there at the same time, sitting on stools. There would be one side for people with infections, and one side for people with injuries, and I would go from person to person in front of everybody, and say "What are you down here for? What can I do for you?" If they needed to be examined privately for a hernia check or something, I'd take them into a back room. But for an upper respiratory infection or sore ankle, I would examine them there, make a diagnosis, give the chart to the nurse and the nurse would treat them. The nurses and the secretary were behind my shoulder, and everybody would hear what was going on.

That was very efficient in terms of time, because at morning sick call (7 A.M.) there are often as many as thirty or forty cadets, all

wanting to be seen in an hour, to get back for classes on time. I'm sure
that's how it got established originally . . . But it was a crazy place to
work . . . There was a sense at that time that, "we're all a bunch of
guys here, and I have nothing to hide from my Brother Rats."

The setup offered no confidentiality for discussing either physical mal-
adies or the mental stresses of the ratline. "I'd have a rat sandwiched in
between two first classmen," explained Copeland, "trying to tell me
some intimate details." VMI had intended to build new examination
rooms well before the Supreme Court's decision. But for a variety of
logistical and financial reasons, hospital renovations had been relegated
to a back burner. With the onset of coeducation, however, VMI had both
the money and the impetus for change.

THE FINAL BUILDINGS AND GROUNDS PROJECT, not scheduled to begin
until after the female cadets arrived on Post, involved the construction of
additional women's restrooms in academic buildings.

The designation of women's restrooms at VMI had always posed
problems, and not solely for women. During a 1995 renovation of
Maury Brooke Hall—a building that houses cadet organizations such as
the band, glee club, student newspaper, and Honor Court—VMI determined that the sole restroom on the main floor should be assigned to
women. The decision proved inconvenient for over 150 male band and
glee club members, who routinely rushed upstairs and downstairs to
find restrooms, while the empty women's room ("empty" because no
female faculty or staff worked in the building) stood adjacent to their
rehearsal halls. Most colleges would have addressed this minor nuisance
by making the bathroom coed, with an interchanging male/female sign.
But VMI's upperclassmen preferred to place a warning sign above the
bathroom door, reminding those cadets who had begun to use the facility that the women's room was OFF-LIMITS.

With plans for additional women's rooms now on the table, VMI's
officials acknowledged that they should equip these rooms with dispensers and waste receptacles for feminine hygiene products—something that had never been done to accommodate female faculty
members. It seemed a relatively minor matter, but it raised again the
awkward subject of menstruation.

One of the most uncomfortable discussions of the year revolved around whether these dispensers should be free or coin-operated. Initially, the Facilities Committee voted for coin-operated machines, but Colonel Rowe, who chaired the group, felt strongly that women should not be left running back to the barracks, or searching for a department secretary, whenever they lacked a quarter. He scheduled a second vote, preceded by discussion. Kathleen Bulger-Barnett recalled the ensuing debate:

> We had a big to-do over the machines . . . There was a lot of almost resentment that the women were getting something that the men weren't. I said "if we can hand out condoms at the hospital, and if Colonel Monsour (a professor and cadet counselor) can hand out condoms in his office, why can't we supply feminine needs?" . . .
>
> I really felt that for at least the first year we should put the dispensers in there, but we all know that dispensers don't work. You don't have a quarter to begin with, and if you do, it's empty. So now what do you do? . . . So someone said "should we charge the women extra tuition, should we build in a few extra dollars for the tampon fund?" And I slammed my hand down and I said "Forget it! I will spring for all the Tampax in Scott Shipp Hall." So we tabled that discussion and started on another topic. . . .
>
> One of the big arguments that came up was that if we were going to have the products in the bathroom, you all know that the men are going to go in there and steal them, and play with them, and make whistles out of them. Of course they will. I didn't want to tell them that women are a lot more clever about how to play with these things than men. Some members of the committee really considered not putting them in the bathrooms because they knew the men would go in and take them. So I reminded them that we have an Honor Code at VMI—and that did *not* go over well. One person on the committee was on the Honor Court when he was a cadet and he did not appreciate my getting the honor system involved with tampons.
>
> But I thought—the women are going to make water balloons out of condoms, and the men are going to make whistles out of Tampax, these things are going to happen . . .

Embarrassing moments were bound to occur whenever VMI's administrators discussed feminine hygiene. At one Executive Committee meeting, a female officer gave a roomful of flinching men a no-nonsense lesson on the difference between plastic and cardboard tampon applicators, using her own experience to illustrate why different women require different products. Her comments emerged as VMI's officials examined the packing list for incoming cadets—an inventory that helps new students anticipate the sort of items necessary for the ratline, from bathrobes to razors. This female administrator believed that VMI should instruct women to bring a three-month supply of feminine hygiene products, because the brands sold at the VMI bookstore might not be appropriate for their needs, and rats have few opportunities to shop off-Post. Colonel Bissell, however, felt that to tell women to bring a three-month supply would make VMI appear primitive, as if the women were journeying into the wilderness. The conversation soon devolved into a discussion of women's underwear, and the need to ensure that no hearts or flowers (or Mickey Mouse! one man piped up) were visible through the women's white trousers, before Bissell was able to conclude the discussion with a few semantic changes.

Clearly, VMI's administrators were in a difficult position. Some discussion of menstruation was inevitable and healthy, since VMI needed to handle a range of delicate issues, from stocking women's toiletries in the bookstore, to providing gynecological care in the Post hospital. There was a fine line, however, between frankness and fetishism.

At a dinner party in early May 1997, General Bunting quietly asked if I had noticed that a number of VMI's administrators had begun to talk about women's periods with remarkable openness. The fact seemed to leave Bunting balanced between philosophical amusement and mild disgust—that VMI officials were now discussing menstruation as casually as if they were pondering military protocol.

VMI's women, however, would ultimately benefit from the school's occasionally excruciating attention to details. The Institute's most conscientious officials were trying to anticipate all of the problems that women would encounter in VMI's male-centered world. The most troublesome issues faced by VMI's leaders—haircuts, uniforms, fraternization, and, in general, how to allow femininity into a masculine culture—occupy the next chapter.

FEMININITY
AND FRATERNIZATION

WHAT SHOULD A FEMALE RAT LOOK LIKE? COULD SHE BE feminine in a crew cut and necktie? And how would VMI cope with the inevitable attraction between the sexes? These were the sorts of questions that plagued VMI during the 1996/97 school year.

When Major Becky Ray, an advisor on gender issues at Texas A&M University, visited VMI in the fall of 1996, she described one of her chief jobs as ensuring that Aggie women could be feminine while also maintaining a professional, military demeanor. As she sat before an audience of VMI administrators and faculty, with her neatly trimmed hair, tasteful makeup, and well-tailored uniform, Ray's concern for women's attractiveness sounded old-fashioned, as if she were the headmistress of a finishing school. But in the months to come, her ideas were reinforced again and again by administrators and cadets at several military colleges. A visit to Norwich University left Major Terri Reddings with one overriding impression: "It was important that women always be identified as women, not as something neuter, or worse, men. We must always allow them to still be women."

But could women be feminine without their hair? That was the question that always lurked in the background. As VMI prepared for the arrival of women, no issue raised more debate, or attracted more media attention, than the matter of women's haircuts. How short would the women's hair be? How soon could they grow it out?

To some, the questions seemed trivial. VMI's women were not a bunch of Samsons, destined to be powerless without their hair. Surely there were more important matters to discuss.

But try as one might to dismiss the subject, haircuts remained a major sticking point. A brief walk down the health and beauty aisle of any supermarket confirms just how much our society cares about hair. Conditioners, dyes, mousse, straighteners, barrettes, scrunchies, Rogaine, all testify to one salient point—*hair matters.*

At one Executive Committee meeting, Major Reddings noted that women's hairstyles were especially important to social status in the African-American community. Would the female cadets' hair be too short to receive any kind of styling? Would VMI's hairstylists be trained in handling black women's hair? Would it be more devastating to women than to men to have a whole year of bad hair days?

Meanwhile, many of the Institute's alumni had a different set of concerns. To them, the haircut was a yardstick for measuring VMI's resolve to remain unchanged. In the minds of some grads, each centimeter of women's hair represented the Institute's growing capitulation to outside pressures. The shorter the dos, the tougher VMI's stance.

VMI took a hard line on haircuts at its September 21 press conference, when the Institute announced its plans to admit women. Questioned by reporters, General Bunting stated that the female cadets would be given a "buzz cut." Exactly what he envisioned by the term was unclear, but when asked if the cut would be as short as The Citadel's (whose women wore a very short, boyish style), Bunting replied: "Shorter." The press took these words to mean that VMI would shave the women's heads—an incorrect interpretation, given that internal memos at VMI continued to distinguish between "buzz cuts" and "shaved heads." The fact remained, however, that VMI intended to give its women one of the shortest haircuts yet known to a military college, a plan which drew harsh criticism from some outside groups.

"They're poor losers" explained Karen Johnson, a retired Air Force Colonel and Vice President of the National Organization for Women. "The haircut is just a way of being vindictive." Kent Willis of the ACLU also objected: "True equality means making some allowances that recognize the differences in the sexes . . . This appears to be a kind of malicious compliance"* In fact, over the next year every outside consultant who visited VMI would advise against buzz cuts for women, finding them unprofessional and potentially grotesque.

---

* Quoted by David Reed, Associated Press Newswire, September 23, 1996.

The Department of Defense cautioned VMI that the continuation of ROTC at the Institute might be linked to the women's hair. If the haircut appeared to be a form of institutional harassment, ROTC could be terminated. From DOD's perspective, there was no need to subject women to haircuts shorter than those used by any of the armed services.

As always, federal criticism merely heightened VMI's resolve. In the minds of Institute officials, VMI's haircut policy was its own business and would be tailored to meet the needs of the school's unique system. Besides, there was enough internal debate over the matter to cover every side of the issue.

For a few staunch advocates of VMI's all-male heritage, haircuts were a punitive matter. Throughout the court case one could occasionally hear older women in the Lexington community remark that "if the girls insist on attending VMI, they should have their heads shaved just like the boys." This was the voice of Southern matronliness, offended at a younger generation of women who did not respect the traditional boundaries between the sexes. For these women, as for some of the Institute's most conservative alumni, the issue was clear: if female cadets wanted equality, let them have it in its most severe forms.

Almost all of VMI's administrators, however, opposed the idea of shaving women's heads. Colonel Leroy Hammond, Headquarters Executive Officer, repeatedly stressed that the only group of women so treated were Nazi collaborators living in France after World War II. If VMI were to follow that lead, the female cadets would look bizarre, and the public backlash would be brutal. No one wanted to see a bald female rat on the front page of the *Washington Post*.

Many VMI officials did not like seeing men with shaved heads either. The practice of subjecting rats to a cue-ball coiffure (known to cadets as a "zero," in reference to the setting on the barber's clippers) was a relatively recent event in VMI history. Shaved heads had been around only since the early 1980s, hardly enough time to constitute a time-honored ritual for the tradition-bound school. Several VMI administrators had long wanted a return to the short, but not shaved, haircut of their own rat years. It was bad for VMI's public image, and its recruiting efforts, to send young men home at Thanksgiving looking, in Colonel Bissell's words, like "ugly ducklings, with billiard ball heads." Now these administrators hoped that the haircut policy could be revisited, reasoning, in part, that if the men's hair was longer, male and female rats might be able to wear similar styles.

In the spring of 1997 VMI officials announced a tentative haircut policy, informing the Corps of Cadets that all rats would be given a "close-cropped" haircut. "Close-cropped" was a conveniently ambiguous term, and the statement did not clearly specify whether the haircut would be the same for both sexes. But with no separate standards announced for men and women, almost everyone assumed that male and female rats would receive the same cut.

The idea of a single standard for rat hair was popular at VMI. Haircuts, after all, were a matter of Corps unity; separate coiffures for men and women threatened the ideal of equality between Brother Rats. Colonel Keith Dickson, a former Special Forces officer who served as Commandant of Cadets from 1996 to 1997, explained the standard wisdom when it came to women's hair:

> What you want is to make those women as anonymous as possible as rats. The more anonymous rats are, the easier it is to bond them, the easier it is to control them, the easier it is for them to come to an identity themselves. Once you leave women with their long hair, and you start separating them, then you are going to cause problems.

Clearly, VMI wanted its women to blend in as much as possible. But at what price? Didn't "anonymity" mean "masculinity"?

Many people at VMI argued that a single standard for rat hair would be unfair to female cadets, noting that when it came to men and women, "equal" did not mean "identical." A close-cropped head was not equally humiliating for a woman and a man. What would be the consequences for women's self-esteem?

Dickson did not pretend to know the answer:

> That was another question with haircuts: If we cut their hair off they won't be women. By cutting their hair we destroy their femininity, we destroy their essence of femaleness, if you will, which I didn't buy. There were a lot of people who felt very strongly about that. But I think the gains you make with anonymity actually help

you. Whether a woman's inner psyche is destroyed or hurt or harmed or damaged by the fact that she has a short haircut and looks like a man, I could never answer. I'm not qualified in that and I don't think anybody else is. Feminist studies go both ways. There's no hard information that would help us make a decision like that . . . I just tended to go with an instinct that if we follow VMI's principles, what do they gain for us? If they help us gain what we want, then we ought to do it.

According to VMI's principles, anonymity helped the rat mass to bond. Identical haircuts promoted anonymity. Women might grow their hair longer after the ratline, but for the first seven months of their cadetships they should mix in with the men as much as possible. Captain Eric Avila, Assistant to the Commandant, put it bluntly: "When it comes to rats, they should almost be eunuchs. Gender, race, religion, whatever—it's irrelevant in the ratline. A rat is almost like being a separate gender. You are a class and culture by yourself."

The notion that a person can shed his or her race or gender might sound absurd, but in the ratline that is the ideal, if not always the reality. One of the first female exchange students to attend VMI said that she felt the Institute would be one of the easiest military colleges to integrate, because the barracks culture "allowed you to take off so much." And yes, she thought that you could "take off" your gender, at least for a while. But even this young woman opposed close-cropped heads for women, stressing that VMI's objective should be equality, not anonymity.

Throughout the spring of 1997 VMI went back and forth with the question of haircuts, unified on only one point—that they should make no more public statements. Statements only gave observers a target at which to shoot. Until the moment when the first female rat sat down in the barber's chair, VMI's Director of Public Relations would have to ad lib on the issue. Meanwhile, the Institute's Co-Curricular Committee, under the capable management of Colonel Tom Meriwether, spent months visiting and revisiting the matter, literally splitting hairs, while Colonel Bissell thumbed through stacks of salon portfolios, hoping to present General Bunting with a few reasonable options.

To help them visualize their choices, Commander Elizabeth Hanson, a Math professor and Naval Reserve officer, sat down at a computer imaging booth and produced multiple shots of herself in various short hairstyles. The results would have made a good joke among her friends: Elizabeth as Sinead O'Connor, Elizabeth as an early Beatle. Colonel Meriwether complained that none of the photos conformed to Army regulations. Nevertheless, two of the pictures eventually made it to VMI's barbershop, a few weeks before the women's arrival. The first showed Hanson in a short-sheared, approximately inch-long cut that was to be worn by female rats from August 15 to October 5. The second was a slightly longer, tapered, behind the ear style, *à la* Katie Couric, designated for the remaining five months of the ratline. Male rats were scheduled to get an initial one-sixteenth-inch cut, to be grown out after the first six weeks of the ratline.

Of course, college-aged students will do what they choose with their own heads. In November 1996 three of the four female cadets at The Citadel attempted to shear their hair down to the length of their male peers. Apparently those women viewed identical haircuts as an important step in bonding with their fellow "knobs." Their actions inspired The Citadel's Public Relations Officer, Terry Leedom, to offer the first in a long year of awkward remarks: "Haircutting is like brain surgery: it's not a job for amateurs."*

VMI was destined to face its own problems with homemade hairstyles once the women arrived. By the summer of 1997 a few VMI first classmen were already contacting their prospective dykes (male and female) at their homes, asking if they would be willing to shave their heads at some point during the upcoming semester. Although VMI's administrators cringed at the thought of women going home at Thanksgiving with "zeros," and warned of severe penalties for any self-styled haircuts, they knew that every year some cohort of rats applies razors to their scalps, and women were liable to be just as cavalier about their hair as the men. One incoming female cadet put the matter simply:

---

* Mike Allen, "Women at the Citadel Get Shorter Hair, and in Trouble," *New York Times,* November 9, 1996.

I just want everybody to know that hair grows back; it's not such a big deal. Everybody is freaked out about our haircuts, and none of the girls here really care about it . . . I think most of them would have shaved their heads if they were asked to, without a problem.

As this young woman stood up and turned away at the end of our July 1997 interview, I couldn't help looking at the long hair that hung halfway down her back, wondering how she would feel when she saw it lying on the floor.

THERE WERE OTHER WAYS to express femininity, apart from one's hair. Jewelry and makeup could help to accessorize a close-cropped head. Here again, however, VMI agonized over the details, questioning what sort of guidelines would constitute equal treatment of men and women.

Colonel Dickson found the discussions exasperating:

It went on and on and on and on. Do women wear makeup? Do women wear jewelry? When do they wear jewelry? Is it appropriate to restrict them from wearing jewelry or makeup? If we say no earrings at all, what are we saying? If we say earrings yes, do we mean male and female?. . . . It would roll and roll and roll in these little loops. Most of us were men, and most of us frankly didn't care one way or the other. I just thought: How do we keep it simple? How do we keep it from getting out of control? . . . But some people said: How will women feel if they're walking around without makeup? Would that hurt their feelings? Would it hurt self-esteem?

VMI's jewelry policy for men was clear enough. Male rats are prohibited from wearing any type of jewelry, except watches, prior to Breakout, partly because of the chance of injury during physical activity. After Breakout, cadets can wear up to one ring on each hand, and a religious symbol or military dog tags around the neck, out of view. VMI eventually decided that these guidelines were fair for women, with one addition. After Breakout, women could wear single gold-post earrings, not more than one-eighth-inch in diameter, for any occasion other than parades, inspections, or athletics.

Even this minor accommodation drew complaints from some male cadets. If women could wear earrings, why couldn't they? VMI grads occasionally return for reunion parades with newly pierced earlobes, and with body piercing all the rage, earrings seemed tame. (In the fall of 1997 one male rat from Band Company returned from Thanksgiving break with a Cheshire-cat smile. When asked what was up, the rat stuck out his tongue. There, in the back of his mouth, the young man was harboring his small, gold-studded rebellion against the VMI system.)

Such transgressions, however, are uncommon at VMI. When it comes to administrative policies and cadet preferences, the watchword is usually "conservative." In VMI's 1997/98 Blue Book of regulations, female cadets were granted permission to wear "conservative cosmetics," as if the makeup itself had an ideological bent. Conservative cosmetics included "noneccentric lipstick" and colorless nail polish. Female rats could use these cosmetics for any social occasion that required a uniform more formal than "class dyke," the shirts and trousers worn in the VMI classroom. After the ratline women could wear their makeup at all times, with one caveat: "Heavy, overdone, or bizarre applications of makeup will not be tolerated."

Apart from hair, jewelry, and makeup, one last feature of the women's appearance remained for VMI to ponder—their uniforms. This matter fell to the members of VMI's Facilities Committee, most of whom agreed that for everyday activities (classes, parades, formations) male and female cadets should look as similar as possible. In 1997, classroom attire for VMI's male cadets included white ducks and white blouse (trousers and short-sleeve shirts) for the warm months, and gray woolen pants, black long-sleeve shirts, and black neckties for the winter. For formal parades, the cadets wear white ducks and gray coatees (short-waisted woolen jackets with brass buttons and long tails). Female cadets, the committee decided, could wear the same uniforms as men— neckties, coattails and all—as long as they were tailored to fit the women's bodies.

The fitting process required a few changes to the normal routine. As Brownlee Tolley explained:

In the military store, before, you had an all-male staff, and the cadets would come in there and just drop their white trousers and put on a new pair of trousers and stand there and get measured for a new coat. With the gals you can't do that. We had to make little changing booths, pretty much like what you would see in a department store. Just a little four-by-four booth, with a floor-length mirror.

What the women were destined to see in those mirrors was not flattering. A young man could look dashing in a gray coatee, with brass buttons spread across his chest and coattails hanging down his back. When a woman tried on the same uniform, she simply looked like a boy.

To allow the women something more attractive for dances, Sunday services, and social occasions, the committee opted for knee-length gray and white skirts, with black pumps. In theory, the skirts were to be worn at the women's discretion. In practice, they were so shapeless and ugly that most of the women abhorred them, and the first female rats who walked out of VMI's barracks in skirts endured so much jeering that they decided not to try it again, at least until after the ratline.

(During the women's third class, or sophomore, year, a brief hubbub ensued when one woman began wearing her skirt to class. A male cadet "boned" her for improper attire, and the Commandant convened the leaders of the first class to discuss the matter. VMI's Blue Book contained no prohibition against skirts in class; although the policy in the Institute's book-length "Assimilation Plan" described the skirts as appropriate primarily for social occasions, the policy's authors had been focusing upon the women's rat year, and they left the matter of upper-class uniforms ultimately in the hands of the Commandant. Colonel Joyner, following the Blue Book, opted to allow skirts in the classroom. The sight of female students in skirts drew complaints from a few male cadets, to whom most faculty members responded by essentially saying: "Get a life." More important, the issue opened a rift between the Institute's skirt-wearing women and those female cadets who believed that strict uniformity promoted class unity. VMI's women—as a friend of mine once mused—were continually confronted by the dilemma she called "equality feminism" vs. "difference feminism." In other words, are women's interests best served by deemphasizing gender distinctions and proving that women can compete equally with men, or by acknowledging the differences between the sexes and celebrating their complementary strengths? The ratline, through its equalizing ethos, pushed women toward the former camp, but once they joined the ranks of upperclass cadets, VMI's women would have to choose their own paths.)

WITH THE INTRODUCTION OF SKIRTS into cadet life, VMI's Facilities Committee also felt obliged to put a panty-hose policy on the books. The task fell to the women on the committee, who approached their job with amusing specificity:

> Panty hose will be worn with the gray skirt and the white skirt. They will match, or be no more than one skin tone darker than color of skin, and will not have any visible runs. There should be enough elasticity to avoid bagging around the ankles and knees; panty hose will be neatly worn at all times. Female cadets may use their own preference in regard to sheen and style of garment top. Panty hose with seams up the back of the leg and other decorative designs are not permitted.

Few alumni could have envisioned the day when VMI would be specifying the elasticity for cadets' stockings. The panty-hose policy, however, proved just how thorough VMI was trying to be throughout its planning for coeducation.

The women on the Facilities Committee also had definite opinions when it came to the female cadets' most controversial piece of attire—their swimsuits. At VMI, all cadets are required to pass one semester of swimming, known in the Corps as "rat drowning." Originally, swimsuits for this class were not a problem, since all cadets prior to the mid-1960s took the course in the nude. Colonel John Rowe, who chaired the Facilities Committee, remembered those days clearly:

> At VMI you went to swim class nude, so you always had your bathing suit with you. Coach Arnold was the teacher of the swimming class . . . and the first class was one on cleanliness. Coach Arnold would, quite honestly, have a bucket of water, and have one of his aides come in and put his buttocks into that bucket of water, and then have the next guy come in and put his face in

there. That sticks with you. He proved the point that once you get in the water, every part of your body is in the water, including your buttocks, and your face is going in the water, so you've got to be clean.

He did it in such a way that it was very professional. You took a shower.

Nude swimming at VMI, however, had long been a thing of the past. Now Rowe and his colleagues faced the awkward task of picking out swimsuits for eighteen-year-old girls.

In keeping with VMI practice, the Committee's initial choices were conservative. Kathleen Bulger-Barnett recalled looking at the pictures:

Of course all the men thought they were fine. I looked at them and I didn't know how to say delicately "gentlemen . . . my *grandmother* would have worn this stuff." It was like the old Catholic thing in the 50s, the low square bottom, folded down way over the thighs, grandma cups—it was horrible, just horrible.

They were concerned about sensitivity for the women and men when the women got cold. They didn't want anyone to be embarrassed. I thought, "Yes, that's a concern, but it doesn't mean you have to put on a suit of armor. Let's not go *Baywatch*, not super-high, but pull it up a little more on the sides, make them look like women."

Eventually the Committee found a design more consistent with current styles on collegiate women's swim teams. When the sample swimsuit arrived, the ever-conscientious Committee dispatched a rather annoyed Bulger-Barnett to the local department store to get a dummy:

They wanted me to go up to Peebles and get a mannequin. So I got a bald-headed mannequin, carried her into Smith Hall, and there I was going up the stairs carrying this naked dummy. And I had to put the bathing suit on her and then show how it worked. I thought "is this necessary? Can't we just hold the suit up and say "Here's what the back looks like, here's what the bra-part looks like?" It was like the old "bring a transparency and a pointer."

After all of this careful consideration, the swimsuits still proved too modest to satisfy VMI's first women. In the fall of 1998 VMI's administrators were told that "the cadets" wanted the women's swimsuits cut higher at the thighs, to which one official replied: "Is it the male cadets or the females who are asking for this?"

Meanwhile, VMI's male cadets got to settle a long-standing grievance against their own swimwear—tight-fitting speedo-style briefs. Such suits were fine for a men's swim team, but the cadets preferred the loose, boxer-style suits, popular with most noncompetitive swimmers. In the equal-treatment aura that surrounded the 1996/97 school year, the male cadets found themselves in a unique bargaining position. They got what they wanted with little resistance, especially since the current trend was to make all cadet clothing as unrevealing as possible.

Some VMI officials seemed to want to create an environment in which they could spare the cadets the embarrassing moments that come with having a body. The Facilities Committee, for example, spent several meetings discussing whether VMI should provide liners for loose-fitting gym shorts, worrying, as Colonel Rowe put it, about "those times when you're doing sit-ups and someone is holding your ankles." It took hours of price-checking and even some consultation with the armed services, before the Committee decided that liners could be a bring-from-the-home, optional item. In the process, Rowe found that "We became experts in the cost of spandex and the availability of red vs. black."

The Co-Curricular Committee went through a similar bout of teeth-gnashing when it came to women's underwear. As Colonel Dickson recalled:

> One of the female members made a very impassioned plea that women needed a place to dry out their underthings, hand wash-ables. When someone came in to inspect, there had to be a place, in VMI regulations, where women could dry their unmention-ables. There was a big discussion about whether VMI should order a drying rack, and how it would be displayed, and what the changes in the Blue Book would look like. And I remember this kind of spread out a little bit more, into a big issue of women needing specific places to put certain things, and were we going to

get something special for the women, because they have special things?

I just said to myself: "Y'know I'm looking around the room here, and there's a Marine combat veteran, there are two Army combat veterans, a couple of unit commanders, a Green Beret, all these he-man killer people sitting around considering whether we dry undies one way or another way." I said "I think what we're doing is getting too wrapped around the axle here" . . . Once you started with a large issue, our committee found that the issue almost always devolved into the minutiae.

It wasn't that the concerns were unwarranted. Within days of their matriculation, three of VMI's first female cadets would be reprimanded for hanging their bras on a barracks window to dry. But the fact that the young women were so nonchalant about their underwear showed that the Institute did not need to treat its women with kid gloves.

Where the kid-glove treatment did arise, it often seemed to result from generational differences. Many Institute officials had spent their educations in single-sex schools like VMI, and had shunned the free-love, "anything goes" spirit of the 1960s. These men were used to maintaining clear boundaries between the sexes. The current cadets, by contrast, were much more casual about the facts of the human body. They had spent their school years in coed gym classes and coed swimming pools. Most had gone through the awkward moments of puberty in a coed environment, and many were sexually active before arriving at VMI.

Yes, embarrassing moments were bound to occur in an environment that allowed for so little privacy. But as the 1997/98 school year unfolded, it would become increasingly clear that VMI's administrators and its students had different thresholds for embarrassment. On one hand, administrators decided that female rats should not wake their male dykes in the morning (a chore routinely performed by VMI freshmen), lest the women find their mentors lying in some state of undress. At evening pep rallies, however, male rats ran around in their underwear, with jock straps on the outside, and on one occasion, when the men took off their shirts to display "98"s (the class of their dykes) painted on their backs, a few of VMI's women followed suit and ran around in their bras.

Despite the best intentions of VMI's administrators, the cadets would inevitably set their own standards for behavior.

VMI's CONCERNS ABOUT PHYSICAL MODESTY were tied to a larger, more troublesome issue—how to handle the attraction between the sexes. Everyone knew that if you crammed young men and women together in an enclosed, intense environment, sparks would fly. In order to maintain discipline in its Corps, VMI needed to establish ground rules for cadet romances. Above all, the Institute wanted to ensure that cadet hormones did not undermine power relations within the Corps.

To begin with, VMI decided that all older cadets (thirds through firsts) would be forbidden from dating rats prior to Breakout. Rats could date other rats, but the authority that upperclassmen exert over new cadets made cross-class dating dangerous. You couldn't have a cadet asking a woman out in one breath, then dropping her for push-ups in the next.

VMI later extended this prohibition throughout the entire fourth class year, to ensure that Breakout did not become the checkered flag for a rush of romances. Also, a year-long prohibition against dating meant that dykes couldn't date their rats while at VMI, a prospect that would have added a flavor of incest to the intensely familial dyke relationship.

Cadets were also forbidden from dating within VMI's chain of command. Company officers could not date within their companies; battalion commanders could not date within their battalions; and the Cadet Regimental Commander could not date anyone in the entire Corps of Cadets (an unenviable position). The dating policy did not prohibit all romances between first through third classmen, an omission that many people feared would undermine VMI's class system. It would have been very hard, however, to eliminate all cross-class dating.

When VMI first announced these regulations in the spring of 1997, cadets were full of questions. Would the Honor Court president and prosecutors, who have great authority at VMI, be prohibited from dating cadets? Could an upperclassman resign rank in order to date someone in his/her chain of command, or could cadets ask for reassignment to another unit outside the chain of command in order to date? What effect did preexisting relationships have on the policy?

On one level, these questions were heartening. In the months following the Supreme Court's decision, many disgruntled cadets had asserted that any women who would come to VMI had to be masculine monsters, without a hint of estrogen in their bodies. Other cadets might do as they pleased, but *they* would have nothing to do with the incoming Amazons. Now, these same young men were studying the details of the dating policy, and not, it seemed, merely to police the behavior of their less scrupulous peers.

Several of the cadets' questions, however, were very difficult to answer. Above all, what constituted a date in the first place? If a male and female cadet went to the movies together, was that just a friendly encounter? Did there have to be physical contact? What if a casual meeting evolved into a date?

In response, Colonel Bissell sat down in June 1997 and attempted to write a definition of "date"—a difficult task in our current society, where entire sitcom sketches revolve around whether two characters are actually "dating." Bissell brooded for an hour in his conference room, scratching out words on a yellow notepad, with several dictionaries before him. Ultimately, his efforts were futile. The dictionaries were little help; each had its own convoluted explanation, and when Bissell submitted a tentative definition to the Institute's legal advisors, they threw it out, saying that it would not hold up to scrutiny in court. Instead, they offered Bissell a paragraph of legal jargon that left him sighing: "I can't use it. I don't even understand it. I had a cadet read it and he said, 'Sir, I don't know what it says.' That's classic." VMI eventually decided that it was easier to say what a date was not than what it was, and the school included in its Blue Book one sentence from the lawyers' paragraph: "Typical cadet friendships based on shared backgrounds, academic or extracurricular interests, or organizational associations, do not constitute dating."

Hand-in-hand with dating came the more sensitive issues of sex and pregnancy. In all of its planning for coeducation, VMI did not pen a policy on sexual activity. It wasn't that sex had never happened at VMI in the past. Homosexual relationships, though rare, had occurred in the VMI closet, and cadets had been known to sneak their girlfriends into the barracks, at the risk of suspension, and to schedule romantic rendezvous in remote areas on Post. Penalties for sexual activity, however, were not specified until after the first female cadets arrived, when the discovery of two rats kissing in a darkened room made the issue more immediate. In the meantime, administrators focused their attention not on the act, but on its outcome: pregnancy.

Few issues irritate military men more than the idea of pregnant servicewomen or cadets. The U.S. Armed Forces maintained a policy of involuntary discharge for pregnant women prior to 1975, when the Defense Department, faced with ongoing legal challenges, ordered them to reverse their position. (One of the lawyers who spearheaded the assault against pregnancy discrimination in the armed services was VMI's recent nemesis, Ruth Bader Ginsburg.) Since 1975, complaints in the armed forces about lost time on the job owing to pregnancy have burgeoned, and no amount of statistics comparing, for instance, the percentage of time that servicewomen have lost for all reasons, including pregnancy, to the larger amount that servicemen have lost owing to alcohol and drug rehabilitation, can assuage the controversy.*

Whenever the subject of pregnancy came up at VMI, the level of tension in some faces around the table rose visibly. It wasn't that the Institute's officials were antibaby. I myself was five months pregnant when I joined VMI's Executive Committee for Assimilation, and after my daughter was born, I often brought her to the weekly meetings. I felt that it was fitting to supplement VMI's in-depth discussions about women with a tangible reminder of the facts of women's lives.

No one seemed to mind the occasional grunting of a newborn infant in the back of the Board Room. When it came to military training, however, pregnancy and motherhood seemed both physically and philosophically antithetical to the mission at hand, and there was no easy way to establish a parenthood policy that would deal fairly with men and women.

VMI had handled a related subject—marriage—on a "don't ask, don't tell" basis in recent decades. In theory, cadets who get married are subject to dismissal, but in practice, they are only required to specify their marital status prior to admittance. Thereafter, no questions are asked.

When VMI's dismissal policy for marriage was originally written, it was designed to discourage both weddings and babies. The two, how-

---

* For these statistics and others, see Linda Bird Francke, *Ground Zero: The Gender Wars in the Military,* New York: Simon and Schuster, 1997, p. 109.

ever, don't always go hand-in-hand, and every generation of VMI cadets has included its contingent of unwitting young fathers.

The imminent fatherhood of a VMI cadet drives the plot of *Brother Rat,* the 1938 movie starring Ronald Reagan that was based on a play by two VMI graduates, and that serves as many Americans' only window onto VMI. In that film, a secretly married cadet learns of his wife's pregnancy ten weeks before his graduation. Of course the word "pregnant" is never uttered, nor does the expectant wife ever gain an ounce. The baby arrives the night before graduation, and the dopey young dad, played by a young Eddie Albert, agrees to name him "Commencement."

Real life is not so corny. In years past, several VMI cadets have been faced with the painful choice of either completing their cadetships or raising their children. Some have left VMI to assume parental duties. Others have watched their children grow at a distance. In the early 1990s one cadet showed no qualms about routinely inviting his girlfriend and toddler to romp on the Institute's parade ground, and in February 1999 VMI's cadet newspaper featured a picture of a first classman posing in front of the Institute's barracks with his nine-year-old son.* Although VMI's administrators did not like the idea of fathers in their Corps, most were content to look the other way, so long as the messy facts of pregnancy and childrearing remained outside the gates of Jackson Arch.

Now, with female cadets on their way, parenthood assumed a new meaning. Pregnancy was clearly incompatible with most rat year activities, including boxing, fighting with pugil sticks, and throwing one's body across obstacle course barriers. Rats frequently exercise to the point of exhaustion, undergoing grueling workouts that could be dangerous even during the first trimester of a pregnancy, when an increase in the mother's core body temperature can cause brain damage to the fetus. The constant sleep deprivation and mental stress of the ratline would also be detrimental to the health of a mother and fetus, and no cadet would be comfortable dropping a woman for push-ups if he suspected that she was pregnant.

For an upperclass woman, however, the matter was different. A woman might fulfill the requirements of her cadetship for one semester,

---

* Todd Kennedy, "Member of Class of 1994: Keith Johnston," *The Cadet,* February 19, 1999.

and even graduate, without any adverse impact on her health or the health of her child. If she was in the early stages of a pregnancy, no one need ever know of her condition. When a team from VMI visited the U.S. Merchant Marine Academy in the spring of 1997, they were told that an obviously pregnant cadet had participated in that college's 1996 graduation ceremony.

Still, the image of a pregnant VMI cadet left several administrators visibly wincing. General Bunting, in particular, believed that both pregnancy and parenthood were incompatible with cadet life. The problem lay not only in the nine months of gestation. Once the baby was born, who would take care of it? Cadets are required to live in VMI's barracks around the clock, with furloughs a rare privilege. Should a mother or father be separated from her or his child for several months at a time? Some VMI officials wondered aloud whether the Institute could be legally required to provide daycare for its cadets.

With these problems in mind, VMI briefly considered a new parenthood policy, designed to discourage motherhood and fatherhood equally. According to this short-lived plan any pregnant cadet, or any male cadet who caused the pregnancy of a fellow cadet or civilian woman, would be dismissed from the Institute. The authors of this scheme hoped to avoid charges of discrimination by dealing equally with men and women, and they explained their position in a three-page document that read more like a manifesto than a draft policy statement. In it, they described in detail each cadet's commitment to VMI and the Corps, emphasizing the incompatibility of parenthood and cadetship, and closing with a moral addendum fit to restage the battle between Dan Quayle and Murphy Brown: "Moreover, causing someone to become pregnant or allowing oneself to become pregnant, while unmarried, is fundamentally irresponsible and unacceptable conduct." (Colonel Bissell later stressed that this draft policy expressed the opinions of its authors, and not necessarily those of VMI.)

The plan raised too many questions to have ever been viable. How could VMI determine the father of a child? Would male cadets who impregnated female civilians be required to turn themselves in? Would VMI establish a grandfather clause to accommodate the fathers already present among its Corps? And what about abortion? Faced with dismissal from college, a young woman would feel great pressure to end a pregnancy. How would VMI respond if, after informing a pregnant woman of her imminent dismissal, she announced that the pregnancy had been terminated? The hypothetical nightmares were endless.

Although the draft policy was scrapped, the worries that inspired it remained in place. When Elaine Donnelly, President of the Center for Military Readiness, visited VMI in the spring of 1997, she suggested that the Commandant's office establish a program to encourage sexual abstinence among cadets. Donnelly believed that abstinence training worked well on the high-school level, and might be effective at a military college.

Those VMI faculty members who heard Donnelly's suggestions at an academic committee meeting privately rolled their eyes. The Institute's chaplain was welcome to encourage abstinence during his Bible study group, but the idea of the Commandant's office preaching abstinence to a crowd of eighteen- to twenty-two-year-old cadets seemed comical. When Donnelly raised the subject again in a speech attended by cadets and administrators, she never used the words "abstinence," "sex," or "intercourse," terms that would have immediately caught the cadets' attention. Instead, she suggested that VMI should encourage its students to "delay gratification" until after graduation. Later, when I asked a few cadets what they thought of Donnelly's ideas about abstinence, they responded with blank stares. The cadets applauded Donnelly's main message—mostly admonitions for VMI to avoid what she viewed as the lowering of standards and proliferation of institutional denial that had accompanied the arrival of women at the federal academies. But when her conservative agenda translated into sexual behavior, the cadets balked. Abstinence would have been a greater change to VMI's world than coeducation.

General Bunting, however, was intrigued by the idea. He placed abstinence training on the list of issues for VMI to consider for the fall of 1997. In the meantime, VMI decided to deal with pregnancy on a case-by-case basis. In consulting with several other military colleges, VMI found that none of them had placed an official pregnancy policy on their books. Although pregnancy was a problem that all the schools faced, the issue was too sensitive to be handled with a one-size-fits-all approach.

VMI's Post Physician, Dr. David Copeland, had always maintained that he would be handling pregnancy on a confidential basis with each female cadet. His inclinations received the official nod in the spring of 1998, when the Institute convened a pregnancy subcommittee. After carefully considering the issue, the subcommittee agreed with Dr. Copeland's plans to advise pregnant rats against continuing in the rat-line, and to handle pregnancies among upperclass women on an individual basis, recognizing that a woman might remain at VMI through the early months of a pregnancy without any impact on her cadetship or her child. After taking a leave of absence a female cadet could return to VMI, so long as adequate arrangements had been made for her child's care.

Ultimately, the issue of pregnancy provided a case study in how VMI made decisions as it planned for the assimilation of women. When faced with sensitive matters—from swimsuits to haircuts to parenthood—the first instincts of VMI's officials were often conservative, sometimes reactionary. As policies evolved, however, administrators and cadets began to recognize just how far they could go to acknowledge the practical realities of women's lives without altering the essentials of VMI.

8

THE VFT

AND THE VARSITY

AFTER HAIRCUTS AND PREGNANCY, THE THORNIEST ISSUE FAC-
ing VMI involved physical fitness standards. Not the physical requirements of the ratline—few people doubted that women could handle
those. Push-ups, sweat parties, and forced marches might be grueling,
but in the ratline there was no set standard that everyone had to achieve.
As long as each rat gave one hundred percent, VMI could ask no more.
When it came to the physical fitness testing in VMI's PE classes, however, the case was different. Could men and women take the same test?
What should it consist of? Push-ups, pull-ups, a flexed arm hang?

There has never been a national consensus on equal fitness standards
for men and women. Each branch of the armed services has its own
tests, most of which were under fire when VMI looked at the issue. In
December 1997 a Congressional panel recommended that all of the services devise tougher physical standards for women and men.

The Army's standards for women were a particularly sore subject.
Prior to July 1998, the minimum fitness test for female soldiers consisted
of eighteen push-ups, fifty sit-ups, and a two-mile run in eighteen minutes and fifty-four seconds. Minimum standards for men included forty-
two push-ups, fifty-two sit-ups, and a run time of fifteen minutes and
fifty-four seconds. For years, women had passed, and aced, their fitness
test at a higher percentage than the Army's men, producing a lot of disgruntled male recruits, as well as female soldiers looking for tougher
challenges. Mia Utz, one of the transfer students from the New Mexico
Military Institute who planned to arrive at VMI with a reserve commission as an Army Second Lieutenant, found her service's minimum fitness

standards "considerably low." In her opinion, eighteen push-ups was an insignificant achievement, and when it came to the time limit for the Army's two-mile run: "You could almost walk it. That's no way to measure physical fitness." She admitted that "Those are the minimums. But I think they need to raise the bar."

VMI's administrators wanted a fitness test for women and men that would be challenging, but fair. They wanted to avoid double standards that would antagonize male cadets, and they hoped to minimize changes to their present system. But how were they going to achieve all of this?

When VMI first established a physical fitness test in the mid-1980s, it had hoped to present its cadets with an exam that would challenge their "self-imposed limits." Dr. Clark King, a veteran of Iwo Jima who was then head of VMI's Physical Education Department, wanted to push cadets beyond their own expectations, in part because he believed that in combat, exceeding one's perceived limits was a matter of survival. King and his colleagues studied the physical standards at the federal academies, they consulted with fitness experts, and ultimately produced a test that included sit-ups, push-ups, pull-ups, and a three-mile run, with minimum limits that were meant to be tough. Where the Marines required a minimum of three pull-ups, VMI required five.

Since King's day, VMI had shortened its fitness test considerably, so that it could be administered during a PE class period. The new version was dubbed the "VMI Fitness Test," or VFT, and in 1997 its minimum standards consisted of sixty sit-ups in two minutes, five pull-ups, and a one-and-a-half-mile run in twelve minutes. A cadet who reached VMI's minimums earned a D on the test. A perfect score required twenty pull-ups, ninety-two sit-ups, and a run time of eight minutes. These standards, especially the pull-ups, were going to be very difficult for women to meet.

Few people, however, liked the idea of a separate test for women. The federal academies' philosophy of "comparable training" for men and women, known in some circles as the "gender-norming" of physical standards, had resulted in a lot of angry male cadets, and the prospect of a similar system at VMI conflicted with the Institute's intention to try, wherever possible, to treat all cadets equally.

With the mantra of "equal treatment" in mind, General Bunting announced at VMI's September 21 press conference that the Institute would use the same physical standards for both male and female cadets. It would be "demeaning," Bunting explained, to offer women anything less. Although Bunting didn't specifically mention the VFT, and "physical standards" encompasses a lot of activities at VMI, the test was included in the gist of his remarks.

This was a tough position to defend. Every other military college in the nation uses separate fitness standards for women and men. VMI's own Board of Visitors, in the text of its resolution announcing the planned admission of women, acknowledged that coeducation might require "alterations necessary to . . . adjust aspects of the physical training programs." Bunting, however, didn't like the idea of a two-tiered system; he was determined that VMI should go its own way.

Outside the Institute the announcement drew a mixture of applause and protest. *USA Today* published an editorial on the subject in which it charged that the Institute's proposed policy on physical standards constituted a "guerrilla war" against women.* Having lost its legal battles, VMI seemed to be using underhanded tactics to discourage women from applying.

The Department of Defense also served notice that it was concerned about VMI's plans. If the VFT had a discriminatory impact on women, the federal government might carry out its ever-present threat: the elimination of VMI's ROTC program. But exactly what constituted discrimination remained unclear, for the debate surrounding the VFT contained more subtleties than most outside observers recognized.

To begin with, many newspapers erroneously reported that VMI was "requiring" women to pass the VFT, "demanding" that they meet the same standards as men. But although passage of a physical fitness test is required at some military colleges (cadets at the federal academies must meet their services' minimum fitness standards), this is not the case at VMI. Successful completion of the VFT is not a prerequisite for admission or graduation; a cadet might fail the VFT on every occasion and still enjoy four successful years at the Institute.

What, then, are the consequences of failing the test?

A cadet's VFT score counts for twenty-five percent of his or her grade in a half-credit physical education course required for each of eight

---

* "VMI Lost Its War Against Women; Why Keep Fighting?," *USA Today*, September 26, 1996.

semesters. In order to graduate each cadet must pass all eight courses, which consist of three electives and five mandatory classes—swimming, boxing, wrestling, principles of physical conditioning, and drug and alcohol awareness. Cadets with low course grades and failing VFT scores have often had to repeat the classes, and there have been a few cadets in the past who, faced with a near-failing PE grade, found that the only thing standing between them and a VMI diploma was the VFT. In those cases, cadets who failed the test (and consequently failed their PE course and could not graduate) had up to ten years from their matriculation dates to return to VMI and retake the VFT.

Such cases, however, had become extremely rare as VMI's grading scale for the VFT had become more lenient. Prior to the fall of 1996, if a cadet failed one event on the VFT, he failed the entire test. Today, although a cadet might receive a zero for a failed event, he or she can compensate by earning A's or high B's on the other portions of the test. In addition, any cadet with a course grade of 80 or above can get a zero on the entire VFT and still pass his or her PE class, and below 80, a cadet can pass the class depending on the number of points scored on the test. For example, a cadet with a course grade of D and a failing VFT score can still pass his or her PE class, if the F on the VFT is high (say, 50 points as opposed to 0). Finally, because these PE courses amount to only 4 credits among the approximately 130 to 150 needed for graduation, their effect on GPAs (grade point averages) is minimal.

These facts help to explain why many people at VMI thought that the VFT might remain unchanged for women. Even if women failed the test in droves, the consequences would be small. True, any woman aiming for a 4.0 would find the VFT a major obstacle, and female cadets who could not pass the test would have to get a passing grade for the rest of the requirements in their PE courses. But male cadets who failed the VFT (as did many of VMI's football players) faced the same challenge each semester, and most seemed to feel that as long as they passed their PE classes, the test had little impact.

One problem did arise from the tie-in between VFT performance and cadets' liberty privileges. Prior to 1997, any cadet who failed the VFT was placed on Limited GP (General Permit) and could not venture off Post or leave for a weekend until after taps on Saturday night. (By contrast, cadets with no limitations could leave the Post on Tuesday and Thursday evenings and Saturday afternoons). In VMI's restrictive atmosphere, where liberty can be essential for sanity, GP can be more precious than GPAs. For that reason, VMI's Physical Education Department had used the threat of limited privileges in the past as an effective inspiration for getting cadets into shape. But the Commandant's office did not enjoy keeping track of cadets' liberty privileges; enforcement of Limited GP was lax, and shortly before VMI's first women arrived, the Institute decided that after the ratline, cadets could take a certain number of special days and weekends off Post regardless of their GP status. In the months to come whenever I asked cadets and administrators about the link between GP status and physical fitness testing, they seemed to find the matter trivial. By March 1999 VMI would eliminate Limited GP altogether.

Male and female cadets who failed the VFT still had to perform one onerous duty: on Tuesday and Thursday mornings from 5:30 to 6:30 A.M. they were required to attend a cadet-run remedial physical training session, intended to help them improve on those VFT events that troubled them most. However, varsity athletes were often exempt from this program, and many of VMI's women were going to fall into that category.

Only one aspect of the VFT clearly needed immediate change. In the past, cadets had to pass the test to be considered for rank. No one who failed the VFT could join VMI's elite Cadre, or assume one of the lower corporal spots in their company.

Once women arrived, that requirement would be gone. The Institute did not want its best female leaders excluded from rank because they could perform only four pull-ups. VFT scores would still be considered during the selection process, along with numerous other criteria, but male and female cadets who failed the test would not be immediately ruled out.

But were women very likely to fail the test? According to Lieutenant Colonel Bob Cairns, who became Head of VMI's Physical Education Department in 1996, the answer was yes. When Cairns discussed VFT standards with the Institute committee assigned to review them, he predicted an extremely high failure rate for women, adding that roughly sixty percent of incoming male cadets also failed the test upon first trial. This failure rate is due, in part, to the grading scale described above, in which a cadet who flunks one event on the VFT gets a 0 for that third of the test, and must make A's or high B's on the remaining two events in order to pass. In other words, a female cadet who could not do five pull-ups would have to compensate by performing eighty-four sit-ups and running one-and-a-half miles in nine minutes (an extremely difficult time to make), just to get a D. Although this grading scale was tough, in the fall of 1996 VMI's PE Department was reluctant to change it, because the Department had already adjusted its scale in the previous year to give cadets credit for the events they passed, and the professors did not want to further "dumb-down" the requirements for men.

Besides, Colonel Cairns did not base his predictions of women's failure rates on the manner in which the test is graded. His impressions came from his experience as a PE instructor at West Point from 1979 to 1984. While there, he had found that most female cadets did not arrive at the U.S. Military Academy with the upper body strength necessary for pull-ups. (They were tested on pull-ups upon their arrival; thereafter they performed flexed arm hangs.) These women could not have passed the VFT, nor were they likely to have mastered West Point's standards for men. As Cairns saw it, the physiological differences between men and women had made the gender-norming of West Point's physical fitness testing a practical necessity, even though it provoked grumbling among male cadets.

However, twenty years had passed since the onset of coeducation at the federal academies, and in that time women had made significant strides in physical fitness, thanks to expanded athletic opportunities from Title IX. As a result, several women who were consulted by VMI on its physical standards were optimistic about women's abilities. Three female cadets visiting from Texas A&M University insisted that the minimum requirements for the VFT, including pull-ups, would be attainable for any physically fit young woman, although A's would be hard to come by. Their opinion was seconded by Cinda Rankin, the Assistant Director of Athletics at Washington and Lee University, who was invited to consult with VMI. Rankin stressed that any healthy young woman, informed in advance of the VFT requirements, could meet VMI's minimum standards. She already required members of W&L's women's tennis team (which she coached) to run two miles in sixteen minutes—the same pace as the VMI standard, but a longer distance.

Rankin's opinion became part of the public record in October 1996, when she was quoted in Lexington's local paper as saying that "I don't think the standards should be different . . . I would think women would get a great deal of satisfaction from being able to meet these standards."* Having made this statement, Rankin felt obliged to prove her point by passing the test herself. No woman had ever attempted the VFT, and Rankin wasn't sure how much training would be involved. But if she was going to advocate unchanged standards for women, she knew that she should back her words with action.

Passing the test was not a quick and easy feat. Although the sit-ups and run posed no problems for the forty-eight-year-old Rankin, the pull-ups were a different story. After three weeks of weight training Rankin attempted her first pull-up and found that she could only lift her arms to a ninety-degree angle; she could not raise her chin above the bar. Disappointed but not discouraged, she returned to W&L's weight room with an intensified plan for upper-body lifting. Twenty-one weeks later, on March 23, 1997, Rankin showed up at VMI, ready to attempt the test. As she recalled, "I don't remember being that nervous about a performance since the time that I actually competed in college."

Three of VMI's PE professors, including Bob Cairns, met Rankin at Cocke Hall. They supported her efforts and intended to ensure that the test was done in the same manner encountered by cadets. The group walked downstairs to the weight room, where, with the help of a footstool, Rankin grabbed hold of the pull-up bar and got to work. By the time her arms had given out, she had performed nine pull-ups. Next, she lay down on the red mats that covered the floor, and with a friend holding her ankles, she rushed through seventy-three sit-ups in two minutes. Finally, the group walked outside, down the steps and across the road to VMI's outdoor track, which surrounds its football field. There, Rankin completed the one-and-a-half-mile run in ten minutes and forty seconds. She had passed every event with room to spare.

VMI's professors, who seemed "surprised and pleased" with their colleague's success, accompanied Rankin back to their offices and performed the good-natured ceremony of entering her numbers on an offi-

---

* Quoted by Ed Smith, "VMI Starts Recruitment Program for Women," *The News-Gazette*, October 2, 1996.

cial VFT score sheet, which they all signed, noting that she could frame it and hang it in her office. The sheet included one line asking Rankin to categorize herself as a first-, second-, third-, or fourth-year cadet. She entered the word "Female" under the heading "Other."

Looking back at her experience, Rankin explained that:

I really don't want to see the test changed . . . Having gone through this myself, I know that I am extremely proud of having received a 73. You might say to me, "Oh, you got a C on the test," and I would say "Yeah, and I'm really proud of it." I think you should get the female cadets to take that mindset . . . prouder of taking a C than getting an A by a different set of standards. . . . There's nothing to really be proud of if you're not evaluated by the same standards.

Rankin was not the only local woman to tackle the VFT. Carole Green, the fifty-one-year-old wife of a VMI alumnus, also decided to train for the test, after hearing much talk among her husband's friends and colleagues about whether women could reach VMI's minimum standards. Determined to prove that the Institute did not need to change its standards on account of women, Green quit her ladies' tennis group and headed for the VMI weight room. "I did it for VMI, as much as anything," she explained. "I felt that to say that VMI should change its physical fitness requirements because women couldn't pass them was wrong."

Stepping into VMI's male-dominated weight room was "very intimidating" for a mom-aged woman who could barely do one pull-up. But Green went back three times a week. She worked on the lat machine, the pull-up machine. She progressed to three sets of twenty-five push-ups every day. In six months she discovered that she could do ten pull-ups, something she found "pretty amazing."

Green became so hooked on building her upper-body strength that her goal changed from passing the VFT, to maxing the test's twenty-pull-up requirement—something she achieved in the spring of 1998. In the process Green gained a legendary status in the weight room:

When I get up on the pull-up bar and knock off fifteen, sixteen, seventeen pull-ups, sometimes everybody just stops what they're doing. It's disbelief, I think. . . . It's amazing the respect I get just from being able to do that . . . I've been told by other cadets that everybody in barracks knows that there is a woman on Post who can do twenty pull-ups. That's actually been fun.

Had Green been a cadet, she still would not have scored that well on the VFT as a whole, because the run gave her problems. Another year would go by before she passed the entire test. Nevertheless, Green, who was later hired as VMI's Deputy Title IX officer, became an enthusiastic advocate for an unchanged VFT:

> I believe that if a woman works hard enough at accomplishing pull-ups, she can do it. . . . I think women have been told for so long that they have weak upper-body strength, and they can't do pull-ups like men, that they believe it in their own minds. I think that's part of the problem. It's a psychological thing.

The successes of a few tough-minded women do not constitute significant evidence for or against single-standard physical fitness testing. Nor are Rankin's and Green's experiences applicable to VMI's female rats, who would not have the time to train as thoroughly as these two women did. Still, these anecdotes illustrate the diversity of opinion that surfaced in Lexington, Virginia, whenever the subject of the VFT came up. Although some outside observers viewed the debate over physical standards as a case of hostile men placing obstacles in the paths of young women, at VMI opinions on the VFT did not divide along male/female lines. Many women, including most of the incoming female cadets, supported a single standard for physical fitness testing, while it was often the experienced military men who made the case for a two-tiered grading scale.

Lieutenant General Winfield Scott, former Superintendent of the Air Force Academy and the New Mexico Military Institute, thought that VMI should adjust its test. He did not question whether women could pass the VFT; he emphasized that women could eventually achieve any goal toward which they strived. But Scott doubted whether the end result merited the amount of time and effort required for women to reach VMI's minimum standards. Did VMI want its women practicing pull-ups when they should be reading Shakespeare or studying chemistry?

Several members of VMI's PE Department were ready and willing to change the test. As Colonel Cairns explained:

> When you set standards, you are doing something that is subjective. . . . There is nothing in combat that says that five pull-ups will save your life and four pull-ups will kill you. The thing we are looking for is guidelines that will keep kids in good physical condition. We have set those for men. Using those for women is going to disadvantage some of those women.
>
> In light of the Supreme Court decision, I am ambivalent; I have no problem changing the standard, or leaving it the same forever. But because it is graded it is a disadvantage to women more than it is to men.

The Supreme Court statement to which Cairns refers is the excerpt from Ruth Bader Ginsburg's opinion often quoted at VMI: "VMI's implementing methodology is not inherently unsuitable to women . . . some women are capable of all of the individual activities required of VMI cadets . . . and can meet the physical standards VMI now imposes on men."

However, Ginsburg prefaces this statement with a significant qualification: "it is uncontested that women's admission would require accommodations, primarily in arranging housing assignments and physical training programs for female cadets." Here Ginsburg refers to VMI's own lawyers, who argued during the court case that the admission of women would necessitate changes in the Institute's physical training programs—a fact that they cited as one reason why women should be kept out. But at a later point in Ginsburg's opinion, she repeats the statement that "some women are capable of all of the individual activities required of VMI cadets . . . and can meet the physical standards VMI now imposes on men," and this time she follows these words by adding that: "It is on behalf of these women that the United States has instituted this suit, and it is for them that a remedy must be crafted." Faced, therefore, with what they viewed as mixed signals, VMI's administrators argued that Ginsburg's opinion gave them the legal leeway to leave the VFT unchanged.

On the whole, Colonel Cairns agreed with VMI's reading of Ginsburg's opinion, but on a personal level he viewed the VFT's impact on
GPAs as the bottom line. Because the VFT affected grades, Cairns and
his colleagues in the PE Department recommended, in the spring of
1997, that the Institute develop separate physical fitness standards for
women and men. They suggested that VMI use the Marine Corps' standards for women as a guide, reasoning that most male cadets would be
amenable to the argument that, "If it's good enough for the Marines, it's
good enough for VMI." The Marines currently require a flexed arm
hang for women instead of pull-ups, and their run times for men and
women take into account the separate aerobic capacities of each sex.

The flexed arm hang (where a woman is measured by how long she
can hold her chin above a bar) was the key issue. A 1986 National Children and Youth Fitness Study, quoted by a few VMI officials during this
debate, found that at the age of eighteen young men could perform an
average of 9.7 pull-ups, while young women could only perform 0.6.
Looking at these admittedly old statistics, it seemed unlikely that most
of VMI's women would be able to do 5 pull-ups.

According to Cairns, a flexed arm hang was also better for measuring
women's improvement:

> It's very difficult to tell your improvement in a pull-up. If you can do
> three-quarters of a pull-up or half a pull-up, it's still zero. You might
> be gaining in strength but it doesn't show yet on the test. In a flexed
> arm hang, by determining the length of time they can hold their
> chins above the bar, you can establish differences among individual
> women. It also doesn't require the same upper-body strength.

Even as they offered recommendations, however, VMI's PE professors knew that they would meet resistance. The mere suggestion of
"gender-normed" standards grated against VMI's egalitarian ideal, and
tended to inflame emotions among both alumni and cadets. Cairns had
spent years listening to West Point's male cadets complain about double
standards, and he had heard the early muttering at VMI:

> You can look somebody in the eye and say these changes were
> made because of physiological differences between men and

women, and they'll look right back and say "Yea, yea, but I'm getting screwed." I've talked to cadets here who cannot pass the pull-ups, and never will be able to in their entire lives unless they have a complete change of lifestyle. And they'll say "Yes, five pull-ups. We've got to have that for women because I can't do five pull-ups and they shouldn't be able to do them either."

VMI felt no need to cater to these cadets' sour grapes. Plenty of their classmates recognized that "equal" did not mean "identical," and that in order to treat men and women equally VMI might have to account for physiological differences. But there was enough Corps opposition to separate physical standards to raise the question of what would ultimately be best for the women's assimilation. Would women be better off with higher VFT scores and embittered classmates? Would lower VFT scores be a fair tradeoff for easier acceptance into the Corps?

"There is a point," explained General Farrell, VMI's Dean of the Faculty, "at which 'fair' may actually compromise the women's chances of integration here":

> The service academies tried to juggle the standards and they have got nothing but animosity and intestinal resentment over it. Many of these women have told us in letters beforehand, "Don't change the standard. We don't want to have to face that complaint too." And I'd be tempted to say "Leave the damn standard." . . . If women are going to earn their way, they need at least to face the standard without asking for it to be changed. . . . Someday a woman's going to make that, and without keeping the standard, her achievement is not going to be what it should have been.

General Bunting, who had the ultimate authority over the matter, continued to support a single standard for physical testing. In the spring of 1997 he informed Colonel Bissell that whatever test was ultimately chosen, it should be applied to both sexes. Consequently, when Colonel Cairns suggested a flexed arm hang for women, Bissell asked if men could do the same. Cairns saw that as a lowering of men's fitness standards. What about push-ups, Bissell asked. Could they be substituted for pull-ups, since they were easier for women? Cairns replied that administratively, push-ups were hard to grade; the only way to accurately measure a good push-up was with a clickerboard (a device in which a student's chest must press down on a clicking mechanism in order for each push-up to count). When Bissell asked if there was one multiple-event test in which men and women could have the same set of standards, Cairns answered with a flat "no."

And so VMI ran into a dead end. When the discussions were over, the current standards remained in place, with one clear qualification: the VFT would be reevaluated at a later date and adjusted if necessary. Almost everyone assumed that some changes would ultimately be needed. If VMI did not alter the components of the test, it would probably have to adjust the grading scale or further limit the VFT's impact on GPAs. Because the physical capabilities of VMI's women were unknown, however, it seemed reasonable to delay final action until the data was on the table.

In the meantime, VMI's single standard for fitness testing would make an interesting experiment. Would women rise to the challenge if the standards remained unchanged? Would male cadets eventually lobby for adjustments if they saw that the women were making a real effort? How much respect would the women earn for attempting to meet the men's standards?

As long as the impact of the test was minimized, the questions could stand.

ALTHOUGH THE VFT was the most controversial item facing VMI's PE Department, it was not the only issue the professors confronted. Boxing and wrestling, required courses in VMI's curriculum, raised eyebrows when outsiders envisioned women punching it out.

You might wonder why VMI requires its cadets to box. Most rats hate the class, and Colonel Cairns refers to it, with a smile, as a mini-ratline. Contrary to what one might imagine, the rationale behind its mandatory status has nothing to do with toughness, or aggression, or the need for military students to master hand-to-hand combat. Instead, Cairns refers to the words of George Garrett, an acclaimed Southern writer of fiction and poetry who heads the University of Virginia's creative writing program.

Garrett once published an autobiographical piece in which he upheld boxing as an important component in the development of his artistic sensibilities. The boxer, according to Garrett, learns lessons in self-discipline, craft, and the wastefulness of anger. Above all, boxing teaches something about courage: "One of the immutable lessons of boxing was that there was no free ride. No free lunch. To succeed you had to be at risk. You had to choose to be at risk. That choice was the chief act of will and courage. After that you might win or lose, on the basis of luck or skill, but the choice itself was all that mattered."* Colonel Cairns keeps a large printout of this quote in his office, occasionally posting it on a bulletin board in an attempt to inspire the grim-faced rats who can be seen trudging toward boxing class on winter mornings.

Words of poets and professors aside, however, when applied to female cadets VMI's boxing requirement did seem unusual. The Naval Academy is one of the only military colleges in the United States that requires women to box. At West Point, female cadets take self-defense courses while their male peers box and wrestle.

Back in 1984, when VMI's PE Department conducted a self-study that acknowledged the possible admission of women in coming years, it, too, assumed that women would have to take self-defense courses in place of boxing and wrestling.† (It is noteworthy that the PE professors, like many other people at VMI, were discussing the admission of women well before the court case ever began.) In the intervening decade, however, more and more women had begun to box and wrestle throughout the United States, and by the spring of 1997 almost everyone at VMI agreed that these sports were fine for both sexes, as long as women boxed women and men wrestled men. The PE Department would need to invest in some chest protectors, but otherwise there should be few problems.

Whether or not the women would be good boxers was another matter. In his years of teaching the sport, Colonel Cairns had found that

---

* George Garrett, "My Two One-Eyed Coaches," in *An Apple for My Teacher,* ed. Louis D. Rubin, Jr., Chapel Hill: Algonquin Books, 1997.
† "VMI Departmental Self Study," Department of Physical Education, October 15, 1984, Virginia Military Institute Archives, Lexington, Va.

boxing required a level of aggression and physical contact not usually associated with women. A boxer needs to step forward and put his body at risk, and most women, Cairns believed, did not have the same "in-your-face" instincts as men. Cairns had already issued plenty of F's to male boxing students, and if VMI's women were not making average grades prior to taking the VFT, they were liable to fail the class in higher proportions than men. As Cairns saw it, boxing might be the straw that broke the VFT's back: "When you have to take boxing a second time because of the VFT, you aren't going to be too happy about it, and then you're going to say 'I'm getting the shaft. I need to have a change made in this VFT.' " That, however, remained to be seen.

In the meantime, VMI's PE Department had one last issue to consider—a program called "rat challenge." Every fall all VMI rats who are not on athletic teams spend two afternoons each week tackling a series of outdoor physical challenges, guided by the upperclass Rat Challenge Cadre. Some of the activities have an "outward bound" flavor: rock climbing and rappelling on the sheer cliffs beside the Maury River, which marks the northern boundary of VMI's campus; walking along high ropes in the upper branches of trees, while strapped into safety hooks; running up House Mountain, the most striking landmark in the Lexington area. Other activities are more overtly military—pugil stick competitions (where helmeted cadets jab at each other with the padded ends of long sticks, using them as though they were rifles with fixed bayonets); the Marine Corps obstacle course (a sprint over metal and wooden obstacles that finishes with a twenty-foot rope climb, which fast cadets complete in less than a minute); and the VMI obstacle course (which includes a lot of running and takes twenty minutes or more to complete).

The objective behind these activities is to promote individual confidence and team-building. Cadets are timed on how long it takes an entire company to complete a five-mile run or to reach the top of House Mountain. Cadets also work in small groups; teams of five scale a high wall, with two cadets at the bottom hoisting up their fellow rats, who then lean over the edge to pull their teammates up from the bottom. These challenges culminate in late November with the Rat Olympics, when representatives from each company compete against one another in everything from tug-of-war to wall-climbing.

Many rat challenge activities were bound to be especially difficult for women. The Marine Corps obstacle course, for example, emphasizes upper-body strength, with cadets pulling themselves up and over high bars and scaling an eight-foot wall. VMI, however, was not eager to make changes. During Colonel Cairns' years at West Point, that academy had attempted to equalize its indoor obstacle course by removing some events that favored men and adding others that they thought would favor women. The results didn't always improve the women's scores, but they did highlight some interesting gender differences. When West Point added a balance beam that turned at three angles, they found that male cadets would tackle it at full speed, crashing, bruising themselves, and jumping up again, while the women moved more slowly and carefully. West Point also established different time limits for men and women on the course, which, as Colonel Cairns recalled, "created a lot of heartburn with the men when they compared their scores."

But unlike West Point VMI has no time limits for its obstacle courses; it never tallies cadets' performances on rat challenge activities. Women might have trouble, but that was OK. Plenty of men would have problems as well, and the cadets would not be competing against one another. Prior to the arrival of women, the only change VMI made to its rat challenge program was the addition of ramps at a few high obstacles, to give a boost to shorter cadets of both sexes. In the upcoming years almost every rat, male and female, would avoid the ramps, preferring instead to get help from their Brother Rats.

AS IT TURNED OUT, most of VMI's women were not going to be participating in rat challenge activities anyway. Rats who compete in intercollegiate sports are exempt from the program, and over fifty percent of VMI's first women were going to fit into that category. As we'll see later, the high percentage of women who participated in varsity athletics would become one of the sorest subjects facing VMI in its first year of coeducation. Not only do VMI's athletes miss rat challenge, they also eat supper after the Corps, avoiding many of the early evening workouts suffered by their Brother Rats. The resulting split between athletes and their peers has long been a source of tension at VMI, and with women added into the equation, the frustration was going to mount.

Nevertheless, if VMI wanted to build a women's athletic program, the school was going to need a high percentage of its female cadets to sign up. Once women populated all four of VMI's classes, the total number of female athletes was still going to be very small for an intercollegiate schedule.

All of which led to some interesting questions. How should a college go about establishing a women's athletic program if it might only have a handful of participants? Where should VMI begin? And what did Title IX's rules on gender equity in athletics require?

VMI is an NCAA Division I school, competing in the Southern Conference. In order to remain in Division I, NCAA rules require coed colleges to sponsor seven sports for men and seven for women (six for men and eight for women is also OK for those schools sponsoring football). At least two of the women's activities have to be team sports.

Obviously VMI was not going to meet that mark anytime in the near future. For the time being, both VMI and The Citadel were granted renewable waivers—two years for the NCAA, and five years for the Southern Conference. But in order to comply with Title IX, VMI would have to ensure from the outset that its women participated in intercollegiate athletics in the same proportions as their male peers. In an average year, thirty-three percent of VMI's cadets participate on the Institute's thirteen athletic teams—a high percentage for any college, possible because roughly eighty percent of VMI freshmen have experience in high-school sports, and many teams at VMI operate on a "come-one, come-all" basis. To match the men's percentages, VMI would need at least one-third of its women to compete in athletics, even though their choice of sports would be very limited.

As with everything else surrounding coeducation, the matter of women's athletics was handled by a committee. The Institute's Athletic Director, Davis Babb, chaired a group that concentrated on a few key questions: What were the exact requirements of Title IX, the NCAA, and the Southern Conference? How could VMI ensure that women received equal treatment in recruiting, coaching, scheduling, and facilities? And which women's sports should VMI develop first?

To help find answers, the committee invited Lamar Daniel, a Title IX specialist who provided confidential analyses of university athletic programs, to visit VMI. Daniel had spent over twenty-one years with the

Office for Civil Rights in Atlanta, conducting over fifty Title IX investigations and authoring one of the chief manuals in the field. As he saw it, VMI had three basic options. They could do nothing and wait to meet the women's athletic interests once they arrived. That, however, would be irresponsible, since VMI knew the athletic abilities of most of its applicants. At the other end of the spectrum, VMI could map out a ten-year strategy to meet the minimum Division I requirements, perhaps planning basketball, soccer, or volleyball teams for women, in addition to a host of individual sports. But without long-range knowledge of the women's numbers or their interests, this would be overkill.

Daniel recommended the middle path, suggesting that VMI develop a select number of women's sports, while planning an expanded program based on the women's interests. Since this was the direction in which they had already been leaning, VMI's officials were happy to continue down that road. Babb's committee outlined two "Five-Year Plans" for women's athletics (never acknowledging Stalin's ill-fated plans of the same name). The first plan included four stated objectives:

1. To offer female cadets athletic opportunities in cross-country, track and field, swimming, rifle, tennis, and golf.
2. To actively recruit female cadets for cross-country and track and field, beginning immediately, and to actively recruit women for swimming beginning with the Class of 2004. (Active recruitment of women for team sports was relegated to the second Five-Year Plan.)
3. To develop other athletic opportunities for women, to be implemented in the second five-year period, based on student interest and the requirements of the NCAA and the Southern Conference.
4. To assess the need for a full-time assistant athletic director to develop the women's athletic program. This person would be hired in the second five-year period.

It made sense for VMI to begin its recruiting efforts with cross-country and track and field. VMI's rats already do plenty of running, and several of the earliest female applicants had expressed an interest in cross-country. In addition, only five women are needed to field a women's cross-country team, as opposed to fourteen for women's indoor/outdoor track, and eleven for a women's swimming and diving program. VMI viewed cross-country as the first sport in which female cadets might compete as a team. The crucial factor, however, in VMI's emphasis on cross-country and track and field came from the strength of the coach: Mike Bozeman, a General in the U.S. Army Reserve.

General Bozeman, who served as VMI's Commandant of Cadets from 1994 to 1996, was VMI's most successful coach. Since his arrival at the Institute in 1986, his track-and-field athletes had brought home ten Southern Conference championships, making them VMI's most victorious team.

Bozeman had coached women on high-school and college teams in the past, but he had never welcomed the idea of female cadets at VMI. He was a Citadel graduate, and as he saw it, he had reason to take the Supreme Court's decision against VMI especially hard: "People say we died a terrible death here. Nobody died twice except for me. All the VMI people that didn't want it felt bad. All the Citadel people felt bad. I'm attached to both, so I felt doubly bad."

Nevertheless, once VMI agreed to admit women, Bozeman was ready to get to work. He had been formulating ideas for a women's athletic program long before the Supreme Court rendered its decision, and despite the fact that he had no operating budget—"we had to build on nothing, really, other than a pipe dream"—Bozeman was determined to turn his vision into a reality.

Bozeman and his staff began by sending questionnaires to high-school coaches throughout Virginia in the late fall of 1996, explaining VMI's plans for women's athletics. They looked at track-and-field results throughout the region and contacted all female applicants to VMI who had any track experience. Bozeman's message to these young women was clear:

> You will build the women's athletic tradition at VMI . . . You will build it on the most solid athletic foundation we have here, and that is men's track and field. They have laid the foundation; now you will build your own tradition. . . . And when you do, when you are successful, those track-and-field alumni will embrace you just as they do the men.

Some women were sold on the sheer force of Bozeman's personality. After Kelly Sullivan, a "thrower" (discus, shot put, etc.) from Jackson, Georgia, visited VMI, her mother complained to Bozeman that "You put a spell on my daughter!" He replied with a smiling "No. It's just VMI. We have this little pixie dust that falls on people when they come here."

Bozeman was especially proud when another young woman turned down the Naval Academy in order to join his team: "When you've got someone with an appointment to the Naval Academy, and they say 'I want to come to VMI, and the main reason I want to come to VMI is because I want to run for you,' then you know that you, as an individual, have made a difference."

With aid from General Bunting and Jeff Morgan (who helps to run VMI's alumni booster club for athletics), Bozeman raised scholarship money for two female athletes. He did not worry about whether his male track-and-field athletes would accept the women. On the first day of coed practice he simply reminded these men of the material benefits of coeducation:

> I went in there and I said "All right guys, your locker room has new carpet. We now have central heat and air. We have the shower fixed. We have more space. And our field house has been painted for the first time in probably fifty years. I've just got to tell you that's mainly because of the women. Look at all of the good things that they have brought to your program. Make no mistake, we would not have had any of that were it not for the women's cross-country team. Period. Exclamation point."

According to Bozeman, "I never had a problem since day one."

The problems were destined to come from all of the questions that could not be answered in the year of planning. How, for instance, would VMI combat the perception that female athletes were "worming" out of the ratline? How successful would the Institute be at building opportunities for women outside of track and field? What would happen to women who preferred team sports? For the time being, VMI planned to invite these women to compete with male cadets on the Institute's non-contact intramural teams, which included soccer, flag football, basketball, and volleyball. In addition, women were free to join some of VMI's club sports, including fencing, racketball, and power lifting. But women could not join the men in contact sports, such as rugby, water polo, and boxing, and as it turned out, one of VMI's first women was going to be an experienced rugby player, looking for a good game.

VMI's status as a Division I school also raised questions. How long would the NCAA and Southern Conference allow VMI to renew its waivers? Would VMI eventually be dropped from both if it could not build a large enough women's program? What would happen if women insisted on joining men's teams? How would other athletic directors in the Southern Conference react?

Lamar Daniel's report to VMI included words of warning on precisely that subject:

> I do not believe these individuals (Southern Conference athletic directors) will go along with women competing against men within the Conference, although Title IX does require you to do that in the case of noncontact sports when there is not sufficient interest to justify a women's team. More specifically, you must allow women to try out for a men's team if there is no women's team. You do not have to let her compete if she is not good enough . . . To illustrate further, if you have one woman trying out for men's golf, you must allow that. She may practice with the team, but if she does not make the top five, she does not compete in the tournaments just as the other men who also did not make the top five do not.

And if she made the top five, what then? Would other Southern Conference athletic directors protest if VMI fielded a coed soccer team?

The Institute's proactive approach toward track and field meant that VMI would at least have some athletic opportunities available for women from the outset. But in regard to sports, as with most of the issues facing VMI, the future was filled with uncertainties.

PREPARING THE CORPS

As all of VMI's preparations moved forward, events at The Citadel provided a cautionary tale. The Citadel had admitted four women into its 1900-man Corps in August 1996. By late October, two had come forward with allegations of hazing, claiming that over the past two months they had been hit, kicked, and sexually harassed. They had been told to stand still while their sweatshirts were doused with nail polish, then lit on fire. Jeanne Mentavlos and Kim Messer resigned from The Citadel's Corps shortly after the New Year, planning lawsuits against their alleged assailants. Over the next few months The Citadel floundered under a swirl of media attacks, criticism that culminated in a devastating *Sixty Minutes* exposé.

One might imagine that VMI would have enjoyed watching its arch rival squirm. Up to this point the Institute had been criticized for failing to embrace coeducation with the same swift fervor as The Citadel. The scandal in Charleston seemed to vindicate VMI's careful pace. But if there was any gloating on the part of Institute officials, it was muted. Most of them realized that the problems at The Citadel would only give the Justice Department more reason to watch VMI with an eagle eye.

VMI's administrators responded to the news from South Carolina by stating, again and again and again, that VMI is *not* The Citadel. Although in the minds of many Americans the two schools blend together into one mass of Southern male militarism, for alumni of these colleges, the distinction between their alma maters is quite clear.

Citadel graduates tend to credit their school with being more rigorous, militarily and academically, than VMI, while Institute cadets counter that what passes for rigor at The Citadel is in fact a culture of sadism, where ritualistic hazing is ingrained in daily life. As one VMI cadet insisted in the winter of 1996, hazing at The Citadel is "ten times worse and ten times more frequent" than the abuses faced by VMI cadets.

It is hard to know what to make of such claims, clouded as they are not only by college rivalry, but by rivalry between the states. Virginians like to envision their Commonwealth as being more civilized than South Carolina, and presumably South Carolinians nurture an analogous prejudice. According to one VMI alumnus: "North Carolina is a valley of humility between two mountains of conceit." Still, as Institute officials watched the national press corps descend upon Charleston, they tended to recognize that "There but for the grace of God go we."

All military colleges have an inherent potential for cruelty. Sophomores in Texas A&M's Corps of Cadets are known today as "pissheads" because of an old practice, now supposedly obsolete, in which fish (freshmen) took revenge against hated sophomores by "balling them up" in their sheets, dragging them to the bathroom, and flushing their heads in the toilet. This, many cadets will tell you, was a relatively playful form of mistreatment. Other examples are more overtly sadistic. During Lieutenant General Winfield Scott's tenure as Superintendent of the New Mexico Military Institute, he was shocked to discover that an upperclassman had been inflicting cigarette burns on a younger cadet. The victim never complained; the problem came to light when an adult noticed the scars.

At VMI, the most notorious case of hazing happened to the Institute's most famous alumnus. During his rat year George Marshall was ordered by upperclassmen to squat over a bayonet. Weakened by a recent bout of typhoid fever, he collapsed and was stabbed in the buttocks. Marshall refused to identify the upperclassmen responsible for his injury, a fact emphasized by those alumni who regularly recount the story. Today, misguided notions of loyalty continue to protect the perpetrators of abuse.

The type of violence that Marshall encountered at VMI was more common in the early twentieth century, when a rash of problems at the school inspired the Virginia General Assembly to pen a statute against hazing. By contrast, today's cadets and administrators explain that the most common forms of ill-treatment faced by VMI rats are unauthorized workouts behind closed doors and unsanctioned exercises that have the potential to cause serious injury.

Take, for instance, the "duck squat," in which a rat is ordered to lock his fingers behind his head, squat, and either jump up and down or walk like a duck. It is an exercise well known to Sergeant Major Al Hockaday, the barrel-chested former Marine and Vietnam veteran who regularly patrols VMI's barracks: "I did it when I was a recruit at Parris Island. The drill instructor would have us duckwalking up and down the parade ground. Shortly thereafter it was outlawed, and it's outlawed here. But cadets want to do it because it is hard, it is painful, so you have to stop them."

It might seem like a harmless joke, to have a flock of new cadets waddling around the barracks, flapping their wings, and occasionally quacking. But after repeated use the duck-squat destroys the cartilage in one's knees, as does the posture required to "assume the position of a chair," i.e., with one's back to the wall and knees bent at a ninety-degree angle.

These exercises are forbidden at VMI; cadets who impose them know that they will be punished if caught. Most forms of abuse, however, are not so clear-cut. Part of the difficulty in policing cadet behavior is that there is often no consensus, among administrators as well as cadets, about the line between horseplay and hazing. The last incident that VMI recognized as a criminal case of "hazing" in its barracks occurred in 1996, when a rat was dragged out of bed by fellow cadets who shaved his head, sprayed Flex-All on his crotch, and, according to some reports, threatened to shave his genitals. In the fury of his resistance the rat dislocated his shoulder, clearly entering the territory of the Virginia hazing statute, which states that it is unlawful to "mistreat so as to cause bodily injury to any student at any school, college, or university." VMI suspended six students, then turned the case over to the Commonwealth's judicial system, where a grand jury refused to indict the cadets, viewing their suspensions as an appropriate punishment.

To most observers, this incident would appear to be a clear case of assault, filled with dark and disturbing psychosexual implications. Had the rat sustained no injury, however, many VMI cadets would have written off the event as a simple instance of roughhousing. Shaving of pubic hair is not unheard of on college campuses. It has occurred at VMI on several occasions, an act that cadets inflict upon their buddies on their twenty-first birthdays. In March 1998 one senior cadet estimated that eleven such incidents had taken place in the previous six months, despite the presence of women in the barracks. (A Washington and Lee fraternity faced a highly publicized encounter of the same variety in the spring of 1998, a case all the more shocking because a woman wielded the razor.)

College students have endless means of appalling their parents, and when presiding over a culture of young men balanced between adolescence and adulthood, VMI's administrators have often been compelled to distinguish between acts that are truly vicious and those that are merely disgusting. As the Institute prepared for women, however, one point was clear to everyone: if a female cadet was physically mistreated, VMI would be dead in the water. The Justice Department and the media would be free to declare open season on the school, and the ratline would likely become a thing of the past.

With this in mind, General Bunting sent a note to Colonels Bissell and Hammond on December 20, 1996:

> Our main task this coming term will be to shape the attitude of the Corps toward the coming of women, and their enrollment this August. Obviously the Citadel did not do that. Obviously too we must stay away from what smacks of "sensitivity training." We must simply demonstrate that the VMI way is the honorable, professional, efficient, self-controlled way, and that the residual ill-feeling must not be directed against the female cadets: they are the beneficiaries, not the makers, of the School's new, coeducational, era.

Words such as "professional," "efficient," and "self-controlled" might not seem to apply to a barracks filled with eighteen- to twenty-two-year-old men. Nor was Bunting naive to the problems in the Corps' private life: "That is the dark underside of 1,400 people living together in a small space, most of whom are male, in this culture. There is too much drinking; there's a lot of bad stuff that goes on in the barracks."

Bunting believed that part of the job of VMI's administrators was to continually battle against the cadets' worst instincts:

> You know, John Adams had basically two halves of his life, and in the last thirty years he began to doubt the possibility of making

people better. But he kept saying that no effort in behalf of the inculcation and encouragement of virtue can be spared. And that's how I feel. I know that for the last thirty years, and one hundred years, bad things have gone on in Barracks, and they probably always will, but (here Bunting lets out a long sigh) we just have to keep fighting it day by day.

Bunting's preferred method of fighting was "to do everything you can to help the cadets identify other cadets who are going to be strong leaders, of strong moral character and who will not stand for that." When The Citadel's scandal first hit the papers, Bunting responded by inviting rising cadet leaders to his home to discuss the news, while he promoted the importance of moral courage among those cadets who witnessed wrongdoing. "Moral courage" was to become one of Bunting's catch-phrases over the next few months, a lesson that needed to be taught regardless of whether the Corps was all-male or coed.

The message, however, could not be broadcast solely from the Superintendent's living room. In the spring of 1997 VMI planned to hold months of formal training sessions, from large convocations down to small workshops, aimed at indoctrinating everyone in the standards of behavior that would have to govern a newly coed, and highly scrutinized, VMI. Such training would not only benefit cadets. A few female professors complained that some of their male colleagues had become accustomed to using sexual jokes and innuendoes in their classrooms. A change was long overdue.

Planning these sessions was the job of Colonel Mike Harris, Head of the Department of Modern Languages. Harris chaired VMI's Orientation Committee, a group that spent months pondering the logistics of Post-wide training. Although the committee proved adept at generating ideas and debating concepts, when it came down to making actual decisions about dates, staffing, and formats for orientation sessions, Colonel Bissell often had to intervene. But through the combined efforts of Harris, Bissell, and several committee members, they managed to address four major questions: who would get the training, what would it cover, who would present the materials, and what timeline would they follow?

The first question was the easiest to answer. From the outset VMI knew that it wanted to include *everyone:* cadets, faculty, administrators, buildings and grounds crews, Post policemen. Anyone who had contact with cadets should be oriented toward the coming of women.

It might seem unnecessary for a school to compel its laundry workers and dishwashers to receive training on new "assimilation policies." But many of VMI's long-time employees were as emotionally invested in the Institute's single-sex status as were the cadets. According to Sergeant Major Hockaday:

> I would go down to the mess hall, and I would talk to some of the guys who were cooks, and they would say "Man, I don't know if I can cook for women." I'd say "What do you mean, you can't cook for women?!" Or the guys who were cleaning would be saying "Well, they're just going to mess the place up." And I'd say: "The guys are vomiting on the stoops. They are pissing on the stoops. And you say that women are going to mess it up? How are they going to mess it up?"

Negative reactions were not limited to male employees. Many of the school's female secretaries and members of the administrative staff had been staunch supporters of VMI's single-sex status. Back in 1990 Vergie Moore, Executive Secretary to the Dean, had told Kevin Kittredge of the *Roanoke Times* that the admission of women "would be the ruination of VMI . . . They might as well tear it down and start over again."* Once the Supreme Court had spoken, Moore was as determined as anyone to see VMI succeed. In fact, after the first year of coeducation she acknowledged that the presence of women was not such a bad thing after all. But it was not going to be easy for all of the Institute's employees to accept the school's new mission.

That was why, in the spring of 1997, VMI planned to include everyone on Post in its orientation sessions—a feat that was possible largely because of the Institute's small size. At VMI, "everyone" includes about 1,600 people, not enough to fill half of the basketball stadium. Indeed, the small size of VMI's Corps and the comparatively generous number of faculty and administrators (the school boasts a twelve-to-one student–faculty ratio) constituted one of VMI's staunchest buffers against a

---

* "Coed VMI OK by Many, Poll Finds," *Roanoke Times*, March 4, 1990.

Citadel-style scandal. Few things can happen at VMI without plenty of other cadets and administrators soon hearing about it.

Once they had determined their audience, Harris's committee pondered their message:

> We had many discussions on what were those issues in modern society that we needed to cover. At one meeting we sat down and I just started taking notes, listing things to include in orientation, just off the tops of our heads. By the end I had two sides of a legal pad filled. I must have had eighty or ninety individual items. . . . So we started out orienting the entire world on everything, every aspect that we could think of, and then we had to zero in and narrow it down.

Gender issues, race relations, drug and alcohol awareness—these were the kinds of things that the Orientation Committee would ideally have liked to address. VMI has a very insular culture, and most administrators agreed that their cadets needed more training in how to "swim in the mainstream." For the time being, however, relations between men and women were VMI's chief concern, so the Orientation Committee chose to narrow its sights to four key topics: fraternization, hazing, new assimilation policies, and, above all else, sexual harassment.

Sexual harassment was the key issue in the minds of most cadets. Even as VMI planned its orientation sessions, a scandal at the Aberdeen Proving Grounds was ballooning into a public outcry against sexual harassment in the U.S. Army. With memories of Tailhook fresh in the public mind, and new stories from The Citadel emerging every month, many VMI cadets feared that they would become victims in a political witch-hunt.

Few people however, liked the idea of workshops on sexual harassment. "A lot of people were uptight that it was going to be sensitivity training and touchy-feely and est and that kind of stuff," recalled Harris. "We didn't attempt to do that. It was simply to get information out, about the legal definitions and so on."

General Bunting was so averse to the notion of "sensitivity training" that Colonel Bissell felt compelled to find synonyms whenever the subject arose. One professor recommended "cultural awareness training," since, as she saw it, VMI's challenge was not so much to assimilate women as to acculturate males. Another recommended "moral education," noting that the issues VMI intended to address were basic questions of right and wrong. Whatever they called it, the content of VMI's orientation sessions would have to be more informative than emotional, more practical than political. "What is it we want to orient everybody on?" asked Harris. "Well, we thought in point of fact it came down to civility. If there were going to be problems with the presence of women here, we thought that the Golden Rule should reign."

Some alumni who shared this view did not see why VMI should waste its time on formal sexual harassment workshops. It would be enough, one administrator said, to simply stand in front of the Corps, give them their orders, and tell them to carry them out honorably. But that seemed to have been The Citadel's strategy, and if anyone doubted that there was the potential for a similar scandal at VMI, the answer became painfully obvious by March 1997, when VMI hired its first female Assistant Commandant, Major Sherrise Powers.

BEFORE COMING TO VMI, Sherrise Powers had served as an enlisted Army recruit for eight years, followed by nine years in the reserves. Among other specialties, she had been trained as a parachutist, a criminal investigator, and an instructor for the Advanced Noncommissioned Officers Course. Throughout her military training, however, she had never envisioned a job at VMI.

When Powers first noticed that the Institute was advertising for an Assistant Commandant, she did not pay much attention. She assumed that the school would be looking for a female officer. Later, when a friend revealed that he was a VMI alumnus and urged her to apply, she remained skeptical. She had recently completed law school, and as she told Colonel Keith Dickson, VMI's Commandant at the time, she was planning a career in juvenile defense. Dickson assured her that "There's plenty of juveniles to work with here," and after enlisting the aid of several Christian friends, who prayed for her guidance, the devout Major ultimately decided that "it was God's will." She would go to VMI, not necessarily because of what she might offer the school, but perhaps for what she might learn there.

The initial lessons were hard. When Powers arrived in March 1997, she was the only woman in VMI's barracks, and the first female with the power to routinely stop cadets on the stoops, to correct them, and to bone them. Her trial by fire came within two weeks, when Colonel Dickson told her to break up an impromptu ballgame in the Old Barracks Courtyard. It was an unpleasant duty under any circumstances—the cadets have so few opportunities for spontaneous fun—and Powers had already become unpopular among many cadets for what they viewed as her abrasive manner when confronting them. When they saw her coming, they responded bitterly.

As Powers moved among the crowd of young men, dispersing the players and confiscating their equipment, she heard, in the background, a clamor of voices gradually getting louder. Looking up, she saw what she estimated at "hundreds" of cadets on the third and fourth stoops, leaning over the railings and yelling "You bitch!" "You whore!" "Get out of here!" Powers was thick-skinned, having spent much of her military career as the sole female among dozens of men. "I just threw it off as folks venting," she explained with a shrug. The episode did, however, make it clear that VMI's Corps was filled with pent-up anger. If the school's orientation sessions served no other purpose, they might manage, as VMI's Dean later explained, "to get bitter, unhappy, confused people to spit out the poison—to get it out in public and deal with it. Even if you can't do anything more than just ventilate it. . . . That stuff does wear down after a while."

The biggest problem that Colonels Harris and Bissell faced in arranging for this "ventilation" was finding time slots for all of the planned events. At VMI, the cadets' daily lives are crammed full of activities, and the Commandant's office jealously guards its own power to alter the cadets' schedules. Orientation on the grand scale that VMI had in mind only became possible in the spring of 1997 because the school's top administrators agreed that everything else on Post should be subordinated to it. In his twenty-four years at VMI, Harris had never seen such a massive group effort:

> The cooperation that we got, from everybody, the supervisors of Buildings and Grounds, the Dean of the Faculty's office, the Commandant organizing the cadets and breaking them down into groups—I thought that was marvelous. If nothing else, it

showed me that this place can come together in a meaningful way when it wants to.

To kick off the months of training ahead, VMI wanted to hold a big media event—something that could draw national attention to the school's efforts. The Institute had already hosted an open house for the media in December, inviting members of the press to spend two days touring the Post, dining at the Superintendent's residence, and attending information sessions on all of VMI's emerging plans for coeducation. The idea had not (entirely) been to butter up the press—reporters are not so easily won over—but to ensure that the writers who would be covering VMI in the fall knew something about the school and its efforts to make coeducation succeed. With the exception of those journalists who covered the Institute on a regular basis, most of the reporters who visited VMI tended to be baffled by the school's rituals and spent much of their time playing catch-up. This was not always a bad thing for VMI's spokesmen; the ignorance of reporters usually prevented them from asking tough questions. But it also prevented them from understanding, let alone sympathizing with, VMI's goals, and before the first female cadets set foot on Post, VMI hoped to both educate and mollify its future interrogators.

Although the December "Media Day" had run smoothly, most of the attendees had been from Virginia and Washington, D.C. Now, with its orientation kick-off, VMI hoped to attract a larger, national audience. To do that, the school planned a big ceremony for Tuesday, March 11, 1997. At eleven o'clock that morning, the entire Post was ordered to "stand-down." For the next hour, no phones were answered, no classes were taught. Instead, VMI's cadets, faculty, administrators, and staff walked down from "the Hill" on which the school's barracks and academic buildings stand, and gathered at the back entrance of Cameron Hall, the Institute's basketball arena.

As they entered the arena, they heard, on the left, a small cadet brass ensemble playing the usual Sousa marches and Holst suites that herald VMI convocations. On the right, a thirty-foot screen featured a slide show of scenes from Institute life. And in the center, on a newly erected stage, there were chairs set up for an ominously large number of speakers, facing rows of television cameras and newspaper photographers.

Here was the public platform from which VMI would begin to modify years of earlier rhetoric opposing the admission of women.

The Institute had chosen its speakers carefully. The first was a woman, Anne C. Woodfin, a member of VMI's Board of Visitors who, on September 21, had reluctantly voted in favor of coeducation. She was followed by an alumnus and fellow Board Member, Robert Crotty, who had voted for privatization. Their words were determined, but not enthusiastic. One professor leaned over to his neighbor in the audience and murmured: "These sound like concession speeches."

With the keynote address, however, the mood changed. Charles Bryant, '69, asked all of the cadets in the audience to stand, forcing them out of their sleepy stupor. He then began to whittle away at the Corps, asking various cadets to take their seats: If you aren't a resident of Virginia, sit down. If you are a liberal arts major, sit down. If you aren't getting a commission upon graduation, sit down. If you are African-American, sit down. By the end, only a handful of young men were standing—the few cadets who would have been able to attend the Institute had the school's original admissions policy remained in place. Bryant acknowledged that coeducation would represent a more substantial change than any VMI had previously faced. But as he reminded the audience again and again: "VMI isn't what it used to be, but it never was."

After Bryant's conclusion, Kevin Trujillo, the President of the Class of 1998, rose to speak. As the elected leader of his peers, Trujillo would be a key player in the coming year. He would serve, in General Bunting's words, as "Mayor of the Barracks."

Scarcely five feet tall and slightly built, he had often been lampooned as "Tiny" Trujillo in the "Beef" section of the cadet newspaper. (His size would prove inspirational for some of VMI's first women, who, when faced with the highest bars in VMI's obstacle course, recalled thinking: "If Mr. Trujillo can do this, so can I.")

Trujillo's height, however, was not his defining feature. As soon as he opened his mouth one could see why his peers had elected him—he was articulate, energetic, and friendly. He would make an eloquent spokesman for the Corps in the year to come. But as he rose from his chair on March 11, it seemed that only the crown of his head would be visible over the microphones. A brief wave of concern passed through the audience, but was dispelled when Trujillo reached behind the podium, picked up a stool, and unabashedly brandished it over his head, in a show of good humor that evoked cheers from several cadets. He then placed the stool on the ground, stepped up, and began to speak in the manner of an officer rallying his troops. "All eyes are on VMI," he told the cadets. "Some are just salivating at the thought of our failure. The Corps of Cadets won't give them the pleasure."

Colonel Bissell concluded the session by introducing all of the committee chairs who had done so much work over the previous year. He described the many meetings and orientation workshops that lay ahead in the next four weeks, essentially giving the "VMI Family" its marching orders. When all of the speeches were done, the band launched into the school's fight song, "The VMI Spirit." As is customary whenever the "Spirit" is played, everyone stood, clapped, and sang (a tradition that ensures standing ovations at the end of most VMI events). After a few closing words, the Corps was dismissed.

Later that afternoon NPR's Linda Wertheimer assessed the scene in Lexington by saying that "VMI staged a pep rally today." The description seemed to belittle the event. Pep rallies at VMI are rowdy occasions in the Old Barracks Courtyard, where rats run wild in jock straps and warpaint, while administrators make rabble-rousing speeches that often culminate in the pummeling of a sacrificial cadet, dressed as the other team's mascot. By contrast, the March 11 ceremony had the same gravity and trappings as a typical VMI graduation ceremony, printed programs and all.

Still, if one stopped to think about it, a pep rally was exactly what VMI needed. Let the public imagine that the Institute was approaching its new mandate with the same enthusiasm and hopefulness that one senses at the onset of a Notre Dame football season. It wasn't an accurate portrait, but it was an interesting one. Could anyone imagine The Citadel, or the Naval Academy, or Dartmouth, for that matter, holding a pep rally to cheer for the arrival of their first women?

PHASE TWO OF VMI'S ORIENTATION began one week later, with the entire community divided into groups of 400 people, which assembled in Jackson Memorial Hall. Sitting on stage before the New Market painting, a panel consisting of Colonel Bissell and several of his committee chiefs explained many of the new procedures that would be in effect the following fall. Some policies, such as those on haircuts and dating, were works-in-progress destined for change, prompting cadets to later complain that the administration was backsliding and hypocritical. Most cadets, however, appreciated that the school's officials were trying to keep them informed.

When the floor opened for comments, a few students asked tough questions: "The Class of 1999 matriculated all-male. Will it graduate all-male?" The short answer was No. Because VMI was accepting female transfer students, some women would arrive as academic "seconds," or juniors. They would endure the ratline and they would wear the ring of their rat class, but VMI would be graduating its first women within two years.

The official who answered the cadet's question, however, framed his answer less bluntly. He explained that just as the Institute had accepted male transfer students in the past, so it would accept female transfer students. The same rules would apply to men and women. And that was the message that VMI's officials continued to reiterate—same, same, same. Although new policies were being written on superficial items such as haircuts and uniforms, the essential features of VMI would remain untouched.

Many cadets didn't buy it. One way or another the admission of women would bring major changes—just look, they said, at the training sessions that lay ahead. Everyone on VMI's Post, except the members of the first class (who would be gone before the women arrived), had been assigned to a twenty-to-thirty-person focus group, and over the course of three days, each of these sixty groups was scheduled to spend two hours discussing sexual harassment, hazing, and fraternization. Cadets and faculty, administrators and grounds workers, all were intermingled within these workshops in the hopes of achieving a lively discussion. To lead the sessions, Colonel Bissell had decided to hire outside consultants from Lane and Associates, a Richmond-based firm that specialized in group moderation.

VMI normally prefers to staff training sessions with its own people; the school's culture has so many odd features that most outside consultants have trouble applying their lessons to the specifics of Institute life. One consultant from Lane and Associates confessed that when he first heard VMI's cadets talk about "flaming" rats, he assumed that they were envisioning setting the new cadets on fire, *à la* The Citadel. (In fact, "flaming" is the art of verbally tearing a rat to pieces.)

Outsiders could never have more than a superficial knowledge of VMI, but Bissell felt that in this case, VMI should open its process to objective professionals, if only to show the Department of Justice that the Institute's efforts were sincere and that it had nothing to hide.

General Bunting decreed that each session should begin with excerpts from Ed Bradley's *Sixty Minutes* story on The Citadel. The piece was scathing, and Bunting wanted everyone to realize that if VMI repeated The Citadel's mistakes, the press would be equally merciless. The cadets' responses to the story were not exactly what VMI's administration might have hoped. Although many were disturbed by Kim Messer's and Jeanne Mentavlos's stories of ill-usage, others said that because men at The Citadel had received the same treatment, and because no one was injured, the women had little cause for complaint. Messer and Mentavlos had wanted The Citadel experience, and they had gotten it. Nevertheless, most cadets agreed that neither men nor women should face the problems that the report exposed.

Once the televisions had been turned off, the mediators broke out their overhead projectors and distributed notebooks full of charts, worksheets, and illustrations of VMI policies that one administrator later dismissed as "these silly cartoons." This was the corporate approach to sexual harassment training, and it was not likely to impress a crowd of military students. VMI's cadets, however, are hard to impress under any circumstances. As one first class leader put it: "Cadets have trouble sitting through anything longer than five minutes."

Following a timeline determined by the Institute, the consultants moved quickly through the first topic on their agenda—dating and fraternization. They distributed VMI's new policy on dating among cadets and reminded the faculty and staff that they were prohibited from dating, or attempting to date, members of the Corps. In all of its planning for women, however, VMI had never established clear penalties for fraternization, an omission that truncated the workshop discussions, since most cadets respond to policy statements by asking: "What, specifically, will happen to me if I get caught doing this or that?"

Although General Bunting had threatened severe penalties for sexual activity on Post, below that threshold the rules were vague. After all, what was the Institute going to do, pen specific policies for first base, second base, third base? Throughout upcoming years the Commandant would be left to struggle with each incident of fraternization on a case-by-case basis. In the meantime, VMI had few answers for cadet questions, and so the consultants from Richmond devoted more time to the key issue on most students' minds—sexual harassment.

They began with a quiz:

True or False:

Two males stop their conversation and look a female cadet up and down as she walks by. That would not be sexual harassment unless the woman knew what the men were doing.

A male cadet makes comments that have sexual connotations at an after-duty-hours party. His behavior is not sexual harassment because that behavior occurred after duty.

A male and female cadet have had an intimate relationship. He stops the relationship. If the female tries to continue that relationship by giving him presents and calling him, that is not sexual harassment.

These scenarios generated some lively discussion; the only problem was that the answers to the quiz usually amounted to "maybe true, maybe false." In the third instance, was the female cadet in a position of power over the male? How often was she calling him? Or in the first two cases, how pervasive was this behavior? And how could anyone police the manner in which young men looked at young women?

Some cadets indicated that they planned to avoid the female cadets as much as possible. A few aspiring officers even claimed that their parents had already instructed them to stay away from the women, lest they be accused of anything that might threaten their commissions.

When the topic turned to hazing, the cadets were equally wary. What, they asked, was the distinction between criminal hazing and behaviors that were unsanctioned at VMI? Did someone have to get hurt for an act to constitute hazing? How much horseplay was allowed in the barracks?

To give the discussion a concrete footing, the consultants offered scenarios that had been constructed with the aid of VMI cadets:

> Cadet Downing has not been able to keep up with his fellow rats in every category. In addition, Downing does not have a good attitude. Although he does not say it, one can tell by his facial expressions and body language that he thinks the ratline is unnecessary.
>
> His chain of command has tried everything to get Cadet Downing to see the importance of the training activities of the Corps. Downing still doesn't get it. His chain of command decides that Downing will get the message if they apply a little "persuasion." They decide to set up a system to ask Downing so many questions at meals that he will not get more than five bites of food per meal. This should make the point to Downing.
>
> Have the members of the chain of command committed unlawful hazing?
> Yes   No   Why?

Several cadets responded to this example with an eye toward money, not morality. Because their parents had paid for their food, they were entitled to every bite. But when it came to the basic question of whether food deprivation was unlawful, they couldn't say. Obviously if a cadet was malnourished the behavior would be illegal, but if it only happened once or twice, food deprivation would probably fall under the category of another miserable day in the life of a rat.

The scenario did serve, however, to make some cadets more self-aware. Why were they harassing rats in the mess hall? What purpose was served in the practice—popular among some senior cadets—of intimidating rats into denying themselves dessert or second helpings of food? What did this have to do with leadership?

VMI's mess hall provided a classic example of the abuses that rats had faced in the past, and of the administration's ongoing attempts to "professionalize" the ratline. In previous decades, mealtime at VMI had been a raucous occasion; the roar of voices from Crozet Hall could be heard a hundred yards away. Stepping through the mess hall door, visitors were bombarded with the shouts of upperclassmen berating rats or the din of entire companies stomping their feet and rattling their silver-ware. Tablefuls of rats could be seen squeezing forks between their knees as they ate, while senior cadets waited for the first utensil to drop. And here and there an unlucky rat was face down in his plate, "snorkeling" Jell-O or—as Colonel Bissell remembered from his own experience—inhaling mounds of lima beans. In the worst instances of abuse, rats had occasionally been pressured to drink cadet-concocted "magic potions," filled with nauseating ingredients.

Ever since the early 1990s, however, VMI had undertaken a wide-spread crackdown on mess hall antics. Although rats were still required to sit stiffly on the last three inches of their chairs, to lift their forks to their mouths in straight lines, and to "strain" if an upperclassman spoke to them, VMI's administrators had decreed that all cadets should be able to eat their fill without serious harassment. This did not mean that meal-time abuses had entirely ceased. Walking into Crozet Hall in the fall of 1998, I promptly encountered a rat with his nose in his plate, slurping up his lunch for the amusement of his dyke. But this young man appeared to be the exception, rather than the rule. New standards were in place, and the penalties for infractions were stiff: in the spring of 1997 an upperclassman received a one-semester suspension for stuffing french fries into a rat's mouth.

Although most of these reforms had nothing to do with the approach of coeducation, VMI's planning for women did inspire a few new twists. General Bunting, for example, was particularly concerned about the potential for eating disorders among female cadets. During his years as Headmaster of the Lawrenceville School, Bunting had witnessed the rav-ages of eating disorders first-hand. He had even gone so far as to write a novel on the subject, featuring a heroine who responds to peer pressure by starving herself. With the imminent arrival of women, Bunting wanted VMI's administration to be alert to the problem among both female and male cadets. In the packets of newspaper clippings that regularly circu-lated among VMI's Executive Committee on the Assimilation of Women, he inserted articles on anorexic teenagers and bulimic ballerinas.

The administration's concerns about the mess hall were not limited to eating disorders. As they planned for female cadets, VMI's officials often raised questions about basic nutrition for women and men. Was there enough calcium in the menu to meet women's dietary needs? Was the salad bar well-stocked? Should they recommend iron supplements for women? How could VMI combine the civility of family-style dining with the efficiency of a buffet line? The school even went to the trouble of dispatching a small team of cadets with Colonel Ron McManus, Director of Post Services, to conduct a culinary tour of other college campuses. The team ate breakfast at James Madison University, lunch at the University of Virginia, dinner at William and Mary. . . . By the second full day of collegiate cuisine, the usually voracious cadets couldn't swallow another bite.

Complain as cadets might about the quality of VMI's food, its accommodations, and its administration, the school's officials did spend considerable time behind-the-scenes trying to make the Institute a more civilized place for everyone. All of which might seem to be an elaborate digression from the issue of hazing, but in order to think about hazing one had to consider the overall nature of life at VMI. With its orientation sessions, VMI hoped to encourage cadets to question behaviors that they had long taken for granted, and to envision the standards of conduct that ideally should prevail at a military college.

IN THE DAYS immediately following the workshops, most cadets dismissed them as a waste of time, nothing more than a legal exercise designed to cover VMI's tracks should anything go wrong in the coming year. The benefits of the training began to emerge, however, over the next few weeks.

First of all, the sessions had gotten the Corps talking, if only to complain about the year ahead. When three cadets from Texas A&M arrived a few weeks later to share their impressions of coed military training and to discuss VMI's plans for an exchange program, over 120 VMI cadets attended the forum—a large number for any voluntary event at the Institute. Attendance was also high when Colonels Bissell and Rowe hosted follow-up dessert sessions in their homes, serving up "the assimilation" with coffee and tea. No one cared whether the cadets had come for the conversation or the cookies.

Some people did complain that the entire year had been filled with too much talk, talk, talk. VMI had spent hours discussing issues that could have been settled within minutes, and each time the school scheduled another assimilation event, it risked stirring the resentment of its more disgruntled cadets. Nevertheless, VMI needed to keep the channels of communication open for those cadets and employees who wanted to speak, and with each dessert session, each committee meeting, and each orientation workshop, the prospect of female cadets grew more tangible, to the point of becoming almost mundane. VMI's year-long conversation (which is what the school's planning for coeducation ultimately amounted to) was, in the end, more valuable for the statements it aired and the questions it raised, than for the policies it produced and the bathrooms it built.

Here again, the seminars with Lane and Associates were important, for they yielded some useful after-action reports that listed the participants' lingering questions and concerns. What, for example, would be the rules governing pornography—could the cadets keep their calendars, their Victoria's Secret catalogues, and the girlie pictures that many of them stuffed in the inside of their hats? What guidelines would govern e-mail language? What were the responsibilities of kitchen workers or grounds crews who witnessed incidents of hazing or sexual harassment? Above all, the consultants had been struck by the sense of fatalism among VMI's cadets, many of whom assumed that the Institute's administration would abandon them at the first woman's complaint. These young men believed that their peers at The Citadel had been "hung out to dry," and they feared the same treatment from VMI's officials.

Over the next few weeks, several VMI administrators, from the Commandant, to the Superintendent, to Colonel Bissell, all tried to reassure the Corps that the Institute's administration would stand behind any male cadet whose behavior remained within VMI's written guidelines. But because much of the ratline is governed by unwritten traditions, the unspoken habits of barracks life were the factors most likely to get the cadets into serious trouble.

Meanwhile, VMI's top administrators wondered how they *would* react if something went terribly wrong. Earlier in the year they had convened a crisis management session, outlining responses to hypothetical incidents of hazing, sexual harassment, and sexual assault. What procedures, they had asked, should be followed in the case of a rape? Who would assist the victim? Who would address the accused? Who would speak to the doctor, the police, the parents, the press? In the end, they had formed a crisis management team that would meet in the coming years whenever trouble seemed to be brewing.

No one could say whether these efforts would be enough to save the Institute from scandal. The U.S. Department of Justice, for one, continued to look upon VMI with dark skepticism. Neither the Institute's big "pep rally" nor its sexual harassment workshops had convinced the federal government that the school's intentions were honorable. In fact, after all of VMI's planning, the 1996/97 school year ended with a minor showdown between the Institute's lawyers in Virginia's Attorney General's Office and the Justice Department, a confrontation that drew some of the battlelines for the year to come.

ON MAY 6, 1997, the Department of Justice sent a letter to VMI's counsel, requesting detailed information on every step the Institute had taken to prepare for women. The letter cited over fifty topics of concern, many of them divided into multiple subtopics. Among other things, DOJ wanted:

> A statement of the total number of women denied acceptance and admission to VMI, and of all reasons for each such denial . . .
>
> The total number of women seeking admission to VMI who were granted and who were denied financial aid by VMI and/or Virginia, and for each denial please state the reasons for such denial . . .
>
> A description and photographs, pictures, or drawings of all uniforms, gym clothing, band uniforms, and shoes for athletic activities and marching that female cadets will be required to wear . . .
>
> A statement of whether and when the position was filled [regarding new hires related to the assimilation of women], by whom, their qualifications, the duties and responsibilities of each position as they relate to the assimilation of women, and the proportion of the time/duties of each position which is expected to be devoted to matters involving the assimilation of women.

The Justice Department also wanted to know what adjustments VMI was planning for women in each of its physical activities, including "stoop runs, running and calisthenic events, rifle runs, training marches, three-mile runs, ravine crossings, rat sweat parties and rat mass parties, push-ups imposed on cadets as personal individual correction, drills, marching." Implicit in this request was the assumption that VMI *would* be scaling down its physical requirements for women, something that neither the Institute, nor most of its female applicants desired.

When William H. Hurd of the Virginia Attorney General's office first received the letter, he did not take it seriously: "I thought someone had purloined a piece of Justice stationery and played a practical joke."* But the Department of Justice wasn't kidding.

Up to this point VMI had not been very generous in supplying information to the federal government. Although the Institute had been trying to keep its own "Family" abreast of new developments at the school (in the fall VMI mailed videotapes to every living alumnus, featuring clips from Institute life, quotes from Robert E. Lee, and images of General Bunting vowing to preserve the school's intrinsic features), when it came to correspondence with the Department of Justice, VMI had stuck to the bare essentials.

One might wonder why VMI would hesitate to inform the Justice Department of its extensive preparations for women; no other military college had done so much to prepare for coeducation. The Institute, however, did not want to give the federal government a foothold in its internal affairs. VMI had already fought a legal skirmish with DOJ back in October, when the latter insisted that VMI provide the federal government with a detailed plan for its assimilation of women. In response, Judge Kiser, of the U.S. District Court in Roanoke, had ordered VMI to produce quarterly reports on its preparations for women. Although VMI had submitted two reports since Kiser's ruling, they apparently had not satisfied the federal appetite for information.

In the present dispute, VMI was fortunate to have outside supporters who rallied to its cause. On June 3, 1997, the *Wall Street Journal* responded to the Justice Department's demands with an editorial titled "Taking VMI Prisoner":

> Remember when federal judges took over the running of entire
> city school systems? Meet Clinton Justice Department lawyer

---

* "Justice Department asks VMI to See More than 50 Assimilation Documents," Associated Press News Index, May 15, 1997, 12:07 P.M.

Judith Kiser [(*sic*), her name is Judith Keith], who now wants to resurrect one of the great, failed liberal ideas by personally taking over the Virginia Military Institute . . . We think we are finally getting a clearer understanding of this Justice Department's current supervisory and senior-management problems.

The editors of the *Richmond Times-Dispatch* took a more indignant stance, attacking the Justice Department's Civil Rights Division as "prim pietists and righteous revolutionaries":

Comes now to VMI from the JDCRD a document so offensive in its import that it represents everything a prudent free society despises. About four dozen pages (actually, eight or nine pages) demanding ASAP everything under the sun, and more: memoranda, notes, guidelines, assessments, statistical data, stipulated goals and percentages of accomplishment, measures against harassment and gender discrimination, discussions of everything from push-ups to pugil sticks—and beyond. Tedium. Trivia. Oppression vast and minute, manic in its reach and sullen in its denial. . . . This is not merely oppressive, and offensive to every sense of fairness and goodwill. It is egregious, pernicious, and wrong. And the federal courts would do just about everyone a favor by ordering the JDCRD enforcers to cease and desist.*

In true Southern fashion, the editors of the *Times-Dispatch* couched the dispute between Richmond and Washington in the language of war: "One might reasonably have thought that, having successfully battled on behalf of a client as yet unnamed, the JDCRD's messianists would seek other fields whereon to reassemble their legions and affirmatively enforce their action." But to soften the editorial's Confederate edge, the Virginians concluded by describing VMI's position with words from Lincoln: "If I were to try to read, much less answer, all the attacks made on me, this shop might well be closed for any other business. I do the very best I know how—the very best I can—and I mean to keep doing so

---

* "VMI Meets the Enforcers," *Richmond Times-Dispatch*, May 14, 1997.

until the end. If the end brings me out all right, then what is said against me won't matter. If the end brings me out wrong, then ten angels, swearing I was right, would make no difference."

After all of the hubbub, the Justice Department decided not to press the matter, and in the months that followed, VMI's quarterly reports were destined to become thinner and thinner. Still, no one doubted that once women arrived on Post, the federal government would be back.

INTERLUDE:

FAREWELL TO

THE ALL-MALE CORPS

IN THE SATURDAY MORNING SUNSHINE OF APRIL 26, 1997, THE officers of VMI's Corps were planning a surprise. Outside of the barracks, alumni were gathering for the annual spring reunion parade, settling their wives into rows of folding chairs. Inside, cadets were getting "dyked out," adjusting rifles, pulling on white gloves, tuning trombones and trumpets. A few fourth classmen were wrapping crimson sashes around the waists of their dykes. Another weekend, another parade.

This review, however, was going to be different. Shortly after it began, Addison Hagan, President of the First Class, approached General Bunting in the reviewing area. He informed the Superintendent that the officers of the Corps had a special message that they wanted to deliver to the alumni, and they intended to use this parade as their forum.

As Hagan remembered it, Bunting did not look thrilled. In the highly politicized atmosphere of the time, with every action at VMI scrutinized by the press and the Justice Department, the Institute's officials did not like surprises. But the cadets had timed their announcement carefully. There would be no opportunity for debate, no chance to convene a committee. Hagan wasn't asking permission; he was serving notice. Bunting would have to wait and see what was in store.

The first half of the parade followed the usual routine. From within the shade of Jackson Arch the band sounded Adjutant's Call—a rousing bugle fanfare followed by a high-pitched cheer. Then the officers of the Corps marched out, with their silver scabbards brushing against their white trousers, and the shiny black chin straps of their shakos resting just beneath their lower lips. Behind them came Band Company's drum

major, twirling his four-foot mace, followed by the brasses, the saxo-
phones, and the drums (no flutes or clarinets in this all-male band).
Finally, two battalions of 1,200 cadets marched out of the barracks' two
main arches and assembled by company on the parade ground's freshly
mowed grass.

Over the next twenty minutes the cadets performed the steps of a military review with habitual ease: Dress Center/Guides Post, Fix Bayonets,
Present Arms. . . . But at the moment when VMI's Regimental Commander would normally have ordered the Corps to Pass in Review, the cadet
announcer read the following words over the public address system, a
statement thereafter known as the "Bagwan Manifesto" in honor of its
author, Cadet Regimental Commander Brian Bagwan:

General Bunting, distinguished alumni, ladies and gentlemen:

> The officers of the Corps this year would like to commemorate
> the passing into history of VMI's all-male Cadet Corps. We recog-
> nize that VMI is about to undertake a brave new mission with the
> assimilation of women beginning with the '97–'98 academic year.
> In facing this opportunity, we believe that VMI will succeed in
> that mission and will show the country just what the VMI com-
> munity is capable of.
>
> The officers, speaking for the Corps at large, would also like to
> commemorate the 157 years of VMI as an all-male military col-
> lege. These 157 years will always be in the Institute's history, and
> it is only right that we, as cadets and as future alumni, recognize
> this fact and show pride in it. We wish to commemorate and pay
> tribute to VMI as an all-male military college and especially to the
> alumni who came before us, who have supported VMI whole-
> heartedly during the last few years. The days of struggle are over.
> VMI will be the most successful military college to assimilate
> women into its Corps of Cadets!
>
> Gentlemen, we salute you and the Institute you represent. We
> do the following to recognize the bright future ahead of VMI and
> at the same time to recognize and to remember the last all-male
> military college in the United States, our beloved Institute.
>
> Thank you—and Rah Virginia Mil!

When the last words had died away, Bagwan's voice rang out across the field: "Sabers post!" All of the cadet officers, from battalion leaders down to the top three sergeants in each company, drew their sabers, raised their hilts to their lips in salute, then drove their blades into the ground. Bagwan's voice called out again: "Shakos post!" and the cadet officers removed their black cylindrical hats, some adorned with twelve-inch plumes, and placed them on the hilts of their sabers. Finally, Bagwan commanded the entire Corps to "Pass in Review," and all of the cadets, including the bareheaded officers, marched by the reviewing officials and into the barracks. When the last cadet had left the field, all that remained were the shakos resting on the sabers, with the black-green feathers of their plumes fluttering in the wind.

The image sent shivers through the crowd. Traditionally, a rifle with a helmet hung on its butt marks the grave of a soldier killed in battle. For those alumni who now stood with tears streaming down their cheeks, the remnants on the parade ground marked a similar passing.

Whether or not this symbolic death would be followed by a grand rebirth was left for each viewer to imagine. Back in January, when Thomas Moncure had resigned from the Institute's Board of Visitors, he had pronounced VMI unrevivable: "the body of the late and great VMI stretched before them (the alumni) is dead, while the majority of the Board hurriedly pours perfume on the corpse. The stench will slowly seep out and over the next few months and years, will be undeniable."*

But even as they abandoned their sabers, the leaders of the Class of 1997 had acknowledged the possibility of a new beginning. Their words had been crafted to salute both VMI's past and its future, which was why Addison Hagan was "upset" and "hurt," a few days later, to find an anonymous alumnus describing the parade to the *Richmond Times-Dispatch* in highly politicized terms: "plumes fluttering in the breeze like flags on so many sad tombstones. Or like uplifted middle fingers stuck in the face of Ruth Bader Ginsburg. Or maybe both, which is what made it so exquisite."†

Although the cadets' actions had constituted a clear protest over

---

* Moncure's Letter of Resignation to Governor George Allen, January 3, 1997.
† *Richmond Times-Dispatch,* Letter to the Editor, April 29, 1997.

FORMAL INSPECTION IN FRONT OF VMI'S BARRACKS. NOTE THE CADET OFFI-
CERS' PLUMED SHAKOS. *(Andres R. Alonso/fotoVISION)*

VMI's fate, they had never meant to insult one of their nation's Chief
Justices. Instead, Hagan offered his own explanation:

> At VMI, there has always been the Old Corps and the New Corps.
> If you graduated you were from the Old Corps, and the New
> Corps included anyone currently in the barracks. But now we
> have a true distinction between old and new with the admission of
> women. And I think it (the posting of sabers and shakos) was just
> a symbol of the passing of the way VMI was and has been to what
> it will become.

Exactly what VMI was going to become would take decades to determine. The early contours are drawn in the chapters that follow.

THE WOMEN
ARRIVE

10

THE DRESS REHEARSAL: VMI'S SUMMER TRANSITION PROGRAM

As the summer of 1997 stretched on, most people curious about VMI were looking toward August 18, matriculation day. On that morning thirty-one women were scheduled to move into the barracks, officially breaking the gender barrier that had existed for 158 years. Depending on each individual's viewpoint, that event would represent either a moment of triumph or the beginning of the end.

What many observers didn't realize was that by June 30 eighteen of those women were already on Post. At dinnertime that evening they were eating in the mess hall. Before breakfast the next day they were on the parade ground, doing push-ups and leg lifts alongside 168 of their male classmates. A few hours later these same women were sitting in VMI classrooms, listening to VMI professors.

They did not look like military students. Their hair was long, their clothes were casual. Many wore jewelry and makeup. Standing next to their male peers, who were similarly dressed in T-shirts and shorts, these women could have been entering freshmen at any school in the United States.

But that was what VMI had in mind. This was the Summer Transition Program, otherwise known as "VMI-Lite," and it was the closest thing to a normal college experience that the Institute had to offer. When it came to preparing for the year ahead, the STP would be one of the secrets of VMI's success.

The STP was started in 1986 by a generous alumnus who wanted to give a head start to "at-risk" students who needed extra help in English and math. Over the years it had evolved into a four-week session designed to give any interested student, regardless of academic performance, a chance to take one class, become acquainted with VMI's Post, and begin getting into physical shape without the pressures of a military regimen.

On a typical July morning in Lexington, Virginia, STP students can be seen jogging around the Institute's Post in PT (physical training) groups led by VMI upperclassmen. After a shower and breakfast they head for the academic buildings, spending two-and-a-half hours in class studying either freshman composition or math, followed by lunch and a two-hour afternoon tutorial designed to reinforce the morning's lessons through whatever creative methods a professor might devise. Twice a week in the late afternoon STP students also compete in one of four intramural sports—basketball, soccer, volleyball, or flag football.

Through it all there is no yelling, no marching, no uniforms. Instead, there is time to lounge in the sun, wander through town, spend weekends traveling to Washington, D.C., or hiking in the surrounding Blue Ridge or Allegheny Mountains. "I had too much fun at VMI"—that was how Tennille Chisholm would later describe the 1997 program to her friends in Richmond. And her reaction was typical. For most students the STP is a blissful calm before the storm.

As VMI PLANNED FOR ITS FIRST COED STP, the school's officials were especially eager for women to attend. During their initial year at the Institute, graduates of the STP normally have a much lower attrition rate than nonattendees. For them, the Post is familiar, some faces are friendly, and the prospect of early morning workouts is not daunting. Although nothing can fully prepare a young person for the shock of rat life, STP students can at least walk from the barracks to the rifle range without getting lost. And as VMI's administrators pictured the coming year, they knew that their first female rats would need every additional ounce of self-assurance that they could muster.

That was why, in the spring of 1997, VMI was selling its summer program especially hard to the Class of 2001—so much so that by late May they had many more enrollees, male and female, than ever before. The previous attendance record was 131; in June of 1997 VMI was expecting 186 men and women.

Housing these students was not going to be easy. In the summer months VMI's barracks also accommodates upperclass summer school students, and with parts of the building still under construction to prepare for women, this year was going to be a very tight fit. More importantly, VMI's administrators wondered whether women would be safe in the barracks. During the summer, none of the Institute's cadet-run systems of self-policing are in place. There is no military regimen, consumption of alcohol can be high, and outsiders have more opportunities to stroll in and out. These were dangerous circumstances for introducing the first few women into VMI's world, and the prospect caused quite a few headaches for Colonel Bill Stockwell, the Associate Dean who runs VMI's summer programs.

The problem solved itself by the end of May, when it became clear that the women's restrooms in the barracks were not going to be finished in time for the program. Construction was behind schedule, and VMI could not allocate one of the men's rooms to the women, since most stoops in the barracks had only one communal restroom that was shared by a few hundred men.

VMI decided to house the eighteen female students in the guest rooms of Lejeune Hall, the cadet activity building adjacent to the barracks. In the spirit of "separate but equal," the Institute's administrators tried to make the women's quarters resemble barracks living. They removed the soft beds from Lejeune and replaced them with cadet hays (racks with thin mattresses). Colonel Stockwell also considered turning off the air conditioning in Lejeune from 4 P.M. to 8 A.M., since he could envision the male students in the barracks, griping in front of their fans in the July heat, while the women slept in cool comfort. But because the windows in Lejeune do not open, air conditioning was a necessity.

Stockwell recruited three female adults to take shifts from 4 P.M. to 8 A.M., posted outside the women's quarters to answer questions, handle emergencies, and ensure that absolutely no one other than the women themselves entered the women's living space. Two evenings a week an upperclass male cadet was also scheduled to visit the lobby next to the women's rooms, to talk about the year ahead, dispel or confirm any rumors about the ratline, and generally show that VMI upperclassmen were capable of being friendly.

This was the best VMI could do to mimic the services and hardships provided in the barracks. Inevitably some of the women were going to complain, resenting their separation from the men. It was a morale crusher, one woman later explained, at the end of each morning workout, to watch the guys in her PT group jogging together into the barracks, cheering and laughing, while she turned her back and walked alone toward Lejeune. But everyone understood that this was a one-time, stop-gap measure; women would be living in the barracks soon enough. In the meantime, the summer program would give VMI's administrators a chance to preview the sorts of issues that they would face in the coming year.

To begin with, there was the matter of physical training. Throughout the planning for coeducation, the women's physical condition had generated a multitude of questions. What shape would they be in when they arrived? Could any of them pass the VFT? Could the women keep up with the men on a run, or on a basketball court? Could they handle VMI's obstacle course?

At an introductory meeting on the afternoon of June 30, the Head of VMI's Physical Education Department, Lieutenant Colonel Bob Cairns, informed the 186 newly arrived STP students that they would be taking the VFT later that evening. Audible groans passed through the crowd. The Institute had been keeping the timing of its first coed VFT very quiet, in order to avoid the prospect of lurking reporters trying to snap pictures of the women as they hung from the pull-up bars. Now, many of the young men and women clearly dreaded the thought of being tested on their physical condition within hours of unpacking. But the test wouldn't be graded. Its purpose was to gauge the students' abilities, give them a sense of where they stood in respect to VMI's fitness standards, and divide them into morning PT groups according to their running speeds.

A few hours later the first ninety-three students had assembled in their shorts and T-shirts outside of Cocke Hall, VMI's main athletic building, where the hallways were filled with ladders and power tools and bags of cement, evidence of the Institute's ongoing efforts to accommodate women. After filing downstairs into the red-matted boxing room, the students lined up in seven rows facing seven pull-up bars. With the help of some chairs, the front line of men and women grabbed hold of the bars, and at Colonel Cairns's command VMI's first coed VFT was under way.

The difference in upper-body strength between men and women was immediately apparent. While many of the men reached the minimum of five pull-ups with ease, struggling as they approached ten, most of the women dropped from the bars before their arms had scarcely begun to bend. There were, of course, exceptions. One woman completed five pull-ups, while some of the men could barely get their muscles to twitch. But as everyone had expected, pull-ups were going to be a problem for female cadets.

When it came to the sit-ups, the men and women were on more equal ground. The students broke into pairs, the women instinctively turning to women and the men to men. They knelt on the mats with one person holding the ankles of another, and after a few words of instruction, the sit-ups began. Within sixty seconds the sound of voices in the room had crescendoed into a roar: "Keep going! Suck it up! Don't stop!" Some of the noisiest young men had already acquired the flair of future drill sergeants, their faces as red as their partners'. Meanwhile, at the back of the room, a recent alumnus turned to me with a broad-faced smile and said: "This is what it's all about."

He was talking about the spirit of the ratline—the ideal of young men, and now young women, encouraging their Brother Rats to push themselves one step further, beyond their imagined limits. And it *was* impressive, in this packed, noisy room, to watch one young man, through the sheer force of his loud-pitched enthusiasm, seem to lift his grimacing partner up from the mat for his sixtieth, test-passing, sit-up.

It was also impressive, a half-hour later, to watch these same men and women complete their one-and-a-half mile runs around the outdoor track that surrounds VMI's football field. Not that these students were setting new records—some could probably have walked the track at a faster pace. But no one quit. And more importantly, several of the swiftest runners stayed till the very end, cheering for their slower classmates, male and female. After many months of listening to upperclassmen lament the impending arrival of women, it was encouraging to see at least a few of the new men patting the backs of their female peers, joking with them as they walked back to their rooms.

Over the next few days the PE Department tallied the results of the VFT, and found the numbers to be disappointing. Seventy percent of the men and ninety-four percent of the women had failed one event or more (a slightly higher ratio for men than was usual). If the test had been graded, all of these students would have received F's, since it is tough to compensate for the zero that each student gets for a failed event.

Even more disturbing was that fact that twelve of the eighteen women (sixty-seven percent) had failed all three events, as compared to twelve percent of the men. Many VMI officials had hoped that, faced with the imminent rigors of the ratline, most women would undergo extensive physical training and arrive at VMI capable of passing at least one segment of the VFT. That, unfortunately, didn't happen. If they wanted to pass the test, VMI's women had a long way to go.

The breakdown of events was approximately what the PE Department had expected. The men and women were roughly equivalent in abdominal strength and endurance, with men averaging 54.7 sit-ups and women averaging 54.2. On the run, the women averaged 12.53.6 minutes, while the men averaged 11.24.03, with eighty-seven percent of them passing the event. The pull-ups posed the biggest problem. Eleven of the eighteen women could not lift their chins to the bar, as opposed to ten of the men. On the whole, the men averaged 8.08 pull-ups and the women averaged 1.28.

Armed with these statistics, PE Professor Colonel Gordon Calkins hoped to persuade General Bunting to implement a flexed arm hang for women once the school year began. But Bunting had been gathering his own data from conversations with the young women and men, the vast majority of whom did not want to see the test changed. One female student captured the prevailing sentiment: "I don't think things should be made any easier for the women. I know that at all the other service academies it is. There is a major curve. The women don't even have to do pull-ups, and that's ridiculous." This young woman, however, ended her comments with a telling, offhand remark: "This is VMI, where the men are men and so are the women."

For the time being the VFT would remain unchanged. VMI's male and female rats would have their entire first semesters to get into shape before the test had any impact. Over the next few weeks Lieutenant Colonel Holly Richardson, VMI's new female PE Professor, planned to introduce the women to those machines in VMI's weight room that would help most with their upper-body strength, and for men and women alike, the many hours of running and push-ups were scheduled to begin bright and early the next morning.

<small>KIM HERBERT PRACTICES PULL-UPS ALONGSIDE A MALE CLASSMATE.</small>

<small>THIS PHOTO WAS TAKEN BY NANCY ANDREWS, A STAFF PHOTOGRAPHER FOR THE *WASHINGTON POST*. ANDREWS'S PICTURES OF VMI'S FIRST COED RATLINE HELPED EARN HER THE NEWSPAPER PHOTOGRAPHER OF THE YEAR AWARD IN THE 55TH ANNUAL PICTURES OF THE YEAR COMPETITION. SEVERAL PHOTOGRAPHS FROM ANDREWS'S AWARD-WINNING PORTFOLIO APPEAR IN THE PAGES THAT FOLLOW. *(Photo by Nancy Andrews. © 1998,* The Washington Post. *Reprinted with permission)*</small>

At 7 A.M. on July 1 the STP students were out on the parade ground, joined by several members of the press, some of whom kneeled in the grass and pointed their lenses directly into the faces of the young women and men as they did their push-ups. The students did not welcome the attention. Throughout the summer they complained bitterly about the presence of the media, while reporters complained about restricted access. (The Institute had designated three female and three male students to answer questions; the rest were off-limits while on Post.) This tug-of-war between student privacy and public curiosity would continue for several months.

If the reporters were looking for changes in the usual PT routine, they were going to be disappointed. The only adjustments to the normal morning ritual came in subtle details. On one occasion the upperclass leader of a PT group ordered his cadets to perform "high knees," jogging in place with their knees bouncing waist-high on each step. The upperclassman walked from student to student with his hand extended, encouraging them to lift their knees to his palm. When he reached the sole female in the group, however, he veered around her. The woman was surprised, but she did not feel ostracized. Instead, she sensed that the cadet was embarrassed, afraid of the trouble he might face if he put his hand on a woman's leg. It took a while, several women explained, for the male cadets to relax.

Nevertheless, most administrators were satisfied with the way the training was going. Three days a week, as the PT groups completed their morning runs, General Farrell stepped out the back door of his office and watched them coming up "Supe's Hill," a long uphill stretch that runs behind the residences of the Superintendent and VMI's other top administrators. Farrell "figured that would be the test":

> The good news is that each of the companies (actually, these were "PT groups") had women. In other words, the fastest company had women, the slowest company had women, and the slowest company had plenty of men, by far the majority. So you'd watch the fast company come up the hill, and the women were up front, doing fine. The fast women ran with the fast men. Then you'd watch the so-called porkchop platoon, the last group coming up the hill, and cadets would be falling out, and throwing up on the side of the road, and puffing and squawking and saying "I can't make it." And the good news is that there were as many men doing that as there were women.

Some of the young men disagreed. A few disgruntled runners, who had been assigned to the slowest groups, went back to the barracks and complained that the women were making their groups even slower. They were falling out in high numbers, or worse, they were speeding up just for the sake of newspaper photographers. Other guys might insist that the ratio of fast to slow females was comparable to the ratio of fast to slow males, but in the minds of these young men, PTing with women was like running around with a ball and chain.

The complaints of individual newcomers held little weight in VMI's barracks. These young men were "prestrains," so called because they had not yet assumed the straining posture of the ratline, and as far as VMI's upperclass summer school students were concerned, prestrains did not have the right to complain about anything. "When you come back here in August," one upperclassman warned a particularly bitter young man, "you are going to have some problems if that attitude is still there."

The upperclassmen, however, had their own reservations about the women. Even Tim Trant, the rising First Captain who was preparing to take command of VMI's Corps in the fall, confessed that when he first surveyed VMI's female recruits "they worried me":

> This is, I admit, not fair to the women, but my first impression was that some of them were overweight, and that really concerned me . . . I felt particularly perturbed at the presence of overweight females because I thought at least if they were going to come and pioneer at this institution, they would have prepared themselves physically and mentally to do it honorably and to prove to everybody that women could do just what men could do. And that wasn't the case, in certain instances.

Trant readily acknowledged that VMI had its share of overweight men. The suggested weight limits for VMI cadets—which are taken from Army ROTC guidelines—are often waived, and every class has had a few graduates who could barely squeeze into their uniforms. But in a culture filled with group athletic competitions, where a rat might have to rely upon his peers to lift him over a wall or, as happened in one case, to take turns pushing and pulling him up a mountain trail, there was little sympathy for slow metabolisms.

Any person, male or female, who arrived at VMI conspicuously overweight was sure to face a lot of negative attention once the ratline began, whether in the form of taunting or extra push-ups. That was one reason why VMI's administrators had hoped that their first female enrollees would be particularly fit; the women's acceptance into the Corps would depend upon their ability to keep up. As it turned out, the women at the STP were very much like women at other colleges. Some were fast, some were slow, some were overweight, some were underweight. Although most were in good shape, they were not, as a group, paragons of athleticism.

This fact was apparent on the intramural playing fields, where the men tended to dominate. Although the games remained friendly, Colonel Cairns doubted whether the women were getting much out of it:

I think the men had a tendency to ignore the women. I think they automatically made the determination that "She's not going to help. I'm not going to pass it to her." So the women were kind of left out on one or two of the teams. . . . I looked at that at West Point [where Cairns taught in the 1970s and 1980s], and to me, you don't get a competitive experience as a woman on a men's team. If you are playing eight-man soccer and you have one woman on the team, she doesn't get a chance to play. To me it would be much more enjoyable to have women play women because you've got relatively the same height differential, the same jumping ability differential, the same shooting ability differential, and you're not towered over physically by the guys or shoved around. At West Point everything is very competitive, like it is here. Nobody wants to lose. And the men can't balance playing as a team against winning and losing. The younger they are, the less well they do that. They want to win, and they don't care what they have to do to win . . . That's going to be a problem.

When the intramural championships took place in the last week of the STP, I wandered over to the gymnasium to see these coed games for myself. Walking into Cocke Hall, with a basketball game on the right and volleyball on the left, one fact was immediately apparent: I was the only woman in sight. The teams were all-male, the spectators were male. The "Blue Balls" volleyball team was competing in homemade T-shirts, adorned with the usual puns on the words "balls," "nuts," and "hard." It looked like the same old VMI.

Outside on the parade ground, where the flag football and soccer championships were under way, the scene was very similar. One woman darted around in the middle of a soccer game, rarely touching the ball. All of the other women, I was told, were on the lower ranking teams—not necessarily at the bottom of the heap, but clearly not in the finals. Having women on one's team was apparently a liability, although no one could say whether that was because of the women's limited skills or because of the men's hesitation about letting them play.

Still, no one seemed to mind. The STP was supposed to be a relaxed experience, and when it came to intramurals, most of the women shrugged: "I'm lousy at basketball." "I can't play soccer worth a damn."

They did not consider whether they would feel more talented or have more opportunities to improve if they were playing against women. Segregation was a dirty word, and for the time being, coed sports were far preferable. Besides, most of these women were not very serious about basketball or soccer. Women who excelled at team sports were not likely to attend a school where the only opportunities in intercollegiate competition were in cross-country and track and field.

When it came to noncompetitive, individual activities, such as VMI's obstacle courses, there was a greater spirit of cooperation between men and women. VMI has two obstacle courses in the wooded hills on the far side of its Post—the standard Marine Corps course, and next to it, VMI's own, longer, version. All of the PT groups were scheduled to visit the Marine Corps obstacle course before the end of the summer, but many students walked over to the site in advance, eager to try it on their own.

What they found was somewhat intimidating. Among other challenges, the Marine Corps obstacle course requires a person to climb a rope, scramble over a wall, run across wooden logs, and pull his or her body up and over a high bar. Still, the students approached it with enthusiasm. "I thought it was a lot of fun," explained Mia Utz, one of VMI's transfer students from the New Mexico Military Institute. "I liked it, and I think we all liked it, but most of us weren't really used to throwing our bodies on top of logs in the attempt to roll over them. A lot of us came back with really bad bruises all over our arms and legs, and rope burns."

More impressive than their miniature battle scars (which the women showed off to one another in the evening) was the helpfulness they encountered among their male peers. It seemed that the obstacle course was an excellent ice-breaker. Many cadets, male and female, required help at the toughest parts, and when the women needed a hand they usually found groups of willing young men to lift them to the highest bars and show them the best techniques for climbing the ropes. After one such chance encounter the students all went running together in the woods, then swam across the Maury River. "It was really neat," one woman recalled. "They treated us the same, which was pretty cool, because at first most of the guys were leery of us. They didn't want to talk to us or anything. And so that was really nice."

Back at the barracks, however, many upperclassmen were watching these fledgling friendships with growing disapproval. For the members of VMI's last all-male classes, this new brand of coed training was an odd and suspicious venture, and they were monitoring it closely. "They all just watched you move around," explained Tennille Chisholm, "trying to figure out what kind of person you were."

On one level, this was nothing new. In past summers the upperclassmen had observed the male "prestrains," especially attentive to anything a young man might say or do that could come back to haunt him during the upcoming months. Often their criteria were arbitrary. Any noncadet who had the presumption to wear a VMI T-shirt or baseball cap, for example, was liable to be targeted for abuse once the ratline began.

With the arrival of women, the main change to this annual game of surveillance and punishment came in its new, voyeuristic flavor. Colonels Stockwell and Cairns received several reports from self-appointed fraternization police, who objected whenever they felt that a young woman was inviting attention, or when they saw a young man, including one of their own upperclass peers, getting too friendly. Their grievances ranged from harmless details—a male student, sitting next to a woman in the mess hall, had been spotted putting his hand on the back of her chair—to full-blown allegations of sexual relationships.

Some of their complaints were frivolous, but a few were legitimate. Kevin Trujillo, in his capacity as First Class President, worried that a few of VMI's more flirtatious women were already hindering their chances for success:

> Because they were in the spotlight this year I was afraid of them making names for themselves before their ratline even began, because at VMI we are very tough on our own, and people don't really forget things. There can be a stigma attached to some people for the duration of their whole cadetships and even past then. I didn't want that to happen to them.

Trujillo recognized that VMI's male cadets deserved just as much censure for any relationships that broke Institute rules. But at VMI, as in most of human society, the women were destined to bear the brunt of the responsibility for romantic misdemeanors.

Although VMI's administrators took charges of fraternization seriously, they did not share the cadets' level of indignation. When an upperclassman reported that two students had been seen walking to the mess hall hand-in-hand, the administrator's first response was: "Please tell me that it was a guy and a girl."

Public displays of affection were prohibited on Post, and hand-holding merited a reprimand. But Colonel Stockwell believed that VMI's upperclassmen were being hypersensitive, both to the behavior of the new students and to the responses of the administration: "It was my impression all summer long that we were being watched by the upper-classmen very carefully . . . They were looking for ways to say that we were favoring the women, and they were really stretching things."

The upperclassmen's concerns were not limited to who was doing what to whom. Throughout the STP, their complaints ranged from significant matters to trivial details.

Early in the summer, for example, VMI's administrators informed the male cadets that they could not wear tank tops to class. Colonel Stockwell had in mind those loose-fitting sleeveless shirts, sometimes made from the mesh of football jerseys, with armholes so wide that a young man's entire side is exposed.

All right, the upperclassmen replied, but that means that the women can't wear any kind of sleeveless attire either. Here, Colonels Stockwell and Cairns found themselves caught in a fruitless cycle, trying to educate male cadets about the differences between men's and women's fashions. Certainly tank tops would be unacceptable for the women. But while a tank top was likely to be the only sleeveless item in a man's closet, a woman's wardrobe might include sleeveless collared blouses, sleeveless knit turtlenecks, and sleeveless dresses fit for Sunday church services. Any of these items would be appropriate for the VMI classroom. Nevertheless, in the minds of several intransigent male cadets it was all a matter of double standards; they protested every time they saw a woman's shoulder.

Still, if the length of women's sleeves was going to be the biggest of VMI's worries, then Colonel Stockwell was happy to face it. In fact, by the end of the STP he could look back and say with confidence that it had been a relatively calm four weeks. The classes had gone well; the students looked happy. Colonel Bissell had briefed all of the students on VMI's assimilation plans, and they seemed prepared for the year ahead. Yes, on one occasion someone had sprayed some obscene graffiti on the wall of the new women's bathroom in the barracks, but that was an isolated incident, and the painters had covered it up before VMI's administrators ever saw it.

There had only been one strange occurrence that served as a lesson for things to come. One morning in the first week of the program, a rumor began to circulate that Colonel Stockwell had dismissed an upperclassman for complimenting a woman on her legs. Stockwell initially downplayed the rumor when he heard it from a colleague. Of course he hadn't dismissed anyone; it was absurd. By that afternoon, however, he had heard the same story three times. To make matters worse, he learned that one of the professors had spent forty-five minutes of class time conducting a heated debate over whether the upperclassman's dismissal had been warranted.

Stockwell checked with the other employees in the summer school office and confirmed that no one had heard of such an incident. He then dispatched Colonel Cairns to speak to the young woman in question, who declared that she had not received any unwelcome comments about her legs. From what Stockwell could piece together, it seemed that a rumor about an upperclassman's inappropriate remarks had surfaced in the barracks one evening, and when that cadet missed class the next day, everyone jumped to the conclusion that he had been thrown out.

Stockwell sent an e-mail to all of the faculty, telling them to spread the word that there had been no such comment and no such dismissal. Several days later, however, some of the male STP students were still complaining that "certain women" were too sensitive about sexual harassment and were getting the upperclassmen into trouble. In a crowded barracks, where students had few intrigues to occupy their imaginations, rumors were as good as reality, and in the upcoming year, VMI's administrators would often find themselves trying to sort through fact and fiction as they mediated the relations between young men and women.

In this case, no permanent damage was done, and by the end of July VMI's administrators were breathing a collective sigh of relief as they watched the STP students depart. "I kind of don't want to go back home," one woman confessed, feeling a deceptive sense of acclimation into VMI's world. The real VMI experience, however, was three weeks away, and by Christmas that same woman would be wondering why she had ever wanted to come.

11

MEMORIES

FROM HELL

On Sunday, August 17, the press began to descend in force. By the next morning over 250 journalists, photographers, video cameramen, and sound technicians were encamped at VMI. Television news trucks lined the residential side of the parade ground. ABC, NBC, CBS, CNN, FOX.... One professor taped a paper plate to the top of his car, in a small echo of the satellite dishes surrounding him.

Elijah Ward watched the scene unfolding on his home TV. He lived only fifteen minutes away, in Greenville, Virginia, and he had known about VMI all of his life. The enrollment of women at the Institute was one of the biggest stories in years, and for the next few days the local stations planned to report live from VMI for their morning, noon, evening, and late-night broadcasts. Ward listened to the interviews with VMI administrators; he watched the crowds gathering in the background; he saw the first women entering the barracks. Then he turned off the TV, walked outside, and got into his parents' car.

Ward was headed to Lexington to matriculate with VMI's Class of 2001. He would have preferred to join an all-male Corps, but he was entering a culture where his preferences would be irrelevant. Now, as he drove down Interstate I-81, Elijah Ward was caught in one of those surreal moments of modern life, moving from his role as a television viewer to one of the many characters on the screen.

He didn't welcome the media attention. Neither did the thirty women who showed up at VMI that morning. "It was very intimidating," explained Gussie Lord, newly arrived from Daggett, Michigan. "We drove in and all we could see were news people. All these vans, it seemed like five thousand. All these satellites. . . . We had no idea that it was going to be like that." As the telephoto lenses snapped shots of new students walking in and out of Jackson Arch, Ward and his classmates had the sinking feeling that they would be "living under a microscope."

VMI, for its part, was doing all it could to keep the press at a distance. Forty yards from the barracks' main entry a rope extended across the parade ground, marking the line beyond which reporters could not step without an escort. Along that line TV news teams reported live, against a backdrop of Stonewall Jackson's statue and four Civil War cannons: Matthew, Mark, Luke, and John.

In keeping with VMI's media pool plan, only a limited number of reporters were taken beyond the rope to witness the day's events. Priority went to those who had covered VMI from year to year and whose readers had the most interest in the Institute—the *Richmond Times-Dispatch,* the *Roanoke Times,* the *Washington Post,* local and regional television stations. They would be responsible for sharing footage with all of the other media waiting along VMI's Maginot line.

A few photographers complained. They wanted their own pictures, not the same photos that would appear on every other paper's front page. But by and large the press were tolerant of VMI's boundaries. They understood that college freshmen should be able to begin the school year without microphones in their faces. They also accepted VMI's decision that all first-year cadets, female and male, would be off limits to the press throughout the duration of the ratline, so long as they remained on Post. Hometown newspapers could catch up with local cadets over the fall break or Thanksgiving, and VMI would schedule two days each month when reporters could tour the barracks and witness ratline activities. For most of the year, however, within "limits gates" cadets would live in a media-free zone.

VMI's administrators knew the risk they were taking in restricting the press. The Institute might be accused of hiding the truth, attempting to carefully orchestrate its public image. But reporters have always had their ways of getting the story "behind the scenes," and the alternative for VMI—an open-access media frenzy—would have been disruptive for all the cadets and especially detrimental to the women, who, throughout the upcoming year, would inevitably be blamed for any changes in the normal routine. As one male cadet explained: "They can cut the grass different, and the guys will say it's because of the women."

Within its boundaries, VMI did all it could to accommodate the media. Throughout the first week, the Institute held daily briefings. General Bunting periodically strolled among the press, talking with his easy charm, and upperclass cadets who had volunteered as media liaisons remained available for interviews and assistance from sunup to sundown. Tom Warburton, the first classman who headed VMI's cadet media team, began matriculation day with four nationally broadcast radio interviews—all before 7 A.M.

Some of the reporters' questions were insightful; others were comical. One employee from VMI's Public Relations Office responded to the media blitz by compiling a list entitled "Stupid Questions—Top 10":

#10
What would Stonewall Jackson have thought about women coming to VMI?

#9
Can I take some pictures in the barbershop for *Sophisticated Hairstylist* magazine?

#8
What has been the past reaction to women getting their hair cut?

#7
What is the point of the ratline?

#6
What was your cadet dating policy in past years?

#5
General Bunting, I understand you have a son who will matriculate Monday. If he were your daughter, what would you tell him?

#4
Is this the first time women have been at VMI?

GENERAL BUNTING ADDRESSES REPORTERS. KEVIN TRUJILLO STANDS SECOND FROM LEFT. *(Andres R. Alonso/fotoVISION)*

#3
So, you can date someone above you in the chain of command, but not below you?

#1 (tie)
Would a male-to-female transsexual cadet be issued a skirt?

General Bunting, did you ever think as a cadet thirty-seven years ago that you would one day be Superintendent of VMI for the first class of women cadets, a class that would include a woman from the former Soviet Union? (General Bunting's answer: "No.")

Meanwhile, the new school year was under way. Ward, Lord, and all their fellow "prestrains" opened their first morning at VMI in the basketball arena, attending to the administrative details that encumber all college freshmen: What is your major? Are you an NCAA athlete? Do you have any need for financial aid? Do you want to join the band? Or the glee club?

A labyrinth of tables and ropes guided the students from question to question. Near the end of the line VMI's Post Physician and his new female colleague were busy recording the concerns of anxious parents. My son has a rash. My daughter has allergies. Whenever my boy is under pressure, it goes right to his stomach. These were the worries of parents about to consign their children to an alien culture—a life of mental and physical stress far removed from the home environment that they had tried to create. Some fathers were VMI alumni, glad to witness the continuation of a family tradition. Other parents had never heard of VMI prior to their child's decision to apply. A few were befuddled as to why their son or daughter wanted to descend the chain of being from a human to a rat.

After the problems at The Citadel, any mother or father might be especially hesitant to leave a daughter at a newly coed military school. But in at least one case the reaction was just the opposite. Tamina Mars, from Prince George, Virginia, explained that her Dad was happy to have her attend VMI because, as she put it, "it's safer here." In her father's mind it was civilian colleges, with their parties, their alcohol, and their unsupervised dormitories, that posed the greatest threat to eighteen-year-olds. Compared to the perilous freedoms at other schools, VMI's ratline didn't look so bad.

Now, as they helped their children matriculate, several parents shared one desire—to look into the eyes of a VMI official and give the Institute a human face. For those people, VMI's Dean, Commandant, admissions officers, and various other administrators and senior cadets were wandering the floor of the arena. General Bunting also walked back and forth through the crowd, offering words of welcome and reassurance. This year Bunting's greetings were all the more heartfelt because he too was a VMI parent. His younger son, Charlie, was matriculating with the Class of 2001. The Superintendent would face the year with the double concerns of a college president and a father.

AS EACH YOUNG MAN AND WOMAN made the rounds of matriculation, they ended with one last task—signing their names in VMI's matriculation roster. Every entering student signs "The Book." The moment can be memorable or relatively insignificant, depending on each student's mindset.

Ebony McElroy had never heard of "The Book." Coming from San Diego, she was scarcely familiar with VMI. McElroy had been completing her second year of college at the New Mexico Military Institute and was determined "never to go to a military school ever again" when she first heard Kevin Trujillo speak about VMI. Trujillo had traveled to NMMI with Colonel Bissell and Major Reddings to encourage applications from any women who were willing to accept VMI's challenge. According to McElroy, "I felt that VMI was trying to do everything right. They were looking at other schools. They had thought of this exchange program. They were trying really hard. And I thought part of doing it right was getting quality women." Now McElroy had come to VMI to see if she could be one of those "quality women."

Standing in line to sign the book, the impact of her decision struck home:

I didn't realize until I was waiting in line to sign, how important signing the book was. For me that was the point where there was no turning back. It's not so much signing your life away, but I guess you can look at it like a certified statement [a signed statement that a cadet certifies, on his or her honor, as true].

It was like: "Here I am. I am part of this history. Many people have gone before and have signed this book." From that point for me, I knew leaving was not an option.

McElroy was not the first woman to sign. That distinction fell to Beth Hogan, from Junction City, Oregon. In one of those odd coincidences of fate, Hogan's last name resembled that of the first male cadet to sign VMI's matriculation roster back in 1839: John S.L. Logan. By January, Beth Hogan, like many of the men and women entering that day, would decide that VMI was not for her. Her name, however, would remain in "The Book" forever.

The next stop for the students, friends, and family members was Jackson Memorial Hall, where they gathered to hear speeches from the Institute's top brass. Behind the speakers hung Benjamin Clinedinst's huge painting, with its image of the New Market cadets charging into battle. For those students seeing it for the first time, the painting symbolized the history that they were joining, and the difficult challenge before them.

Bunting tried to quell their anxiety with an uplifting message:

> Today you are joining the family of VMI. . . . this should be a day of joy in your lives, not dread; of brimming confidence and delight in a fresh adventure, not anxiety or fear; of pride in the courage of your decision to enroll at VMI, and not regret that you do not enroll in a civilian university; of resolve, even at the beginning, to look out for and take care of your Brother Rats. The less you think about the challenges VMI will lay before *you,* and the more you think about how you may help *them,* the better for all of you.

Bunting avoided any acknowledgment that this class was different from those that had come before. His only recognition that the students assembled before him included women came in one sentence: "We do not care if you are poor or rich, black or white, female or male, Taiwanese or Virginian. We care about your heart and your determination. We care about your integrity."

It was a sentence designed to downplay gender, class, and ethnicity. Indeed, if any of the incoming women were looking for special words of welcome, they were going to be disappointed. VMI had decided that, throughout the year, the Institute would not single the women out, nor would it herald the Class of 2001 as a unique group. The administrators' intention was not to ignore the women—a strategy that some wary upperclassmen initially planned to follow. Instead, VMI hoped to give the women a low profile and to maintain an aura of business-as-usual, if that was possible with a crowd of photographers waiting outside the door.

General Alan Farrell, who as man-in-charge, was especially good at describing exactly what constitutes business-as-usual at VMI. He was the second speaker that morning, prepared to deliver his unique blend of brutal honesty and colorful diction.

Anyone who has visited Farrell's office at VMI knows that he is not the type to mince words. Inside this room, French World War I rifles lean in one corner while the opposite wall displays a large photograph of Farrell as a young recruit in Vietnam, brandishing his M-16 with a big, white-toothed smile. Elsewhere, there are pictures of Farrell with his Special Forces buddies and Farrell posing with assorted shiny cars. On his desk, an antipersonnel mine faces all petitioners, reading "Front Toward Enemy."

The office would seem like an unyielding monument to machismo, were it not for the stacks and stacks of books—volumes of modern poetry and philosophy and (lo and behold) feminist cultural theory. Alan Farrell is a man who moved from life as an enlisted Green Beret to a career in academia. After getting his Ph.D. in Modern Languages from Tufts University, he went on to teach French for twenty-six years at Hampden-Sydney College in Virginia. (His interest in French rifles derives from beloved passages in French World War I novels.) While at Hampden-Sydney he met then-President Josiah Bunting III. When Bunting came to VMI, Farrell came too, and like his boss, he acquired the title of General in the Virginia Militia.

Now Farrell, the only top administrator at VMI who is not an alumnus, was going to participate in one of the Institute's most historic ventures. On this occasion his message to the future Class of 2001 was clear cut:

WELCOME TO THE VERRRRRRY MILITARY INSTITUTE . . .

. . . You'll notice that everything is *square* here. We live in Barracks *Square*. We cut *square* corners, we *square* away these uniforms and cubicles, and we cling to a *square*-headed old system of values that has given our lives the same intensity of purpose as those of the men whose statues you walk past out on the Parade Deck. This is a place of *tradition*, of habit. For Honor, Ladies and Gentlemen, *young* Ladies and Gentlemen, is a *habit*, a habit that one practices over the small things of daily life till it becomes second nature and inevitably commands our response to the *larger* questions of human commerce and ultimately of life and death.

This world may be unfamiliar to some of you, with its rituals, its language, its symbols, its customs, its pomp, its ferocious nostalgia, its occasional, well . . . *brutality.* Now by brutality, I do not mean battery or laying on of hands. That is proscribed here and absolutely. I mean a certain *intolerance* of human frailty that can *appear* brutal, an intolerance spawned by a confidence that most human beings can overcome that frailty and in doing so gain a spiritual ascendancy over things and their own *human* condition.

And it is about *humanity* that I speak now, at the beginning. I have not, Ladies and Gentlemen, *young* Ladies and Gentlemen, spent more than thirty years of my life as a professor of *Humanities* to come here and preside over *in*-humanity or *de*-humanization in any form. What is about to happen to your young person is a systematic *affirmation* of human essence through the denial of superficial, insignificant, and meaningless expressions of human identity: hair, clothing, gesture, speech, mode . . . the petty velleities and indulgences of day-to-day life in an opulent nation, the miniscule distractions that help us through the day.

We have found—and put that finding to the test—over 158 years that once a young person can no longer assert personal identity through such shallow manifestations of individuality, that young person must confront what's left: *character bare and unadorned;* must live on its essence alone; must embellish its contours alone; must face judgment on its strength alone. But in facing such judgment—we have discovered over the years since our founding—one gains the power to sustain a lifetime. A power renewed and enhanced by one's communion with others who've undergone the same initiation, an initiation so dark and scary that it's almost unbearable alone.

But your sons and daughters *will not* go it alone here. I suspect that there will be times when they think they have only *too many* friends in stripey-legged britches and black belts, that they are *only too often* the object of attention. But you should know that many dedicated people will monitor the progress of each entering cadet. (emphases in original)

And so Farrell continued, winding his speech down into final words of welcome. After the speakers had concluded, family and friends bid tearful goodbyes to their sons and daughters, handing their children over to VMI in a sacred trust.

NONE OF THIS was news to the press. They didn't care about speeches or the tours of the Post given by friendly S-5 cadets, who would serve as sympathetic peers for the new men and women in the difficult week ahead. To the assembled media, the day's main event was yet to come: haircuts. Would women and men receive the same haircut? How short would it be? How would the women react?

In years past, haircuts had been a high-stress event at VMI, conducted on the first day that the rats entered the ratline. Cadre members lined the rats up with their noses to the wall and yelled insults into their ears, or dropped them for push-ups, while they awaited the barber's chair. As each newly shorn rat emerged, the taunting intensified, all part of the humiliation of the ratline.

In 1996, however, VMI had decided to push haircuts forward to matriculation day, to get this time-consuming ritual out of the way before the ratline officially began. This was the plan for 1997 as well. And so, as the first company of "prestrains" assembled outside the barbershop on Monday afternoon, there was no yelling, no push-ups, no abuse. Just pressure of a different kind—the eyes of multiple onlookers.

General Bunting was standing inside the barbershop. So was the Dean, the Commandant, and a small entourage of assistant brass. VMI's new female counselor was also there, in case any of the women broke down at the sight of their close-cropped heads. In the past, the press had also been allowed to position themselves right next to the barber's chair. This year VMI had decided to keep the cameras out. As Mike Strickler, Director of Public Relations, explained: "What we didn't want the six o'clock news to have on it was a picture of a woman with a really close-cropped haircut, bawling in the barbershop, before we even got things going."

As it turned out, there were very few tears. The first woman to sit in the chair, Brooke Greene, from Shirley, New York, endured the two-minute clipping with nonchalance. She was one of four cadets in the room, sitting in front of four female hairstylists. All of the VMI's lady barbers had years of experience cutting the hair of women and men. Connie Hostetter, the hairstylist who handled Greene, had run her own salon in Lexington for twenty-six years before joining VMI in 1991, and she was undaunted by her current task: "The fact that we were going to be cutting women's hair was no earth-shattering thing for us."

The haircut that Hostetter administered was short, very short. According to General Farrell: "What the Supe eventually said was he wanted a haircut that would make even the hardest-core objector [to coeducation] say (here Farrell theatrically bites his knuckle): 'They've gone too far.' And the gesture goes with it. He seems to have gotten that."

Shortly after Greene left the barbershop, someone from the VMI Museum arrived, hoping to collect a sample of her hair for posterity. But by then, the hair of many cadets was mixed together on the floor. The only souvenir that remained was Greene's black scrunchie, hanging on a hat rack along the wall. Throughout the next year it would stay there, untouched.

Most of the women were well-prepared for their haircuts. Many had cut their hair prior to matriculation, adjusting to their new look in increments. Angela "Nicki" Myers, from Virginia Beach, had gone so far as to shear her hair all the way down to VMI's length. She figured that the mental pressure of the ratline would be bad enough, without the combined shock of looking into the mirror and seeing an unfamiliar face. That daily jolt might be the factor that would make her "crack," and she was determined not to quit. Myers' father had been one of the first blacks to join the Marine Corps, serving for thirty-two years and attaining the rank of Master Gunnery Sergeant. Now, Myers wanted to follow in his footsteps by attending a military college, especially one in Virginia. As she put it: "West Point? That's not even *in* Virginia."

All in all, VMI's new men and women faced their haircuts with the same variety of emotions. Some were saddened. Some felt foolish. One woman laughed through the event, finding the sensation of a razor at the back of her neck surprisingly ticklish. Another scooped up her hair as she left the room, a keepsake from a previous life. But by and large, they were stoic. This was VMI; the haircut was a well-advertised part of the system. In the next few days, their hair would be the least of their worries.

Haircuts continued late into the night. With four barbers shaving 457 heads, the lights would stay on in the barbershop long after the crowd had dispersed and CNN had broadcast the first footage of a close-cropped female. Outside VMI, reactions to the cut varied. Up until the

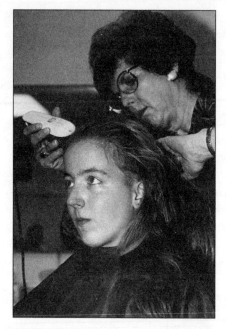

BROOKE GREENE BEFORE . . . *(Andres R. Alonso/fotoVISION)*

last moment VMI had implied that women and men would get the same haircuts. Now, several alumni and reporters pointed to the one-inch difference in the hairstyles and claimed that VMI had already begun to slip. Males had been shorn to the scalp; women had an inch of hair. Here was the first drip in an inevitable mudslide of double standards. (Give them an inch and they'll take a mile.) In upcoming weeks General Bunting would dismiss complaints about unequal haircuts by stressing that the men and women looked equally bad.

As the sun set on Monday evening, VMI viewed its first day of coeducation as a success. The media pool was working. The men and women had survived their haircuts. Only one event had cast a shadow across the day. Over the weekend, a group of VMI and Citadel alumni had announced that they were raising money to open their own private, all-male military college—the Southern Military Institute. Mike Guthrie, the VMI grad leading the effort, informed *The State,* a newspaper in

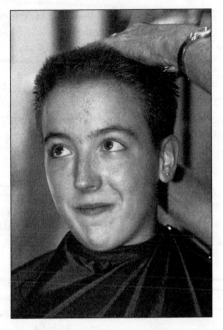

. . . AND AFTER. *(Andres R. Alonso/fotoVISION)*

Columbia, South Carolina, that SMI would be an "overtly politically incorrect institution," a Christian college that would emphasize military traditions of the Confederacy.*

The announcement was a clear protest against the arrival of women at VMI. In the opening words on their Internet home page, SMI backers described their disappointment at the fate of the Institute:

Welcome

The education and training of military officers of the United States have fallen victim to the tyranny of the U.S. Justice Department and its accomplice the Supreme Court of the United States in their efforts to use the military as a tool to force social reforms on

---

* Associated Press, "New All-Male Military School Proposed," *USA Today,* August 17, 1997.

the American public. The grand tradition of the Virginia Military Institute, the last all-male military college in the U.S., fell victim to this tyranny in September of 1996.

The site goes on to propose a new college deliberately based on VMI, with its own "ratline," a class system, and a "dyke" system. The proposed logo for SMI features the same statue of Virginia Mourning Her Dead that stands near Jackson Memorial Hall on VMI's Post.

As news of SMI spread, reactions in Lexington were largely negative. Now was the time for alumni to rally round the Institute, not to split their forces. Several cadets expressed disgust that some alumni were so quick to abandon their alma mater without giving the Corps a chance to prove itself over the course of the year. And when one VMI faculty member heard that SMI intended to emphasize "*military* traditions of the Confederacy" he responded with: "Like what? Losing?"

SMI's ideological focus was also too extreme for most peoples' tastes. When Sybil Fix, a reporter for Charleston's *Post and Courier,* published a feature article on SMI on September 21, 1997, she presented the college as one component in a larger political agenda. According to Fix, Guthrie and several other leaders of the SMI campaign were members of the League of the South, "a 6,000 member secessionist, Southern nationalist organization whose goal is the creation of a new Southern nation." Although Guthrie himself denied being a secessionist, for most SMI backers the Civil War was clearly not over. "I can see this institution turning out people who are as close as you can get to the Lees and the Jacksons and the Forrests and the Davises," said Michael Hill, an Alabama College professor, League of the South member, and SMI supporter.*

News about SMI was destined to creep up occasionally in the coming year, as its backers searched for a location for the college. Although many people doubted the long-term financial viability of such a project, the efforts of SMI supporters served as a thorny reminder that in the minds of some alumni, women would never be welcome at VMI.

Meanwhile the sun rose on VMI's second day of coeducation, a day devoted to assessment tests. Throughout that Tuesday the Institute

---

* "SMI: Southern, military and politically incorrect," *Post and Courier,* September 21, 1997.

gauged its new students' abilities in math, science, and foreign languages, settled their academic schedules, and, as Jennifer Boensch recalled, encouraged them to drink water: "Every time we turned around it was 'drink water and take this test.' . . . I was thinking we were drinking so much water, what are they planning to do? I figured they were going to run us into the ground before the week was over."

She was right. Important as these examinations were, everyone knew that the true test lay ahead. At one o'clock on Wednesday afternoon the new men and women were scheduled to meet their Cadre. That hour would mark the beginning of the ratline—the inaugural event in the next seven months of mental and physical stress, and the first among many moments of truth.

Before that moment arrived, however, VMI had to address one more small incident, the strangest episode of the week. In the dark, early hours of Wednesday morning, someone dumped twenty-six dead laboratory rats into a pile on the parade ground. A white cloth lying beside them proclaimed "Save the Males" in large red letters.

As word spread, photographers rushed to the scene. Here, it seemed, was the first sign of VMI's latent hostility to women—a thinly veiled death threat for the incoming females. Mike Strickler, VMI's PR man, remembered the initial commotion:

> When that first got out, the phones just went nuts. Everybody was calling. . . . And the first reports that came out were very, very negative: "Oh boy, VMI is showing how unfriendly they are to women coming. Somebody at VMI has dumped these dead rats, and there were thirty of them." Of course there were only twenty-six, but they had to make it thirty, so it sounded like the thirty women that were here. One paper even took an AP story and had General Bunting as the one that dumped the rats on the parade ground.

Luckily for VMI, a *Washington Post* reporter and *Roanoke Times* photographer who had visited a Lexington bar the previous night informed the Institute that a young man who had identified himself as a Washington and Lee student had told them that he and some fellow students were considering dumping dead rats at VMI. Although the student was never caught, there was enough evidence pointing to W&L that the

University's President, John Elrod, apologized to General Bunting later that week. An incident that had the potential to become very ugly went down as one in a long history of pranks between rival schools, and attention once again returned to the real story at hand—the beginning of the ratline.

IF YOU ASK A GROUP of VMI cadets to recall the most memorable event from their opening days at the Institute, most will say "Meet Your Cadre." This ceremony marks the beginning of "Cadre Week," also known as "Hell Week." Prior to that moment, the incoming students are "prestrains"; afterward, they are "rats."

VMI's Cadre consists of third class corporals through first class executive officers, with various sergeants in between. All are chosen by their company commanders—the cadets who will give them their orders. Men and women qualify for Cadre positions by maintaining strong academic records, good physical standards, and excellent peer evaluations. These are some of the top cadets in VMI's Corps, and they are tasked with training the rats for their companies. Throughout the course of the ratline, they serve as the drill sergeants. Their job is to find each rat's physical and mental limit and to push him or her just beyond it.

Cadre members teach the rats how to march, how to dress, how to look, sound and act like VMI cadets. They run with the rats; they eat with the rats. The best of them drop and do push-ups with the rats. And, notoriously, they yell. Cadre members have the most leeway to "flame" rats, heaping verbal abuse upon them. Some people at VMI don't approve. They find it unprofessional for cadet leaders to scream into the faces of their charges, and a few Cadre members agree. But for most, flaming is an essential part of the game.

To prepare for the arrival of women, this year's Cadre had received extra training. They had listened to a talk on sexual harassment, reinforcing the sessions that all cadets had attended the previous spring. They had learned about new details for room inspections, such as how the female rats should fold and store their underwear. They had snickered as the Post Physician spoke to them about feminine hygiene, describing what to do if one of the rats had "female problems." And Tom Warburton, one of the leaders of the first class, had added a few dos and don'ts about language:

It was a psychological thing with women that they were very, very sensitive to comments about their weight. So I told the Cadre "Listen. You do whatever you want. You call them whatever you want. But there are a couple of things you don't say. You don't go sexual, you don't go cuss words, and you don't go weight."

Their training period had also provided the Cadre with a chance to meet the female and male exchange students from Texas A&M and Norwich Universities. These exchange students would serve as valuable resources in VMI's opening weeks, helping with the numerous small questions that could arise when bringing women into a male-oriented environment. Warburton recalled a typical example:

We were talking about morning PT, and I went ahead and said, "When you get them out there on the parade deck for morning PT, put the girls in the back, so that when they're doing push-ups none of the guys are shooting their eyes straight up into their crotch area." And one of the Norwich girls just stood up and said: "Listen. You are overreacting. You don't need to do that. Just do it regularly. When they are doing push-ups no one's going to be thinking about looking up into somebody's shorts." That was a classic example of me overreacting a little bit, and that exchange student providing some input. I was thankful that it happened.

Given the importance of VMI's Cadre, it is appropriate that the rats meet these upperclassmen in the most theatrical ritual of the year. Visually, the mood is stark. Aurally, the ceremony resounds with a mixture of well-orchestrated roars, silences, and drumbeats. It is a scene that sends chills through one's blood.

"Meet Your Cadre" occurs in the courtyard of VMI's New Barracks. It takes place while most of the upperclassmen are still out of town, but those athletes, band members, and regimental leaders who have arrived early assemble on the stoops surrounding the courtyard. Usually the cadets are joined by a few faculty, administrators, and one or two local photographers. This year, members of the media pool spread throughout the third stoop.

Outside the barracks, the soon-to-be-rats of 1997 exchanged encouraging words and motivational cheers as they gathered in their yellow T-shirts and red shorts, with big name placards hanging around their necks. On each placard, a cartoon-style rat stood in a VMI uniform, a tail protruding from the back of his trousers while an upperclassman yelled into his rat-snout. Beneath the picture, the placard noted each rat's company, his or her room number, and a few sentences that encapsulated the depersonalization of ratdom: I am Rat *Smith, J.* If I am lost, please return me to Sgt. ———— and Cpl. ————.

The rats had just emerged from a pep talk in Jackson Memorial Hall, where Sergeant Major Al Hockaday had told them about the British square—a fighting formation used against the Zulu—which he viewed as symbolic of the power the rats could exert in their coming ordeal if they chose to protect one another:

> I took four rats and I put them shoulder to shoulder in the square and I said to the rest, "Any time one of you becomes weak, the rest of you must move that person to the center of the square and protect him." Then one by one I would rotate them (putting someone new into the center of the square to symbolize their weakness in running, weakness in academics, weakness in room inspections). I told them: "Everybody in this room has a weakness. Everybody. There are very few guys or women who can come to VMI and make it through by themselves. So everyone at some time will find themselves in the center of the square, being protected by everybody else."

Above all, Hockaday wanted to leave the rats with one clear message before they faced their Cadre:

> The upperclassmen have a lot more clout among themselves than rats will ever have. Upperclassmen know all the ins and outs of VMI, so they know how to make rats fail. Rats have to be smarter than the upperclassmen to keep from failing. You've got to protect each other.

Now, as the rats were corralled into the New Barracks, a roar emerged from the upperclassmen. This was the Coliseum, and the Christians were about to be fed to the lions. S-5 "good-guy" cadets herded each company of rats into four rows along the two long sides of the rectangular courtyard, while the rest of the upperclassmen yelled taunts: "You're gonna lose, rat!" "Prepare to die!" At the encouragement of their upperclass escorts, the rats added to the din with chants of "Brother Rat, Brother Rat" and "We Want Cadre! We Want Cadre!" (Afterward, a few male and female rats confessed to their true thoughts: "We *don't* want Cadre! We *don't* want Cadre!")

One rat had pumped himself into such a frenzy that he was jumping up and down waving his fists like a madman, hurling insults back at the upperclassmen. Up on the second stoop, a group of cadets were pointing at him, laughing hysterically. They were clearly the young man's friends, for they waved at him to calm down, knowing that the worst thing a rat can do is to make himself conspicuous. At their signal the rat nodded and seemed to try to focus, still swaying from foot to foot.

Then came the drums, a row of snares and a bass, echoing through the courtyard while the shouts dwindled into silence. Each year the drums play a simple, stark cadence, the same beat that was used in the nineteenth century to march a condemned man to the gallows.

At the sound of the drums the Cadre entered, 105 men marching in two straight lines, wearing gray blouses, white ducks, polished black low quarters (translation: wool tunics, cotton pants, and plain leather shoes). They seemed to move in slow motion, their feet gliding, their jaws fixed, their bodies rigid with their hands hanging in loose fists at their sides. When they reached the end of the courtyard, the drums stopped. One row of upperclassmen turned to the left, the other to the right, and suddenly the Cadre were face to face with the rats, staring them down with the most intimidating expressions that each young man could muster. Angelia Pickett from Glasgow, Kentucky, who stood directly in front of her company's executive officer, looked into his eyes and remembered thinking, "That's the meanest look I've ever seen anybody have on their face."

One stoop above, at the west end of the courtyard, Mike Lorence, the Regimental Executive Officer, placed his hands on the railing and leaned forward. In a deep, harsh voice, with each sentence clipped to achieve the effect of a verbal punch, Lorence delivered the same essential message heard at VMI year after year: "Look at the men who are standing

TENNILLE CHISHOLM LAUGHS WITH A BROTHER RAT WHILE WAITING TO MEET HER CADRE. *(Photo by Nancy Andrews.* © *1998,* The Washington Post. *Reprinted with permission)*

before you. They are your Cadre. They represent the essence of VMI. . . . From these men you will learn everything you need to know to survive here. You will not fail them, and you have no choice!"

Lifting his voice to a forte, Lorence shouted:

Because they will teach, and YOU WILL LEARN!

With these last three words all of the upperclassmen along the stoops joined in, punctuating each syllable by jabbing their fingers down at the rats and ending with another massive roar. The volume subsided long enough for everyone to distinguish the annual call to battle:

RATS!   MEET   YOUR   CADRE!

With this, the Cadre leapt into motion, running forward into the ranks of the rats, almost knocking them down. They moved from rat to rat, yelling into faces, "Why are you here?" "What makes you think you can be a cadet!" "Don't look at me!" "Never look at me!" "Drop and give me twenty!" And within seconds a few of the rats were running in place, or attempting the first of thousands of push-ups they would do over the next few months.

That night anyone watching the evening news in Roanoke, Virginia, could see Matt Baldwin, Executive Officer of Band Company, screaming into the face of Brooke Greene. It was a clip that Matt treasured. He got a copy from a friend and intended to keep it forever as a memento.

Watching Baldwin yell at the diminutive Miss Greene, anyone unfamiliar with VMI might assume that he was a brute. A sadist. A woman-hating thug. But Baldwin's case provides one of those examples, common at VMI, of the difference between outward appearances and underlying truth.

In fact, Matt Baldwin had spent much of his summer on the phone with these same women, recruiting them for the band. Baldwin didn't welcome coeducation. Like most of his peers, he would have preferred for VMI to remain all-male, and he resented having the outside world tamper with his school. Once the Supreme Court had spoken, however, Baldwin was determined to get to work. As he saw it, the sooner his company became accustomed to women, the better off it would be:

> I had a list of 160 prospective people who put down on their applications to VMI that they had band experience. And on that list I think there were sixteen females. I wanted them all. If I could have gotten them I would have taken them. I thought, the more we get the better. Especially if there were more than one or two, the better it would be. . . . My number-one goal for the females was to have the highest number of females in any company, which I succeeded in getting. At the beginning of the year we had eight, and that was a cap that the administration put on us. We could have had ten or twelve. . . .
>
> As I saw it, girls would be good for our unit. The earlier we could adapt and overcome what problems we might have, the better. Get them in here in let's get done what we need to do.

Now that the women had arrived, Baldwin confessed to being "just as nervous as the rats." This was his first time on VMI's Cadre. In years past, he had viewed Meet Your Cadre as a rat or as a drummer playing the snare cadence. This year was very different. Not only did Baldwin serve on the Cadre, he was his company's executive officer, the guy who was supposed to look meaner and yell louder than anyone else, while maintaining accountability for the fifty rats in his unit. It was a lot of responsibility for a young man who, four years earlier, had been throwing boxes into the back of a UPS truck, doubting whether he ever wanted to attend college.

Baldwin recalled how he dealt with the pressure as "Meet Your Cadre" was about to begin:

> I got the guys together right before "March In" and we prayed. We said: "God, this is something that no one at this school has ever done before, and please give us the strength to do it well." It never hurt to get His help too. After we did that the guys looked at each other like, "I can't believe we are about to undertake this, but we have to do it right."

Watching VMI's Cadre charge at the rats, one would never guess that some of them had come straight from praying; most Cadre members are far from being choirboys. But when you pose a question at VMI, the answer is often surprising, as when I asked Baldwin to describe his thoughts as he stood stone-still before the rats:

> I was really pumped up. I was breathing hard. I was staring down this one kid in front of me and I remember these splotches coming into my eyes, and it hit me: "You'd better slow down, because you are about to pass out. And if you don't calm yourself down, it's really going to be hard to recover as an officer when you fall on your face in front of these people. They are always going to remember that." So I just relaxed for a few minutes.

When the Cadre charged forward, Baldwin stopped first at a male rat, choosing him for one reason—because there were three females directly behind. Baldwin was determined to ensure from the start that the women in his company had a ratline just as tough as their male peers'.

His first problem with a female rat came shortly thereafter. After about ten minutes of yelling, the Cadre members for each company lined up their rats and sent them running—to be fitted for uniforms, to get room fans, to find some niche in the barracks where they could be yelled at again. Band Company's rats had just been corralled on the fourth stoop when Baldwin heard a troubled female voice. It was a moment he remembered well:

We were trying to get the accountability squared away, and the corporals were trying to keep it hot. I was chewing some rats out, when I heard this (here Baldwin lifts his voice an octave) "One sir, two sir." I thought "Oh my God what's going on?" It was the first girl I had heard pushing [doing push-ups]. I was thinking: "This is odd." I went over and checked with the corporal, and he said, "We're just dropping them, keeping them on their toes." So I said: "Just do whatever you have to do."

We kept on going and this girl got to about six and she started crying. I thought "Oh no. I can't take this. I'm a softy, I can't take it." So I was just yelling at the girl, saying:

"What's your problem!"

"My stomach hurts."

"What? What do you mean your stomach hurts!"

I thought, just get her up, get her down to the hospital, let her worry about it down there. I told her to get up, and I said again, "What is your problem?" She goes, "I'm going to be sick."

I thought "Oh no. I don't need this. Not with a 150 news cameras focusing on me flaming a female." So I said "Come with me."

You have to understand that there were all of these cameras inside Barracks. All the top brass in the world could have been there. Then you have the cadets monitoring it . . . I think everybody and their brother saw me throw this girl into the guys' bathroom, because I was just trying to get her to a toilet so she could make herself feel better. . . . So I took her into a stall, and just as I put my hand on the door to open the stall for her, her lunch was all over my hand.

I was saying "Calm down, everyone does this." Every year there's always at least one rat that throws up. It's just nerves. That's all it is. I said "Calm down. It's your stomach. It's nerves. You just need to relax. We'll get through it." . . . It seemed like an hour had passed, but not even a minute had passed and about that time I had a news camera, a Colonel, I think a General, and two or three cadets come through the door at the same time. They were yelling: "What is going on in here!" I said, "She's sick." You could hear her . . . Then the EMT [Emergency Medical Technician] cadet came in and said, "Good job. I'll take care of her."

Many incoming students assume that the physical requirements of the ratline will be the hardest part. They worry about falling out at runs or failing to do the required number of push-ups. In reality, the mental stress is what gets to most rats—the shock of being in a new, stark environment, surrounded by angry strangers, where nothing you can do will ever be right. For this young woman, as for many, many rats before her, the pressure went straight to her stomach.

Shannon Faulkner claimed to have had a similar experience at The Citadel. By the end of her first day of Cadre Week she was in that college's infirmary, unable to keep any food down. She explained that the pressure of being the only woman in a high-stress environment contributed to her problems.

Mental stress, tears, and physical breakdowns are not limited to women. Each year at VMI male rats experience the same troubles. Brad Arnold, a member of VMI's Officer of the Guard Association (the first class privates charged with monitoring behavior in the barracks and investigating all disciplinary offenses) recalled seeing a male rat face a similar moment of crisis:

All the OGA members had to stay on the fourth stoop, all the time, for Cadre Week, and I remember seeing this rat. He stood out, so four Cadre members were around him, and he was doing the "left face, right face, about face, right face, left face," while being ordered to yell things. So I walked over there to make sure that they were within the six inches rule, away from his face [upperclassmen are supposed to maintain a six-inch buffer between themselves and any rat that they are confronting], and this kid started to cry, so I knew that they were going to flock to him now. I said "You're within the boundaries, Cadre, but watch him." About five minutes later the eyes rolled back in the kid's head, and he fell straight to the ground, passed out. That's when the Cadre looked at me, the OGA rep, and they just went nuts: "Oh no! What have we done? Am I going to get kicked out?" They were within VMI's limits, but they had pushed the kid pretty hard, and I just wanted to make sure he was OK.

. . . He was fine. Within thirty minutes he was back on the fourth stoop. They took him to the S-5 and counseled him a little bit, but he came back up.

In this case, there was no workout. No physical contact. Just the dizzying effect of having multiple voices yelling into the rat's ears while he was turning from left to right, right to left. On top of that, you have to add the effect of the August heat in Virginia.

Brad Arnold knew, from his own experiences, the sort of feelings that were probably running through the young man's mind:

Even when it's not hot outside, a lot has to do with heat. Because you are so nervous. You're just generating heat; your heart is pounding. You're really confused. Everybody is around you and your mind is flying. You don't know what to do. An outlet is to just lay on the floor, whether you want to or not.

Vomiting, passing out—these are the most extreme examples of how the human body can respond to the stresses of the ratline. Ninety-five percent of rats never have these problems. For most, Cadre Week is not a matter of distinct traumas, but a constant blur of activity, hurrying from one thing to the next, not knowing what day it is, what time it is. (Rats are denied watches during Cadre Week, which increases their sense of disorientation.) The memories that linger are often mundane. Staring at the wall while your Brother Rats are getting chewed out. Squeezing a $10 bill between your elbows, hoping that it won't fall, while holding a Rat Bible up to your nose. Sitting cross-legged on VMI's grassy parade ground, listening to Cadre members recite, in robotic fashion, instructions on how to salute, how to march, how to shoulder a rifle. (In order to ensure that each company of rats receives identical training, Cadre members memorize a standard script and stock gestures for teaching each "drill block." There is no room for pedagogical subtleties.)

The presence of women had little effect on most of these activities. Cadre members soon learned that a rat was a rat, and the 427 males embarking upon the ratline did not have time to worry about coeducation. According to Elijah Ward: "You weren't thinking about gender issues. You were thinking about personal survival."

In instances where gender made a difference, the impact was usually superficial, not touching the essence of the rats' training. Take, for example, the matter of showers. During Cadre Week rats are traditionally subjected to "rat showers," running in and out of the water in anywhere from thirty to ninety seconds, with upperclassmen yelling at them to hurry up. It's an ordeal suffered by recruits at various military training camps, a procedure that barely allows a person time to get wet. At VMI, any rat quick enough to lather up is usually herded out of the showers before he or she can rinse the soap off.

VMI's Post Physician, Dr. David Copeland, had long objected to the practice, arguing that it was unhygienic for anyone exercising in the August heat to be denied a proper shower. Many administrators agreed. They had often tried to stop what Colonel Bissell calls "this bottle-cap factory" in the showers, but senior cadets kept reinstating the practice. With the onset of coeducation, some administrators anticipated that rat showers would be a special problem for women who were on their periods. As it turned out, their predictions came true. After the first day of Cadre Week some female exchange students discreetly informed the cadets in charge that a few of the women needed more time to wash. The Cadre, facing pressure from the Commandant's office, decided to grant those women a ten-minute shower. Once that decision had been made, however, they had to contend with complaints about preferential treatment for females. Soon, all the rats were given the same luxury.

Yulia Beltikova, VMI's first Russian rat, remembered that moment clearly. Most of the hardships at VMI had not fazed her. The cramped living quarters in the barracks were nothing new; in Russia she had shared a one-bedroom apartment with four other family members. And due to cultural mistranslations, Beltikova had entered VMI expecting that the pace and pressures of Cadre Week would last for the entire year. The ratline, as it turned out, was going to be less grueling than she had expected. Ninety-second showers, however, were a surprise she had never anticipated, and when the rats were given their first opportunity to thoroughly wash, she recalled the women's response: "We were like, 'Oh my god, ten minutes! That was like two hours.' So we took a shower in about three minutes, and we said "Ok, we're ready." And our corporal said: "No! I told you! You can take a shower! Go back! It's good for you!" The women dutifully trotted back into the showers.

The women's presence also resulted in slight alterations at the QMD (Quarter Master Department). Every year during Cadre Week rats spend hours lined up outside the QMD, waiting for their entire company to try on shoes, get measured for their uniforms, and receive the various accoutrements of military life, from belt buckles to shoe polish. This year the process was especially slow, since the rats could no longer strip and dress in one open mass. Small changing booths had been built to accommodate the women, and if the women were going to use them, so were the men. On top of that, women had much more variety than men in their neck and waist sizes, requiring more time for measurements, and VMI soon learned the lesson known to all female shoppers, that a size six from one manufacturer might equal a size eight or ten from another.

The fall of 1997 was destined to be the worst semester for uniforms that VMI could remember. According to Colonel Ron McManus "Anything that could go wrong, went wrong." Because of a computer error, the machine that cut the women's shirts measured the cloth incorrectly, and the pieces did not fit together. And because the women's skirts were not made with the fabric that VMI requested, their lining turned yellow when washed. Nor were the majority of the problems limited to women's clothing. When pants arrived for all of the rats, VMI found that they had not been hemmed, and once hemmed (by one very efficient prison inmate), they were too short. The manufacturer hadn't accounted for hems. In addition, a major UPS strike meant that Institute employees had to drive to Pittsburgh and New Orleans to retrieve uniforms.

These were only a few of the sartorial headaches VMI was destined to face in the coming year, all of which convinced the Institute that during the next Summer Transition Program they would fit all participants with their uniforms and provide them with shoes that could be broken in over the summer. The wait at the QMD would then be cut in half. For the time being, the Class of 2001 would look back at Cadre Week and remember hours of standing in line with their laundry bags in front of them.

The only clear break in the QMD routine occurred on Wednesday afternoon, August 20, when Bravo Company assembled outside the shop. Gussie Lord remembered hearing a sudden commotion among her Cadre members: "Everyone was yelling at us from every angle, so I thought 'I'm just going to stare at the wall.' And someone said 'Look up there!' And I looked, and I thought 'Oh *NO*.' "

Three sports bras were hanging in a barracks window, clearly visible from the QMD.

"Is that your window!"

"Yes sir!"

"What are you *Doing!*"

Earlier that morning Gussie and her roommates had washed their bras in their room sink and had hung them out to dry on the bars that extend across the lower half of each barracks window. The women had meant to remove the bras prior to that afternoon, but they had forgotten. Now, the media began clicking pictures of the offending lingerie. As Gussie explained: "We were pushing for a long time for that one."

BETWEEN THE PUSH-UPS, the verbal abuse, and the hours spent with one's nose to the wall, the ratline might appear to be an unbroken span of misery. Behind their stern demeanors, however, most Cadre members are looking for a chance to laugh, and when approached in the right spirit, the ratline is usually filled with humor.

Walking through the barracks in the opening weeks of the school year, one administrator remembered seeing a group of male and female rats lined up facing the wall outside an upperclassman's door. The administrator feared that he was about to witness a case of hazing, when suddenly the beat of "Disco Inferno" ("Burn baby burn") came pounding from the upperclassman's room. "Dance," yelled the senior cadet, and the rats started to move. "Dance more like the seventies!" and the rats struck John Travolta poses and began spinning on the floor. Soon everyone was laughing.

Another playful form of degradation is self-flaming, when rats must stand in front of a mirror and yell insults at themselves. Nicki Myers performed a variation on this theme with two roommates during Cadre Week, after someone came into their room and planted a plastic bear filled with honey. When Matt Baldwin saw the honeybear, he required

YULIA BELTIKOVA PRACTICES HER SALUTE. *(Photo by Nancy Andrews. © 1998,* The Washington Post. *Reprinted with permission)*

each woman to take the little animal into her hands and flame it, yelling "Strain! Get your chin in! What do you think you're doing! You're nasty!"

Charlie Bunting, the Superintendent's son, remembered similarly comic results when he and a few friends were ordered to teach a Brother Rat from Thailand how to sing the American national anthem, so that he could perform it in the morning: "The kid could barely speak a word of English. So Cadre says 'Forget that! Have him sing the Thai national anthem!' And then the Cadre comes to attention and starts saluting while this kid is singing (badly) in another language, and the whole company starts to laugh."

A sense of humor was especially important for Ebony McElroy, who had the distinction of being one of the shortest people in her class. When asked her height, McElroy readily responds "Four ten and a half," with the emphasis on the last fraction of an inch. McElroy's height would normally have guaranteed her a spot in one of VMI's shorter companies; cadets are usually assigned to companies according to their height, with the average male cadet standing at approximately 5'10". These assignments help to ensure that cadets in each company march with a similar stride and do not appear uneven when assembled on the parade ground.

A FEMALE RAT STRAINS WHILE HER HAT IS ADJUSTED. *(Photo by Nancy Andrews.* © *1998,* The Washington Post. *Reprinted with permission)*

But in one of the many cruel ironies of the ratline, McElroy was placed in Bravo Company, among some of the tallest cadets in the Corps, and she had to endure a lot of kidding.

When standing in formation, Bravo's Cadre members would sometimes yell: "Where is McElroy? Where are you? Jump up and down so we can see you!" Or they might start in with: "McElroy! Look left! Look right! All you see are shoulders! How did you get in Bravo Company?" On one occasion McElroy remembered being assigned her nickname (a common trait for rats) by a Cadre corporal:

> He said "McElroy, you're so small I'm going to call you McNugget. Do you know how much McNuggets cost?" They happened to be on sale during the summer. They were $2.99 for a lot of them. "Does that mean that you are only worth $2.99?"

McElroy didn't mind. She knew that a sense of humor would be crucial to her survival throughout the ratline. As she put it: "Me and my roommates spent a lot of time laughing, and I know some people spent a lot of time crying."

BY SUNDAY MORNING, August 24, as Cadre Week approached its end, one woman and twenty men had left—many of them on the opening day of the ratline. It might seem strange for young people to seek out VMI's harsh system, only to exit at their first taste of rat life. But each year the initial shock of the ratline hits some people especially hard. The last thing that Elijah Ward remembered prior to "Meet Your Cadre" was giving a "high five" to a friend he had met during the Summer Transition Program. The two young men were happy to have been assigned to the same company and were waiting excitedly for the ratline to begin. Within six hours, however, Ward's friend was checking out, leaving an indelible impression: "To remember him being so motivated at one o'clock that afternoon, and by seven o'clock that night he had resigned his cadetship. That's something that has stuck with me."

The first woman to leave VMI was subjected to a lot of unwelcome media attention. Like every rat who decides to go home, she was required to consult with student and professional counselors, a member of the Commandant's staff, and the Dean of the Faculty. After all of this outprocessing, the press were curious to know what the young woman had said. Tom Warburton, who had spent the previous afternoon driving her from building to building in the alley behind VMI's Post, so that she would not be spotted by the press, phrased the matter carefully. Speaking to reporters, he explained that: "She didn't feel she could flourish as a person in a military system." General Farrell, however, gave the press a more blunt assessment: "She said she was totally unprepared for the violence of the ratline, the assault of it. . . . It overwhelmed her emotionally."

Most VMI administrators try to avoid words like "violence" and "assault" when describing the ratline, but Farrell isn't the type to pull punches. Still, physical violence did not seem to be a factor in this woman's withdrawal. Like everyone who leaves, the woman was asked to sign a statement specifying whether she had been physically abused or forced out by upperclassmen. Farrell stated that she had responded "no" to both questions.*

For those rats who remained on Sunday morning, the day was destined to be especially memorable. At dawn the rats piled into buses and traveled north to New Market, Virginia, where they marched their first parade down the town's main street. Normally the parade attracts a scattering of viewers; this year, the streets were lined with onlookers, curious to spot the females. They were difficult to distinguish—a sign that their haircuts were probably at a good length. After the parade, the cadets performed the annual visit to the New Market Battlefield, where they learned about VMI's role in the Civil War and reenacted the charge of the New Market cadets. For Yulia Beltikova, the event was especially stirring: "That was a great honor for me, being a rat, the first of the females, and plus I'm Russian. It was a great honor because I could participate in something from American history."

This was the rats' first chance to relax, to talk to their classmates, and to get away from the VMI Post. It was a break all the more welcome because, as the rats were well aware, that evening they would endure "Hell Night," a ritual that would include their first "sweat party," their first lesson in the awkward pose known as "straining," and their first encounter with the rest of the Cadet Corps.

Cadre members like to scare rats with threats of the misery that will descend once the Corps returns from summer break. Tough as the Cadre are, the pressure they exert pales in comparison with the daily presence of hundreds of upperclassmen, stopping rats on a whim.

This year, VMI's administration had its own worries about the return of the Corps. They knew that the Cadre included the school's best-disciplined cadets, the ones most likely to carry out the assimilation of women in a professional manner. The entire Corps, by contrast, included those cadets known among their peers as the "dirtbags," the ones with nothing to lose. Some of them were angry to be returning to a barracks that now housed women, and most of the third classmen (i.e., sophomores) were eager to wreak upon the rats the same punishment they had suffered the previous year.

---

* Warburton and Farrell quoted by Wes Allison and Rex Bowman, "First Woman, 13 Men Quit," *Richmond Times-Dispatch*, August 22, 1997.

As a result, on Sunday evening, August 24, the atmosphere at VMI was tense. Most of the rats were too anxious to fall asleep. Outside of the barracks, administrators were busy making sure that no reporters or uninvited guests were among the gathering of observers. This was to be a closed ceremony.

Shortly before midnight the small cannon known at VMI as "Little John" went off in the barracks like a bomb, followed by the rattle of blank machine gun fire. Cadre members began kicking in doors, yelling for the rats to get out of bed, gathering them on the stoop. As soon as each company of rats had assembled, they ran down to Jackson Memorial Hall, their backs straight, eyes forward, fists balled with their arms stiff at their sides, wearing the yellow shirts and red shorts known at VMI as "gym dyke."

As the rats filed into the Hall, they were flanked by members of the Rat Disciplinary Committee, yelling: "Get in there, rat!" "What are you looking at!" "Get your eyeballs off of me!" The RDC is one of the most dreaded groups on VMI's Post, a tribunal that responds to ratline infractions—from undone buttons to insubordination—by summoning delinquent rats to early morning hearings, followed by physical workouts. In past years RDC meetings had featured audio–visual effects—darkened rooms where red lights cast shadows over the faces of upperclassmen. This year, in the name of professionalism, VMI would have none of that.

Now, as the rats crowded shoulder-to-shoulder into the pews of JM Hall, stiffly perched on the edges of their seats, RDC members threatened anyone whose eyes flitted around. When all of the rats were settled, three leaders of the RDC strode up the center aisle and onto the stage. Jon Spitzer, RDC President, introduced the committee to the rats and explained how to answer disciplinary charges. He rattled off the instructions too quickly for them to be absorbed, part of the mental game that keeps rats in a constant state of confusion and fear. With the RDC, like everything else, the rats would have to learn through experience, not through verbal instruction.

Suddenly a few RDC members pulled one rat out of the audience and onto the stage. It was Charlie Bunting, the Superintendent's son. With five upperclassmen yelling from all angles, they molded Bunting's body into a straining position, shoulders hunched with his chin buried in his neck. One RDC member put his palm immediately in front of Bunting's forehead, making the young man lean the top of his body farther and farther back until his torso was arched at a painful angle. Then, at Spitzer's command, all of the rats in JM Hall jumped to their feet and assumed the same contorted position—hundreds of young men and women teetering back and forth, their bodies stiff as warped wood. The posture was especially awkward for the women, requiring them to thrust their chests forward. As one of them later recalled: "The first time we started straining we all thought 'Wow. That looks bad . . . I'm not walking around like that for six months!' But you just get used to it." During the previous year, some administrators had worried about the problems that might arise from a system in which upperclassmen could require women to stick out their chests on command. The posture, however, was a traditional part of the game. Straining, the rats were now told, was the one "privilege" they would be allowed during the ratline.

Next, the rats trotted down to Cocke Hall while upperclassmen yelled the usual threats: "YOU'RE GONNA LOSE, RAT!" Huddled into a mass at one end of the gym with their eyes facing forward, the rats could not see what was waiting behind them at the opposite end of the floor. There was the newly returned first class, or at least all of the senior cadets who wanted to work out the rats (some cadets prefer to sleep). At the beat of a drum, the first classmen took one step forward, pounding the gymnasium floor. The drum sounded again and they took another step (the intended melodrama was thwarted by a few first classmen who were deliberately out of sync). Again and again their feet pounded the floor, each drumbeat accelerating until the class ran forward with a roar, running into the backs of the rats, dragging them out in ones, twos, and threes. Within a few seconds, the gymnasium was a mass of moving bodies—rats pushing, rats running in place, rats lying on the floor doing leg-lifts. One first classman had chosen to torment a particularly heavy male rat, who jogged in place with such an expression of red-faced terror that an observer could only think: Why did you choose this? What did you expect?

Mike Meads, another first classman, had come that night with the specific intention of working out a woman. Meads wanted to see how his dyke, Melissa Graham, would handle her first sweat party. Graham had come to VMI after two years at the New Mexico Military Institute, and she was already commissioned as a Second Lieutenant in the U.S.

Army Reserves. In the outside world, Meads would have called her "Ma'am."

"I don't know what I expected," Meads explained, looking back at his first encounter with Graham:

I just wanted to see what would happen. So I went and got her. I knew where she was. I pulled her aside and she still didn't know who I was, or that I was going to be her dyke. And I started working her out.

She was doing push-ups and flutter kicks and all of these exercises, and I was impressed from the beginning . . . I looked to my left and right and there were guys that couldn't keep up with what she could do. I was really working her out, making her do push-ups and sit-ups, get up and get down, and she hung right in there with no problem whatsoever. I just thought: "Oh my goodness."

Meanwhile, a row of rats stood silent along one wall, exempt from the physical workout, although not the verbal abuse. These rats were "on the gim," separated from their BRs owing to injury or sickness. Seven were female—a high enough percentage to feed rumors throughout the upcoming weeks that the Institute's women were "worming" out of the ratline by "riding the gim." VMI's Post Physician later explained that he had never specified that those seven women could not participate in Hell Night. That decision was made by the Cadre. Perception, however, is more poignant than reality, and on this first night of the Old Corps' return, many cadets perceived that the rats were getting off easy.

The sweat party in Cocke Hall lasted for less than thirty minutes. Afterward, the rats were herded up to the New Barracks, where they pressed together in one crowd as Kevin Trujillo introduced them to the General Committee—the main branch of the cadet government—as well as the class officers and the entire crowd of "firsts," who pronounced their dominance by knocking their rings on the stoop railings. (The class below them would not receive their rings until November.) Trujillo delivered his version of the traditional speech heard at VMI on every Hell Night: "The leaves will fall from the trees and you will *still be rats*. Winter will come, the snow will fall, and you will *still be rats*. Spring will come, the flowers will bloom, the leaves will return and you will *still be rats."* Afterward, he dismissed the rats with a curt: "Take them to the showers."

Hell Night was over, and for some of the upperclassmen, it was not enough. As one cadet later complained, "That wasn't Hell Night. It was I Love You Night." The third class was especially disgruntled. The only Hell Night they had for comparison was their own the previous year— an unusually grueling ordeal that had erased reforms made throughout the previous decade. It had started later and lasted longer, with all-night workouts from the second and third classes that left the rats facing the next day sleepless and exhausted.

Now, that misery was fresh in the minds of the new third class, and by comparison, this Hell Night was a weak imitation. Inevitably, many cadets assumed that this year's rite had been watered down to accommodate women.

In fact, the first class had given the rats the same Hell Night that they had experienced three years before. Each year, VMI's senior leaders attempt to pass the traditions of their class down to posterity by giving their rats the same Hell Night, the same Breakout, and the same ratline that they survived. Although it might have looked like a sign of change, VMI's first coed Hell Night was actually a continuance of tradition. As Kevin Trujillo explained: "You don't want to climax your entire ratline in one evening. You want to build to a kind of crescendo and finish off with Breakout. Last year they had a huge operation on Hell Night, and it kind of fizzled out from there. I didn't want that to happen." Trujillo had thought about giving the other classes a more active role in Hell Night, but he was persuaded that this ceremony should be a special occasion for the first class and "their rats." The other classes could be incorporated into subsequent rituals. Regardless of Trujillo's motivations, however, it would take months to dispel the growing impression that this year's rats weren't getting a true ratline.

For now, the male and female rats returned to their barren rooms with their stiff wood furniture and thin hays, bracing for a new challenge: the day-to-day anguish of the ratline. Cadre Week was over, and the rats could be proud to have survived it. But bad as it might seem, Cadre Week is not so trying as the monotonous abuse of the normal ratline. Most rats advance through Cadre Week on a rush of adrenaline. After that excitement wears off they must find other inner resources to

CADRE MEMBERS "FLAME" MEGAN SMITH. NANCY ANDREWS EXPLAINS THAT, "I MADE THIS PICTURE BY SHOOTING ACROSS THE LENGTH OF THE NEW BARRACKS ON THE FOURTH STOOP, ABOUT FIFTEEN MINUTES AFTER THE CADRE HAD ARRIVED." *(Photo by Nancy Andrews. © 1998, The Washington Post. Reprinted with permission)*

help them endure the routine degradation of a rat's life. Lieutenant Ryan McCarthy, '97, a recent VMI grad who was working in VMI's Assimilation Office while awaiting his Army assignment, looked at the rats and pitied them for what they had in store:

> When the Old Corps is there, it's relentless. During Cadre Week you were going so fast you didn't know what time it was, what day it was. Later on, it was the day-to-day that got to me—when you woke up in the morning and there was a guy screaming at you, hustling you down to the courtyard for a sweat party. Then you're herded up to the fourth stoop to take a shower with 400 people at the same time. You probably don't get a decent shower because you've got to go down and wake up your dyke before morning roll call. Then you're marched off to breakfast where the screaming makes your head buzz. You go to class all day and you

stink, you're tired, and you're hungry. All you want to do is sleep, but no one will let you. You can't go down and use the phone because someone is going to stop you. That is the true test.

Meanwhile, in the basement of Smith Hall, VMI's Public Relations Office commemorated the Institute's first coed Cadre Week by Xeroxing a photo from the *Washington Post* and taping it to an interior door. It was a shot of Megan Smith, a petite young woman from Monument, Colorado, staring blankly forward while four hulking upperclassmen screamed down at the top of her sheared head, veins popping from their temples.

Beneath the photo, the office placed a quote from a mother who had just left her daughter at a very different college:

Like all young people, they are entitled to space and privacy [and] . . . should be left alone to mature as sanely as possible.

Hillary Rodham Clinton

PROBLEMS

AND PROCEDURES

WHEN SERGEANT MAJOR AL HOCKADAY LOOKED BACK AT CADRE Week one moment immediately came to mind:

> I was standing in Jackson Arch, about the third or fourth day, and there were two or three guys from the media. One of them was saying: "How are things going?" And the other one replied: "Man, we are getting the hell out of here. Nothing is happening."
>
> That was the highest point in my entire week. I loved that.

Nothing would have pleased VMI more than to have an uneventful year—no scandals, no sexual harassment lawsuits, no front-page head-lines. The hope was to maintain such an undisturbed aura of normality that neither the press nor the Department of Justice would be interested. On one level, VMI succeeded. Although several problems emerged dur-ing the year—charges of hazing and challenges to the school's honor system—none of these involved women. When it came to "the assimila-tion," the months ahead were destined to be scandal-free. Of course, that did not mean that they were trouble-free. Rather, VMI's administra-tors and cadet leaders became adept at putting out the many small fires that were inevitably sparked in a coed barracks.

Even as the reporters were packing their gear, the first minor crisis was brewing. Two days into the ratline a faculty member walked into his office and found a senior cadet, utterly distraught. A Cadre member under the cadet's command had allegedly made a crude remark to one of the women. Now she was camped in VMI's hospital (one of the only refuges for rats), talking about heading home.

In the mind of this young man, the Institute's entire year of planning was about to crumble. The woman would go home complaining about mistreatment. She would tell reporters about those horrible people at VMI. She might bring charges of sexual harassment. Months of preparation would collapse under the weight of one inappropriate comment, and it had all happened under this cadet's command. As he poured out the details, the young man was on the verge of tears.

The faculty member tried to reassure him. One rude remark did not constitute a case for sexual harassment. A whole pattern of such language was needed to meet the legal definition of a "hostile work environment." If the woman was really thinking of leaving, she must have far more serious reasons than a single comment. Besides, any rat who could be chased away with a few words would never complete the ratline.

After a long conversation the cadet regained his composure, picked up his hat and went on his way, leaving the faculty member with much to ponder. On one hand, the encounter showed how seriously some of VMI's male cadets were taking the task before them. Here was a young man who had personally dedicated himself to the successful integration of women and who was appalled at the possibility of failure.

At the same time, the cadet's reaction showed how much pressure the leaders of the Corps were feeling. They had been told, in frank terms, that the reputation of the Institute was in their hands. One false move and, as Jon Spitzer put it: "The entire 157 years—it's going to be screwed up."

Perhaps the cadets were taking themselves too seriously. Perhaps they were overestimating their role in VMI history. But they were taking their cues from the school's administration, and at the beginning of the year, most VMI officials were on edge.

When the Institute's administrators heard of the disgruntled female rat, they streamed to the hospital. Over the next twenty-four hours the woman was, in one official's words, "visited by everybody except Santa Claus." From top administrators down to the Institute's professional counseling staff—everyone was eager to assure her that they took her concerns seriously. By the time Colonel Bissell heard of the problem, the accused male cadet—who was very upset and claimed to have no idea of what the young woman thought she had heard him say—had been removed from the Cadre and temporarily assigned to another company.

Meanwhile, the Corps' most pessimistic cadets were watching from the sidelines, saying "See, I told you so. At the first sign of trouble the administration will sell us down the river."

Bissell was dismayed. He was responsible for investigating any Title IX complaints, and this, he realized, was not proper procedure. During the summer VMI's administrators had received training on the correct way to handle sexual harassment complaints. Now it seemed that their training had flown right out the window. In their eagerness to demonstrate their good faith, VMI's officials had overwhelmed the young woman with their concern, threatening to blow a minor incident way out of proportion.

VMI is a small college, where it is common for top officials, including the Superintendent, to become personally involved in the problems of individual cadets. This hands-on approach, however, was not going to work for anything that even hinted of sexual harassment. Bissell knew that the first step in resolving such complaints was to try to bring the two parties together to settle the matter face to face. In this case, there was enough confusion in the various reports of the incident to persuade him that the whole thing might have been a misunderstanding. He called the two cadets into his office, with a female exchange student present to ensure that the female rat was treated fairly. In a short time, the young man and woman were on friendly terms, glad to put the matter behind them.

Unfortunately, the issues their case raised would not go away so quickly. First, there was the matter of language. "I worry about language continually," explained VMI's Commandant, "only because when passions are heightened, then obviously verbal conflict is what precedes some kind of physical act. And when you start at a language level that is confrontational to begin with, then obviously it's easier to escalate quickly thereafter. So we are continually trying to correct the language in Barracks."

At the beginning of the year, most cadets were trying hard to hold their tongues, if not their tempers. A typical incident occurred one morning in September, as one of the company commanders stood in front of his rats, chewing them out for a stupid mistake. In the midst of his diatribe he threw out the word "fuck." Suddenly the cadet stopped. He hesitated. He mumbled a brief apology. And then he resumed his yelling.

That, according to Band Company's Matt Baldwin, was the new sign of the times. Again and again Baldwin would see a Cadre member begin to flame a rat, raising his voice, pointing his finger, gesticulating in the air. And then the upperclassman would stop in midsentence. He would either take a different approach or promptly dismiss the rat, leaving Baldwin impressed: "It takes a really big person to be able to think about what you say before you say it. My hat's off to my staff because I saw them do it a million times, and they caught themselves before they'd say anything. They did an excellent job."

Baldwin also recalled an incident where a cadet did not catch himself in time:

> I saw someone who went off on a tangent and starting cussing at this woman. In the line of cussing, he threw in some of the female genitalia, and then stopped immediately. He put down his books and took the rat aside and said "Look at me. I am so sorry I said that." He totally apologized to her: "I was not thinking. I did not mean anything."
>
> A lot of people are scared, literally scared about what they will say and where they will find themselves if they end up getting a sexual harassment case put on them. In the news today you always hear people talking about sexual harassment, and the guys are scared that "I'm here on scholarship, and if I get sexual harassment in my file, I'm never going to be an officer."

As the year progressed, most of the cadets started to relax. They gradually learned what level of language both the female and male rats would tolerate, and most of the women didn't mind profanity. "These girls talk worse than most sailors I know," explained one male cadet.

When it came to words, problems usually didn't arise from obscenities, but from remarks that were simply inappropriate. At the beginning of the year, for example, a few upperclassmen repeatedly referred to Yulia Beltikova as a "commy." Beltikova knew that insulting nicknames were routine for rats, but this word was too sensitive. She protested that her parents were not members of the Communist Party; neither was she (not that rat nicknames require any basis in fact). After a brief investigation by the cadet-run Executive Committee, "commy" disappeared, and most upperclassmen returned to their other nickname for the Russian woman: Beltivodka.

According to Major Carole Green, whom Bissell hired in October as VMI's Deputy Title IX officer, most of the complaints her office received stemmed from miscommunications: "It goes back to that *Men Are from Mars, Women Are from Venus* thinking. Something a male says can be misinterpreted by a female, and vice versa. That's been the biggest challenge."

There were, nevertheless, instances of more hostile language. Sometimes a female rat might hear it from an anonymous voice in a hallway or on an upper stoop: "You don't belong here." "Go home." "Bitch." Other times, as Kendra Russell discovered, the hostility could be more direct. "I was minding my own business, walking down Letcher Avenue (the site of VMI's academic buildings), and some guy walking next to me turns and says 'You're the reason why my school sucks.' What do you say to that?"

Russell had no reason to take the comment personally. She was, in her own words, a "ghost rat," a deliberately inconspicuous young woman from Chattanooga, Tennessee, who kept her head down, her grades up, and generally did what she was told. Silent acquiescence was the most common formula for success in the ratline, and Russell held to that mode. Because she was a woman, however, she could never hope to fully blend in. "You can shave all the rats' heads bald," one official explained. "The women will still stand out."

When antagonism surfaced, it usually came from VMI's second and third classes. On one occasion a male rat was disturbed to see a group of cadets gathered at a bulletin board in the sally port (a corner portal between the Old and New Barracks), reading a newspaper article that had been written by a woman. They were, in the rat's words, "laughing, smirking, making comments about women, saying 'I told you so.' " The rat instinctively looked at the stripes on the cadets' shoulder boards and saw that these were second and third classmen. His own class, the young man believed, was much more accepting of women, as were those first classmen who encountered the women on a daily basis. The seconds and thirds, by contrast, were more removed from the rats, and because they had not been deeply involved in the planning for women, the success of "the assimilation" was not a matter of personal pride for them. Some were angry that a few of the female transfer students might be graduating with their classes; one cadet described the prospect as "a slap in the face." On classroom desks and barracks walls one could occasionally find a third classman's defiance scribbled into an old phrase that had taken a new life: "2000 LCWB" ("Last Class With Balls").

Of the thirteen women interviewed for this book, the two who felt the most hostility emanating from VMI's Corps—overhearing rude comments and noticing antagonistic looks—were both black. One white male rat added that he believed that a black woman in his company had been singled out for extra abuse because of her race. In the fall of 1996, a black faculty member and alumnus who had worked on minority affairs at VMI explained that, based on his discussions with black cadets, male and female, he felt that race relations in the Corps were at an extremely low ebb. In a school with historical ties to the Confederacy, where African-American students constitute only seven percent of the student body, and where many cadets keep pictures of the Confederate flag in their hats or lockers, to be female and black was doubly difficult.

Nevertheless, the two women who sensed the most tension among VMI's Corps also stressed that the majority of the Institute's cadets seemed very accepting of female cadets. Negativity toward women appeared to be most pronounced among cadets whose fathers and grandfathers had attended VMI, and who thus had the strongest emotional ties to the Institute's single-sex history. But these young men were a clear minority, constituting about eighteen percent of VMI's student body. For those cadets who came to VMI with no preconceptions, coeducation was the norm. Overall, most male and female cadets reported that friendships were spreading across gender lines, and that those young men who felt particularly angry about the presence of women were tending to keep their mouths shut.

As it turned out, open attacks were more likely to come from people outside the Corps.

One fall day a pair of alumni entered the barracks without the administration's knowledge and began to flame a group of female rats, demanding to know what these women were doing there. Similar confrontations have occurred every year at VMI, whenever recent graduates, back for a football game, decide to march up to the barracks' fourth stoop and yell at a rat, for old-times' sake. This year, however, the confrontation had a mean-spirited flavor, with the usual interrogation taking on a new, malicious tone.

The alumni were never identified, and on the whole, there was little VMI could do to control the occasional hotheaded graduate. Nor could they prevent people outside the Institute from finding other channels to express their anger toward the female cadets. According to VMI's Commandant, Colonel James Joyner, hate mail was a particular problem at the beginning of the school year:

> We had a meeting of the women because they were starting to receive letters that were anonymous from all over the United States. When they were identified in the press, someone would send letters to these women that were not only unflattering, they were very threatening. So I got the women together and said that if they got something and did not know the address, or they didn't know the individual who was writing them, or they got some mail that was particularly offensive, I told them to turn it in. We would try to find out where it came from and take steps to ensure that it didn't happen again in the future.

Joyner himself was overwhelmed with negative mail during the first few months of the school year. He kept a large cardboard box piled high with letters in the corner of his office, and, thanks to the Internet, he was also receiving an average of eighty-six new e-mail messages a day.

Among all of these messages Joyner recalled only two that were supportive. The rest were filled with angry complaints, not usually directed at the women, but at VMI. One letter was written by a man who had seen the *Washington Post* photograph mentioned in the previous chapter—the shot of four upperclassmen screaming down at one woman. The indignant writer complained that VMI was producing a bunch of "Neanderthals." In his opinion, the cadets' behavior looked "criminal." Another anonymous writer asserted that VMI needed to be "exorcised." The particular ceremony the writer suggested was a ritualized "sexual healing."

Joyner kept a few of the more vitriolic letters in the top drawer of his desk as a reminder of what was at stake in the upcoming years: "When you understand the perception outside of the Institute of what your institution is, it makes you want to protect it that much more. And protecting the Institute from itself, and the Corps from itself, is a full-time job."

But what did it mean to "protect the Institute"? What level of supervision was necessary to "protect the Corps from itself"?

As the year unfolded, these questions became much more pressing than VMI's problems with language. Verbal confrontations occur at all military colleges, and at VMI they could usually be resolved through brief investigations by the cadet-run Officer of the Guard Association. But the question of how much control the administration should assert over barracks life was a perennial argument that became all the more acute once women arrived on the scene.

AT THE BEGINNING OF THE YEAR many cadets complained that VMI's administration was keeping a stranglehold over the Corps. The Commandant's staff, which had grown considerably in recent years, was patrolling the stoops more than ever before. Upperclassmen were being told that "You can't do this, you can't do that," and were being assigned penalties for what they viewed as menial infractions of ratline procedures.

Deputations of cadets filed into the Dean's office, complaining that upperclassmen had been threatened with reductions in rank, removals from office, and transfers out of their companies simply for administering the ratline in the normal fashion. Their most common refrain, according to General Farrell, was that: "I'm not going to risk my cadetship over this. There's not going to be a ratline."

By mid-September tensions in the barracks were running so high that some upperclassmen began to circulate rumors of a possible "step-off"—a mutiny in which the the first class suspends the military order within the barracks. During a step-off the rats are released from the ratline, which means no more flaming, no more push-ups, no more marching down to meals. The last step-off at VMI occurred in 1989, sparked by a similar dispute about administrative controls over barracks life. Throughout that conflict the Corps had continued to attend classes, but the upperclassmen had refused to play the military game. The rats did their best to maintain their own discipline, voluntarily straining, walking the ratline in the barracks, and marching in formations (a reminder that students who come to

VMI seek out strict discipline and will impose it upon themselves if necessary). Eventually the administration had settled the crisis by replacing the cadet leaders with other upperclassmen, whom their classmates had denounced as scabs.

Power struggles between cadets and administrators are a routine part of VMI life. Although the barracks is described as a "leadership laboratory" governed and policed by cadets, administrators are always present to enforce boundaries, and cadets always complain.

With the arrival of women VMI's upperclassmen felt that the usual struggle had taken on a new intensity. In their eyes VMI was facing an unprecedented crackdown on cadet authority. Both the class system and ratline, so they felt, were being threatened by an overly protective administration, afraid of lawsuits, afraid of the media.

On one level, they were right. In the early weeks of the school year the cadets *were* facing more stringent controls than they had seen in recent years. The Commandant's staff was more visible on the stoops, quicker to stop cadets who were not following the written rules. Contrary to perception, however, these controls had little to do with the arrival of women and everything to do with the personality, the priorities, and the specific orders given to the new Commandant, mentioned above: Colonel James Joyner.

The previous spring, VMI's rising cadet leaders had become accustomed to the leadership style of Joyner's predecessor, Colonel Keith Dickson. Under Dickson's command they had begun to hammer out the ground rules for the upcoming school year, revising the charters for the Rat Disciplinary Committee and the Officer of the Guard Association. More important, they had spent many hours getting to know Dickson's style. Throughout his one-year tenure, however, Dickson had butted heads with the Institute's other administrators, and at VMI, there is no grace period for Commandants. Dickson was VMI's sixth Commandant in nine years, and by the summer of 1997, General Bunting was looking for the seventh.

On August 5, two weeks before VMI's first coed class was scheduled to arrive, Bunting phoned Colonel Joyner, who was then serving as Director of Cadet Affairs, and asked him to take up the reins as Commandant. Joyner did not jump at the chance: "My immediate response was 'I'm happy doing what I'm doing.' I did not want the task." But

Bunting told Joyner that "VMI needed him," and that, according to the Colonel, was what made him take the job.

Administrative upheaval was the last thing VMI needed on the verge of a difficult and historic year, but that was precisely what it faced, and for the cadets, the result was several weeks of confusion and frustration.

Dickson and Joyner were very different men, with very different leadership styles. Dickson was a former Special Forces officer, a tough-minded man in his mid-forties who had worked for the CIA, and who could be seen marching through the hills of Rockbridge County with a hefty rucksack on his back. Joyner, by comparison, was an older officer, a Vietnam veteran with decades of experience commanding large Army units throughout the United States and Korea. He had returned to VMI twice during his active duty career to teach ROTC classes, and his vocabulary was now filled with words such as "restraint" and "control." Inevitably, Dickson and Joyner had contrasting approaches toward cadet life.

Over the summer Dickson had sent a letter to the rising first class, outlining the rules for the upcoming year. When Joyner looked at the letter, he disagreed with at least eight of the points, especially those dealing with the ratline. Joyner had not been happy with the way the ratline had been administered over the previous several years. He had seen it evolve across four decades, during his years as a cadet, as a professor of military science, and as the father of a cadet in the 1990s. When he took command in August 1997 he was told by his superiors that the ratline had been suffering from an increasing lack of structure and discipline, and he agreed. If he was going to be Commandant, things were going to be different.

As soon as the cadets arrived in mid-August, Joyner began to lay down the new law, both as he saw it and as it had been prescribed to him:

> I started working with the class officers and the regimental system in order to make sure that they understood that we were going to have not only professionalism, but controlled professionalism this year. To make sure that the rats had a chance at success, rather than failure. I started preaching that during Cadre. And because I had not set up and worked with the selection of any of the leaders of the Corps of Cadets, I controlled them an awful lot, because I

didn't have the confidence, because I had not chosen them. So I kind of kept my thumb on them for the first three to four months of the school year, to make sure that what we did accomplished our major missions at VMI, that it lived up to the bargains that we had made with all of our rat candidates that had come into this class, that it lived up to the spirit of our assimilation plan, and not just the letter. And because of that I think that we had some growing pains together.

From the cadets' perspective, "growing pains" was an understatement. They objected to what they saw as micromanagement by the Commandant and his staff. Jon Spitzer recalled going back to revise the RDC charter that he had worked on with Colonel Dickson. He didn't mind making a few changes, but he was annoyed at the new administration's focus on details:

> At the beginning of the charter I had a list of eight things that the ratline would do, like "make a morally sound and efficient cadet" and "provide a cadet with the traditions and history of VMI." I had them numbered one through eight, and I had to literally take it back three times and change the actual numbering, because someone didn't feel that the numbering was correct.

Cadets also complained that the Commandant's staff was placing too many limitations on physical activities in the ratline. Each year the first class leaders negotiate with the Commandant to establish some basic guidelines: What will sweat parties consist of? How many push-ups will the members of each class be allowed to demand of rats? How long will the ratline last? The answers vary from year to year, according to the preferences of the cadet leaders and the Commandant. Because there are no set standards, each class boasts of the toughness of its own ratline, and tries to surpass previous benchmarks of physical rigor once they take charge.

Colonel Joyner felt that VMI's cadets tended to place too much emphasis on the physical aspects of the ratline. They were turning it into an ongoing test of bodily endurance, the trial that dominated one's cadetship, when in fact Joyner believed that the ratline should serve a different purpose. Throughout the year he had one central message that he preached until he was "blue in the face":

> VMI is a four-year program. It's not a ratline and then it ends. The ratline is only one step in this four-year trail that they have to walk. And that one step is not a physical step. It is a hard step. It requires time management. It requires organization. It requires doing many different tasks at different times to a standard that they have never been held to in the past. It requires mental agility. It requires memorization. It requires all those kinds of things. It is more mental than physical, and always has been.
>
> You cannot stress someone physically to the breaking point every day and expect him to succeed in an academic environment. It just cannot be asked of anyone . . . I would not ask any soldier to do that kind of thing. I cannot ask these college students to do that either.

And so, when the leaders of the first class—Regimental Commander Tim Trant and First Class President Kevin Trujillo—approached Joyner with their ideas for any physical event, they usually met opposition.

Joyner recalled the cadets' plan for the first barracks sweat party as something exorbitant, much too long, with dozens of allowable exercises: "The best trained soldier, marine, or airman in the world could not have accomplished what they wanted these rats to do. They would have killed them." Over the next week Joyner was caught in an ongoing argument with Trant and Trujillo, whittling away at the planned workout. The proposed date for the sweat party came and went, while the cadets haggled with the Colonel. Eventually they agreed to a twelve-minute structure (which the cadets usually extended to fifteen), in which the rats performed three sets of three-minute exercises, with one minute of standing at attention in between, while upperclassmen yelled at them. A typical sweat party would begin in the early morning or late evening, with a voice on the barracks intercom announcing "Rats! Get up!" The walls would then come alive with echoing shouts as Cadre members roused the rats from their rooms and herded them down to the courtyard. The upperclassmen waiting below would select two or three rats to focus on (a few had a notable propensity for always choosing women), and after a brief speech from Jon Spitzer, admonishing the rats for some failure, real or imagined, the twelve-minute workout would begin.

Twelve minutes might not seem long for a sweat party, and some cadets pointed to this limitation as one example of VMI's lowering of standards to accommodate women. But the structure was similar to that used in 1991 and 1994, and Joyner liked the final product:

> That twelve minutes is enough to bring anybody to total muscle failure. It was something that you could train the Corps on, get them used to. You could coordinate it; it was easy to supervise. Everyone knew what the standard was. The cadets knew what was allowed and what was not allowed, so they could police themselves. I was always present at the sweat parties. I always had my staff present.

In Joyner's own words one can see the tension between allowing cadets to "police themselves," and having an administrator "always present." The omnipresence of the Commandant's staff was the cadets' main grievance throughout the first semester of coeducation. According to Kevin Trujillo, the upperclassmen "were being watched like hawks":

> It really was kind of personally offensive because we have some excellent people in the Class of 1998. We have systems in place like the OGA and parts of the Regimental system, to watch out for one another, and we had been doing that all along, taking care of our own and disciplining them if we had to, and I felt like we weren't trusted. . . . We have been doing great things and I believe we have made the Commandant's office look good because we could have done a hell of a lot worse, that is for sure . . . It's amazing what people can do for you if you just give them the resources, pat them on the back, and let them go do it. But if you start constantly nagging somebody, you're going to get in their way. You're going to be a roadblock to their success.

The cadets described Joyner as an "overly protective father," and indeed, "protect" was one of the Commandant's favorite words. When asked why his staff was keeping such a close watch over cadet activities, Joyner explained that it was partly to "provide the Corps protection" from legal challenges: "So for whatever lawsuits, whatever actions, we have someone who was watching the event and can protect the Corps at large."

The previous year many cadets had complained that even the routine, sanctioned activities of the ratline were likely to get them into trouble. If they yelled at a woman, insulted her, and subjected her to the same physical treatment as a man, they feared that they would be charged with sexual harassment. Mike Meads, a rising first classman who helped to oversee a cadet committee on the assimilation of women, heard the same complaint from his peers day after day: "I'm worried that if I do one little thing wrong I'm going to go to jail." As Joyner saw it, the presence of the Commandant's staff at sweat parties and other rat activities might help to give the Corps the legal protection they wanted.

Still, VMI's administrators could not shield the Corps from any scandal that might result from the unsanctioned activities of individual upperclassmen—unauthorized workouts behind closed doors, duck-walking, finning out (with hands palm upward beside one's armpits), or physical violence in any form. Every cadet can tell you that at VMI there is an official ratline and an unofficial ratline, with the unofficial side filled with abuses that administrators must constantly battle. One of VMI's greatest concerns going into the first semester of coeducation was that one or two particularly angry cadets would use unofficial ratline "traditions" to try to force women out. "All it will take is the mistake of one person," Kevin Trujillo had warned at the spring orientation, words which echoed repeatedly throughout the upcoming year. As Colonel Joyner stressed: "I do not want the Corps of Cadets to be placed at risk because you have a crazy guy who does something dumb."

To appreciate VMI's version of "a crazy guy," and to understand the precise nature of the administration's worries, one needed only to sit down and have a conversation with Joseph Bates, a cadet from nearby Buena Vista, Virginia, who began the 1997/98 school year as the Executive Officer of Charlie Company, and later assumed the rank of Company Commander.

Bates was the sort of cadet who thrived on the ratline's confrontational nature. "My rats say I am a devil," Bates once explained to me in an interview. "I am Satan . . . I flamed rats when I was a rat. I flamed my own Brother Rats."

At the beginning of the school year Bates was at the top of the administration's list of cadets to watch, attention which he clearly enjoyed:

In the first month of school Colonel Williams (VMI's Deputy Commandant) had a conversation with my company commander, and he told him that they had their eye on me, and that basically I had a target on my chest, because they were expecting that, were anyone to mess up, it would be me. . . . Every year they identify certain people who, to quote Colonel Williams, "take this place too seriously. Or take their job too seriously." And this year I am the member of my class that they said takes it too seriously. And I do.

For Bates, taking his job seriously meant devoting considerable effort to creating an "evil" reputation: "The difference between being mean, as I tell my Master Sergeant, and being evil, is being smart . . . And by being smart I mean being able to do the things that you are not supposed to do and not get caught. And that's something that we do well."

Yelling when they were not supposed to, holding private sweat parties at unsanctioned times and places, pushing individual rats to the point of crying or quitting—these were the sort of practices that Bates, and other cadets like him, tried to dish out to their rats. Bates did draw the line at what he described as "hazing," which included "hitting, pushing, finning out, ice chair":

You get into a law of diminishing returns if you do that. You are counterproductive. Rather than earning their respect and their trust, you are making them hate you. And hatred, if you are earning it in a different aspect, is not all bad. But if you are abusing the power you have, then that's when you get into problems. . . . That's like the difference between being mean and evil. Mean is hazing.

Listening to Bates, it is difficult to say to what degree his words have been calculated in advance for shock value. Here is a young man who clearly appreciates the ratline's theatrical potential; few cadets have ever worked so hard to cultivate their personas. When I asked Colonel Williams for his impression of this cadet he responded with a smiling "I like that kid," apparently finding Bates's bark worse than his bite. But yes, Williams had fingered Bates at the beginning of the year as a young man to be monitored, because, like so many other cadets at military colleges nationwide, Bates was the sort of upperclassman who took pleasure in high attrition rates.

Much as VMI's administrators might try to convince their cadets that good leadership involves helping one's worst recruits to improve, many upperclassmen view the object of the ratline not as group survival, but as survival of the fittest. In the minds of these students, the Corps should be a self-selecting society from which the misfits are weeded out early. According to Colonel Williams:

> Some upperclassmen like to condition their rats to reject the weakling in that unit. They try to turn the strong cadets against the weak ones and force the weak cadet out of school. And that should not be happening. . . . It's not right; it's not part of the VMI spirit. But yet there are some upperclassmen who think that's the way things should be done.

Part of Colonel Joyner's mission in the fall of 1997 was to curb the cadets' Darwinian instincts and to stop upperclassmen from preying on the weak. The weak, however, were not necessarily female.

Even Joseph Bates, who was completely opposed to coeducation at VMI, confessed to being "very impressed" with the women of Charlie Company:

> They really, really surprised me with how well they did. There were mornings when we would get up to go for the morning PT, and I would look in their window, and they were already awake, with their hays rolled, and their racks up, and they were sleeping with their heads on their desks, ready to go out and PT. And to me, that was weird. This is my third year on Cadre, and I've never seen that. But they knew what they were getting into, so they were

ready. . . . And when I'd ask them, they said "Well sir, we woke up and ya'll weren't up, so we just did what we had to do."

As the first semester progressed, VMI found that its male and female rats were roughly comparable when it came to holding their own within the barracks' culture. It was not for the sake of women that members of the Commandant's staff could be seen walking the stoops, looking into the windows on cadets' doors, searching empty rooms where an upperclassman might be dropping a rat for unsanctioned push-ups.

When cadets charged that certain members of the Commandant's staff were too zealous, Sergeant Major Al Hockaday simply shrugged. Official supervision of the barracks was a practical necessity, especially on those occasions when dozens of upperclassmen began to hone in on one group of rats: "It's a feeding frenzy," explained Hockaday. "It's like sharks after a corpse in the water."

Hockaday's own bottom line was that anyone who wanted to join the frenzy must first read the rules of engagement. Many upperclassmen had never bothered to read what was and was not allowed in the ratline, and when Hockaday saw someone breaking the rules, he often delivered a simple message: "You can have a hard ratline, but before you do anything else with any rat, I want you to go back to your room, get the charter, read it, come back and tell me that you have, and then you can join in again. But until then you can't play."

Young men in their early twenties did not like being given time-outs. By late September the cadets had filed so many complaints against the Commandant's staff that the Superintendent said something had to be done. Even the visiting exchange students from Norwich and Texas A&M had begun to lobby on behalf of VMI's cadet leaders, urging the administration to let the Corps run itself. From what these students had seen, VMI's senior cadets were more than capable.

Colonel Joyner responded by making an announcement over the barracks-wide intercom to the effect that if anyone wished to talk to the Commandant he would be waiting in Jackson Memorial Hall later that evening. Approximately one hundred and twelve cadets from all four classes showed up that night, including Brad Cooke, President of the

Officer of the Guard Association, Tim Wirth, President of the Honor Court, and Jabar Beane, Vice President of the First Class. Joyner was grateful for their presence; when the cadets began to dispute his version of events, these leaders of the Corps often stood up to verify his responses. Looking back, Joyner attributed the tensions in the Corps to "misperceptions as to what was going on":

> Rumors were flying around about everybody and his brother getting thrown out of the school, and that it was all because of women. We answered the questions, showing that there weren't women involved in any of the instances. It was men, doing things that they should not have done.

After that Wednesday night meeting Joyner announced that he would hold weekly forums in JM Hall over the next few months, so that cadets could continue to air their concerns. On the second week eleven people showed up; on the third there was only one. After two months Joyner announced that anyone wishing to speak to him could come to his office—an invitation few cadets accepted.

In the weeks ahead, the Corps' aspiring journalists continued to voice their grievances in the cadet newspaper, publishing weekly report cards for the Commandant's staff, where they routinely doled out C's, D's, and F's. Joyner and his staff were also regular targets for satire on the paper's humor page, where cadets complained that there was no Joy in Joyner. Nevertheless, the immediate crisis was over. The Commandant's open-door policy had eased the tension for the time being, and by the end of the school year Tim Trant was able to recognize some value in Joyner's cautious approach:

> Kevin Trujillo and I are a very strong-willed pair, not easily beaten down or convinced to do something differently than what we believe in. And we like to do things very physically. We are fire and brimstone types, and I won't say we were not concerned for safety, but we were less concerned about the meticulous nature of precautions for this or that, or media concerns. So the Commandant, I think, served as a good balance for us, because we might have stepped on our own toes had we just gone hog wild like we

probably would have wanted to, and gotten our way in everything. . . . Kevin and I probably wanted too much one way, and
the Commandant probably wanted too much the other way, and
what we ended up with was doing it the way it should be done.

With these struggles temporarily smoothed over, Joyner's office
focused on more pressing issues. At the top of the list was fraternization.

IN LATE SEPTEMBER VMI faced its first case of fraternization between a
female and male cadet, when two rats were found kissing under a desk
in a darkened room in the barracks. The unromantic location for their
rendezvous showed just how little privacy cadets have at VMI. The desk
hid the couple from the window that spanned their door, but they were
nevertheless discovered by a member of the guard team, who entered to
investigate the darkened room. Their encounter soon made headlines,
inspiring such titles as "Rats, You've Got to Hide Your Love Away."*

VMI had no prohibition against rats dating rats. All of the Institute's
who-dates-whom rules were geared toward the rank structure within the
Corps. Displays of affection, however, were forbidden on Post, and
when visiting in the barracks with members of the opposite sex, cadets
were required to keep the lights on and shades up. In this case, the incident was handled by the Executive Committee, a group of nine class
officers and the President of the OGA, who serve as the Corps' chief
governing body. The EC recommended that the rats be placed on confinement for a month, marching penalty tours with their rifles, back and
forth in front of the barracks.

The punishment might seem harsh for a common behavior, but the
penalties for on-Post love affairs had always been stiff, and with the
arrival of female cadets, they became even stiffer. VMI's cadets live in
such an open environment that any displays of affection were bound to
be witnessed by other cadets, and for the sake of Corps morale the
administration wanted all romantic encounters to occur off Post and out
of sight. General Farrell already lamented cadets' tendencies to hold
hands with their civilian girlfriends while walking in town: "That's what
a uniform denies you—the right to express yourself in that way. And

---

* Matt Chittum, *Roanoke Times*, October 8, 1997.

that has nothing to do with Barracks. I see cadets in town with their girl-friends walking hand-in-hand or hugging. That's not done." Still, most administrators, however, preferred to reserve their wrath for the more serious offenses, which were soon to come.

Late in the fall of 1997 VMI faced its first alleged sexual encounter in the barracks, which involved the same female who had been caught in the kissing incident. The EC recommended suspension for both rats, noting the woman's status as a repeat offender. However, when the administration reviewed the case, they reduced the penalty to a "Number One," or "1" (fifteen demerits, four months of confinement to the barracks, and sixty penalty tours, each of which typically involves fifty minutes of marching in front of the barracks, although penalty tours can be worked off in other ways).

The decision left many cadets outraged. The Corps assumed that VMI's administration had lessened the punishment because one rat was female and both were track-and-field athletes. The Institute, many thought, feared the media attention that would come from suspending a woman for sexual activity. The Commandant, on the other hand, insisted that there was not enough concrete evidence to merit suspensions. Both of the rats had taken the fifth, and in Colonel Joyner's opinion, most of the case was based on rumors and incomplete identifications of faces in dark-ened rooms. Ultimately the rats were found guilty of conduct unbecoming a cadet, visiting repeatedly after taps.

The case remained a sore subject for months to come. In addition to the ongoing controversy over the rats' punishment, the incident under-scored problems that the Corps' system of self-governance might face in a coed environment. At VMI if a student is "boned" by an Institute offi-cer or authorized cadet, the penalty is assigned by the administration. But certain infractions may be reported by cadets to the cadet-run OGA, and in those cases, the alleged violations are investigated by senior cadets and, if warranted, referred to the Corps' EC. Although VMI's administration reserves the right to reject EC recommendations, the Institute's officials try to use their veto sparingly. And while this two-tiered disciplinary structure produces inconsistencies, in most cases it seems to work. Charges of sexual activity between cadets, however, were bound to put this system to the test.

Prior to the arrival of women, VMI's cadet leaders had no training or experience in handling sexual offenses. No case of homosexual activity had ever come before the EC. Those incidents had been handled discreetly, according to the judgment of individual administrators. On one occasion, when an off-duty official had walked into a cadet's room and found two young men lying naked in bed together, he had responded by turning his back and walking out. In another case, when a Commandant had been faced with ongoing complaints about a particular male cadet, he had dealt with the matter by calling the young man into his office and warning him to "knock it off" for the sake of his own safety. Because incidents of homosexual behavior were uncommon and embarrassing, VMI had no written rules for handling them.

Now, with the arrival of women, sexual activity was going to be an ongoing concern, and although VMI's cadet leaders insisted on maintaining authority over the life of the Corps, sexual behavior opened up a whole Pandora's box of questions. If the OGA began to investigate a female cadet's sexual activities, could they be accused of sexual harassment? And if the EC was going to adjudicate cases of heterosexual activity among cadets, would they be prepared to address cases of homosexual activity?

The EC was an awkward forum for discussing sexuality of any kind. In the case of the alleged sexual encounter mentioned above, the young woman explained that she found herself standing before a video camera in Jackson Memorial Hall for forty-five minutes, with a row of ten male upperclassmen dressed in coatees sitting above her on stage, asking questions about her personal feelings and sexual behavior. There was nothing unusual about the format of the proceedings. The accused male rat was asked similar questions, and Major Carole Green witnessed the meeting at the request of the Commandant's office, and found the questions to be relevant. Still, it was an uncomfortable scene. "When I was standing up there," recalled the young woman, "I was thinking 'have you guys ever read *The Scarlet Letter*?' "

For the rest of the year this young woman was destined to be the Hester Prynne of the Corps, with other cadets informing her that "You disgraced my school. You're a piece of shit." The male cadet involved in the encounter was also criticized, but, according to the young woman, he had the sort of temper that few cadets were willing to provoke; she was an easier target for abuse. She considered leaving VMI, but decided instead to weather the storm. Attention would begin to shift once the next case came about, and that didn't take long.

In the last few weeks of the school year, a VMI official walked into a barracks room and discovered a first classman in a sexual encounter with a female exchange student. This time there was no argument over the facts. Both cadets were clearly identifiable, they were caught in the act, and General Bunting, who had been espousing a zero-tolerance policy for sexual activity, determined the punishment himself. The male cadet was expelled two weeks prior to graduation, and the woman was sent back to her own college to face formal proceedings.

The harshness of the penalty took some by surprise. In the spring of 1998 VMI's Blue Book contained no specified punishment for sexual activity; sex fell under the category of "conduct unbecoming," which merited penalties up to and including dismissal. Several cadets felt that the punishment in this case was unfair, given that the rats in the previous incident had received a "1."

Some other cadets, however, supported the expulsion, emphasizing the need to keep sex between cadets out of the barracks. "That's all of our homes," explained first classman Mike Meads. "It's not just that one person's room. . . . We have no locks; you can go right into rooms. I think you're doing a real discredit to the Corps if you do stuff like that." Another upperclassman summed up the popular sentiment by saying that "A barracks is not a college dormitory."

VMI's disciplinary standards have always been far removed from civilian norms. During Bunting's youth a cadet could be peremptorily dismissed for drinking a beer, on or off Post (a prohibition that accounts for many alumni's memories of jumping out the back windows of Lexington bars whenever a VMI official came through the door). Cadets who choose to attend VMI understand that they must submit to a "minute regulation of behavior" alien to most college students. Still, General Farrell did not enjoy his new status as the bestower of punishment for sexual offenses: "I have to call two kids in here who have engaged in a perfectly common, if not necessarily legitimate, relationship, which at any other college a Dean of Students would laugh at, and I have to impose some kind of horrifying penalty."

The penalty was all the more striking because VMI habitually doles out suspensions for incidents as serious as physical brutality. Why, many observers asked, should sexual acts result in a tougher punishment than acts of violence?

Farrell acknowledged the incongruity:

> Over the past couple of years there have been a number of instances where the Institute struck more severely at sexual activity than at destruction of property, or even laying on of hands in barracks. And I have been called on to explain that inconsistency to parents and cadets, and I don't think I've done a very good job. . . . All I can say is that we've dealt with violence in barracks for a long time. It's a constant issue and it's not going to go away as long as we have this so-called "doubting" or "adversative" system. But we are new to the problem of sex, and we are exposed on it. And I suppose that's the sense in which the first encounters of that kind are being met with such ferocious repression.

By the fall of 1998 General Bunting would try to alleviate this disciplinary inconsistency by expanding the rules for expulsion to include cases of "hitting." But regardless of how strict VMI attempted to be, fraternization was destined to be an inevitable part of its future. In the coming months cadets would continue to talk about who was meeting whom in the Physics Department study rooms, or what romances were budding at the indoor track and field. None of this was unexpected. Troublesome as cadet hormones might be, the most memorable disciplinary problems of the 1997/98 school year would come in forms the Institute never anticipated.

ONE SURPRISE CAME at the beginning of the year, when VMI suspended a female rat for hitting a senior cadet. The young woman apparently lost her cool while being disciplined by the upperclassman. She shoved him, then threw a punch that accidentally landed on the Sergeant of the Guard, who had tried to intervene.

Although the incident had a comical ring, the EC took the matter very seriously. VMI's administration had already suspended a third classman for striking a rat with a broomstick after the rat, acting on orders from another upperclassman, had entered the third's room and thrown his mattress onto the stoop. With the administration taking a hard line on disciplinary infractions, the cadets were determined to be equally tough. Above all, they wanted to show that a female cadet would not receive preferential treatment. They recommended that the woman be suspended for two semesters, and the administration concurred. (One semester would not have been practical since a rat cannot reenter the ratline in January after missing the entire fall.)

The U.S. Department of Justice immediately began to ask questions. Citing their obligation to ensure that VMI's women were not discriminated against, they requested all of the details of the case, including the full circumstances surrounding the incident, any related incidents that had preceded or followed it, copies of VMI's rules and regulations regarding such matters, and all records on cadet suspensions for the past three years, including every case in which one cadet had been accused of striking another. DOJ was especially concerned about whether the female rat had made any allegations of sexual harassment.

VMI refused to tell them anything. The Institute did not want the federal government investigating its internal disciplinary matters; as they saw it, the Supreme Court's decision gave DOJ no such mandate. Doomsayers among VMI's alumni had long predicted that coeducation would be accompanied by a wave of federal micromanagement. Now, VMI wanted to stop that specter in its tracks. William H. Hurd, with the Virginia Attorney General's office, sent DOJ a letter on September 16, 1997, stating that "It appears that you and VMI have different views on what authority, if any, your agency may have in matters concerning the disciplining of individual cadets." Hurd enclosed copies of newspaper articles about the incident, a tactic that annoyed the federal lawyers, who stressed that such reports often contain errors.

For a while VMI's officials speculated that the matter might have to be settled in court. But the Justice Department eventually backed down. The young woman's father had publicly stated that he was satisfied with VMI's handling of the incident, and his daughter had accepted her punishment without protest, asserting that she would be back next fall. (True to her word, when the Class of 2002 matriculated in the fall of 1998, she returned to endure her second round of Hell Week.) With no complaints filed, DOJ stepped back for the rest of the year to let VMI handle its own problems.

The most serious incidents to emerge thereafter did not involve women. Over the next several months VMI faced two highly publicized cases of upperclassmen striking their male dykes across their buttocks and thighs with belts and coat hangers. The first case surfaced when George Wade, a rat from Henrico County, Virginia, alleged that he and five fellow rats had been struck with belts nearly three times a week from mid-September through early October. The incidents occurred in the rats' "dyke room," where they were told to line up and bend over while one of the senior cadets living in the room administered several cracks of his belt to each rat. When the beatings first happened, Wade accepted them as a one-time initiation. The rats soon learned, however, that over the next few weeks they would have to take ninety-eight licks to honor the class of '98, licks which, according to Wade, raised welts and bruises.

The problem came to light when the mother of Wade's girlfriend made an anonymous call to VMI. After an investigation by the OGA, the EC recommended two weeks of confinement and twenty penalty tours for the guilty seniors, but when Wade did not return to VMI after Thanksgiving, Colonel Joyner began his own investigation, and found that the EC had not looked into the case completely. The administration decided to suspend three senior cadets for two semesters, while a fourth was given a "1."

Many first classmen disputed VMI's decision to overturn the EC ruling, charging that the administration was catering to outside pressures associated with coeducation. But Kevin Trujillo supported the suspensions. Looking back, Trujillo explained that if his committee had been given all the facts, it would have recommended the same punishment: "I felt like the guys who went up there before the EC painted a rosy picture, didn't give us the full story. That upset me pretty badly. It turned into a huge fiasco when we could have taken care of it at the lowest level."

Wade's father was not satisfied with the suspensions. He wanted VMI to charge the upperclassmen with a criminal offense under Virginia's law against hazing. That law, however, requires proof of bodily injury, and because the anonymous caller who first reported the incidents did not identify specific rats, by the time VMI discovered who the victims were, their alleged bruises were gone. According to VMI, the Institute did not have the proof needed to invoke Virginia's hazing law. The irate father was left to pursue his own justice, and by the spring of 1998 he had filed criminal charges against the first classmen.

One interesting outgrowth of the case came from the number of VMI administrators, from General Bunting on down, who, when questioned by reporters, confessed to having been struck during their cadetships. Although they deplored the repeated, sadistic nature of the beatings in this latest case, it seemed that an occasional whack with a belt was not unusual at VMI. In fact, belt beatings were part of the Breakout ritual that had been endured by the Institute's present generation of administrators. In the 1960s the rat mass broke out of the ratline by running from the barracks' Old Courtyard up to the fourth stoop through a gauntlet of belt-wielding upperclassmen. As Colonel Joyner explained:

> You ran through this beltline, and they used their web belts and gave licks as you went up to the fourth stoop. They shot shaving cream on you, and that kind of stuff. But nobody impeded you. No one stopped you. I was probably hit about three times the entire time going up the stoop. It wasn't a vicious kind of thing.

Viciousness, however, is in the eyes (or flesh) of the beholder. Although for George Wade the beatings he endured went well beyond the realm of horseplay, another rat claimed that it was all in good fun. "We weren't pressured at all," explained Wilson Mustian. "If we didn't want it, we didn't have to. There was no intent to hurt or injure; it was just horseplay." *

Of the thirteen women interviewed for this book, none experienced the sort of problems that Wade encountered. In fact, most were completely surprised when his case came to light. "Hazing, to me, was nonexistent," one woman declared. "I never saw it, I never encountered it, never witnessed it. As far as I am concerned, it doesn't happen." VMI's women benefited from having mature dykes who were hand-

---

* Dan Alvarez, "Rats Say VMI Spankings Were Consented Horseplay, Not Hazing," *The Cadet,* February 27, 1998.

picked by the Institute's administrators and leaders of the Corps. In fact, many of the women credited their success as rats to VMI's dyke system. "My dyke has helped me out so much," explained Angela Winters, a young woman from Quinton, Oklahoma. "He didn't help me worm through the ratline. He wouldn't walk me up to my room or anything. It was just the little things. If I was sick in the hospital he would come and visit me. Sit there and talk to me for a while. Bring me back things that I needed from the store, if I wanted anything. Take me out to dinner if I was having a bad week." By contrast, VMI's male rats were exposed to the best and the worst that the dyke system had to offer. Nevertheless, most male cadets claimed that the sort of repeated beatings Wade faced were an aberration.

Unfortunately the problems were not rare enough. One afternoon in the spring of 1998 a VMI official sensed a particular tension among the Institute's top administrators. When he asked General Farrell what was up, the Dean responded with disgust: "We've uncovered another nest of butt-whackers."

It seemed that three more upperclassmen had been running a "whacking system" in their room, doling out licks to their dykes for posted infractions, such as bad grades or spilled drinks. The case took a terrible twist when the first classmen and rats lied about the beatings during an investigation by the OGA. In written, certified statements, the cadets claimed that the beatings had not occurred, and when they tried to reverse their statements later, the episode expanded into an Honor Court case, with the rats transformed from the victims into the accused.

All six of the cadets hired out-of-town lawyers who filed motions in federal court trying to stop the Honor Court proceedings. The lawyers for the rats argued that their clients had been instructed that loyalty to one's dyke trumped the VMI Honor Code. This argument was not likely to change the course of a VMI honor trial, since all cadets are told from day one that the Honor Code supersedes everything else at the Institute, including the dyke system. The lawyers for all six also argued that the manner in which their statements had been taken was unconstitutional. The cadets had been roused from their beds on February 16 near 1 A.M. to be interrogated by members of the OGA.

Outside observers often question VMI's tendency to hold Honor Court and OGA investigations late at night, but within VMI's gates midnight inquisitions rarely raise an eyebrow. Cadets explain that while investigations also take place during the day, often the only time you can gather all of the necessary people together is after taps, since most cadets' schedules (which frequently include six courses a semester and a host of military activities) are usually booked from sunup to sundown. Because OGA officers need to act quickly to resolve complaints and to ensure that the statements they get are not rehearsed, they cannot schedule their interrogations a week in advance. VMI officials also explain that late-night Honor Court investigations originally evolved from the need for confidentiality. In previous decades VMI's Honor Court met in a building far from the barracks, and whenever cadets were seen walking in that direction in their coatees, everyone knew that one of their peers had been accused of an honor offense. By conducting some investigations at night, officials explain, cadets can be called while most of the Corps sleeps, and defendants found to be innocent can continue their cadetships without a stigma.

Previous Honor Court cases had been handled with such confidentiality that most administrators never heard of a problem until after a cadet was gone. In the case described above, however, the usual code of silence was broken. The lawyers discussed the matter openly with the press, apparently trying to garner public sympathy for their clients. In fact the publicity did not sway VMI's randomly selected cadet jury, who, on May 1, found all of the cadets guilty of lying. In accordance with VMI's single-sanction Honor Code, six drumouts were scheduled for later that night.

Shortly before the drums began to roll, an explosion occurred in the barracks. Cadets rushing to the scene found the room of the accused upperclassmen in flames, and the state police were called in to investigate. Some cadets suspected that the upperclassmen, who had left VMI earlier that day, might have rigged the explosion as a form of protest, but the case was never solved. Meanwhile, the drumouts continued as scheduled, although they did not mark the end of the legal battle. The litigation continued and the six former cadets were permitted to take their spring exams without credit while they prepared to appeal their case to the Institute's Board of Visitors, and then to federal court. At the same time, a former cadet who had been dismissed the previous year filed a complaint against VMI's honor system, claiming that he had been drummed out on falsified evidence. He would later drop the case.

There was a certain irony in these legal challenges to VMI's honor system. Opponents to coeducation had long predicted that the arrival of women would threaten the Institute's Code, as romantic relationships conflicted with personal ethics. During the planning for coeducation the honor system was one of the primary features of VMI life that administrators had sworn to preserve. Now that system was under attack, but not from women. The problems had stemmed from men abusing their authority over other men.

AND SO VMI ENDED ITS SCHOOL YEAR amidst a legal tangle far different from anything its administrators had been expecting. The previous fall VMI's officials had braced for charges of sexual harassment, or complaints from women who might not be prepared for the ratline's harsh reality. By and large, however, such complaints never materialized. There had been false alarms—cases where cadets had made claims of scandalous behavior, launching administrators into hours upon hours of investigation, only to have the original complainants admit that the incidents had never happened. But, on the whole, when it came to "the assimilation," VMI was still in its honeymoon phase.

During the Institute's planning for women, administrators from other military colleges had frequently warned that the most serious problems associated with coeducation were not likely to surface in the first year, when everyone at VMI would be on his or her guard. If the Institute followed the pattern of similar schools, crises were more likely to come in subsequent years, as VMI became complacent and as its women became less tolerant of the daily struggle for respect in a masculine culture.

In the meantime, the most subtle and difficult questions facing VMI's women would have little to do with administrative policies and disciplinary procedures. They would stem, instead, from the difficulty of maintaining a sense of feminine identity in a predominantly male world. At the beginning of the school year no one at the Institute, least of all the female cadets, could say what it would take to be a woman at VMI. In the next chapter, we will look at the sacrifices involved in becoming a female Brother Rat.

13

RAT/WOMAN

ON THE MORNING OF OCTOBER 18, 1997, EIGHTEEN OF VMI's women arrived at Arlington National Cemetery. They had come to share in the dedication of the Women in Military Service for America Memorial, the first national monument devoted solely to the achievements of U.S. servicewomen. It was a hectic moment; VMI's group was running late. The cadets from the other military colleges were already seated, 100 yards behind them. The ceremony was about to begin.

Lateness, however, can sometimes have its advantages. With the start of the dedication only minutes away, VMI's women were granted a block of unclaimed front-row chairs. From their VIP seats, they listened to speeches by Vice-President Al Gore and several female veterans. They heard Frieda May Hardin, 101, recall her experiences in the U.S. Naval Reserves during World War I. And later that evening, after a midday visit to DC, they joined a crowd of female veterans, active-duty servicewomen, and cadets from other schools, marching from the Lincoln Memorial across the Potomac and back to the Cemetery, where a tearful memorial service was followed by a display of fireworks.

It was a banner day for America's servicewomen, but not everyone was happy to see VMI's group attend. Back at the Institute, the trip had provoked some grumbling. Rats are rarely allowed to enjoy special events away from Post; this excursion was a privilege the women had not yet earned. VMI also prefers not to separate any group from the rat mass. To distinguish the women because of their gender seemed to set a bad precedent. Prior to the event, some administrators had wondered if the women were even prepared to represent VMI. These girls were raw recruits; if they went to Washington, perhaps they should travel in civilian clothes.

The opportunity, however, had been too rare to miss. The ceremony offered a unique chance for the female rats to share in an historic event and to witness the tradition of service that several of them would be joining. It also gave VMI an occasion to show the country that the Institute had accepted its new mandate as a college that trained both sexes.

There was only one catch. Here was a group of young women, selected because of their sex to join in a celebration of women's achievements. And yet, when one older woman at the ceremony spied the female rats, she walked up to VMI's Tamina Mars and said: "I know that this is a women's memorial service, but I'm really, really glad to see you men here supporting us." Mars didn't know how to respond: "I didn't want to say 'No, we're *not* men.' I didn't want to make her feel silly. So I just said 'OK.' "

That exchange proved to be the first in a series of awkward moments, as one person after another mistook VMI's "close-cropped" females for young men. Nicki Myers remembered hearing the pervasive question: " 'Do ya'll have any of the women up here with you?' Some of them were serious, and some of them were being smart. . . . After the sixth or seventh time it was like, grit your teeth, keep marching, and don't say a word."

To make matters worse, the emcee of the ceremony mistakenly introduced VMI's group as young men—from West Point. That was what they looked like, at a distance. When VMI's women actually encountered the female cadets from West Point, the moment was awkward. Although the uniforms of the two schools are very similar, the haircuts left no question as to who was who. And while the tone of West Point's women ranged from sincerity to sarcasm, the substance of their remarks was pretty much the same: "Oh my *gosh*. I can't believe your hair."

The comments did not ruin the day for VMI's women. Most looked back at the event and were "glad" and "touched" to have attended. During the march across Memorial Bridge, a female veteran, who appeared to be from the Women's Army Corps, had walked up to VMI's group and started calling cadence. Soon several other female vets from the same era had joined in, until the two generations of women were echoing each other, the rats following the veterans' lead. Major Sherrise

Powers, who helped to chaperone VMI's women, remembered the expressions on the veterans' faces: "There was just a different sparkle in their eyes when they could see the female cadets. They were really so proud of them."

The rats were equally proud to be there. "I was awe-inspired," explained Ebony McElroy. "You listen to these women who actually prepared steps for us. Everybody thinks we are pioneers, but those women came so much before, and without their preparation we would have never been here. And when we got there people gave us standing ovations . . . It made us proud and it made us want to do so well."

But even McElroy acknowledged "the flip side." That day provided the first glimpse of how the female rats would be perceived outside the Institute, and the confusion about their sex was not encouraging.

In the months to come, almost every woman at VMI could tell a story about the time she was mistaken for a man. Nicki Myers' most memorable occasion came when she was riding home to Virginia Beach for fall break:

We stopped at a rest stop. I had my gray blouse on [a dark gray woolen tunic], and I went into the restroom. When I was getting ready to leave this old lady comes in, and she was like:

"Young man, you can't be in here!"

"Excuse me, ma'am, I can be in here. I'm not a man."

"Young man, you can't!"

"Ma'am, please."

And the next thing I know, I see this handbag coming at my face. I was yelling, "Ma'am stop!" and I've got my hand up. And I think her daughter or somebody comes in, "Mom, mom stop!" "But this young man shouldn't be in here!" And I'm saying "Look, I'm sorry. I didn't mean to cause any problems." The daughter said "Don't worry." And I'm scooting out of the bathroom, and the lady is just staring at me, and I said "I'm sorry, ma'am. I'm sorry." I put my cover [i.e., hat] on and I hightailed it to the car . . .

I felt so bad after that. I went home and I thought, "I've got to do something with my hair." I went to every hairstyling place in Virginia Beach that I could go to. They all said "It's too short. We can't do anything with it." . . . I walked into two hair salons and they were like "Excuse me, sir?"

I thought, "That's *it* for this short hair thing."

From that point forward, Myers determined to avoid the VMI barbershop. According to the Institute's rules, male and female rats could grow their hair longer after the first six weeks of the ratline, and Myers intended to stick to the book.

VMI's administrators had written the six-week clause into the haircut policy hoping that male and female rats would be "walking tall" by Thanksgiving. They realized that the Institute's short hairstyles looked strange outside of Lexington, and they had heard about the troubles the women were having in public restrooms. The incidents were so common that Colonel Bissell once initiated discussion at an Executive Committee meeting by saying "OK, apart from getting kicked out of women's rooms right and left, what other problems do we have?"

Bissell did not take the matter lightly. He knew that androgynous cadets did little to enhance VMI's public image. A confident young woman like Tennille Chisolm might find humor in the confusion— "When somebody would call me 'son' or say 'Excuse me sir, can you direct me,' I'd just pull out the biggest girlie voice that I could, and leave him wondering: 'Is that guy a little feminine, or was that one of those girls?' " But many VMI watchers were not amused. After the trip to Arlington, Bissell received letters from a few angry alumni, complaining about the women's appearance. What, they asked, was VMI doing to these girls' femininity?

Some VMI officials feared that the female rats' masculine look might begin to attract the "wrong sort of women" to VMI. "Wrong sort" was usually defined as "Amazons." (The idea of a self-sufficient, all-female culture known for conquering male tribes did not appeal to the VMI imagination.) An additional fraction of hair, it was hoped, might bring VMI's women closer to traditional standards of femininity.

But while the Institute's administrators looked forward to seeing the rats' hair grow out over the first semester, VMI's upperclassmen had other ideas. They continued to "flame" rats for long hair, sending them back to the barbershop, and occasionally "boning" them. Colonel Ron

Williams, the Deputy Commandant to whom all "boned" cadets must report, threw out every complaint against the women's hair. Nevertheless, many upperclassmen remained intransigent.

In part, their behavior stemmed from ignorance about the exact policy on haircuts. Many upperclassmen had never bothered to read the new rules on hair length for men and women, and had the haircut policy been ingrained in their memories, most would not have cared. VMI's Corps of Cadets likes to enforce its own standards when it comes to haircuts, trying to keep the rats' hair as short as possible for as long as possible.

Within the confines of VMI, this passion for short hair was not a problem. "I thought it was better that our hair was short," explained Angela Winters. "It was so much easier to take care of. And no one cared what you looked like, which is what I loved. I loved the fact that no one cared, because everyone looked like crap and so did you."

A couple of women took the haircut even further. When several dozen rats from Alpha and Bravo Company decided to shave their heads in October 1997, Kim Herbert and Gussie Lord were among the ringleaders. They applied their clippers to their scalps, then left their Brother Rats in Bravo Company to play the role of Adam, wondering whether to follow the women's forbidden lead. Lord described how it happened:

> It was Sunday night and we were bored. We had been talking about it within our company for a month. They'd ask: "Would you guys shave your heads if everybody did?" And we said: "Yea, why not?" It was something that I guess Bravo Company has done for the past eight or ten years—to have their heads shaved. So we said: "Well, you think we're not going to shave our heads? We'll do it too." But then we couldn't get our company to do it.
>
> So on Sunday night we went next door, and we said: "Do you guys want to shave your heads?" They told us: "You go shave your heads first." So we thought, "All right." We just got out our clippers and we shaved them, right to the skin. And people were coming in, saying "Oh my Gosh!" Half of our company was mad because we hadn't gotten together as a company and discussed it. They were saying: "You guys just can't make decisions like that," which was right. But I didn't think anybody would care because they didn't have any hair anyway.

When Bravo's Cadre got the news, they stormed into the women's room: "Oh my God! Look at each other! Turn around and just look at each other!" The upperclassmen ordered the women to stare at themselves in the mirror, while they shouted "Look at you! You are so ugly!" Herbert and Lord, however, couldn't stop laughing.

VMI's administration did not find it funny. Although plenty of male rats had shaved their heads, with the all-male Alpha Company taking the lead, the women's new look caused the most heartburn for the Institute. "They were really mad at us because it was a big media stink," Lord explained. "I remember Tom Warburton, who was the cadet in charge of PR. Oh my god, he was so mad. He said, 'You are so stupid! Why did you do that? Go down and tell your dyke what you did!' "

Lord's dyke accepted her appearance with good humor, but Kim Herbert did not fare so well. Her first class mentor symbolically kicked her out of the "dyke room," an unenviable fate for a rat. Until she regained his favor, Herbert could no longer use his room as a sanctuary from the ratline. Worse, she had to eat lunch alone in the mess hall, where, as a bald-headed female, she was a constant target for insults.

Whether bald or close-cropped, VMI's women felt the impact of their haircuts more profoundly than their male peers. Women's hair took longer to grow to an acceptable length, and in the outside world, hair played a greater role in women's identity. Of course VMI had never catered to the outside world. The Institute relished its status as an enclave at odds with contemporary norms. Still, VMI's stubborn spirit had never before taken the form of gender-bending, and that was precisely how some of its women experienced reentry into the civilian world. "When you went home you were feeling like a little boy," recalled Jennifer Boensch, "thinking that you were wearing the wrong clothes because these were girls' things, and you didn't look like a girl anymore."

One female exchange student from Texas A&M tried to persuade her company commander to let the rats grow their hair longer before Christmas. If the rats looked bad, VMI looked bad, and the effect of the haircut, she explained, was not equal for women and men. The first classman wouldn't budge. Going home with an embarrassing haircut was a routine part of the ratline. The humiliation of being the oddball around the family Christmas tree, explaining oneself to curious cousins, and perhaps scaring off one's high-school girlfriend forever—these were trials that male rats had endured for the past two decades. VMI's upper-classmen insisted that women should face the same ordeal.

But was it the same? Male rats might feel ugly or ridiculous when they returned home on furloughs, but their haircuts did not blur their sexual identity. A male rat with a shaved head did not look like a woman.

What, however, defined a "woman"? General Farrell insisted that VMI's women, like its men, needed to dig deep to explore their identities:

> The point of removing your identity from you in the form of hair, and clothing choice, and gesture, and language is to force you inward. It appears to those who have never been in the machine as though it is an attempt to remove permanently that part of you, or to change moral outlook even. That's not it. It is to force you inward where the real substance is. Goddammit, high-school kids get obsessed with hair out there. Take the hair away and force them to look at what they are. That's the game. Being a woman has got to be something internal, and not merely a question of appearances. That seems to be part of feminism.

In the seven months of the ratline, many of VMI's women would embark upon the self-exploration that Farrell valued. For Ebony McElroy, the result was a questioning of the nature of femininity "out there" in the world beyond VMI:

> You become a different person in here, and in here it's safe. Out there sometimes you don't feel as safe. In here you're just a rat. But out there you are a girl. Or you are supposed to be a girl. But what's a girl? What defines femininity? Is it because I have my hair cut that I'm not a girl anymore? That shouldn't be true. Just because I don't wear earrings and makeup, I'm not a girl? . . . I think that society's views are pretty bad then too. It's not VMI, just because they want to cut my hair. I mean, it's *growing*. That doesn't make me any less a female, to have my hair cut. Maybe society needs a few changes. Maybe it's not just VMI changing us into men, but it's what society views as what is feminine or not.

These questions would linger well after the women's hair had grown out. And it *was* going to grow out. At VMI, rat haircuts are only a temporary humiliation. Everyone knew that the women's hair would be longer after the ratline, although the exact length was unclear.

VMI had originally envisioned a tapered hairstyle for upperclass women, above the ears and off the collar but with a thickness and shape clearly feminine. However, during the spring of 1998 a committee of male and female cadets recommended something longer, suggesting that upperclass women be allowed to grow their hair to jaw length. This was still shorter than all branches of the U.S. Armed Forces, and in the coming years several of VMI's women would lobby for longer, service-style cuts. But, for the time being, a jaw-length haircut would be long enough to distinguish women from men, upperclass females from female rats.

Many male cadets looked forward to seeing "their women" in a more feminine style. Despite their hard line on rat haircuts, most upperclassmen got little pleasure from looking at women with hair that stood straight up, or pointed in odd directions. As one male cadet put it: "Some of these girls scared me when I saw them in the morning."

General Bunting was also pleased to accept the cadets' recommendation for the women's hair. Here was one instance where the ideal of cadet self-governance seemed to have worked. Given time, VMI's cadets were usually capable of making fair decisions, and having spent many hours listening to hard-core alumni who thought that the women's hair should match the men's throughout their years at VMI, Bunting could now point to the cadets' preferences and say "The Corps has spoken."

But would longer hair make the women's lives any easier? At least one young woman recognized that there was no easy choice between the embarrassment of looking like a man and the problems that would arise once VMI's women became more attractive:

We used to sit in our room at night and talk, my roommates and I, about whether we were ever going to be feminine again. We still do. We still wonder whether or not when we go home are we going to be pretty? It's so strange when you go home because everyone looks at you like you're strange if they don't know you, and they don't know where you're from. You wonder while they're looking at you if there are ever going to be people that think that you are pretty again, because it was so much easier when you had long hair. . . .

I kind of want to grow my hair out, but then again I kind of don't, just because I'm at VMI and I'm kind of scared about what will happen if we become pretty. I think that we should be here mainly for academics, and for VMI. Not to come and pick up guys. I know that's going to happen because guys and girls attract. And I'm not saying that it's not going to happen to me either. But there are times I wish it didn't have to.

In their unisex look, with buzz-cuts and uniforms that flattened the curves of their bodies, VMI's women could become "*Brother* Rats." They didn't want to be "Sister Rats"—a term they emphatically rejected. They didn't want the distractions of sex to send fissures through the unity of their class and their Corps. Once they began to look more feminine and had more freedom to date, gender would inevitably become a more disruptive factor in daily life. But through it all, the women hoped to maintain that spirit of brotherhood.

BROTHERHOOD had its price, and short hair was only the most superficial toll the women had to pay. Becoming a "rat mass" involved not only looking like one's peers, but acting like them, and for young women, that was very difficult.

Colonel Joyner anticipated the problem from day one: "I had a rather animated discussion at the first of the year with some of the cadet leaders, that we did not want to develop a group of women who were trying to out-butch the guys. We needed to make sure that they had the freedom to maintain their identity, as every guy has his freedom to maintain his identity."

Individual identity is a concept more applicable to upperclassmen than to rats. Most rats strive to fit in, and in a masculine culture, conformity often entailed setting aside one's femininity.

Major Sherrise Powers saw the results every day:

The women feel that they have to do the very same things [as the men], to the point that they will acquire language that they would not normally use; they will start spitting on the stoop. . . . I've been told by several fairly reputable sources here at VMI that some of the women, when they've been out on their weekends, and out with some of the guys, have been trying to keep up with the guys in drinking. And the anatomy of a woman typically cannot take the same amount as a man can take. But there's that point that "I've got to be one of the guys." . . . Now if you were to ask them "So does that mean that all the guys have to match up with your GPA, or your track-and-field record?" They would say "Well no, that's different." It's not different. It's just the mentality.

I think a woman can be a cadet and still be a lady. We're not teaching that just yet, partly because many of the women feel that they have to be just like the men.

Major Powers understood the women's position, having lived through similar situations during her Army career. When Powers taught at the Non-Commissioned Officers' Academy at Katterbach, Germany, she had been the only female out of about forty instructors, and among the roughly 200 students that had passed through the school at any time, there might have been five or six females, if there were any at all. Given her odd status, Powers had felt considerable pressure to fit in:

There was a week at PLDC [Primary Leadership Development Course] when you had to go out and live in the field environment in pup tents and do small infantry tactics. That was all part of the leadership training. And the guys that I worked with were all either ranger qualified or Special Forces qualified, oo-rah type guys. They would kind of act crazy out in the field. So I gathered that mentality, because I felt that in order for the folks I was teaching and even the folks I was working with to totally accept me, I had to be like them. When they went out into the field it was nothing for them to bite the head off a lizard, or eat worms, and I did that, to be one of the guys . . . with *little* lizards.

I was twenty-two. Now in retrospect I look back and say, "Y'know, did I really have to do that?" No. I didn't. Some things I could have done differently, but I thought I had to be one of the guys.

This lizard-biting episode was not an aberration unique to Major Powers. Carol Barkalow mentions a similar case in *In The Men's House,* where she describes her years as one of the first female cadets at the U.S. Military Academy. During West Point's "Recondo" infantry training in Barkalow's sophomore year, one female cadet felt inspired to bite the head off a live chicken, apparently sensing that fitting in with the guys meant going to extremes.*

Fortunately, during VMI's first year of coeducation there were no reports of female or male cadets decapitating small animals with their teeth. When it came to women behaving like men, most administrators' concerns were limited to cursing and drinking—behaviors which are not, one might add, defining characteristics of maleness. Profanity and alcohol are popular vices among college-aged women nationwide, while some male cadets at VMI carefully avoid them. They might seem more indicative of morality than masculinity.

Still, there were other examples, without the moral taint, of what it meant for a VMI woman to become "one of the guys." Colonel Joyner, for instance, worried about the appetite for roughhousing among his "young ladies":

When you have an all-male college, there is a certain amount of horseplay that goes on. Men normally grapple, they wrestle. They go around and hit each other on the arm. All of those kinds of activities happen as a normal course of events . . . and at the first of the school year we started to see those kinds of behaviors. Groups of cadets would run in and tussle as they always have in the past.

Well, we had young ladies who wanted to be part of the group who would get involved in that. They would run into these rooms to go tussle as well . . . But our young ladies weigh 110 pounds. The guys that are tussling weigh 160 to 170. So when a man is grabbed on the arm by someone, and slings them off, he is expecting something to happen when a man is on there. That man is not going to be shaken off. . . . One of our young ladies, who weighs 110, when a man slung his arm like that, went flying across the

---

* Carol Barkalow, *In the Men's House,* New York: Poseidon Press, 1990, p. 90.

room and hit her head. They weren't doing anything that was not expected in that kind of environment, but obviously someone becomes at hazard when the different sexes are involved.

According to Joyner, VMI had never experienced these problems with lightweight men. A male cadet who weighed 110 pounds could still hold his own in a wrestling match; boys had years of practice in roughhousing. "Perhaps the women will do better once they've taken their wrestling class," I half-jokingly suggested to Joyner. (All VMI cadets are required to pass one semester of wrestling.) But in VMI's PE classes, women wrestle women, and men wrestle men.

Several cadets, male and female, viewed coed roughhousing as a sign of the women's acceptance at VMI. According to Tennille Chisholm, the first coed "pile-on" in the barracks had been a liberating event. In a pile-on, cadets suddenly leap onto one person who is lying down, forming a heap of sprawling bodies with the blue-faced victim at the bottom. At the beginning of the year VMI's female rats had stood back and watched these antics, until one memorable occasion when an upperclassman had yelled "What the heck! Grab a female and throw her on top!" From that point on, the women had joined in.

Compared to the early weeks of the ratline, when most male cadets had been afraid to accidentally touch a woman, this kind of physical contact seemed healthy. One first classman hailed, as a badge of open-mindedness, his readiness to hold his female dyke in a headlock. Nevertheless, Colonel Joyner cringed at the potential for serious injury. Throughout the year he tried to convince VMI's cadets that roughhousing in the barracks had to change. Cadets needed to be safer, more aware of what was going on. Wrestling was fine, he explained, "As long as we don't have the women thrown on the stoop so they get concussions, and we have to evacuate them to the hospital, which we have had to do twice this year."

There were no traditionally "feminine" activities that corresponded to the rough play, rough language, and rough edges in VMI's barracks. The one time that a television cameraman seemed to catch two women in a stereotypically feminine act, Kendra Russell was annoyed: "One of my female BRs and I were working on the spirit banner up on the fourth stoop and we were sewing it, because you have to sew all of those sheets

A FEMALE BROTHER RAT LOOKS BACK. *(Photo by Nancy Andrews. © 1998,* The Washington Post. *Reprinted with permission)*

together. And zoom, there was the camera, watching these two female rats sewing."

What the cameraman didn't realize, as he captured this seemingly placid image of women at their stitchery, was the violent nature of the banner they were helping to create. Every fall each company of rats makes a spirit banner by sewing together their bedsheets, painting a huge mural across them, and unfurling them off the back roof of Cocke Hall, where they hang in full view of the football field. As is traditional at VMI, the spirit banners of 1997 were strewn with scenes of carnage: opposing football teams impaled, three and four corpses high, on VMI guidons; the thirty-foot decapitated body of a rival player, kneeling over a huge pool of blood. Skulls, swords, snarling rats with blood-drenched fangs. Every year VMI's companies seem to compete to produce the most graphic images of mutilation and gore, and the presence of female rats did nothing to soften the practice. "I thought it was pretty funny," Russell confessed. "I guess by the time you get around to making your spirit banner, the Cadre have been talking about blood and guts and gore for several weeks already."

The contrast between the domestic image of two women sewing and the violent scenes on their final product underscored the cultural divide facing VMI's women. It was difficult for female college students to bridge the gap between traditional notions of femininity and the masculine realities of a military culture. As one female cadet put it: "I don't know whether I want to be feminine for the outside world, or whether I want to be tough for VMI. I don't know which world I need to live up to . . . There's no middle, either."

The dilemma was not unique to VMI's women. The veterans whom the female rats had honored at Arlington Cemetery had faced similar challenges, as had the female cadets who had pioneered at other military colleges. Any woman who chose to enter a military setting had to adjust to the lifestyle of a masculine world. VMI's determination to keep its system unchanged had made the road for its young women especially difficult, but most of them had chosen it for precisely that reason. They wanted the VMI experience with as few accommodations as possible, and despite the pressures of living with 1,300 men, most appeared to preserve a clear sense of their womanhood.

"I don't see them turning butch," explained Jennifer Buettner, an exchange student from Texas A&M University who spent the fall of 1997 living in VMI's barracks. "At A&M we've had a problem with women who turn into men. Most of the ones who do turn into men, all the rest of the girls end up hating them. I don't see that happening yet at VMI, which is good."

Even within the limits of the ratline, the women's distinct natures managed to surface. General Bozeman, VMI's Track Coach, saw it in the way that the women's cross-country team relaxed while traveling to their meets: "The women are just crazy. They're always giggling, and upbeat, and cutting up, and making jokes about something—the music on the radio, what they are eating—always. Men kind of carry this game face. The women put it on when it's time to run, but after that it's like a carnival atmosphere."

Other administrators saw the women's femininity emerge in a playful flirtatiousness: an inflection in one woman's voice, a bounce in another's step, a wry smile. Male cadets were just as adept at flirting; the women simply did it in a different way.

It was also possible to be nurturing while in the ratline. Rats must look after one another in order to get by, and for women this culture of mutual dependency sometimes sparked maternal instincts. "I felt a lot like a mom," said Kim Herbert, describing the atmosphere in her dyke room. "I'd say 'Are you OK? Are you sick? You better go to the hospital.'"

Only one stereotypically feminine trait caused VMI's administrators serious concern—a tendency toward bickering among themselves. In a culture that was hard on women, the women were especially hard on each other, and the results sometimes turned ugly.

ONE FALL EVENING a VMI Tactical Officer (the officials who inspect companies during the day and patrol the barracks at night) placed a cadet sentinel outside a woman's room after learning that some of her female Brother Rats were planning a blanket party for her. "Blanket parties" occur at all military training camps and colleges. In the typical VMI version, a group of cadets will enter a room at night, "ball up" the victim in his or her sheets, and inflict some form of punishment (blows, shaving cream). The tone behind such actions can range from humorous to vicious, depending on the participants and their motivation. In most cases, rats use blanket parties as a benign form of competition between companies and rooming groups or as a method of revolt against unpopular third classmen. But these "parties" assume a much more dark and cruel aspect when cadets attempt to use them to intimidate one of their classmates, as was the case with the female rat.

Many members of the Corps believed that this young woman was trying to "worm" her way out of the ratline. She had been plagued with physical injuries that had prevented her from joining in many ratline activities, and she did not seem to have a burning desire to be at VMI. Throughout the fall semester she was a frequent target of verbal hostility from her male and female peers.

Placing a sentinel outside the woman's room only increased her visibility; he was removed after about an hour, and the blanket party never took place. Still, Colonel Joyner was troubled enough by the incident to convene one of his rare single-sex meetings:

> I called the women together in JM Hall and I told them that Brother Rats help Brother Rats. . . . You don't eat your own. You don't sit there and prey upon them. You sit there and help them in order to get through their trials, and get through the ratline. When the fourth class starts picking on a fourth classman, it's wrong. Any rat is a Brother Rat, and your whole focus should be on helping them succeed, rather than fail.

A few officials suspected that upperclassmen might be exerting pressures to turn the women against one another. Unscrupulous upperclassmen sometimes encourage rats to torment those classmates whom they view as misfits. This is the ugliest aspect of life at a military college, and it is not unique to VMI. Carol Barkalow describes the same phenomenon in her account of life at West Point: "Machiavellian by tradition, the upperclassmen wouldn't hesitate to turn our classmates against one another. The rule was to target the stragglers in order to effect the end result, which was to get them out of the Corps."*

At VMI, unpopular rats can face ostracism, verbal harassment, destruction of personal property. Although administrators deplore the behavior and can combat individual acts of cruelty, there is little adults can do to make cadets embrace a rejected classmate.

In the case of the aborted blanket party, no upperclassmen seemed to have been involved. One first class cadet claimed to have been furious when he discovered that his female dyke was a leader in the plot. But although VMI's upperclassmen might not have instigated this particular incident, they did exert subtle pressures that tended to divide the women.

Like any small minority within a larger community, VMI's female rats were viewed by most male cadets as a group, not as thirty individuals. If one woman was "riding the gim," then all of the women were slackers. If

---

* *In the Men's House,* pp. 34–35.

one woman was caught in a romantic encounter, then all of the women were whores. "Any time any one of the women acts in any way that brings scorn upon herself, she brings it on all of us," explained Kendra Russell. "Everybody looks and they don't see that particular female; they see *a* female, and that can lead to some serious disagreements."

The more the men bunched them together, the more VMI's women hoped to distinguish themselves—and some of them were quite distinguished. Chih-Yuan Ho, from Taiwan, was cited by several upperclassmen as a model rat—smart, quiet, and hard-working. By the end of the year she was appointed to the Institute's color guard, a great honor for any cadet. The sort of praise she received, however, was revealing. One second classman who was particularly impressed with Ho explained that: "If you were in a classroom and things were going on, you would never even realize that she was there." And that was what many male cadets valued—the inconspicuous female. Invisibility was a virtue in the ratline, and all the more precious for women. If female cadets must come to VMI, let them be as unobtrusive as possible.

Ho's ability to maintain a low profile derived, in part, from her upbringing in an Asian culture that valued homogeneity. She was accustomed to blending in, and with her English skills still shaky, she was not eager to speak out. VMI's American-born women, by contrast, were more inclined to assert their individuality. Nevertheless, some of them also earned respect from upperclassmen—for their good humor, their motivation, their running ability. (Few cadets ever praised any of their peers, male or female, for their intellect.) The triumphs of individual women, however, did not translate into respect for their sex. Every female cadet had to earn her place separately, and this sort of pressure was not conducive to group bonding. Although friendships flourished among small clusters of women, the female rats showed no special allegiance to their sex.

Such allegiance would not necessarily have been a good thing. The goal of the ratline is to mold 420-or-so young people into one cohesive "mass." Separate bonding by any group interferes with that process, and when it came to the female rats, VMI was careful to discourage any form of segregation. When VMI's chaplain suggested hosting a women's tea in the fall of 1997, his idea was quickly vetoed. VMI's administrators informed the chaplain that he could invite male and female rats, but that to distinguish the women in any way would be a mistake. Attention from the media already threatened to drive a wedge between the women and their male peers, and on the rare occasions when the Commandant's office called the women to single-sex meetings—to discuss feminine hygiene or hate mail—upperclassmen assumed that they were being coddled.

Most of VMI's women saw little need for separate social functions. Kelly Sullivan, from Jackson, Georgia, explained at a mid-March press conference that the female rats had plenty of "quality time" in the women's restrooms to get to know one another. But bathroom conversations rarely yield close friendships, and several of VMI's faculty and administrators worried about the long-term psychological effects of the women's position.

"I wonder," Colonel Joyner once mused, standing in his office in the spring of 1998, "if our women will look back twenty years from now and say 'VMI ruined me.' " It was a valid question for VMI's men as well, but Joyner's point was clear. He had been speaking recently with an acquaintance who was one of the earliest female graduates of West Point, and she was concerned that VMI's women should not suffer from the same emotional scars that she and some of her female friends had come away with when they left the Academy. The female pioneers at the federal academies had faced opposition both during their college years and in the military careers upon which they had embarked. VMI's women, by contrast, were fortunate to be entering a military college at a time when women's presence in the U.S. Armed Forces was well established, and for those female cadets who did not intend to pursue military careers, this foray into a predominantly masculine culture would be short-lived.

Still, the impact of being female in a school that had so vehemently opposed the admission of women was bound to have lingering effects— effects that would be all the more profound if the women did not support each other. Identification with one's sex is important for establishing a healthy sense of identity; it was something that VMI specialized in for young men. However, the unusual status of "female Brother Rat" (a status that these women, admittedly, had sought) not only made sisterhood an unlikely prospect within VMI's Corps, it often placed the female rats at odds with other groups of women.

RELATIONS BETWEEN VMI's women and the women from the Virginia Women's Institute for Leadership were especially cold. VWIL—which, as I noted earlier, had been started at Mary Baldwin College during the court case in a bid to provide a publicly funded single-sex military education for women—had not ceased functioning with the arrival of women at VMI. VWIL cadets were still taking ROTC classes at the Institute, alongside VMI's male and female students. Jen Jolin, a young woman who resigned from VMI's Corps in March 1998, described the resulting tensions:

> I remember the first time I saw these "cadettes" in AS 101, about one week after my BRs and I met CADRE. As I sat there with my close-cropped hair, filthy BDUs and boots scuffed from numerous trips up and down Sally Port, I watched the VWIL girls file in. Each walked in with varying lengths of hair, makeup, fresh BDUs, and "shiny-happy" boots. And though I felt superior to these girls, they looked at my female BRs and I and wrinkled their noses before sitting as far away from us as possible. . . .
>
> I finally realized just how different we were on the day the matriculation video for next year's rat mass was being shot. When the camera crew began setting up their equipment around the room, the VWIL girls helped each other fix their hair. I found this particularly annoying mostly because I had no hair to fix. Then, to the surprise and shock of most of the class, they whipped out compacts and applied makeup—during class.
>
> Since then I have fumed about the unimportance of this program . . .*

Jolin received a lot of criticism for writing this piece, especially from male upperclassmen who were dating VWIL cadets. A few VWIL women protested that Jolin's account of their peers applying makeup in

---

* "A Rat's Eye View: VWIL—Need I Say More?," *The Cadet,* October 31, 1997.

class was pure fiction. Nevertheless, Jolin's article illustrated the tension between groups of women at VMI.

Jolin's doubts about the usefulness of VWIL were shared by several women and men who questioned whether the program should continue to exist, now that the Institute had opened its gates to women. Colonel Joyner, for one, believed it was time for VMI to sever its connection with VWIL:

> I think, and this is heresy, that we need to break our ties with VWIL in order to be proud of our women, because the VWIL women are examples of something outside, and the more we treat them as guests, with preference, it shows that our female cadets don't have any preference, and they should. They should have that feeling of community. They should have that feeling that "I'm a VMI cadet and I know that other VMI cadets around me will defend me. I know they are proud of what I have done and I am one of them, and I am part of this family." I don't think they have that yet because they see our cadets embracing other people. . . . The more we defend VWIL, the more we attack what we have here.

VMI had helped to found VWIL under the assumption that women needed a method of education far different from what VMI offered, and the VWIL cadets tended to agree. Most had no desire to join VMI's ranks; they had served as partners in the Institute's legal bid for single-sex education, and they embodied a different approach to military womanhood than the female rats who had chosen VMI. To place these two groups of women together in a classroom, with male cadets observing and inevitably judging the contrasting styles of femininity, was asking for trouble.

VWIL's future, however, would take years to settle. The Institute had obligations to the program that could not be resolved quickly. Besides, removing VWIL cadets from VMI classrooms would not address the larger issue—i.e., the cultural gap between VMI's female rats and women outside the Institute.

Whenever the female rats watched the Keydet cheerleaders (imported, for the time being, from Mary Baldwin College); whenever they listened to women from neighboring schools giggling at VMI's coed

Bible study group; whenever they saw the male cadets' dates waiting outside the barracks in their short skirts and makeup, they were reminded of how different they were from other college-aged women. "When I see the squeelie girls, and what they're doing, I kind of feel like I'm more mature," one woman explained. "I don't know if it's because VMI has taught me to be more mature."

Male rats had similar feelings of separation. A sense of distance from one's civilian peers was an inevitable by-product of the ratline; new cadets often return from fall break complaining about the childishness of their high-school friends, while remaining blind to their own brand of immaturity. For women, this distance was all the more distinct because of their unique position.

Civilian women who visited VMI tended to reciprocate feelings of separation. Some of them looked upon the female rats with pity, telling their dates at the year's first dance that they felt bad for VMI's women because they couldn't wear pretty dresses. Other women viewed the female rats with contempt. One second classman explained that his sister, who had visited him at VMI in the past, was so disgusted with the presence of female cadets that she now refused to set foot on Post.

In most cases the line between female rats and civilian women was not so stark. A few of VMI's women developed friendships with female students at Washington and Lee University, and felt comfortable mingling in W&L dorms. Alexis Abrams, a female cadet from Alexandria, Virginia, had a twin sister attending W&L, but their two worlds were very different. At a March press conference Abrams noted that whenever her civilian friends would talk about their latest, greatest party, she could only think: "Well, we had a great *sweat* party."

If VMI's women felt removed from their civilian peers and VWIL classmates, what, you might ask, were their relations with the female exchange students from Texas A&M and Norwich? In the fall of 1997 eight women and two men from these universities were living in VMI's barracks, eating in the mess hall, attending class side-by-side with the Institute's cadets. With them, one might imagine that VMI's women could have found common ground.

Several of the female exchange students had come to VMI with a specific desire to help the female rats. Brigette Paddock, a junior from Norwich University, was especially enthusiastic:

When I came down to visit and I saw this place, I thought it was great. I knew that great things were going to be happening. I also understood that if the first woman hadn't gone through Norwich, we wouldn't be where we are now. I knew that this new freshmen class, these females, were going to be the first ones coming through. And I was thinking, if there is any way that we can make it easier on that transition, and I could have something to do with that, I want to do it. These women are going to need all the help that they can get, and so are the guys, accepting it. I thought, "if I can have something to do with this, I want to be there."

The male and female cadets from Texas A&M were equally determined to see coeducation succeed at VMI. Their Corps was still suffering the pains of an especially difficult transition to coeducation, marred by the school's original decision to place the women in separate units and separate dorms, and later aggravated by sexual harassment scandals. As one young woman put it:

Even though we've been integrated for twenty-six years, our problems are far from being solved. More importantly, I wish someone would have been around when my school integrated, because I know a lot of the problems we are having today wouldn't even be an issue. Hopefully, by giving up a year of my life, twenty-six years from now, or twenty-seven, these girls' granddaughters or daughters won't go through any of the things that I've had to go through at A&M.

The idea behind the exchange program was to introduce cadets from coed military colleges into VMI's environment, to help answer questions, share experiences, and in the case of the women, serve as big sisters. At the same time, upperclassmen from VMI would attend Norwich and A&M, for a taste of life in a coed Corps.

In theory, the exchange was a great idea. In practice, it was full of pitfalls.

Originally VMI's administrators had thought that the female exchange students might serve as "co-dykes," supplementing the Institute's mentoring system whenever a female rat needed a woman's ear. The dyke relationship, however, is very intimate, and filled with Institute traditions. Exchange students could not indoctrinate rats into the ways of VMI, and by midsemester most of the female rats felt comfortable talking to their male mentors about even their most personal troubles. "I think they underestimated the maturity of the guys," explained Kendra Russell. "Especially the first class."

While this bond between first classmen and their female dykes was very good for VMI, it left the exchange students without a specific function. During the first few weeks of the school year, VMI's Cadre had been eager to use the exchange students as sources of information, but after that point their role seemed unclear.

On one hand, the exchange students served a useful purpose by simply being at VMI. It was reassuring, one female rat said, to know that there were other women in the barracks and to occasionally glimpse an upperclass female out of the corner of her eye. The exchange program also helped to show VMI's critics that the Institute was willing to invite young women and men from other schools to observe and comment on "the assimilation." Throughout the 1997/98 school year, Colonel Bissell held weekly meetings with the exchange students, soliciting their input. "Whenever you try to proofread your own work," explained Mark Andrews, from Texas A&M, "it's kind of hard to find the mistakes. Whereas if you give it to someone else to read, the mistakes are going to come out, and they are going to be glaring."

Still, without a clear sense of direction, the exchange students were destined to step on some toes, especially when it came to their interaction with rats. What part, they had asked upon arrival, should they play in the ratline? Should they "flame" rats? They had earned that privilege at their own schools, but could they do it at VMI?

Initially VMI's cadet leaders told the exchange students to follow the advice of each company commander, some of whom encouraged them to jump right in. But when a few women actually began to yell at the female rats, VMI's upperclassmen did not like what they saw. Jennifer Buettner, from Texas A&M, remembered the results:

> The first night we did showers, and of course showers are supposed to be a very intense time for the rats. So there were several of the girls who were actually in the showers yelling, and flaming

the rats to get them in and out in their allotted amount of time. And that night we had the biggest pow-wow session with every single Commanding Officer and X.O. [Executive Officer] on every level in the Corps. They basically told us that we were not even allowed to so much as instruct the rats, which I was very offended by. . . . But that was their system and that's what they said, and we've really tried to respect that.

Buettner believed that by denying the exchange students any sort of instructional role, VMI's cadets were shooting themselves in the foot. As she saw it, there were many small occasions when the female rats might have benefited from a woman's experience.

One morning in class, Buettner noticed something odd about a woman's belt buckle. She glanced at the buckle of a nearby male, which seemed fine, but when she looked at the waist of another female rat, the problem was there again. Buettner pulled the two women aside and said "Do you realize that you are wearing your belt buckles backward?" Apparently the mistake was a result of the women's pants being folded differently from the men's, something the male upperclassmen had never noticed. Although Buettner asked the women to pass the word among their peers, weeks later she was still seeing women walking around the Post with their buckles reversed.

This was a minor problem, and one that Buettner might have solved by asking an upperclass leader if she, or a VMI cadet, could give the women a quick lesson on their attire. But Buettner had tried that approach on a different subject, with negative results:

We wanted to teach the female rats how to sound off. Men typically have an easy time doing it, whereas with the women you end up getting this really loud screeching voice that just makes our skins crawl. . . . So we went to the class system and the regimental system and asked them if we could please instruct the women as to how to sound off.

With us, we've actually had to learn how to drop our voices a couple of octaves and use our diaphragms and sound off. So we wanted to teach the women, and they (VMI's cadet leaders) said "No. You're not allowed to because that would be instructional.

We don't want you doing it." But they never took care of teaching it. So now they have all of these female rats running around, sounding off like little screeching birds, and all the guys are upset about it, and then they wonder why.

Part of VMI's resistance to the exchange students stemmed from the rivalry between competing cadet corps. The cultural differences between Texas A&M's spit-and-polish cadets, in their knee-length leather boots, and the comparatively lackadaisical VMI upperclassmen, were especially striking. "I've never seen so many shoes that had the heels half worn off of them," one Texas A&M student complained after two months at VMI. "I've never seen so many pants that were wrinkled and had spots on them and loose threads hanging out all over the place, and duty jackets that were dirty, or wrinkled, or the back belt of them was hanging out underneath the duty jacket because they didn't take the five seconds it took to pull it down. Their shirts are always hanging over their belts!"

Another Texas Aggie was dismayed by the habit, pervasive among VMI cadets, of complaining about *everything,* from their classes, to their parades, to their food: "At VMI the alumni are proud, but not the cadets. . . . These guys hate every single day of their lives."

When confronted with these criticisms, one VMI first classman simply shrugged. It was easy, he explained, to keep your uniform spotless and your demeanor cheery when you were, in his words, "a part-time cadet." (Texas A&M cadets are not required to be in uniform while in their dorms or off-campus.) VMI's Corps could sparkle just as brightly as any other on special occasions. But when you lived in one uniform or another twenty-four hours a day, without the presence of civilian students whom you wanted to impress—as is the case at Norwich and A&M—both your appearance and your mood were likely to sag. (When this cadet rose to leave the room, the smudges on his black jacket and white pants were immediately apparent.)

Despite their occasionally disheveled appearance, most VMI cadets insisted on their superiority over the visiting exchange students, stressing that their Barracks was more spartan, their Honor Code more stringent, and their ratline more brutal than anything faced at Norwich or A&M. Many VMI upperclassmen were disdainful of outsiders, who had not proven themselves within the Institute's system. Faced with foreign influences, several first classmen became protective of their rats, essentially saying: "These are our women. Keep away." A few senior cadets went so far as to inform the exchange students that they should not even speak to their female dykes without asking their permission.

To a certain extent, this possessiveness was an unforeseen and very beneficial outgrowth of the exchange program. In their determination to maintain sole authority over their rats, VMI's first classmen pulled "their women" into their emotional enclave. Rather than viewing the female rats as the intruders, those cadets who were especially angry about coeducation tended to direct some of their wrath toward the exchange students. They were the "Other."

The female exchange students served, in part, as the "flame shield" for VMI's women. Some of the harsh comments, glaring looks, and rumors about women's sexual behavior that might otherwise have been directed toward female rats were instead targeted at the upperclass visitors. (One exchange student added that Major Sherrise Powers, the other conspicuous female in the barracks, also served this purpose. Powers' enthusiasm for correcting "unprofessional" upperclassmen had made her very unpopular among the Corps, and as a result she was trying to steer clear of VMI's women: "If I was a lightning rod, I didn't want them to get hit.")

VMI needed lightning rods. As one A&M woman explained: "I'd rather them abuse me, make rumors about me, and pin me down for things I didn't do or say, than taking it out on the girls. That goes back to the whole reason that I am here. I wish somebody had done that for my school." The insults were particularly hard to take, however, when they came from the female rats.

By the end of the first semester it was VMI's women, not its men, who had become especially antagonistic toward the exchange students—criticizing them, snubbing them, refusing to call them "ma'am." Some of the female rats saw no need for an exchange program, echoing the sentiments of those upperclassmen who believed that the Institute could handle coeducation without help. Other women, who did not know about the restrictions placed on the exchange students by VMI's upperclassmen, felt personally insulted when they saw the women from Norwich and A&M keeping their distance.

There was also the very basic problem of jealousy—jealousy at the freedom of the exchange students, jealousy at the modicum of limelight that they diverted from the female rats, and even romantic jealousy. There was a conflict inherent in having one group of women in close-cropped haircuts and unflattering uniforms, constantly on their faces doing push-ups, while another—in long hair, makeup, and skirts—was living on upperclass stoops, enjoying upperclass privileges, and, as the semester evolved, forming friendships with VMI's upperclass cadets. "Those are *our* first classmen," one female rat insisted, complaining about the flirtatiousness of a few exchange students. (According to several VMI cadets, some of the female visitors had come to exchange more than ideas.)

Colonel Bissell viewed the inhospitable attitude of many VMI cadets as an embarrassing by-product of the Institute's insular culture. From all reports, it seemed that those VMI cadets who had gone to Norwich and A&M were being treated like royalty; one VMI cadet had been invited to serve on Texas A&M's regimental staff. By contrast, the one time that a female exchange student took a turn as VMI's Sergeant of the Guard, she was met with vocal resistance, and when the same woman read a list of "turnouts" (announcements) over the barracks intercom, VMI's Corps erupted with shouts and jeers: "Shut up!" "Go home!" The young woman interpreted the roar of protest not to her sex, but to her status as an outsider. But Mark Andrews from Texas A&M, who was in the barracks at the time, looked at the male cadets yelling around him, heard the unpleasant remarks that they would not make to a woman's face, and for the first time since his arrival at VMI, felt a sinking sense of dread: "Just when you thought everything was going well, all of the sudden, at least for the time being, it seemed that everything went out of the window." (In the coming months, whenever one of VMI's female cadets would read turnouts on the intercom, the scene would repeat itself, a reaction one male upperclassman found particularly ironic, considering that in the past, when a cadet would persuade his girlfriend to speak over the intercom, the Corps had often responded with cheers.)

One final snub for the exchange students occurred at VMI's weekly parades, where the Institute's cadets passed in review with their bayonets fixed, while the exchange students marched by with bare rifles—

what one observer called "the castrated look." Parading with fixed bayonets is an honor reserved for military units that have seen combat; VMI earned the privilege at the Battle of New Market. Although the exchange students had joined VMI's unit for that semester, the Institute's first class leaders refused to extend them this honor.

NONE OF THIS MEANT that the exchange program was doomed to failure. Most of the exchange students had come to VMI anticipating some resentment, and they attributed the problems that they faced to the Institute's growing pains. At the end of the fall semester, a few declared that they planned to lobby for features of VMI life at their own schools, and two women asked to remain at VMI for a second term.

At the same time, several of VMI's upperclassmen claimed to have benefited from the exchange students' presence, and by the spring of 1998, even the chilly relations between VMI's women and the female exchange students were beginning to thaw. Once the Institute had decided that the visitors would not play a mentoring role, and that they should simply come to the Institute to watch, to learn, and to make friends, most VMI cadets lost their resistance to the presence of outsiders.

Nevertheless, the first semester of the exchange program showed yet again how tough VMI's female rats could be on other women. In the coming months, one Institute administrator after another expressed pity for the new women who would face the wrath of VMI's upperclass females in the next few years. To some extent, their concern was justified. As one female cadet explained at the year's end:

> I remember reading on an alumni page an article about this girl who is coming next year, that said she can't wait to get here because she is looking forward to us helping her, and she knows that we'll be here for her. And I know that that was a really wrong thing for her to do. Let's just put it that way. I'm not saying that we are going to totally rip everyone apart. But I'm sure there's going to be a little bit of hostility. We are going to have to prove ourselves. . . . We have to prove the point that we can be here and be mean. We are not little girly-girlies.

No, they were not "girly-girlies," but just what sort of women these female cadets would become remained to be seen. Would VMI produce any traits in its women that differed from those found in women at other military colleges? How would a female cadet officer at VMI conduct herself in her relations with her male peers? What impact would the presence of women have on VMI's culture? These were the sorts of questions that could not be settled by the Institute's Blue Book of regulations, nor were they lessons that VMI's women wanted to learn from visiting exchange students.

Ultimately, it would be easier for the Institute to produce a female rat than to create a "VMI Woman." The ratline was designed to downplay gender differences, along with differences in class and ethnicity, and in practical terms, downplaying gender meant molding the rats into one predominantly masculine group. This immersion in a male-oriented lifestyle was something that most female cadets were willing to tolerate for seven months. After that, the distinctions between men and women would emerge more clearly.

In the coming years the "VMI Woman"—if such a being were ever to exist—would have to evolve slowly, as each female cadet's personality responded to the pressures of the Institute's system. That evolution would begin at the conclusion of the ratline, after the annual ritual known as "Breakout."

BREAKOUT

BREAKOUT CAME SLOWLY TO THE CLASS OF 2001. AS FEBRU-
ary 1998 drew to a close, the leaders of VMI's first class were locked in
an ongoing argument with Colonel Joyner about the precise date on
which the rats would claw their way up the muddy face of VMI's Breakout Hill, joining the ranks of full-fledged cadets. Joyner wanted the ratline over before spring break, which was scheduled to begin on February
28. As he saw it, the rats were ready; the first class had nothing more to
teach them; to send these young men and women home on spring furlough still burdened with the shadow of the ratline would be debilitating
to their morale; some rats would not return.

Each year, however, the timing of Breakout must be agreed to by
VMI's senior cadets, and prolonging the rats' misery is one way for the
first class to flex its muscles. In this case, Kevin Trujillo and Tim Trant
held onto their last playing card, delaying the event until mid-March.
When it came to sheer length, no one could say that this year's ratline
had been easy.

Once VMI's Corps returned from spring break, the delays were over.
Of the 430 men and 30 women who had matriculated in August, 361
men and 23 women now remained. One last week of intensive physical
and mental trials lay between them and Breakout, a time known to some
cadets as "Resurrection." The first class had planned a series of events
for the rats, outlined in a schedule that Jon Spitzer had titled "Operation
Spitzkrieg." Among other tests, the rats would endure a sweat party
from each class, beginning with the thirds.

For three consecutive nights in March, shortly after eleven o'clock, the barracks' walls came alive with the shouts of upperclassmen herding the rats out of their rooms, down the stairs, and into the Old Barracks Courtyard. Seen from the upper stoops, the courtyard was transformed into a mass of moving bodies, divided into twos and threes, with rats doing high knees, push-ups, and flutter kicks, while upperclassmen alternated between yelling at them and pushing with them. Although these parties were meant to be exhausting, the mood behind them was congratulatory. "When I got worked out by a third classman," explained Yulia Beltikova, "it was hell. But after that he shook my hand twice. And I was surprised. . . . He said 'You've done a great job.' " The next night Beltikova was worked out by a second classman, who also concluded by shaking her hand, a small gesture of acceptance that left her amazed: "I thought: 'That's twice!' "

Like all of her Brother Rats, Beltikova spent much of her second Hell Week receiving extra attention from her dyke. First classmen traditionally push their rats hardest in the final days before Breakout, and for Beltikova and her co-dyke, this meant performing an exercise called "the killer," starting with twenty push-ups, and one squat thrust, nineteen push-ups and two squat thrusts, eighteen push-ups, and so on. Although the exercise was painful, it was also exhilarating. Cadets often confess to feeling a bond with the upperclassmen who work them out the hardest, something like the ties between an athlete and an uncompromising coach. In this case, Beltikova's dyke worked his rats out in front of his own dyke, so that the three "generations" of cadets could bond together.

As the pressures in the barracks accelerated, some administrators were holding their breath. The last few days before Breakout are always a difficult time at VMI, darkened by the possibility that some irresponsible first classmen might push their rats too far. Stories abound at this time of year of rats dispatched to perform late-night stunts, such as climbing House Mountain after midnight. The first-class privates who run VMI's OGA must be especially vigilant during these days, watching their peers, thwarting planned abuses, and investigating alleged incidents of hazing.

This year, VMI's first class leaders ensured that there would be no hazing on the night before Breakout by scheduling their own exhausting ordeal: a fifteen-mile forced march. The rats had been taken on forced marches before, but this one was designed to be an unforgettable inauguration into a day of misery and jubilation.

AT MIDNIGHT ON MARCH 16 the entire rat mass gathered in front of the barracks with their unloaded M-14s, wearing combat boots and fatigues. It was freezing cold, and their breath rose from the crowd like a mist.

Almost 200 first classmen were gathered nearby—Cadre members, class leaders, dykes who wanted to share the march with their rats. Some had packed cigars to smoke along the way. Others were passing out sticks of gum, knowing the importance of having some small thing to take their minds off the trial ahead.

Several faculty members and administrators also began to arrive, including the Superintendent, the Commandant, a few PE professors, the band director. Those who hoped to preserve their feet were wearing running shoes; those who preferred to set an uncompromising example for the cadets were sporting heavy rucksacks. Colonel Dickson, who was now teaching in the History Department, arrived with nearly eighty pounds on his back.

As they assembled for the march, the rats were arranged by company, with the long-legged men from Alpha in the lead. There had been talk of placing a shorter company at the front, so that the female rats and their shortest male peers would not be struggling to match the stride of the tallest men in the Corps. All year long VMI's administrators had been encouraging their cadet leaders to place women near the front of any marches or runs; other colleges had warned the Institute of the potential for pelvic stress fractures among women who were required, day after day, to maintain a too-lengthy stride. However, on this night the lankiest cadets were setting the pace.

After a pep talk and a few rousing cheers, the columns set out at a slow trot with General Bunting, an avid marathon runner, in the lead in his jogging suit. They trotted down "the Hill" on which VMI stands, taking a back road behind the Superintendent's mansion, past the tennis courts, past a row of faculty houses, following the "Chessie" nature trail to the edge of Lexington, where a two-lane bridge crosses the Maury River. Once over the bridge, the cadets turned left and started along the wooded road that follows the Maury into the hills of Rockbridge County.

At first the mood was jovial. Some cadets were telling jokes. Some were laughing. One first classman ordered Yulia Beltikova to sing the theme song to *Titanic*. Strains of "Near, far, whereeeeeever you are," floated by in a Russian accent.

After the first three miles, the mood was less cheerful. Several first classmen began to complain and lag behind. Before they reached the five-mile point, many decided to drop out, planning to wait there and meet the rats on the way back. For them, Sergeant Major Al Hockaday had nothing but contempt: "I thought that was disgusting. I thought it was horrible." Hockaday had endured much worse than this during his years as a sniper in Vietnam, and he had no tolerance for senior cadets who could not take what they dished out: "I believe in leadership by example. . . . You don't *send* your men out to do something like that. You *take* them out. . . . Here you are yelling and screaming at rats, and now you can't do the one thing you are telling them that they must do. It was shameful, sinful."

For those Institute officers and cadet leaders who continued with the rats, the march was destined to be long and painful. It was 3 A.M. by the time they reached the halfway point, doing an about face at a small Lutheran chapel overlooking acres of stubbly cornfields. Most of the rats were already tired, and there were still seven-and-a-half miles to go.

They got a boost of adrenaline when a local man, angry that his mother had been awakened, got out his shotgun and started shooting. Kevin Trujillo remembered the scene well:

> I was scared. I didn't know what the hell was going on. I ran to the front of the column and I see these locals out there with their car parked in the middle of the march, yelling. At first they were talking to Colonel Joyner, and then he walked off. I went in there and I said "Ma'am, we're moving out. It's OK. We're going to be out of here shortly. I apologize for the inconvenience." And she just started going crazy on me. She told me I didn't respect my mother. There were people out here sleeping . . . She was throwing out the four-letter words like I don't know what. And that just fired up the rats more. They saw this lady yelling at them for something

they were doing, and for some strange reason at VMI, people love that. That makes people a little bit more pumped up. So they started yelling, "Whooo! VMI! 98 + 3" and it carried on through the whole column, and they started getting louder, and dogs were barking. And then they had cousin Jimmy Joe out there, and uncle Bob, and all kinds of people. It was crazy. . . . You get some guy out there drinking moonshine with his shotgun—that's what I was scared about. But once we got past them, it was almost a unifying experience for everyone involved: "Yea, man, we got shot at while we were marching! It's the second time in the history of VMI. We were in battle again!"

Earlier in the week VMI had informed the state police that the march would be taking place; the local residents were supposed to have been warned. But apparently the word hadn't gotten out.

The gunshots were the highlight of the morning until the columns began to approach the Maury River Bridge. Then the snow began to fall.

Snow was the last thing that Colonel Joyner wanted to see. Later that afternoon the rats were scheduled to crawl up a muddy hill doused with tons of water. Joyner had previously declared that if the temperature was not going to be at least 50°F, he might call the whole thing off. The high temperature for the coming day would be 36°F.

As Kevin Trujillo watched the snow coming down he remembered thinking, "Please God, we've got to break these rats out." But aloud, he joked with the other cadet leaders at the head of the march: "Man, I tell you this snow is going to mess up our Breakout plans. It's unfortunate they're not going to be able to do it today." Trujillo spoke these words for the benefit of the nearby rats, then watched the motivation of the entire rat mass sink as his words spread from company to company.

It was 5 A.M. when the columns got back to VMI. The rats lapped the parade ground, holding their rifles above their heads and cheering. After twenty push-ups, they were told to drink no less than five glasses of water, and were sent to the barracks to get one hour of sleep before breakfast. Back in her room, Jennifer Boensch peeled off her boots; her feet had bled so badly during the march that she threw her socks away.

A few hours later the rats were back in the Old Barracks Courtyard, doing push-ups in the snow flurries, chanting and cheering. A few yards away, inside the Commandant's office, the mood was less jubilant. VMI's Post Physician, David Copeland, deplored the thought of college students crawling through puddles of mud in freezing temperatures. Yes, it had happened in the past, but Copeland had never been happy about it. General Bozeman agreed. His track athletes would already be suffering from multiple blisters on their feet; he didn't want them in the hospital with hypothermia as well.

Colonel Joyner didn't like the current Breakout ceremony to begin with. It was a relatively new tradition at VMI—this practice of having rats crawl on their bellies across a field of mud, then inch their way up a thirty-foot, slimy hill, with upperclassmen at the top alternately pushing them down, and then, in a final gesture of acceptance, pulling them up. In Joyner's day, the rats had run up the barracks' steps, from the first stoop to the fourth, while belt-wielding upperclassmen gave them licks along the way. Before that, would-be cadets had wrestled their way each year through a gauntlet of upperclassmen.

VMI's current muddy ceremony had originated in 1981, in an attempt to produce something safer than the previous stampede up the barracks' concrete steps. At the time, the Institute's administrators had been especially eager for a change, since some upperclassmen seemed to be developing the "tradition" of disrupting the annual race up the stoops by pelting the rats with the most disgusting filth that they could gather.

By contrast, the muddy scramble up Breakout Hill encapsulated much that was good about the ratline. In order to reach the top, the rats had to form human chains, climbing up one another's bodies in the spirit of Brother Rats helping Brother Rats. Upperclassmen also helped, reaching down from the top of the hill, sometimes meeting the rats halfway and pulling them to the top. There was an emotional symbolism in seeing mud-splattered upperclassmen extending their hands to welcome the rats into their ranks.

But like the Breakout rituals before it, this ceremony was open to the abuses of mean-spirited individuals. As the rats crawled across the muddy field that lies in front of Breakout Hill, first classmen traditionally impeded them, usually in a benign fashion (rubbing mud on their backs and in their hair), but sometimes in more vicious form (pressing a rat's face into the mud, jabbing a knee into his back, kicking him).

During the planning for coeducation a few cadets had argued that

Breakout would have to change. John D. Cocke IV, '98, penned an editorial for the cadet newspaper in which he asked his fellow students to imagine a young woman suffering from the cuts, bruises, and sprained ankles that had resulted from Breakouts in years past. Imagine too, he said, the sexual harassment lawsuits that could arise if upperclassmen stuffed mud down women's clothes, as they often did to the male rats. "It is simple male brutality in its purest sense," insisted Cocke, and if it continued in a coed environment, he predicted serious damage to VMI's reputation.*

VMI's administrators had fretted over Breakout as they planned for women the previous spring, and although the muddy ritual had its problems, they knew that if it were abandoned, the women would be blamed. Breakout, they had decided, could continue in its present form, so long as the crawl across the muddy field was carefully supervised by administrators, with the number of first classmen on the field strictly limited. The weather, however, remained an unpredictable factor, and that, according to Colonel Joyner, was his primary concern: "I did not want any hypothermia. I did not want any injuries as a result of the fact that we had a system that allowed people to get too cold, and become injured. . . . It was still a college activity, and college activities should not result in physical injury, as far as I was concerned."

And so, as the snow flurries fell on the morning of March 16, 1998, VMI's administrators were caught in a dilemma. The ratline had gone on for too long; the rats were desperate to break out; parents and reporters were already arriving. Clearly, the ceremony could not be postponed. As a compromise, Joyner considered holding Breakout without water. The rats could crawl across the frozen field and up Breakout Hill, but they would not be coated in mud. Joyner realized that this would be an unpopular decision, but given the looks of the weather, it seemed the safest way to go.

At that moment, however, General Bunting entered the room in his jogging suit, clearly invigorated by the outside air: "It's not so bad out there," he pronounced. "Let's do it." And with that, the discussion ended. Breakout would occur in its usual, wet fashion, with one point of agreement: the total time that elapsed from when a rat first dove into the

---

* "The Brutality of Breakout," *The Cadet,* February 14, 1997.

mud, until he or she stood in the heating tents atop Breakout Hill, should be no more than approximately ten minutes. The rats would be soaked, but they would be in and out as quickly as possible.

By 1:00 P.M. (1300 hours, VMI time), the rats were once again assembled in the Old Barracks Courtyard, sporting the same fatigues and combat boots they had worn the previous night. Some had painted camouflage on their faces. Others had written nicknames on their foreheads, or '98 (the class of their dykes) on their cheeks. Kelly Sullivan, from Jackson, Georgia, was wearing the letters "K-I-L-L" in black paint from ear to ear.

A few rats had taped down their pants legs and sleeves and wrapped their ears with duct tape, hoping to keep out the mud. (New fourth classmen typically find mud dribbling out of their ears for several days after Breakout.) Once at the Hill, they would discover that duct tape was not allowed.

Clapping and cheering, the rats trotted into JM Hall for one last motivational speech from Kevin Trujillo, who told them how proud he was of their accomplishments. Then, with a noisy yell, they were back out in the chilly air, headed across the Post to Breakout Hill, one company at a time.

Those parents who had come to witness this minigraduation assembled with binoculars on an overlook several hundred yards away from the site. From that distance, their children were going to look like insects scrambling up an anthill. But VMI had always limited access to Breakout. This was traditionally a closed ceremony, belonging to the first classmen and their rats. The previous year had been the first time that the ritual had been opened to the press, and those few reporters who had attended had overheard the muttered curses of senior cadets who were angry to see their private rites made into a public spectacle.

This year, the throng of reporters was much larger. Mike Strickler, from VMI's Public Relations office, mingled with the press at the far side of the field, making sure their needs were met as they waited for the first wave of rats to arrive.

Before Breakout could occur, everyone had to await the local fire truck. Each year Lexington's volunteer fire department obligingly douses Breakout Hill with several tons of water. This time, when the truck didn't arrive promptly, some upperclassmen standing at the top of the frozen hill began to complain, fearing that Colonel Joyner might have gotten his wish for a dry Breakout. One cadet took out his canteen and poured the contents down the hill, shouting, "We've got mud, bring 'em up here!" Others chanted "Water, water!" and threatened to leave if the truck didn't arrive soon.

When the red engine finally drove up, honking its deep horn, the firemen sent an arc of water shooting high over Breakout Hill. They pointed their hose to the right, then the left, scattering most of the upperclassmen, except for a few stoic souls in rain gear who stood directly beneath the freezing shower. The truck sprayed less water than usual (one more excuse for upperclassmen to complain in the days to come), but the field and hill were nevertheless soaked. By the time the firemen had wrapped up their hose, a light snow was once again falling.

Within seconds the first wave of rats came onto the field. Most had their dykes at their sides, and got a friendly pat on the back before being tossed into the mud. Some dove into the newly made puddles, sliding ten feet forward on their bellies, only to have their dykes pull them back by the ankles. Others, at the command of their first class mentors, rolled all around in the mud, so that they were immediately covered from head to foot. Then the rats began to inch forward, many using only one arm, keeping their faces pressed into their left elbows to shield their eyes from the mud that was being kicked up right and left.

First classman Mike Meads remembered standing with his dyke, Melissa Graham, at the start of the muddy field, hoping to pass along a few traditions from his own Breakout:

I pointed at a spot at about the middle of the mud field, and I wanted her to run and slide and jump right into the pool. "Yea," she said. "No problem, no problem." She was really keyed up. She ran and jumped in the mud.

My dyke, Chuck Story from the Class of '91, he spun me around. He let me crawl toward the hill and then he spun me around, and I didn't realize it, but he let me crawl backward off the hill. So I was doing the same thing with her. She didn't like that. She was kicking, and she started kicking me. And I was just piling mud on her head, and packing mud on her back. Making it a little bit

BREAKOUT 1998. *(Photo by Nancy Andrews. © 1998,* The Washington Post. *Reprinted with permission)*

heavier for her. And she just kept going and kept going and kept going. Pulling herself up the hill, and helping her Brother Rats.

The first rats to ascend the hill were pushed back by the cadets at the top. Soon enough, however, these same cadets were dangling their legs, letting the rats grab hold of their boots, and pulling them up. A couple of upperclassmen had tied their camouflage jackets into a long rope, and were throwing it down to the rats.

Once they had crested the hill, the rats faced another unpleasant surprise—baptism in "the pit," a deep pool of muddy water. Some upperclassmen tossed the rats into the water with a great heave-ho. Other rats, exhausted from their climb, slid into the pool like water snakes. Members of the Commandant's staff were posted in the pit, making sure that no one drowned. One captain in short sleeves stood waist-deep in the muddy water for over an hour. If anyone was destined to get hypothermia, he was the most likely candidate.

As it turned out, no one got sick. Dr. Copeland, who stood at the top of the hill observing everyone for signs of illness, was pleasantly

A FEMALE RAT CRAWLS TOWARD BREAKOUT HILL. *(Andres R. Alonso/fotoVISION)*

surprised with how well the ritual was going. VMI's administration, together with the leaders of the first class, seemed to have been successful in their joint determination to get the rats up the hill as quickly and safely as possible. Several upperclassmen later complained that the Commandant's staff had been overly intrusive, stopping them from performing even the basic rites of rubbing mud into their dykes' hair. A few cadets were so disgruntled that in the coming year, the Class of 1999 would decide to forgo this muddy ritual altogether, opting instead to march their rats eighteen miles from Harrisonburg, Virginia, to New Market, where they would reenact the New Market charge amid the smoke and clatter of cannon fire. For the next few years each senior class at VMI would have to decide upon their preferred format for Breakout.

For now, however, the dazed rats of the newly forming Class of 2001 stood at the top of Breakout Hill, looking like the bronze soldiers at the Vietnam Veterans' Memorial in Washington. Every inch of their bodies was brown and glistening—their hair, their clothes, their eyelashes. As they emerged from the pit they were guided toward coolers, where senior cadets poured Dixie Cups of water over their eyes. Those rats who looked particularly cold were directed toward heating tents, which

A RAT CLINGS TO AN UPPERCLASSMAN'S BOOT. *(Andres R. Alonso/fotoVISION)*

were blasting hot air. Surprisingly few took advantage of the offer. Instead, they stood hugging each other, embracing their dykes, posing for pictures by upperclassmen who congratulated the women just as warmly as the men. Most rats said afterward that they never felt the cold until the end, as they waited for everyone in their company to reach the top—and then they were freezing. Once the last rat from each company had ascended the hill, they hurriedly jogged back toward the barracks for a hot shower.

All-in-all, this was one of the fastest, smoothest Breakouts VMI had ever staged. There were no injuries, no cases of hypothermia. The press was content; they had plenty of photos of mud-drenched women crawling on their bellies. Afterward, reporters interviewed happy parents as the new members of VMI's fourth class stood in the Old Barracks Courtyard in their gray sweats, giving the inaugural Old Yell for the class of "zero one."

RATS CELEBRATE AFTER BREAKING OUT. *(Andres R. Alonso/fotoVISION)*

These young men and women were no longer rats; they were cadets, and with their new status came new challenges.

IMMEDIATELY AFTER BREAKOUT, the first priority for many cadets was to catch up on their sleep. For the past seven months these young men and women had been averaging five hours of sleep a night, often less, with afternoon naps a rare luxury—cadets must roll up their hays and put their racks against the wall on most mornings. Like all rats before them, they had compensated by sleeping in class, in assemblies, in library carrels. (When teaching freshman composition at VMI, I once walked into the classroom to find a young man curled up on the cold floor in the back of the room, sound asleep.) Now, having gone for almost forty-eight hours without rest, the rats could settle into a long winter's nap.

When they woke, they would be free to indulge in the small gestures of individuality that they had suppressed during the ratline. Colonel Joyner was surprised to find stuffed animals and freshly picked flowers in some of the women's rooms immediately after Breakout. Nothing in the Blue Book prohibited such things, but in his four decades of contact with VMI, Joyner had never seen it before.

Earrings, makeup, and longer hair were also in store for several of VMI's women, changes which inspired complaints from some male cadets, and improved efforts at personal hygiene from others. When asked to cite one noticeable change in the barracks after Breakout, one female cadet smiled and noted the whiffs of cologne that were now emanating from certain upperclassmen.

The aftermath of Breakout was not entirely rosy. Having arrived at their newly free and conscious state, some of VMI's women became more aware of the negative feelings emanating from several upperclassmen. During the ratline, these women had kept their heads down, their eyes averted. Now that they could look up and assess the world around them, they were disturbed to note hostile expressions in faces that they passed on the stoops. Was this, they wondered, how these men had been looking at them for the past seven months?

The increased presence of the media immediately following Breakout added to the resentment of many male cadets. Throughout the year the reporters had been patient, waiting until the end of the ratline for a chance to interview VMI's first female cadets. Now that day had come, and the national press corps had once again returned to VMI's gates. In an attempt to be evenhanded, VMI scheduled a press conference on the day after Breakout, featuring equal numbers of male and female fourth classmen. In the weeks ahead, however, VMI's male cadets would be cropped from the picture.

To make matters worse, on March 20 one male fourth classman published a cartoon in *The Cadet* newspaper that many female cadets found insulting. He had sketched a picture of Breakout Hill, with signs directing men to the right and women to the left. On the women's side, a ladder extended up the hill, with Colonel Joyner waiting at the top, saying: "By far the hardest Rat-Line."

"It's just a cartoon," several upperclassmen responded, when they heard of the women's indignation. Someone was always being insulted on the "Beef" page of *The Cadet*. But whereas the newspaper's satire was usually directed at individuals, this cartoon targeted an entire gender, and the drawing was all the more painful because it had been done by a Brother Rat. As one angry young woman put it, the cartoon showed "how little respect the females in the Corps are ever going to get. Not only do we have to prove ourselves to the Corps, as a class, we have to prove ourselves to our own Brother Rats. . . . We don't have any respect whatsoever. . . . Not unless you are really good friends with someone do you feel like it's worth it here."

The cartoon reignited the emotional debates that had raged all fall, and that would surface again the following year. Were men and women getting the same experience at VMI? Had the ratline been watered down for both sexes, because of the presence of women?

For generations, VMI cadets have insisted that "My ratline was tougher than yours. The Institute is going downhill." It wasn't a phenomenon unique to VMI. "Every class at jump school hears that it was a Mickey Mouse class," explained General Farrell. "My class was the last hard class. You're a wienie. It's not hard anymore."

This year's complaints warranted concern only because so many alumni were watching, sensitive to the slightest signs that VMI might be easing up to accommodate women. Those alumni looking for answers, however, were liable to hear a different story from every cadet in the barracks.

When it came to the treatment of men and women, most cadet leaders stressed that VMI's first coed ratline had been gender-blind. "After three weeks into it, it was commonplace," said Jon Spitzer. "I didn't think twice. I saw a rat. I didn't see male or female; their gender was just transformed into one single rat. . . . Now, it's nothing. I don't even think about the last three years of my cadetship, not having women there. And so I think that's truly a testament to how VMI has done things."

Nevertheless, some female cadets doubted whether VMI's Corps could ever be entirely gender-blind. Although they felt that they had been treated fairly, their sex had been inescapable. "When you're a girl, if you do nothing it's still impossible to be a ghost rat," explained Jennifer Boensch. "There are so few of you that you just stand out, and everybody knows your name. . . . When you're a guy you can walk around with 400 other guys and be completely unnoticed. You're just another face that's wandering the stoops. When you're a girl, you walk differently; your hair is cut differently; you're just so much easier to pick out."

The easier you were to pick out, the more likely you were to be stopped on the stoops, quizzed on Rat Bible knowledge, asked for the day's menu, or dropped for push-ups. Ebony McElroy knew all about that. When asked whether VMI's women were getting off easy, McElroy pointed to her own experience, not only as a woman, but as the shortest cadet in the Corps, with a lively personality that immediately attracted attention: "They always say 'You're going to lose in the ratline.' And I lost."

Assuming that VMI's men and women had been treated equally badly, there still remained the question of whether the ratline as a whole had been weakened as a result of coeducation. It was an impossible question to answer, since VMI has no hard and fast standards for every ratline. One first class private, who measured toughness according to group physical activities, stated that the Class of 2001 had endured the most difficult ratline in years, including three forced marches and numerous "stoop runs" (where the rats jog up and down the barracks' steps and around each stoop). But other upperclassmen, who gauged the ratline's toughness according to their own freedom to torment rats, complained that this year's indoctrination hadn't been rigorous enough; the Commandant's staff had imposed too many controls. To this, Colonel Ron Williams, one of the Corps' most highly respected administrators, replied that: "Nothing significant changed . . . The rules we used were the same rules that were agreed to back when Bozeman was the Commandant a few years earlier. . . . I think that was the first time some of those new first classmen had even read the rules. They didn't realize rules were written, probably."

One of the most common refrains of the year was that the ratline had been lacking in intimidation and menacing theatricality; the rats were no longer afraid of the upperclassmen. Whenever Major Sherrise Powers heard that argument, she responded by emphasizing the realities of the military world:

> One of the big things in the military is that you can't lead by fear, because there is always going to be a bigger fear. At the time that you need your people the most, there is going to be a bigger fear, and they are not going to follow you. . . . The cadets who went to New Market, they did not charge those fields out of fear; they charged those fields out of respect for their leaders. That's what I don't think a portion of the leadership in the Corps understands

right now, because for the past seven, eight, nine years they've waddled into this thing of "I've got to make this tough, and tough means I have to make them scared of me." But that's not it. You have to make them respect you.

In the end, all that could be agreed upon was that this year's ratline had been different from its immediate predecessors. The leaders of the first class had spent more time planning for the year, envisioning their ideal ratline. Well before Colonel Joyner had been appointed Commandant, these cadets had opted for a more restrained style of leadership. And according to Kevin Trujillo, their preferences in no way constituted a lowering of standards:

> Just because we are professionalizing, it is not a sign of weakness. There is a way you can discipline somebody without even raising your voice, by simply looking at them, and talking to them, and they will get the point quickly. I think sometimes people respond better to that. We were looking at that quite a bit this year, watching how people interacted with rats, and if we saw something wrong we'd step in and actually do something about it instead of turning our backs. So people thought that the ratline was weakening, but that's a bunch of crud. We weren't professionalizing because women were here. We were professionalizing because that's what we wanted as leaders.

Whether the other cadets in the barracks, and the VMI alumni outside of Lexington, would buy this argument ultimately depended on their individual biases.

Some VMI alumni were convinced of the Institute's downfall as soon as the women arrived and could never be persuaded otherwise. In the fall of 1997 a few of these men went so far as to seek out a member of the Virginia House of Delegates to submit a bill proposing that VMI's name be changed to VMA—the Virginia Military Academy. In their opinion, VMI was now a different school, and beginning in May 2001 they felt that graduates should no longer receive a VMI diploma. These alumni even found a willing messenger for their cause, Delegate Robert Marshall, who offered the legislation to the Virginia General Assembly on January 26, 1998. However, no one expected it to pass. Most VMI cadets dismissed the proposed name change as the epitome of sour grapes.

At the other end of the spectrum, some alumni were very accepting of VMI's first female cadets. When the Class of 1958 met Yulia Beltikova at their fortieth reunion, they were so impressed that they decided to adopt her, offering to pay for her to visit her parents at least once during her cadetship, or to have her parents flown to the United States. (Owing to a lack of funds, Beltikova had no plans to visit her family during her years at VMI.) Their generosity overwhelmed Beltikova, reinforcing one of her most common refrains: "I love American people!"

In the end, the presence of women had no effect on alumni contributions to the Institute. From July 1, 1997, to June 30, 1998, VMI raised $14 million for its endowment, the second highest total on record. The Institute also set another record for its smaller, annual giving campaign, collecting $2.74 million in unrestricted funds. Whether their alma mater was all male or coed, the majority of VMI's alumni would continue to support it.

LOOKING BACK AT
THE YEAR

WITH THE RATLINE BEHIND THEM, THE CLASS OF 2001 could focus on their academic work—a central, but often unheralded, part of VMI life. This book does not deal extensively with academics at VMI, largely because almost everyone on the Post agreed during the planning for women that coeducation would have a more immediate impact on barracks life than on life in the classroom. Nevertheless, one of the most important questions for the 1997/98 school year, and for the years to come, was whether the presence of women would affect the Institute's intellectual life.

Statistically speaking, it was too early to tell. In the initial weeks of coeducation the academic news had seemed particularly good. VMI reviews its students' grades (and sends them home to parents) four times a year, and at the end of the initial grading quarter it looked as if VMI's first coed class might be doing better than usual. The cumulative GPA for the Class of 2001 stood at 2.227 in October 1997, as compared to 2.088 the previous year. 2.227 was in fact the highest GPA VMI had recorded for the opening grading period in the previous fifteen years. (If these averages seem low, that's owing not only to the pressures of the ratline, but to the fact that VMI has none of the grade inflation common at most universities today. There are no pluses or minuses in VMI's grading system, only As, Bs, Cs, Ds, and plenty of Fs.)

Still, by the year's end, there seemed to be no substantial difference in GPAs between the Class of 2001 and previous classes. The women's GPAs were only slightly higher than the men's, and there was no significant gap in the percentage of women vs. men who had made the Dean's list. VMI would have to wait for several years, and introduce many more women into its system, before it could accurately gauge the academic impact of coeducation.

Nevertheless, some professors believed that the presence of women had made an immediate, and very positive, difference in VMI's classroom atmosphere. Most of these professors had never been sold on all-male classes. Although one hears much about the academic benefits of single-sex education for women—some educators believe that women can get more attention, develop more self-esteem, and speak more freely in women's colleges—this line of reasoning had not always applied to college-aged men. Quite the opposite.

When Captain Blair Turner joined VMI's Department of History in 1982, he found the Institute's classroom environment to be reminiscent of his days at an all-male boarding school:

> I taught for years at a large coed university, and one of the first things that struck me when I came here was that there was a completely different atmosphere in the classroom. It was an atmosphere that reminded me of my prep school days. . . . There was just a lot of hooting and macho stuff going on that had nothing to do with being in a classroom. It can all be amusing, and I understood it, and it never offended me, but it was just a certain type of attitude that the cadets generated, and it was constant.

Once the women arrived, Turner sensed a clear change in attitude: "I think it's quieter; it's more serious about academics; it's not so goofy."

Exactly how the women evoked this change was not clear. Some professors in the humanities enjoyed having a new viewpoint to enliven class discussion. "Whenever you get stuck as a teacher," explained Colonel Dickson, "you can always turn to Miss Miller and say 'What do you think about this?'. . . . You can count on the women to say something."

Most of the time, however, the women didn't need to say anything at all. According to a few professors, the silent presence of females was enough to make the male cadets perform. Even in classes with one or two women who rarely spoke out, the male cadets seemed to be more prepared, more serious, less willing to appear foolish.

Some of these changes might have been generated by the professors themselves. One English lecturer, who claimed to see a clear distinction between his coed and all-male classes, acknowledged that "Maybe it's me. Maybe I respond better to a coed class." Faced with female students, many professors had become more conscious of their language and their professionalism; there was less profanity in the classroom, less horsing around. In years past, when faced with a roomful of sleepy young men, one professor confessed that he had sometimes gotten the cadets' attention by using sexual metaphors:

> There's a verb tense, and it's composed of two elements. And what you do when you make it negative or ask a question is you play around with the helping verb, and leave the participle alone. So I would say "Look folks, the participle is a virgin. You don't change her. You don't trifle with her. You do all your playing around, all your trifling, all your manipulation with the helping verb. She's the whore."

With the arrival of women, this professor had switched to the language of chemistry, comparing the participle and helping verb to two molecules. It was a less memorable metaphor, but also less likely to offend.

A few professors, nevertheless, still managed to insult their students. One woman complained that a certain older faculty member had an obnoxious way of prefacing his statements with a thinly veiled form of sexual harassment: "I used to say something else, but now that we have a young *lady* in the room, I can't do that." Another male rat expressed surprise when, in a private conversation, a faculty alumnus informed him that he was not going to get the same VMI experience as his forerunners, because coeducation was changing everything at the Institute. The rat had expected this sort of complaint from upperclassmen, but not from his teachers.

Still, most cadets found the academic environment at VMI to be fair, open, and engaging. The women did not feel intimidated by their minority status; as with their male peers, any classroom inhibitions tended to arise from their position as rats, sitting in a room with upperclassmen. (New cadets at VMI tend to speak more freely in all-rat classes.)

But while the women were not intimidated, they did not always shine. When asked about the academic performance of the female cadets, one professor simply shrugged: "They're assimilated all right. They sleep in class just as much as the guys."

General Farrell had a similar response. In addition to his duties as Dean, Farrell teaches French in VMI's Department of Modern Languages, and unlike some of his colleagues, he saw little difference between his coed and single-sex classes. In fact, he was pleased to find some women performing just as poorly as the men:

It always gratifies me in class to see women who are doing as badly as the guys. That sounds like a dumb thing to say, but you worry about newcomers in a culture like this being obliged to be a credit to their gender, a credit to their race. . . . Somewhere I made a statement that when the first woman gets a "1" [VMI's severest disciplinary penalty below a suspension], we'll know they're OK. In other words, when they can screw up, when they can be imbeciles, when they can be adolescents, when a woman can graduate last in her class and giggle about it, then we're OK.

Whether VMI's curriculum would be altered by the presence of women remained to be seen. There was no sudden move to include more female authors in literature courses, or to delve more deeply into women's history. In the humanities, VMI's course offerings have always been traditional, filled, in contemporary parlance, with the works of "dead white males." Despite the occasional, off-beat courses taught by younger professors, VMI's conservative curriculum was not likely to change anytime soon.

VMI did attempt to bring more female lecturers to its Post during the 1997/98 school year. Most of these women were of a conservative bent, including Jeanne Kirkpatrick, former U.S. Ambassador to the United Nations; Christina Hoff Sommers, author of *Who Stole Feminism: How Women Have Betrayed Women;* and Lieutenant General Carol Mutter of the U.S. Marine Corps. VMI required its entire Corps of Cadets to attend these women's lectures.

There was also a small effort (spearheaded by myself) to update the library's collection of books by and about women. Prior to 1997, anyone searching VMI's library catalogue would not have found Sylvia Plath's *The Bell Jar* or Charlotte Perkins Gilman's *The Yellow Wallpaper*. There was no mention whatsoever of Phyllis Wheatley, and although for years VMI's history professors had included Mary Wollstonecraft's *A Vindication of the Rights of Woman* on their list of recommended readings, they had never realized that the work was not available in their own library. When it came to women's health and psychology, the gaps were equally glaring.

In part, these omissions had been overlooked because VMI cadets have access to Leyburn Library at neighboring Washington and Lee University, a school that specializes in the liberal arts. There, an undergraduate can find more than enough material to research the lives and literature of women and men. At the same time, Washington and Lee's students can walk the 400 or so yards to VMI's Preston Library to find specialized works in engineering and science. With the onset of coeducation, however, VMI would have to pay more attention to maintaining canonical works on the lives and literature of women.

ONE "ACADEMIC" MATTER at the top of VMI's list of concerns related to the VFT. Fitness testing might not seem to be an academic issue, but because physical education is part of the Institute's required curriculum, and because the VFT counts toward every cadet's GPA, the test falls under VMI's academic umbrella.

Throughout the year, VMI had stood firm in its controversial decision to administer the same fitness test to men and women, with the minimum standards remaining at five pull-ups, sixty sit-ups in two minutes, and a one-and-a-half-mile run in twelve minutes. By the year's end, the PE department had compiled data on the men's and women's performance, and the results were pretty much as expected.

At the close of the spring semester, 96 percent of VMI's male fourth classmen were passing the pull-up event, as compared to 30 percent of the women. On the run, the men also had an edge; 97.5 percent of the men could pass the run at year's end, as compared to 85 percent of the women. When it came to sit-ups, the women performed slightly better than the men, averaging seventy-eight sit-ups while the men averaged seventy-six.

Passing an event, one must remember, only gives a cadet a D, and although a few women could perform over ten pull-ups by April 1998, none could approach the seventeen to twenty required for an A. As a group, the women were averaging three pull-ups by April, which gave most of them a zero for that event, and brought their average VFT grade down to forty-nine, as opposed to the seventy-eight average for VMI's men.

The good news among these statistics was that the women showed noticeable improvement over the year. When they first matriculated, only ten percent of them could achieve the school's minimum for pull-ups; by April, thirty percent were passing the event, and many of them who couldn't perform five pull-ups still wanted to try.

Angelia Pickett's attitude was typical:

When I came to VMI I couldn't do any pull-ups at all. I wasn't even close to being able to do them. But I've worked all this year, and my dyke has really helped me out a lot. I would do "personal workouts" with him [all cadets are required, at least twice a week, to spend an hour doing a three-mile run and twenty pull-ups], and he would teach me how to do pull-ups, with different techniques. . . . Where before he would have to help me do all twenty of them, now I can do all twenty of them by myself. I can't do them in a row, obviously, but I can do three, and then hop down for a little bit, and get back up and do three more. I never thought I would be able to do that. If someone had told me at the beginning of the year that I could do my twenty pull-ups by myself in a personal workout, I would have thought that they were crazy. But it's just one of those things, that if anybody works hard enough toward it they can do it.

Despite their general support for a single-standard VFT, in the coming year some of VMI's women would question why the test was included in their PE grade. "I'm taking 'drug and alcohol awareness,' " said Mia Utz, describing her PE course for the spring of 1999, "not drug, alcohol, and pull-up." Gussie Lord added that taking the VFT at the conclusion of a PE course was "like taking Spanish all semester and then having a French exam at the end."*

VMI planned to convene a cadet committee during the 1998/99 school year to consider possible changes to the VFT. (As of October 1999 the test had not been changed.) One option for the future was to lower the women's pull-up requirement while raising their minimum for sit-ups. Another was to give some points to cadets who could perform between one and four pull-ups; at the present time, there is no difference in grade for cadets who do four pull-ups and those who cannot bend their arms. VMI's PE professors still supported a flexed arm hang for women, even though several female cadets didn't like the idea. Many of VMI's women performed flexed arm hangs for their ROTC fitness tests, and they felt silly hanging from a bar while the men nearby pulled themselves up and down. The women also enjoyed the sense of accomplishment and the praise they received from VMI's men for being able to do two or three pull-ups.

In the end, the VFT debate was probably best summed up by one female cadet, who looked at the Institute's requirement for five pull-ups and shrugged: "When you think about it it's not realistic. But we're at VMI. Not everything here is based on reality."

DURING THEIR FOURTH CLASS YEAR most of VMI's women did not seem bothered by the possibility of failing the VFT, in part because none of them were failing their PE classes. During the first semester, when all of VMI's women, and many of its men, took a required swimming course, it was the nonswimmers, not the VFT failures, who flunked the class in droves. Similarly in the spring, when the rats took their required boxing class, all of the women passed, although some of the men did not fare so well.

Few cadets actually enjoyed boxing. It was depressing, one male cadet explained, to wake up on the morning of boxing class and know that within a few hours you were going to get hit in the head. One female cadet added that it was not the pain of boxing that bothered her, so much as the smell of it:

---

* Quoted by Jack Hagel, "VFT Policy Targeted by Justice Department," *The Cadet*, February 12, 1999.

All of the equipment stinks. You put this thing on your head and it's just nasty. You know that 5,000 other people have been sweating into it. The gloves and everything are stinky. We have to wear these big plastic chest protectors, which are really funny, because you put on your sports bra, then you put this plastic insert into it, and it ends up making you look like Barbie.

Unpleasant as boxing might be, it posed no real problems. VMI's boxing instructors had to be very persuasive to convince some women to throw hard punches at their opponents' faces. Most of the women seemed more inclined to aim for their partners' gloves than for their noses. But they eventually got the hang of it, and after the novelty of the first few weeks, during which some male cadets were spotted trying to peek into the boxing room to watch the women jabbing at one another, boxing was a routine part of life.

In fact, when it came to women's sports, the problems that surfaced did not usually stem from VMI's PE classes, but from the large number of women who had signed up for the varsity track team. According to several male cadets, the high percentage of female athletes at VMI was the most divisive issue associated with coeducation.

During the 1997/98 school year, over half of VMI's women participated either in cross-country or track and field—the only varsity sports in which VMI offered a women's program. By contrast, thirty-three percent of VMI's male cadets typically participate in one of the Institute's fifteen varsity sports. When VMI's male cadets saw the comparatively large percentage of female athletes, they assumed that many of these women had joined the track team in order to avoid the most rigorous aspects of the ratline. Some male cadets even suspected that VMI's administration might be encouraging women to sign up as athletes in order to give them an easier ride at VMI, and to reduce the women's attrition rates.

At VMI, there has always been a split between athletes and "nonathletes." Athletes are exempt from VMI's rat challenge program, and many also eat supper after the Corps, missing the early-evening workouts that regularly disrupt their peers' digestion. "It completely changes your day," one woman explained, "when you know you've got half an hour between when you get done with dinner and when study hours start, and that the Cadre are free to do their will with you."

VMI's cadets tend to be particularly bitter toward those full-scholarship athletes who display little interest in the Institute's military regimen—who do not keep their shoes shined and their rooms impeccable, and who, in the most privileged cases, can be seen wearing running shoes in the early weeks of the ratline, while their Brother Rats accumulate blisters in their combat boots and black "low quarters." As a result, athletes are often derided by upperclassmen for "worming out of the ratline."

The criticism is painful for those cadet athletes who work especially hard at their sports, and who make the extra effort to adhere to VMI's military standards. Ben Stanley, a track-and-field rat from Atlanta, Georgia, explained the frustration faced by VMI's most conscientious athletes:

> I would go to practice, and I would run so hard—until I about fell out in the grass . . . I would be hurting so bad, and then I'd get back to the barracks, and you're so dizzy, you can't hardly walk, you've got to go study, and you feel like sleeping but you can't put your bed down, and you might be sweating still. And they'll start yelling at you: "You're a worm!". . . . It really makes you mad to work so hard at something—for me, it's something I've done since I was in the eighth grade, and I put my heart into it. To have someone tell me that I'm just a worm, I'm just riding a permit, it really frustrates you.

The frustration was destined to become all the more acute when gender was factored into the equation.

It did not help that a few women on VMI's track team joked about how much fun they were having, and how they pitied their less athletic peers. Nor did it help that the remaining women who participated in the rat challenge program were so few in number that when their companies assembled for single-sex activities—fighting with pugil sticks, wrestling in a mud pit—the sole female in each group was left standing on the sidelines. On one occasion, after watching the men in her company grapple in the mud pit, one young woman was encouraged to get into the pit by herself. She obligingly jumped in and coated herself in mud, but with no one to wrestle, her good-natured effort seemed rather pitiful. To compensate, VMI gathered all of the female "nonathletes" and exchange students together one afternoon for a bout of wrestling and pugil-stick fighting. The Institute's intentions were good, but the end product had the flavor of a sideshow. It was awkward to watch mud-coated women wrestling in a pit, while dozens of young men, who had been invited to cheer for their female BRs, stood at the sides hooting and yelling.

ALTHOUGH THEY WERE SORELY missed at rat challenge, VMI's female athletes deserved credit for helping to get a women's athletic program off the ground. General Bozeman found it amazing that the Institute was even able to field a women's cross-country team in time for the October 1997 Southern Conference Championships:

> People will never understand what a miracle it was that we were able to run a full team at that conference meet—to get five women, and we actually had six, standing and running at the end of October, after having to do all that training, and still go through the ratline. There is nothing more difficult than being a cross-country rat. . . . Every day I'd just hope and pray they would survive.

To illustrate the unique problems facing VMI's cross-country rats, Boze-man pointed to the women's feet:

> During the summer we had all of our women buy low quarters and break them in. I personally went up and sized them; we went into the military store and they tried on all those shoes and I per-sonally made sure they fit. They took them home to break them in, and I'm thinking, "Man, am I smart." Then we come in here in August, and lo and behold they [the Cadre] throw them in boots. And their feet were just destroyed. I mean there were *blisters*. . . . Erin Claunch, you talk about tough—she had a triple blister. She went up to the hospital and they lanced it, and cut it off, peeled off a layer or two, and she said "I think I can run today." Two days

later she was running like she hadn't had anything like it. If we had had that done to some of our men, they would still be in the hospital.

At the Virginia Invitational Cross-Country Meet, which was held at the University of Virginia in September 1997, UVA's Sports Information Director congratulated Bozeman for producing a team after only one month of coeducation. UVA was then celebrating its twenty-fifth year of women's athletics, and according to this man, it had taken that university four years after the admission of women to field its first varsity team. VMI, by contrast, not only fielded a team, it also managed to beat one Southern Conference competitor during the course of the fall semester. "I have never been prouder of any team than I was of them," declared Bozeman.

Few male cadets at VMI had a quarrel with the women's cross-country team. Most would never have wanted to attempt the many miles of running that these women jogged every day. What bothered VMI's male cadets were those women on the track-and-field squad who competed in less strenuous events, such as sprinting and throwing. Some of these women had little previous experience in track and field, and at a normal college they might not have made the cut for a varsity team. Even some of the male track-and-field athletes, who tended to be supportive of their female teammates, were angry when it came time to hand out varsity letters. "A lot of people are mad," explained Ben Stanley, "because they see women walking around with letters on their jackets, and they got them because they were the only women on a certain team. A lot of athletes who really worked hard, and came so close to getting a letter, didn't get one. There has been some tension from that."

General Bozeman stressed that those women with letters—all of whom were on the cross-country team—deserved every bit of credit that they received. In the year to come the women's cross-country team would finish seventh out of twelve teams at the Southern Conference Cross Country Championships—an impressive performance for a very new squad. (The men's team, by contrast, finished ninth.) Bozeman also noted that some of the female "throwers" on the track team, who had been criticized for having little prior experience in the sport, would be scoring very well in their events by their second year of competition, propelling the women's indoor track squad to a sixth-place finish out of nine teams at the 1999 Southern Conference Indoor Track-and-Field Championships. According to Bozeman, if anyone had cause to complain about varsity letters it was Kelly Sullivan, VMI's All-Southern Conference discus and shot-put thrower, who did not get a letter during her freshman year because the women's track-and-field athletes were not then competing as a team.

Despite these successes, complaints about the large number of female athletes at VMI were not going to go away any time soon. So long as VMI continued to build its women's track-and-field program, Bozeman was going to accept walk-ons, and with few opportunities at VMI for women to join together in any group activity, the track team was going to remain popular. In addition, in order to meet the NCAA Division I requirements for a coed college, VMI would eventually need to field *seven* women's teams. If one estimated that it might take an average of ten women to fill a team (fourteen are required for indoor/outdoor track, eleven for a women's swimming/diving team, five for cross-country), with some women doubling on two teams, VMI would eventually need to attract somewhere from sixty to seventy female athletes. Since VMI did not ever expect to have much more than 130 women in its Corps, the Institute would always need about fifty percent of its women to compete in varsity sports, if it wanted its men's teams to remain in Division I. For the time being, VMI was operating under a two-year renewable waiver of NCAA and Southern Conference requirements, but the Institute would have to show that it was making progress toward building a substantial varsity sports program for women.

Apart from the women's track and cross-country teams, there were not many other opportunities for female cadets who wanted to compete in intercollegiate sports. In the fall of 1997 two women signed up for VMI's swim team and practiced with the male cadets. But although the Institute had talked about finding women's meets for female swimmers, these competitions had never materialized. Instead, the sole female who remained on VMI's swim team in the spring of 1998 described the embarrassment of competing in men's meets and always being the last one to finish, rewarded by the audience with token, courtesy applause.

The other chief athletic opportunity for VMI's female cadets came in the form of women's rugby. Natasha Miller, a young Marine Corps candidate with years of rugby experience helped to build a women's club team after being told by the Institute that she could not play with VMI's men. The male cadets would have been happy to accept Miller; she was a good player, and she had practiced with their club team at the beginning of the year. VMI's administrators, however, believed that rugby was too rough for coed play. They did not want to face the consequences if Miller got hurt. (Ironically, Miller later suffered a minor neck injury in a rat challenge activity, when a few men in her company hoisted her, head first, over a fence.)

In the spring of 1998 two senior rugby players, Sam Bernier and Brad Cook, began to organize a women's team, using Miller as the chief instructor for a group of enthusiastic, but inexperienced, women. Within a few months these women were looking forward to playing against other local colleges, and they were attracting some curiosity among their male peers. According to Kendra Russell, "There are a lot of guys who have said 'If ya'll have a game here at VMI, let us know because we want to see.' I don't know if it's because they are supportive of women playing rugby or because they think it would be funny."

AS THE RUGBY SEASON NEARED ITS END, so did VMI's first year of coeducation. For Kevin Trujillo, Matt Baldwin, and all of the first classmen who had helped to carry out the assimilation of women, this venture into new territory was soon going to be over. For VMI's female cadets the work was just beginning. Over the next few years these women would face the dull grind of sophomore year, the excitement of Ring Figure (a weekend of celebration when second classmen receive their rings), and the challenge of leading VMI's Corps while perpetuating the annual struggle against the school's administration. For VMI's women, each year would bring new questions: What sort of upperclassmen/women would they make? Would they be "flamers"? Would they be friendly? Would they assume leadership roles in their class? How would male rats respond to having female tormentors and female dykes?

No one assumed that the semesters ahead would be easy. If anything, they would be more difficult than the year that was now drawing to a close. With women assuming upperclass privileges there was going to be more friction in the Corps, especially while the last two all-male classes waited to graduate. "It's almost a matter of rolling the dice as to whether it all blows up," explained Tom Craig, a third classman who had spent much of his year volunteering on committees, hoping to help with the successful assimilation of women. The question was not whether troubles would arise, but whether VMI would deal with each crisis effectively.

The epilogue that follows surveys some of the problems and challenges that VMI was destined to face in its second year of coeducation. In the spring of 1998, however, VMI's status was best assessed by two cadets, one male, one female, who offered their personal reflections on the months that had just passed.

The first was Tim Trant, sitting on a sofa in VMI's Protocol Office in late April, thinking back over the previous semesters. Trant came from what he called an "old Virginia family." Since the 1930s every generation of Trants had produced a VMI cadet, and when it came time for him to apply to colleges, Tim knew that it was his generation's turn.

Before the arrival of women, Tim Trant viewed VMI as "a finishing school for Virginia gentlemen." Now, with female cadets firmly ensconced, Trant's greatest worry was that coeducation would eat away at the Institute's core:

What I think has been lost, and this is my concern for the future, are the intangibles about the school which, in my opinion, a lot of males were attracted to the Institute for. Those intangibles are hard to explain, sort of the brotherhood of VMI. The feeling when, late at night after taps, the entire Corps is in JM Hall for some sort of formation, and everybody is tired and has got studying to do, and nobody wants to be there but everybody just kind of makes the best of it, and smiles and cracks jokes. The atmosphere in JM Hall at those times, prior to this year, was to the point of being electric. I don't know whether everybody felt that, but I'm certain that the people that I've expressed this to did. It was just a feeling of 1,300 brothers. As different and diverse as the Corps was at that point, still, being all-male, we all had something special in common, a bond among men that was electric, that created that atmosphere.

This year I have found that to be undetectable in those same situations. There was, I feel, a notable distraction among the fourth class this year, which I attribute directly to the presence of the opposite sex. There was a clarity of mind in the past among rat classes. They were dedicated entirely to being rats, doing the ratline, doing their sport, doing whatever it was that they came to VMI to do—one hundred percent, study, eat, sleep, do the ratline . . . And it may be in a very tiny way, but certainly in a very real way [this distraction] has inhibited this class's ability to fully absorb . . . what it means to be a VMI cadet, what it means to be a VMI graduate, what it means to be a VMI person. Not that there aren't people every year that graduate, that are VMI alumni and cadets in all-male classes, who fail to do the very same thing. But I think that on a larger scale that distraction has inhibited that ability. And because they have failed to absorb it entirely, they will fail to pass it on entirely. Their dykes will fail to get the full appreciation of what VMI is about. It will be lost sequentially, until those intangibles that are so important to VMI will be nonexistent.

Similar fears had been voiced by VMI alumni throughout the court case, and it is difficult to know whether Trant's assessment of the 1997/98 school year was a confirmation or an echo of earlier predictions. But the words of one female cadet, who could not comment on the Institute of years past, and who could not say whether any "intangibles" had been lost, offered some hope for the future.

She was sitting in Sergeant Major Al Hockaday's office in April 1998. Hockaday liked to bring each of VMI's rats into his office at some point during the year, to solicit their impressions of the Institute. In this case, he spoke with the young woman for five or six minutes. She told him about her "VMI Experience," her relations with her roommates and her dyke, how hard it all was. There were times, the young woman admitted, when she was miserable.

But just as she was about to leave, Hockaday asked: "How would you sum it up? How would you sum up your stay here at VMI?" The young woman hesitated. She turned her head and looked out the door that leads to the offices of the Commandant's staff. She stood up and walked to the second door in Hockaday's office, which opens out onto the barracks' first stoop. Glancing to the left and right, she made sure that no one was listening. Then she turned back to Hockaday and left him with one brief sentence:

"Sergeant Major, I love this place."

EPILOGUE:

THIRD CLASS YEAR

On May 15, 1999, two years after the initial admission of women, VMI graduated its first two female cadets. Chih-Yuan Ho, from Taipei, Taiwan, and Melissa Graham, from Burleson, Texas, received their diplomas alongside 223 members of the Class of 1999. Ho and Graham were cheered by a block of their female classmates, who were sitting amidst a packed crowd in the upper rows of VMI's basketball stadium. Their voices drowned out the halfhearted booing of at least one man nearby, and left a positive imprint on an historic event.

The women's show of spirit was a welcome outgrowth of the preceding months. Throughout their first year at VMI, the gender-neutralizing pressures of the ratline had left the Institute's women little opportunity for group bonding. Now, as third class cadets, they had more occasions and inclination to support one another. One week before the commencement ceremony, the women of the Class of 2001 had gathered for a dinner to honor Ho and Graham. For many of them, the friendships growing around that table were becoming their most precious asset.

The female cadets' enthusiasm for their first two graduates was especially important, since many of VMI's male cadets were less supportive. Although VMI routinely accepts male transfer students, it is uncommon for cadets to receive their diplomas after only two years at the Institute. Several members of the Class of 1999 felt that Ho and Graham had not paid their dues.

Male transfer students often face similar criticism. VMI, they are told, is a four-year trial; anything less is incomplete. In this case, the arguments were all the more pointed because VMI's senior cadets took pride in their status as one of the Institute's last all-male classes, and although Ho and Graham would remain members of the Class of 2001 (like other transfer students, they would have to return to VMI the following November if they wanted to receive their rings with their classmates), their participation in the graduation ceremony was viewed by several senior cadets as an intrusion.

Throughout the spring semester handfuls of disgruntled first classmen had threatened to stand up and turn their backs as Ho and Graham received their diplomas. "All it will take is one person to set off a chain reaction" one graduating senior explained. "You'll have dozens of guys turning their backs." When the time came for the women to "walk the stage," however, VMI's male cadets behaved with restraint. The degrees were conferred without a hitch, and VMI's "Family" ultimately found itself less ruffled by the graduation of women than by the Class of 1999's selection for their commencement speaker—G. Gordon Liddy.

Liddy's impending visit had cast a shadow over the last few months of the 1998/99 school year, inspiring dismayed editorials from cadets and alumni who stressed that an unrepentant felon was not an appropriate graduation speaker for a college that touted its honor system as its *raison d'être*. VMI's faculty had been particularly upset, prompting General Farrell to distribute an eloquent e-mail message in which he expressed support for the professors, but warned against the frustrations of "impotent rage":

Before you get to puffing tooooooooo ferociously, you might remember this: you've had four years to impress your values upon these cadets, four years to imbue them with your sense of maturity and proportion, four years to endow them with your dignity and judgement. You've had a fair shot. This is their response to you, whatever it means. You can take it as a repudiation of abstract intellectuality, if you care to, or at least of the stridency and occasional sanctimony with which some of us ply that intellectuality. Maybe. On the other hand, it might be better seen as a last gasp of joyful adolescent titanism and a light breath of relief at an ordeal's end. This is a school, after all.

Liddy's commencement address, which included admonitions on everything from the proper use of the English language to "how to pray so as not to annoy God," ultimately drew a standing ovation from two-thirds of the commencement audience, while others sat with folded hands. The most awkward moment came when Liddy chose to expound on the proper duties of U.S. servicewomen. He celebrated the role of America's military women in World War II, implying that since that time U.S. policy on female recruits had gone awry. Separate billeting, separate training, noncombat assignments—these, in Liddy's opinion, were the best ways to accommodate women who sought military careers. Later, when asked by reporters what advice he would give to VMI's Melissa Graham—who was scheduled, after graduation, to report to Fort Sill, Oklahoma, for field artillery training in the U.S. Army—Liddy replied: "Do your very best to stay out of combat. You don't belong there."*

Although Graham and a few of her female classmates were bothered by Liddy's comments, they soon shrugged them off. School was out, and with the conclusion of the commencement ceremony VMI ended a year that, for the Class of 2001, had not been easy.

Third class, or sophomore, year is traditionally a time of misery at VMI. Most cadets endure the ratline with the hope of better things to come, and are often disappointed to find that promotion to the third class is a very small step in the VMI food chain. Third classmen enjoy few privileges; some continue to suffer the taunts of upperclassmen; and like all cadets, they face the constant threat of being "boned," of marching penalty tours in front of the barracks, of living confined to the Post for weeks, sometimes months, at a time.

This year, the trials of third class life had been particularly acute for VMI's women. Some had expected that with the completion of the ratline they would earn the respect of the entire VMI Corps, and were unhappy to find that those male cadets most stridently opposed to co-education could not be won over easily. Pockets of chauvinism were especially apparent among members of the Class of 2000, who publicly relished their position as VMI's "Last Class with Balls." Some of them

---

* Quoted by Sherri Tombarge, "First Women Graduate from VMI," *Lexington News-Gazette,* May 19, 1999.

had engraved the letters "LCWB" inside their class rings; many others had engraved a circle and arrow beside their names. The cadet committee which designed the ring had added an arrow to the last zero in "2000," to symbolize the class's manhood. A saber with a shako resting upon it had also been incorporated in the ring's design, recalling the salute to VMI's all-male tradition that had been staged by the Class of 1997 two years earlier.

VMI could not assume that this brand of defiant masculinity would fade from its Post upon the graduation of its last two all-male classes. The Institute's dyke system enables first classmen to instill their prejudices in new generations of rats, and this year a few cadets seemed intent on propagating their opposition to coeducation. "It's frightening," Charlie Bunting explained, looking at the classes before him. "It's like some sort of vindictive rebellion against the Supreme Court at the expense of their own alma mater. If they don't bring up their dykes right, and teach them that they better go ahead and take ownership of this process, then we're going to have some serious problems and they are going to be really hard to fix. Once something gets sunk into a dyke line, it's really hard to correct it."

There was little VMI's women could say or do in response. During the previous year, the Institute's female cadets had enjoyed the protection of carefully chosen dykes who had shielded them from the negativity of some upperclassmen. Now, there were no big brothers to fight the women's battles. The arrival of thirty-three new female rats did little to help their cause, since rats and thirds are traditional opponents, and the new women had to contend with their own problems, as we'll see below. VMI's female pioneers did benefit, however, from the efforts of conscientious male peers, who tended to speak out when they saw problems arise.

During the fall of 1998, Colonel Bissell estimated that ninety percent of the complaints his office received were from young men looking out for the interests of female cadets. While most of the Institute's women tended to endure the occasional insults of VMI life with stoic resolve, many of their male peers were ready to speak up whenever they saw a female cadet being unfairly singled out in the mess hall, or subjected to inappropriate language. It was heartening for VMI's assimilation office to encounter so many male cadets committed to the successful integration of women. The bad news, however, was that this office received over twice as many complaints in the fall of 1998 as it had at the same time the previous year. Of course, with twice as many women on Post, gender-related problems were bound to multiply, and during their rat year, the male and female members of VMI's first coed class had been less inclined to assert themselves. A rise in complaints was an inevitable part of the process, and the assimilation office took it as a good sign that the cadets felt free to air their grievances.

The cadets' complaints ranged from trivial concerns to serious allegations. There was, for example, the matter of VMI's cheerleaders, a minor issue that attracted considerable media attention. In previous years VMI had imported female cheerleaders from nearby Mary Baldwin College, pairing these women with upperclass cadets to support the school's football and basketball teams. VMI's assimilation plan had recommended that the Mary Baldwin cheerleaders be phased out gradually, while the Institute gathered upperclass female cadets to fill its own squad. Shortly before the 1998 football season began, however, VMI opted for a more sudden change. VMI dropped the cheerleaders from Mary Baldwin, recruiting instead a group of incoming female and male rats, whom they sent to a five-day cheerleading camp. Two third class women and a handful of upperclassmen agreed to lead the novice squad, and by the opening kick-off of the 1998 season, VMI was sporting its own, homegrown cheerleaders.

Unfortunately, they were not well received. When the Institute's Corps of Cadets (who are required to attend every home football game) found themselves facing a row of female rats in short skirts, bare midriffs and buzz cuts, their reaction was vehement. At game after game, they laughed, they hissed, they jeered. Charlie Bunting, who had been elected Class President the previous spring, voiced the common sentiment: "The idea that a rat is going to try to stand in front of me and make me feel better about my school, when they have no idea of what they're getting into, and they haven't proven themselves to be a part of it yet—it's putrid, it's stupid, and it's ineffective." VMI's third class women were equally dismayed. Several complained that the rat cheerleaders were an embarrassment to VMI and a blow to the assimilation cause.

Some of the arguments against the cheerleaders were contradictory. On one hand, several upperclassmen claimed that the contrast between the female rats' feminine outfits and masculine haircuts made them look grotesque. But at the same time, many of these cadets complained that the cheerleaders were too attractive; their short skirts provoked sexual feelings that were inappropriate for upperclassmen to feel toward rats. A petition that circulated throughout VMI's barracks stated, among other grievances, that watching the rat cheerleaders provoked "sexual tension" among the Corps. The cheerleaders aggravated the situation by routinely performing a cheer called the "Keydet Rumble," in which they all, male and female, turned their backs to the Corps, bent over, and wiggled their bottoms at their fellow cadets.

Had the football games been more compelling, the cheerleaders might have attracted less notice. But VMI's team floundered through its 1998 season with only one win—a record particularly disappointing at a school where each football victory brings a temporary suspension of the ratline and the granting of weekend privileges. As the losses mounted, so did the Corps' frustration.

VMI's upperclassmen were especially disturbed because in the past, cadets had been prohibited from participating in club activities (such as cheerleading) during the first semester of the ratline. Now, with their new club "permits," VMI's cheerleaders (along with a handful of rats in other club activities) were often eating separately from the Corps and missing rat challenge events. In the eyes of many upperclassmen, the cheerleaders were "worming" out of the ratline.

The cheerleading debacle reached its zenith after a late November football game, when the cadets booed the cheerleaders and pelted them with peanuts. A few days later the Corps found its poor behavior detailed on the front page of the *Washington Post*. The article inspired a crackdown by Institute administrators and generated a few chagrined editorials in the student newspaper. Throughout the coming basketball season, hostility toward the cheerleaders would be minimized, and VMI determined that it would not use rats as cheerleaders in the future.

Cheerleading is, of course, a minor affair in the sphere of college life, but VMI's cheerleading woes were symptomatic of two larger problems—the question of how to introduce the trappings of femininity into the Institute's world, and the perils of changing any aspect of VMI's routine throughout the early years of coeducation.

During the previous year, while VMI's female rats had maintained their androgynous appearance, gender differences had been muted. Now they were more visibly apparent, not only in the form of cheerleaders, but in the debate that arose when a few third class women began to wear skirts, and, most notably, in ongoing arguments over the cut of the women's hair.

Throughout the 1998/99 school year, haircuts remained a thorn in VMI's side. Most of the Institute's third class women agreed that all female rats should suffer the same close-cropped style that they had endured. They were unhappy, however, with their own jaw-length locks, which proved just long enough to hang in their faces, without being adequate either to braid or to arrange neatly with barrettes. Although Colonel Bissell noted that the jaw-length cut had been approved by VMI's women the previous year, it seemed that the style had been better in theory than in reality. U.S. servicewomen are allowed to grow their hair much longer, so long as they put it up while on duty. Why, several women asked, did VMI have to be different?

By the end of the school year, the Commandant's office seemed likely to grant the women's wish for longer hair, despite the objections of many male cadets who viewed the haircuts as a matter of principle. During the planning for coeducation, VMI's administration had advocated a philosophy of minimal change. Now, the male cadets argued, changes were creeping in.

In this particular instance, VMI's Assimilation Office sympathized with the male cadets. Colonel Bissell had been selling the Institute's alumni on the idea that nothing significant would change with the arrival of women, and although life in VMI's barracks is constantly subject to flux, with new administrators advocating new practices, Bissell would have preferred for any alterations to wait until after the first class of women had graduated. But although VMI remained committed to its major promise—the continuance of its adversative method—changes were coming in more subtle matters, whether in the form of service style haircuts or in VMI's revised policy on club permits for rats.

Even when the new policies had nothing to do with women, VMI's female cadets were easy targets for blame. When the Class of 1999 settled upon a new format for Breakout, substituting a march to New Market and a smoke-filled charge across the "Field of Honor" for the usual muddy scramble up Breakout Hill, several alumni attributed the change to the presence of women. Similarly, when Colonel Joyner proposed a new rooming scheme for the fall of 1998—thirds through firsts would now live according to company, instead of being allowed to choose their roommates from their entire class—a few female cadets received antagonistic phone calls from VMI alumni during the summer, blaming them for the upcoming change. Although Colonel Joyner eventually chose to apply the policy only to sophomores, quelling the complaints of VMI's top two classes, the women were still in an awkward position. Since most companies had too few females to occupy VMI's typical four-man room, third class women from various companies were grouped together, with their rooms scattered throughout the barracks.

One additional problem facing VMI's women came as they began to exert authority in the barracks. At the beginning of the school year a few third class women met resistance when they attempted to discipline rats. In one case, a female cadet who confronted a male rat was thwarted by one of her own male classmates, who told the rat that he didn't need to stop for a woman. On another occasion, when a third class woman tried to stop a male rat, the young man simply walked away, explaining later that his dyke had instructed him to ignore the female cadets.

Colonel Bissell responded to the problem in characteristic fashion—by forming a committee. He instructed a very capable third classman, Brett Carter, to bring together approximately eighteen of his classmates, male and female, to discuss assimilation issues on a weekly basis. Carter was told to deliberately include male cadets who opposed the admission of women into VMI, so that the committee might serve as a forum for hashing out major grievances within the Class of 2001. Although the initial meetings were tense, Carter found that by breaking the committee into smaller units of six or seven cadets, they were able to form an amicable and constructive group. The problems with disrespectful rats soon disappeared, and although Carter's committee could not claim sole credit for this improvement, their work did serve to ease tensions among the Class of 2001.

Still, the success of this committee did not translate into Corps-wide acceptance of the female cadets' growing authority. In the spring of 1999, when VMI's first two women rose to the level of Cadre—after male corporals who outranked them dropped out of the Cadre for disciplinary and personal reasons—VMI's cadet newspaper published a front-page article questioning the qualifications of Angelia Pickett and Mia Utz, charging that they had been placed on the Cadre by the Institute's administration. The paper also attacked those male cadets who had made rank despite failing the VFT, but in the case of Pickett and Utz, their gender seemed to attract the criticism. (Utz could pass the VFT without a problem.) In subsequent letters to the editor, several male cadets insisted that Pickett and Utz were deserving candidates who had advanced up the ladder of company corporals in routine fashion. Nevertheless, the article once again demonstrated the resistance that some cadets felt toward the image of women giving orders to men.

These problems were not unforeseen. They existed at all military colleges, and VMI had no easy remedy. In accordance with its assimilation plan, the Institute scheduled sexual harassment training sessions for its entire student body in the fall of 1998, hoping to promote mutual respect among its cadets. VMI divided the Corps into four groups, each of which was required to attend a presentation given by Dr. Chris Kilmartin, a frequent lecturer on the subject of gender relations. VMI also required all of its second classmen to attend a special leadership training seminar in March 1999, consisting of three ninety-minute sessions on interpersonal skills, consensus building, and how to create a foundation of trust among one's workers/recruits. The sessions were led by some of VMI's most successful alumni—men who came from corporate, military, athletic, and ministerial backgrounds. Anne Whittemore, a lawyer and member of the Institute's Board of Visitors, also headed a seminar. One goal of these meetings was to prepare VMI's rising first classmen to lead a coed Corps, and to enter a coed work force, but the school kept the words "sexual harassment" out of it, knowing that the cadets were becoming inured to the term.

While the sessions went well, VMI could not inoculate its Corps against the offenses of individual cadets. By the end of the 1998/99 school year, VMI had handed out two suspensions and a "1" to male cadets for sexual harassment, and it had drummed out its first woman for an honor offense. Meanwhile, the most serious incident of the year arose shortly before graduation, when VMI dismissed one of its top cadets—the rising senior who was scheduled to serve as Regimental

Commander and Vice-President of the Honor Court in the coming year—for using his perceived powers to try to establish romantic relationships with several female freshmen. The cadet's disgrace came as a particular shock to General Bunting, who had placed his trust in the young man, citing him among a list of friends that appears in the acknowledgments of his book, *An Education for Our Time.*

All in all, the events of the 1998/99 school year showed that despite its careful planning, VMI would have to contend with the same sorts of problems that have faced military colleges nationwide. The road would inevitably be bumpy—it was difficult to administer any system of education in which young men and women can exert such substantial power over one another—and in the future VMI would have to move forward without the help of Colonel Bissell. In April of 1999 Bissell announced that he would be leaving VMI to devote himself fully to his role as Commandant of Cadets for the Virginia Women's Institute for Leadership at Mary Baldwin College. That single-sex program not only continued to exist, it continued to attract more women than VMI. In the fall of 1999, VWIL welcomed fifty new cadets into its ranks, while VMI in a disappointing setback, enrolled twenty-eight. Although VMI was no longer helping to fund the VWIL program, the State of Virginia continued to support it, a fact that left many VMI cadets philosophical. After their school's long struggle to remain all-male, the legacy of VMI's legal battle seemed to be that Virginia would offer single-sex military education to its daughters, but not its sons. "Was that fair?" the cadets often asked. Perhaps. Perhaps not. But in the end, the most important questions facing VMI would have little to do with VWIL. Instead, as VMI's administrators, faculty and cadets looked to the future, they were curious to see whether all of their discussions about gender, and all of the lessons they were learning about the ups and downs of coeducation, would ultimately result in a college better prepared to train officers for a coed military, and better suited to produce citizens for a country that continued, decade after decade, in a state of transformation.

AFTERWORD:

VMI REVISITED

"IN THE BEGINNING IT WAS LIKE DRIVING DOWN AN INTERSTATE covered with ice, and your hands were on the steering wheel, and you had to concentrate all the way, simply because you were so worried about what might go wrong, or what had gone wrong."

General Bunting was sitting in his office in October of 2000, looking back at VMI's first year of coeducation. "In that atmosphere, tiny things assumed an almost cosmic significance. You know the metaphor of the sacrament being an outward sign of an invisible grace . . . [that's how it was with] the length of a woman's hair. All those things were cosmic."

Now, in its fourth year of coeducation, VMI was no longer operating in a state of crisis management. The Class of 2001 was presiding over life in the barracks, and in Bunting's opinion, this fact marked a crucial turning point in the college's history: "We now have a school which is fully coeducational in the sense that the seniors have only known VMI as a school that has had women. The atmospherics are completely different from last year and the two years before that. Coeducation—and that word is now used forthrightly instead of the term 'assimilation'—is now a settled fact of life at VMI. People are comfortable with it. People may or may not like the concept, but it is now a fact of life. . . . I would say that the school is now fully and amicably coeducational. Period."

Clearly, Bunting was eager to put the day-to-day concerns of coeducation behind him. He was a man who, as he often explained, tried to live life in the present. For now, the task at hand was the public launching of a $175 million capital campaign, designed to bolster VMI's academic programs. Outside on the parade deck, grounds crews were pitching seven white tents for a gala dinner, where hundreds of VMI's top contributors were scheduled be plied with food and wine and fundraising pitches. It was a far cry from the fall of 1997, when the same parade ground had been covered with journalists and television news teams. The switch from reporters with their insistent questions, to alumni with their powerful checkbooks, typified the shift in VMI's energies. Within the administrative offices of Smith Hall, gender issues were no longer a priority.

The story was different, however, within VMI's barracks, where women still constituted only five percent of the Corps. In conversations with male and female students, the common refrain seemed to be that while VMI was making progress, the school was far from being fully coeducational, and whether or not it was amicable depended upon what class you were in.

For the Class of 2001, the news was generally good. Hostility toward women seemed limited to pockets of cadets—"the womanhaters," as they were sometimes called—men who were easily identified, and carefully avoided. Their presence had little impact on the women's spirits. Several of VMI's senior women expressed a newfound sense of confidence and ease. Perhaps, they explained, it was merely the benefit of being first classmen in a hierarchical system. When you were at the top of the food chain, the occasional glare or muttered comment was easily sloughed off.

VMI's senior men echoed the same feeling that, when it came to coeducation, the Class of 2001 was on the right track. Elijah Ward—who was now a member of VMI's regimental staff, and a devout leader of what cadets called "the chaplain's God Squad"—noted that this year much of the grumbling about women had subsided. Complaints that, he confessed, used to be rampant among his classmates behind closed doors, were now rarer. He attributed the change to the passage of time; the presence of women had lost its novelty.

Some credit also had to go to the determination of Ward's female classmates, several of whom held positions of rank. Most notable was Erin Claunch, a physics major from Round Hill, Virginia. During her time at VMI, Claunch had been a top scholar, a cross-country runner, an ace at pull-ups (that odd measure of female virtue at VMI), and the founder of an equestrian club that had recently borne fruit in the formation of a mounted color guard. Now she was serving as commander of VMI's second battalion. At Friday afternoon parades Claunch could be seen dressed in her crimson sash, sword, and plumed shako, shouting orders to the 600 cadets under her command. The uniqueness of her position had caught the media's imagination. *Talk* magazine had featured Claunch as one of the top ten women most eligible to marry Prince William.

One of Claunch's roommates, Kendra Russell, provided another example of a woman who had made a positive contribution to VMI. She too was an outstanding student, who had chosen to devote some of her intellectual energies to the job of editor-in-chief of the cadet newspaper. The results were visible. Although its irreverent humor still served as a thorn in the side of VMI's administration, the paper's grammar and spelling were no longer an embarrassment to the school's English Department.

Cadets such as Claunch and Russell had no hesitation recommending VMI to other women. Russell had even recommended the Institute to her younger sister. The best thing about VMI, she explained, was the closeness of the friendships that were forged within the school's rigid system: "I wouldn't give up the friends I've made here for anything in the world." But not all of VMI's senior women were willing to endorse the school.

One female private, who claimed to have no regrets about attending VMI, nevertheless shook her head sadly when asked if she would recommend it to others. Being part of the first coed class had been something special, she explained. It was not like attending college; she felt she had been doing something important for women, something historic. But that original luster was gone and now she would not promote VMI to women or men. Regardless of gender issues, the school had "too many problems." There was "too much misery."

Misery had always been a factor in VMI life, lamented by generations of young men who had condemned the place as a prison. The real question was how these young people would view VMI ten years hence. In the past, men who had hated the Institute during their cadetships had often returned for reunions brimming with nostalgia, heralding their time at VMI as the most valuable experience of their lives. Whether any women would respond in similar fashion remained to be seen.

Another key question for the future was whether the successes of VMI's first coed class would be shared by any classes to follow. Most of VMI's senior women seemed confident that their class was instilling a positive approach toward coeducation in the current rat mass, but when they looked at the class immediately behind them, they just shook their heads.

Negativity toward women was more widespread and more open among VMI's second coed class. According to one male member of the Class of 2002, his peers seemed split between a right wing and a left wing, with no middle ground.

Problems tended to surface whenever male second classmen were faced with the fact of female difference. One female member of 2002 described the response when, after more than two years at VMI, she decided to wear a skirt:

> I walked out of my room, and my room is right between all of these guys that are very anti-female. It just happened to work out that way. They saw me and I could hear them cussing and making all of these comments. And as I walked down the stairs every single person just turned and looked at me, like they just couldn't believe it. And I thought: "This is so ridiculous. This is so petty. This is just a skirt." I just felt like saying: "The maturity level is not there."

This young woman did not hold a grudge against VMI. Her day-to-day life at the school, she explained, was "not so bad." She had "plenty of male and female friends," especially among women in the class above her, and overall she would not "take away a negative experience." Her years at VMI, however, had opened her eyes to the face of human prejudice: "If you stay it makes you a stronger person, because you learn how to not let that kind of thing bother you."

According to most cadets, the problems among the Class of 2002 stemmed from the atmosphere within VMI's barracks during the school's second year of coeducation, when these cadets had been rats. "I

look at that year and I really feel lost," explained Tennille Chisholm—
who was now a member of VMI's Officer of the Guard Association, and
an outspoken advocate of VMI. "To see people's real opinions of you
being there, taking your blinders off, realizing that your dykes weren't
there to protect you anymore, was a bit of a shock, and very scary."

Chisholm knew that third class year was traditionally a time of hardship at VMI. But the normal pressures of sophomore year had been
exacerbated by a resistance to women that seemed to come from all
fronts:

> I think it was from everybody. Rats who didn't want to drop for
> you, didn't want to listen to you. Upperclassmen who were telling
> their rats "Don't drop for women." Your BRs who felt that they
> had been born a year too late were voicing their opinions. . . .
> There was chaos coming from all directions.

Part of the problem went back to VMI's year of planning for coeducation. As Elijah Ward viewed it, VMI "had every contingency planned
for women as rats, and none once women were upperclassmen." He
cited the debates over skirts and haircuts that lingered throughout his
sophomore year as evidence of a lack of preparedness on VMI's part.
More importantly, VMI had not primed the Class of 1999 (who were
seniors during the second year of coeducation) to serve as leaders of a
coed Corps. Whereas the Class of 1998 had been encouraged to take
ownership in "the assimilation," recognizing that their legacy would
depend on its success, for the Class of 1999, their defining feature was
their maleness, and they had little desire to emulate the class before
them.

Under their watch, resentments toward women that had festered the
previous year boiled to the surface. Erin Claunch remembered the "verbal wars" that used to erupt between her room and the seniors on the
first stoop. The confrontations were triggered whenever a woman made
announcements on the barracks intercom. First classmen would invariably yell for the woman to shut up, prompting Claunch and her roommates to respond with the same admonition. Soon a barrage of insults
would be flying back and forth, an occurrence that, explained Claunch,
"would probably happen once a week." The exchanges might have

seemed humorous, were it not for the surrounding atmosphere of tension. According to Claunch, her sophomore year was the time when women received "the most angry stares," and were most often derided as "sluts."

One might have expected VMI's administration to silence all barracks shouting matches. But that, according to one member of the Class of 1999, would have made matters worse. Edicts from the Commandant inspired resentment from male cadets, some of whom already complained that the administration was too easy on VMI's women. And so, while some observers charged VMI's administration with complacency, others charged it with favoritism. The result was an atmosphere for women that was difficult for thirds, and worse for freshmen.

According to one male member of the Class of 2002, VMI's first classmen actively "discouraged" his female Brother Rats. Cadre members would often segregate women from men, in order to concentrate their negative attention upon the female rats. These gender-targeted workouts were not allowed under VMI's rules, and upperclassmen who were caught could be severely punished. Nevertheless, the young man explained, cadre members who were intent on targeting women would simply wait until there were no VMI officials in sight.

A more grotesque example of "discouragement" was experienced by the women in Golf company, who returned to their room one afternoon to find it defaced with human excrement. The guilty cadets were never caught, but the incident typified the hostility women faced in one of VMI's two companies that had remained all-male the year before.

Some of these problems might have been avoided if the women of 2002 had been assigned dykes who were prepared to champion their cause. The previous year, VMI's first group of women had benefited from the support of senior mentors handpicked by the administration. Within the Class of 1999, however, many cadets had not wanted to mentor female rats, and some who had been assigned women were deliberately antagonistic. Erin Claunch recalled the experiences of one young rat who was assigned to a room with men who "absolutely hated her." "They would be rude to her, they ignored her. They would send her out on the stoops to be worked out by somebody every day. They would send her out on the stoops to be yelled at by someone. It was absolutely horrible what they did to her. . . . But she stuck it out. She's still here."

Other women had not stuck it out, in part because of the most disturbing incident of the year, when VMI's rising Regimental Commander was expelled after it was discovered that he had been using his status as an honor court prosecutor to approach female rats. According to one young woman, this second classman used to call her to his room frequently, on the pretext of discussing honor court business. She had thought little of it, since, in her case, the encounters were limited to offers of conversation and food. But when she learned that the young man had been summoning other women to his room, using honor court business as a ploy for establishing romances that had sometimes lasted for weeks, she had been struck with a sense of her own naivety: "You realize that when you're a rat you don't really know what's going on at all, and people can lead you to believe whatever they want."

It would be unfair to blame all of the difficulties in the 1998–99 school year upon male cadets, or upon the VMI system. Complicating the whole scenario were problems among the new women, several of whom had a knack for attracting negative attention. Complaints against the female rats throughout the 1998–99 school year ranged from excessive flirtatiousness, to excessive demerits, to a penchant for body piercing. "I was hoping their class would be more focused on learning the system," explained Tennille Chisholm, looking back at the women who had succeeded her group. "Instead, they appeared to have preconceived ideas painted by the media. They were like: 'We're here and we're going to let everybody know we're here.'"

To make matters worse, the women of the Class of 2002 were very divisive amongst themselves—a fact obvious enough to be noted by administrators, male and female cadets, even women within the class. Apparently the female rats were split into unbreakable factions.

Perhaps these problems were predictable. Every expert with whom VMI had consulted had warned that VMI's greatest challenges would not come in the first year of coeducation, when the school was on its guard. They would arise in subsequent years, when the administration was less vigilant, when the women were less stoic, and when resentments that had been suppressed under the watchful eye of the media began to surface. Still, the predictability of the problems did not make them any less painful.

Of the thirty-three women who matriculated with the Class of 2002, only nine remained in the barracks by the fall of 2000. Three had graduated the previous spring, and another had been suspended. If the class lost no more female cadets, it would graduate thirteen women—a sixty-one percent attrition rate.

This level of attrition for women was not unknown at military colleges. As noted earlier in this book, Texas A&M's Corps of Cadets lost fifty percent of its freshmen women during one particularly bad year, and VMI had been expecting attrition rates to be higher for women in subsequent classes than they had been for the school's first group of females. (As of November 2000, the Class of 2001 was on track to graduate nineteen of its original thirty women, with the possible return of a twentieth woman who had left for academic reasons. This attrition rate was close to the traditional numbers for VMI's men, and lower than the school had anticipated.)

The central question for the school's future was whether the unusually high attrition for the women of 2002 would prove to be an aberration. General Bunting, for one, did not seem ruffled by the numbers. When asked if he was concerned about the rate of attrition among VMI's second group of women, his response was philosophical: "A college lasts for four hundred or six hundred or eight hundred years. You can't judge these things year to year." Indeed, there were signs that when it came to problems with coeducation, the worst might have passed.

One might reasonably have expected the troubles in VMI's second year of coeducation to have resurfaced the following fall, since the seniors that year were particularly vocal about their status as the "Last Class With Balls." But according to Elijah Ward, by the time the Class of 2000 had taken over, the tide had already turned:

> 2000 talks about being the last all-male class, but really 1999 was the last time that you really had that overwhelmingly male atmosphere in barracks. Once 2003 [the rat mass mentored by the Class of 2000] was coming through, coeducation was here to stay and I think the grumbling stopped a lot. For our rats, I think they are not even noticing things like gender issues.

By November of 2000, VMI's hemorrhage of female cadets seemed to have been staunched. Attrition for VMI's third female cohort stood at thirty-two percent, and the school had lost only one of its new female rats.

This did not mean that the problems had evaporated. There remained one issue that was particularly troublesome in the minds of many cadets: dating among the Corps.

Dating was allowed at VMI—except for those romances that conflicted with the school's power structures—and when five of VMI's women were asked how many female cadets had dated or were currently dating fellow students, estimates ranged from fifty percent to ninety percent. If the percentages seemed high, one woman remarked, it wasn't the fault of the female cadets. It was an inevitable outgrowth of VMI's male-female ratio: "We are surrounded by guys and they are constantly hitting on us."

None of these women was troubled by the idea of cadets dating one another. They seemed to feel that dating was a natural part of college life that should not be disruptive to the VMI system so long as it was handled in a professional manner. But among VMI's male cadets, the issue was more divisive.

Matt Brooks, a member of the Class of 2002 who was comfortable with the presence of women at VMI, nevertheless felt that there was no place for dating within the Corps of Cadets:

> I don't think it should happen at all. Friendships are fine, but I don't think serious relationships and dating should go on at all. I think it is destructive to the Corps. . . . We are all BRs [Brother Rats], we all depend on each other, and if we start forming these other relationships, that go outside the BR unity, then it undermines that BR relationship.

Brooks acknowledged that if VMI's women did not date within the Corps, they would be at a great disadvantage when it came to meeting young men. Although there were several women's colleges located within an hour of VMI, there were no equivalent men's schools, and Brooks imagined that young men from coed colleges might be intimidated by the entire VMI milieu. Nevertheless, many male cadets, and a few faculty members, believed that VMI's women and men should abstain from dating each other.

VMI's female cadets recognized that women who dated within the Corps were open to unfair criticism. As Kendra Russell put it: "The women are sluts and the guys are studs." One young woman, who had been a cadre corporal, had encountered particularly harsh criticism during her third class year when it was revealed that she was dating a cadet in the class above her. In the midst of the uproar, she and her roommates found "dipspit" (chewed tobacco juice) thrown on their door. Although she was assured by a VMI official that the romance did not violate the school's rules, she decided to give up her rank to avoid more controversy. One year later, however, the animosity had not entirely disappeared. At a meeting for the 2002 Ring Figure ceremony, her classmates had broken out in a round of booing when the class Vice President announced that there would be one first classman attending the dance (a pointed reference to this woman's date).

With dating, as with most issues surrounding coeducation, the Class of 2002 was a hotbed of emotion. All of which made some people wonder what leadership the class would exert during its first class year. What atmosphere would they encourage in the barracks? What attitudes would they instill in their rats? Looking at VMI's second class, one senior woman phrased the problems bluntly: "Those guys do not respect us at all. . . . I feel sad for my friends in there, especially my female friends next year. I hope they make it through in one piece."

The future would depend, in large part, upon the leadership of a new Commandant, Colonel Eric Hutchings, VMI '77. Hutchings, a veteran of the Army's Rangers and Special Forces, had moved into the Commandant's office during the summer of 2000, after Colonel James Joyner returned to his previous position as Director of Cadet Affairs. Like most of VMI's administrators, Hutchings had lamented the Supreme Court's 1996 ruling against the Institute. He remembered being "terribly distraught" when he heard the news while serving at Fort Benning. But according to Hutchings: "When the Constitutional authorities tell you to do something, you salute the flag and you do it." Now, his task was to establish his own standards for how young men and women should behave at a military college.

From the outset, Hutchings had made an unforgettable impression. Upperclassmen returning to VMI's barrracks on the night of August 20 had been confronted by a broad-chested man in a black beret, with his trousers bloused in his combat boots, surveying the cadets with a squint in his left eye. Hutchings recalled with particular pleasure the flustered gestures of one young cadet, who was hurriedly unscrewing a silver stud from his tongue while the new Commandant barked into his face.

Hutchings deplored "the sloppiness of the cadet Corps, their lack of military bearing." Under his command, he had determined that there would be more personal inspections, more room inspections. All cadets whose weight exceeded the Army standards for body-fat ratio would be assigned to his "elite physical training unit" (i.e., the pork chop platoon). They would be required to submit to biweekly weigh-ins, special dietary restrictions, and physical training sessions five days a week.

Hutchings also held strong opinions about rat haircuts. He despised the shaved heads and close-cropped hair that VMI's freshmen had sported over the past several years: "They all look like a bunch of Hitler Youth. . . . What is the message that we are sending? We've become freaks for people to look at in alarm."

Hutchings had little concern for the months of discussion that VMI had devoted to haircuts for female rats. During the initial assimilation of women it might have been necessary to keep everyone's hair as short as possible, but in Hutchings' opinion, now was the time for change. Inside the VMI barbershop, he posted pictures of himself and General Bunting during their rat years, to show VMI's male cadets that shaved heads were a recent development in the college's history. This year the Institute's male rats were going to enjoy the meager bit of combable hair that Hutchings had sported as a freshman. (His haircut had changed very little since that day.) Meanwhile, the hair of VMI's female rats would be cut above the ear and midway down the neck, in a style still boyish, but consistent with military standards elsewhere.

Surprisingly, the new haircuts did not seem to phase VMI's senior women. The main protests came from those third classmen who wanted the rats to suffer the same humiliations that they had recently faced. Hutchings, however, did not believe in debating policy with undergraduates. "I've had some resistance," he admitted. "And the way you deal with that, in my view, is you immediately crush it. You say, 'Wait a second. I'm not negotiating anything with you. Are you listening to me? This is what we're going to do, and this is why.' That's what I told the young men."

When a delegation of sophomore women tried to convince Hutchings of the benefits of close-cropped hair for female rats, the Commandant remained inflexible:

> I said "Why is your hair, now that you're a third, as long as it is? It's absolutely as long as the regulation will allow. If you think short hair is such a hot idea why isn't your head shaved like last year?" And they just didn't have an answer. So I said "You know what? It's because we're mean to people around here with no compelling reason. We're just mean because that's become a tradition, and I'm sick of it."

"Meanness" was, in fact, one of Hutchings' greatest concerns as he assessed the current state of his alma mater. He didn't care if the meanness manifested itself between men and women, men and men, or women and women; they were all symptoms of the same disease. Hutchings remembered the VMI of his cadetship as a kinder, more humorous place. Whether or not this VMI ever existed, or was the product of a nostalgic mind, he was determined to recreate it:

> The meanspiritedness of this place is what I am most focused on. It was not like this twenty-three years ago. And I believe that in the last few months we have already made great inroads, with the help of the current first class. But I'm appalled by the lack of civility I've seen between cadets. I don't know why people do these things to each other. I always wanted a tough rigorous place when I was a young man. I wanted to be challenged. . . . But when I was a cadet there was a joking atmosphere . . . there was a silliness, and a camaraderie that has dissipated. And I'm trying to revive that.

The new Commandant disliked, for example, the violent rhetoric that some cadets had recently adopted. He heard it in the early days of the ratline, when VMI's cadre were drilling rats in front of the barracks. At each turn of "left face," or "right face," the rats had been told to yell "Kill!"—an instruction that irritated Hutchings. Passersby, walking their dogs, looked up as the word rang out. Joggers turned their heads. After a few days the Colonel had had enough:

I called everybody over into JM Hall and I said, "Stop it. We look like morons." I said, "Look at your squad realistically. The fat guy in the third row—he's going to go to school here for four years and then he's going to be a stockbroker in Richmond. The only thing he's ever going to kill is a submarine sandwich at Spanky's."

Hutchings also decided to get rid of the violent banners that each company of rats had traditionally made from their bedsheets and hung at home football games. He formed his resolve after attending the first game of the season: "There was a saber going through someone's skull. It said 'Duquesne sucks!' There was 'Baby-Eating Bravo,' which had this skeleton that looked like it's munching on a young infant in Pampers. I saw this and I said 'What in God's name is that?!! . . . Somehow bloody slaughter is taken around here as being neat and cool—being blood-thirsty somehow denotes a higher form of masculinity, and I say that's a lot of crap."

The censoring of football banners was only a chip at the rock of VMI culture. When it came to VMI's dyke system, Hutchings was attempting a more profound change.

According to the Colonel, during his cadetship the relationship between a first classman and his dyke had been "brotherly" and "friendly." Rats performed menial tasks for their seniors, retrieving laundry and putting up beds, but they were never mistreated: the dyke system provided "a harbor in this terrible sea." In recent years, however, the dyke system had been threatened by cadets who abused their power:

> Today there is a significant minority of first classmen who think that their fourth classman, their dyke, is a slave. He's to clean everything up—like Cinderella—to work in their room for hours, and then to be berated, to be played with. Occasionally they have these unauthorized sweat parties, and work their dykes out. And if I catch them I will put them out of school.

To overhaul the system, Hutchings had announced that first classmen could no longer physically discipline their own dykes. They could yell; they could expel fractious rats from their rooms for a limited time. But push-ups, sweat parties, and any form of physical violence were strictly prohibited. Instead, first classmen and their rats were now free to throw footballs and Frisbees in the barracks' courtyards—something unheard of in the past.

Hutchings didn't mind if women mentored men, and men mentored women. Although the idea had left him initially skeptical, VMI's senior women were adamant about the benefits of "cross-dyking" for breaking down gender stereotypes, and as of November, Hutchings had seen no problems. There remained, however, the question of how cross-dyking would fare the following fall, when the strained gender relations among the Class of 2002 came into play.

Hutchings had already been alerted to the potential problems among the Class of 2002. At the Ring Figure dinner for that class, which Hutchings had attended, someone had thrown food on one of the female cadets. She had not seen who was responsible, and no one was punished, but Hutchings was forming his own ideas about who the troublemakers were. He had recently handled a case where a third class woman had received a very threatening anonymous email. The message had been traced to the computer of a second classman whose anti-female bias was well-known. The young man swore that he had not written the note, and because several cadets had access to the computer, VMI could not prove otherwise. But Hutchings claimed to have done his best to "terrify" the young man. "I said I didn't want him spreading his brand of hate at my school. I didn't want to see his crap in the *Richmond Times-Dispatch*."

Hutchings did not believe that the second class as a whole was prejudiced against women. As he saw it, there were "five to eight" men who were intent upon conducting their own "guerilla campaign" against female cadets, and it was his intention "to neuter them." He wanted the cadets to understand that he alone had the monopoly on meanness at VMI.

Whether this tough talk would yield results remained to be seen, but thus far Hutchings had struck the cadets as a man of action. One male cadet believed that Hutchings' priorities were already producing a better atmosphere for coeducation: "It's made a lot of cadets forget about their bad feelings towards the females, and keep track of their own self first." Others asserted that there would less cause for complaints about disciplinary double standards under Hutchings' regime. From what they had seen of Hutchings and his new Deputy Commandant, most cadets agreed that these men were likely to be equally harsh toward everyone.

The chief concerns about double standards now seemed to come from VMI's senior women, who feared that Hutchings, backed by a new female assistant commandant from West Point, might try to hold them to Army standards of femininity. The new rat haircuts provided one example, though the women more often pointed to an instance, earlier that fall, when Hutchings had objected to a wrestling match between two female rats, that had been staged by the women's dykes. VMI's senior men had often staged wrestling matches between their rats, and the women complained that Hutchings was trying to hold them to a separate standard.

Hutchings admitted to distaste at the "specter of forty or fifty young males watching two ladies wrestle—that's something out of the World Wrestling Federation." There was a "gratuitous sexual tension" involved that he felt was "inappropriate for a military college." VMI's women pointed out that in their coed wrestling classes, women wrestled women while their male classmates watched. But those matches, Hutchings objected, took place in a carefully controlled environment after weeks of preparation, with the intent of promoting physical fitness. Besides, the real issue in courtyard wrestling matches, he argued, had nothing to do with gender. It had to do, once again, with meanspiritedness: "It's like a cockfight. Nobody's volunteering to do this. This is something that an Asiatic despot does with his minions, where you go, 'Hmmm. This rat is strong. My rat can beat your rat.' It's not like two kids wanting to horseplay. . . . We are pitting people against each other, and the loser gets a public and humiliating butt-whipping."

Hutchings was willing to permit spontaneous, friendly wrestling matches between cadets in their own rooms. But from now on, all staged matches would be left to the PE department.

Hutchings had no control over the final, and most challenging, issue facing VMI in the fall of 2000—the recruitment of female cadets. Over the past two years, the number of VMI's female matriculants had dropped. After enrolling thirty women, then thirty-three, in its first two coed classes, VMI had watched the total count for new women fall to twenty-eight, then twenty-four. Some observers had been predicting such a drop, once the initial media rush was over, and they lamented the fact that VMI's culture had been irrevocably changed in order to accommodate a very small number of women. Others, however, believed that with effort, VMI could attract more women.

The low number of women among the Class of 2004 might have been due, in part, to a staffing change in the admissions office. When VMI's first female admissions officer, Terri Reddings, left in the summer of 1999 to become Dean of Admissions at Hollins College, VMI had taken several months to find a strong replacement. By the spring of 2000, however, the admissions office had settled upon Claudia Pirkle, a former instructor in the Chemistry Department, who approached her new task with visible enthusiasm.

Pirkle was determined not only to increase VMI's number of female enrollees, but to reduce women's attrition. Whenever she heard of a VMI woman who was thinking of leaving the school, Pirkle was one of the first people on the scene, making sure that if a young woman wanted to go, it was for the right reasons. Pirkle could not predict what sort of woman would thrive at VMI: "You'll find this spunky little girl who you just think has all the spirit and fire in the world and she lasts 48 hours. Then you'll find one who seems more delicate, who just flourishes here. There's no stereotype that applies to VMI's women." Pirkle wanted all female applicants and cadets to know that there was a female official at the school who took a personal interest in their success, and who could serve as a contact for them and their parents.

As she looked toward the following year, Pirkle was hopeful that VMI's number of female matriculants would increase. The inquiry pool from women was substantially higher than it had been the previous year, rising from 2861 inquiries in October of 1999, to 4286 in October of 2000. Of course, turning inquiries into applicants, and applicants into matriculants, was a hard task. Many of the women who inquired about VMI were considering military careers, and the top candidates would invariably be swept up by the federal military academies. Those who wanted to attend college in Virginia would also courted by Virginia Tech—which was trying to increase the size of its Corps from 600 to 1000, and by the VWIL program at Mary Baldwin College, which was continuing to attract between forty-two and forty-nine women each year, and commissioning about forty percent of its graduates, mostly into active duty service.

Pirkle had no special funds for attracting women. The scholarship money that VMI had used to draw women into its initial program had now dried up. Now, men and women were competing for the same limited resources.

Nevertheless, it was going to be crucial for VMI to increase its number of female cadets if it ultimately wanted coeducation to succeed. Twenty-four female rats had been barely enough to integrate each of VMI's nine companies in August of 2000, and without more female cadets, VMI could not build a strong women's athletic program.

In the fall of 2000, the only varsity sports offered to female cadets were still cross-country and track and field. VMI had begun a fledgling soccer program for women (after the rugby club folded), and the players were enthusiastic, but the team had scarcely enough members to survive. For their first home game the women had to recruit a last-minute volunteer to complete their squad.

A few cadets questioned whether VMI was serious about women's sports, noting that the school had made no progress in expanding its varsity program, and had failed to hire a new soccer coach over the summer of 2000, as had been promised. Meanwhile, the athletic department argued that it could not start more teams without more women, and the admissions office countered that it was hard to attract more women without a strong athletic program.

And so all eyes were on the following fall, to see if VMI could increase its number of female entrants, and to see what sort of ratline the Class of 2002 would provide for these women. When asked to summarize their impressions, several cadets stated that things were better now with coeducation than they had ever been in the past; the challenge, they added, was to keep moving forward. VMI was confident that it had laid a strong foundation; the future would tell what sort of house would be built upon that bedrock.